RESHAPING THE WORLD TRADING SYSTEM
A HISTORY OF THE URUGUAY ROUND

Reshaping the World Trading System

A History of the Uruguay Round

Second and Revised Edition

John Croome

KLUWER LAW INTERNATIONAL

The Hague • London • Boston

WORLD TRADE ORGANIZATION
ORGANISATION MONDIALE DU COMMERCE
ORGANIZACION MUNDIAL DEL COMERCIO

Published by Kluwer Law International,
P.O. Box 85889, 2508 CN The Hague, The Netherlands.

Sold and distributed in the U.S.A. and Canada
by Kluwer Law International,
675 Massachusetts Avenue, Cambridge, MA 02139, U.S.A.

In all other countries, sold and distributed
by Kluwer Law International,
P.O. Box 85889, 2508 CN The Hague, The Netherlands.

ISBN 904111263

Table of contents

Foreword

The Uruguay Round of negotiations in the GATT took over four years to prepare, and seven more years to complete. Failure often threatened; success was not certain until the very last days. The most ambitious worldwide negotiations ever attempted on trade matters – perhaps, indeed, on any economic subject – the Round covered an enormous range of questions, many highly sensitive. Over one hundred governments took part, defending the interests of countries of all sizes, stages of development and economic structures. Unlike previous GATT negotiations, this one spilled over into the political arena, sparking sharp controversy, international tension, and in some countries even riots. The agreements reached are expected to influence world growth and development for decades to come.

Since the Uruguay Round agreements were signed in April 1994, they have been widely discussed and analyzed. Studies have sought to estimate their impact: additional world economic growth worth hundreds of billions of dollars has been forecast, as well as large shifts in patterns of production and trade, and challenging problems of economic and social adjustment. This book, however, has a different purpose: to trace the history of the Round. It seeks to explain, in as accessible and non-technical a way as possible, how the Uruguay Round came about, why it covered the subjects that it did, what the participants sought and the twists, turns, setbacks and successes in each sector of the negotiations. The present work makes no claims to scholarship. However, it is based on essentially the same sources that scholars will use when the time comes to write a definitive history. These include the many hundreds of official and unofficial documents generated by a huge international negotiation, supplemented by memoranda exchanged inside the GATT (now WTO) Secretariat, press reports, private notes jotted at meetings and – not least – personal memory of events.

A brief explanation of the structure of this history may be helpful. The story is told here basically in chronological order. The Round divides into five fairly distinct time periods, separated by three ministerial meetings (Punta del Este in 1986, Montreal in 1988 and Brussels in 1990), and by the presentation of the first comprehensive but tentative package of results in 1991. The book's structure reflects this pattern. The chapters dealing with the preliminary and closing phases of the negotiations, as well as the four turning points, look at developments in the Round as a whole. The intervening negotiations were so complex that the narrative must, to a great extent, focus on developments in each separate area. Chapters III, V, VI and VII, which describe these negotiations in detail, are therefore divided into sub-chapters which take up each sector in turn. The reader wishing to trace what happened in a particular sector (for example, agriculture or services) is advised to use the table of contents as the principal guide, with the index serving, if necessary, to trace references to that sector outside the detailed narrative.

Arthur Dunkel, Director-General of GATT up to 1993, originally suggested that I should undertake this history. Peter Sutherland, his successor, confirmed the arrangement. They took the risk of giving me a free hand and the cooperation of the Secretariat to tell the story as I saw fit, to quote private conversations and internal notes, and to pass personal judgements on events. I am grateful to Renato Ruggiero, Director-General of the WTO since May 1995, for his readiness to publish the result. Many of my former Secretariat colleagues, and a number of Uruguay Round delegates, helped me by providing valuable insights into the course of some of the more tortuous negotiations. They corrected many errors. Those that remain, and all the views expressed, are mine alone.

John Croome
Geneva, 1995

Foreword to the second edition

Advantage has been taken of the republication of this history to bring the story down from early 1994, when the Uruguay Round agreements were signed, to the beginning of 1998. A new chapter, "Epilogue – The WTO three years on", offers a personal view of how the agreements have been brought into force, of some successes and problems encountered, and of the possible ingredients and prospects for another round of multilateral trade negotiations.

John Croome
Geneva, February 1998

Prologue

An Agreement at Marrakesh

"Hungary..."; "Iceland..."; "India...".

Each time, a ripple of applause and a barrage of electronic flash. Another head of delegation moves to the table at the centre of the ornately decorated meeting room, is seated in a scarlet and gold chair, signs below the name of his or her country, shakes hands and withdraws.

On the table, linked by long streamers of blue ribbon to the slim open text that is being signed, are a dozen or more stacks of documents, 26,000 pages in all of agreements and promises to overhaul the rules and institutions of the international trading system and to create a more open world market.

The signing ceremony has already been running for two hours, and has another two hours to go, as well over 100 national delegations take their turn to sign the Final Act of the Uruguay Round of multilateral trade nego-tiations. The delegations come and go, along with a changing audience of journalists, television crews and photographers, as well as of officials national and international, past and present, who have seized the opportunity to see the immense enterprise in which they have shared come to fruition. Only Peter Sutherland, Director-General of GATT, Conference Chairman Sergio Abreu Bonilla of Uruguay – both shaking hands with each signatory – and GATT Secretariat colleagues who guide the delegations through the formalities, remain throughout.

Almost unbelievably, the Uruguay Round is at last coming to a successful end, well over a decade after it was first broached and after seven and a half years of actual negotiation.

The sense of unreality is heightened by this final meeting in Marrakesh. For four days, government leaders have delivered speeches recalling the labours of these past years. They have celebrated the agreements reached: the deep cuts to be made by all countries in their barriers to trade; the coming liberalization, at last, of world trade in agricultural products, textiles and clothing; the far-reaching overhaul of the rules for international trade in goods; the new rules to govern and encourage trade in services and the protection of intellectual property; the strengthened system to settle trade disputes among governments; the new World Trade Organization that will put the whole trading system on firm foundations for the first time. They have spoken of the prospects of economic growth and development, and of better international relations that the results of the Uruguay Round hold out. Some have criticized shortfalls in the agreements and put forward proposals for continuing or new negotiations on some subjects. Virtually all agree that the Uruguay Round has been the largest, the longest, and – if the promise of its results is fulfilled – the most successful international trade negotiation of all time. But these speeches in Marrakesh seem far removed from the reality of the Uruguay Round. Three earlier ministerial meetings have each seen tough negotiations. Two out of the three were failures, accompanied by bitter mutual recrimination. This one is a pure celebration. The rooms set aside here for negotiations to overcome any last-minute hitches stand unused. All has been settled in advance. Not a word in the Marrakesh Declaration to which ministers subscribed this morning has been changed from the draft on which the officials agreed more than a week ago in Geneva. There is nothing in this meeting to recall the days and nights of effort, the clashes of policies and personalities, the national pressures on the negotiators, the repeated solemn declarations of heads of state and government, the frustrations and breakthroughs, that have led to final agreement – nothing except shared memories and the presence among the spectators of a distinguished handful of earlier negotiators: people such as Sutherland's predecessor, Arthur Dunkel, some of his former colleagues, and ex-ministers and ambassadors, veterans of Uruguay Round battles years ago, from Brazil, Colombia, the European Union, New Zealand and elsewhere.

Tonight, a final sumptuous ceremony will take place at the royal palace. Tomorrow, the participants will disperse. Within 48 hours, the 26,000 pages, weighing not far short of 200 kilos and lodged securely in eight wooden packing cases, will have been shipped back to Switzerland, where they were first drafted, fought over, and finally agreed. The fate of the agreements will rest on national parliaments who over the next months will decide whether to approve them, and then, if all goes well, in the hands of the diplomats and trade officials who bring the World Trade Organization to birth in 1995. But in any case, the Uruguay Round is over.

How did we get here?

Chapter I

Towards a new round: 1979-86

In November 1979, the governments of 99 countries formally completed the Tokyo Round of negotiations, held under the auspices of the General Agreement on Tariffs and Trade (GATT). These had been the most ambitious worldwide trade negotiations ever undertaken up to that time. Launched in Tokyo in September 1973, with the probably unrealistic expectation that the Round could be completed within 27 months, the negotiations had taken more than six years of work in Geneva to bring to conclusion. Their success, often in doubt, had demanded a degree of political attention and commitment from world leaders for which there was no precedent in international trade relations. Several participants declared that the experiment of negotiating on so many trade issues at once should never be repeated. Even those who were convinced that the Tokyo Round's results could only have been won as a package deal looked forward, in 1979, to a long respite from major negotiations. The 1980s were seen as the years in which GATT, now reshaped to meet the current needs of international trade, could peacefully bring into effect the tariff reductions agreed to in the Round, apply and extend the new disciplines negotiated for non-tariff distortions of trade, and work out the implications of the agreements reached on the role of developing countries in the trading system and on the settlement of trade disputes. Many developing countries, disappointed at what they saw as meagre results from the GATT bargaining process, turned their attention to negotiations among themselves, and to the more congenial forum of the United Nations. Trade negotiations threatened to slip off the agenda of international policy makers, already grappling with the direct consequences of the second great oil-price shock, and soon to be faced by the debt crisis of Africa and Latin America.

Exactly six years later, on 28 November 1985, GATT member governments took the key decision to start preparations for a new and even more ambitious round of multilateral trade negotiations. This chapter traces the steps by which the international community moved from the Tokyo Round to the Uruguay Round.

1

Aftermath of the Tokyo Round

The end of the Tokyo Round left GATT members with no lack of work to be done. The results had to be put into force – a far more substantial task than with previous GATT negotiations. Earlier GATT rounds had been largely devoted to reducing import duties, a task which, once agreed, fell on the individual governments concerned. The Tokyo Round also achieved large tariff cuts: the industrialized countries agreed to reduce their import duties by an average of about one third. However, the core of the Round's results consisted of separate multilateral agreements whose main aim was to reduce or control non-tariff distortions of trade. These "codes" were not self-executing; they had to be brought into effect by their signatories (for the most part, the developed countries) and steered by their individual management bodies. Seven such agreements were to come into effect at the beginning of 1980, and two more in January 1981. Further new "framework" agreements called for regular review of developments in the trading system, and in particular of protective measures affecting the interests of developing countries. Moreover, part of the agreed bargain in concluding the Tokyo Round, and in accepting the tariff-cutting results, the codes and the framework agreements was that the door should be kept open for later action on issues which had not been dealt with effectively. Thus negotiations were to continue on reform of the GATT rules on safeguard action (the use of temporary restrictions against imports that are disrupting domestic producers), an issue generally agreed to be the main piece of unfinished business of the Tokyo Round. Countries heavily dependent on exports of agricultural products, who had obtained little from the Round, won agreement that GATT should look more closely at how greater progress could be made in future in this sector. "Structural adjustment", at that time a code-name used primarily for policy proposals that would encourage a shift of some industries from developed to developing countries, was to be studied. All these matters were embodied in an agreed work programme, with a final promise that GATT's Consultative Group of Eighteen, a small but representative group of senior trade officials, could look into such other proposals for future work as might be put forward by governments.

The new work programme got off to a good start, with the first of the eight rounds of annual tariff cuts applied on 1 January 1980, seven codes put into force, and the other issues quickly taken up, as appropriate, in the GATT Council of Representatives or elsewhere. As GATT's Director-General, Olivier Long, pointed out, worldwide trade liberalization had been resumed for the first time since 1972, when the final tariff cuts of the previous GATT round had gone into effect. However, the economic outlook was bleak, and with it the outlook for cooperative action to maintain an open world trading system.

In principle, at least, the GATT member governments agreed with their 1979 Chairman when he told them that a practical and immediate way of overcoming protectionism and promoting economic adjustment was "to implement the results of the Tokyo Round quickly and vigorously, to monitor their implementation, and to make full use of GATT as a negotiating forum to see that the agreements become a permanent catalyst for liberalization in the world trading system". They were ready to live up to their contractual commitments: to cut tariffs on schedule, and to apply the new rules. Repeatedly, in intergovernmental meetings at all levels, they also agreed that they must continue to resist protectionist pressures and use the procedures of GATT to resolve their trade problems. But they were not prepared to go further. The GATT bodies charged with new studies went through the prescribed motions. The Committee on Trade and Development agreed to examine prospects for trade liberalization. The Consultative Group of Eighteen undertook to look not only at the familiar or traditional problems of dispute settlement and origin rules, but also at possible trade difficulties arising from export restrictions, and in the fields of restrictive business practices and services. Such examinations, however, required no commitment from governments. Where multilateral agreement and commitment was needed, it could not be found: the safeguards negotiations remained totally blocked, as they had throughout the greater part of the Tokyo Round. Meanwhile, trade tensions grew. Protectionist pressures – never easily measurable, but evident enough in political speeches, draft legislation, protest demonstrations and newspaper reports – ran high. The number of trade disputes brought before the GATT Council, one of the better indicators of international trade tension, reached a record level of 13 in 1980: significantly, ten of the disputes concerned agricultural trade.

As the year 1980 advanced, the international economic situation deteriorated further, with widespread inflation and unemployment, monetary instability, and large payments imbalances. Increasingly, oil-importing countries in particular found themselves unable to handle the debts they had run up to finance their sharply increased fuel costs. Over the year as a whole, trade growth slowed to barely 1% in volume. The worst was still to come. The years 1981 and 1982 were to be even more difficult for the world economy, for world trade, and for international economic relations. However, they were also to see the first concerted efforts by the trading nations to restore purpose and direction to their joint efforts in GATT. Although the launching of new multilateral negotiations was still more than half a decade away, the Uruguay Round's conception, and much of its agenda, stems from events and discussions in 1981 and 1982.

Stocktaking

In October 1980, Arthur Dunkel, Switzerland's chief Tokyo Round negotiator and representative at GATT, took over from Olivier Long as GATT's Director-General. During the following months, he undertook a series of visits to Asian, European and Western Hemisphere capitals, as well as discussions at GATT's home base of Geneva. His aim was to sound out the views of GATT members on the state of international trade relations, and what could be done to improve them. At the same time, Dunkel carried through a series of "brainstorming" sessions with his own senior staff.

Virtually everyone Dunkel talked to agreed that the trading system was drifting dangerously. Although the Tokyo Round reforms and liberalization were being put into effect, and protectionist rhetoric was fortunately not fully matched by protectionist action, the momentum that had carried governments, and the world trading system based on the GATT, through successive negotiating rounds had been largely lost. The authority of the GATT rules, and above all of the central rule of non-discrimination among the member countries, had been undermined by the failure to resolve the safeguards issue and by increasingly restrictive application of the Multifibre Arrangement that, negotiated within GATT itself, provided an alternative safeguard regime for trade in textiles and clothing. Developed country governments were looking for solutions to problems in particular industries by negotiating trade-restrictive agreements entirely outside the framework of the GATT rules. A very important new bilateral restraint, involving Japanese self-limitation of automobile exports to the United States, was actually adopted while Dunkel's consultations continued. Some dispute cases brought before GATT seemed to reveal, as a GATT Secretariat publication noted, a lack of agreement on issues "too wide in scope, and too important in terms of national policy, to be dealt with effectively by the semijudicial panel procedures" of GATT. Not all the Tokyo Round codes were working well. Agricultural exporters continued to feel that GATT failed to address their concerns.

Developing countries for a time had placed their hopes on a total reshaping of the international trading system, as part of a wider "New International Economic Order". However proposals for "global negotiations" on both financial and trade problems, and other initiatives in the United Nations in the so-called North-South dialogue, had brought no results except a growing recognition by developing countries that the industrialized nations, even if they sometimes betrayed their own principles, would not give up their fundamental preference for a trading system shaped and driven by market signals rather than by government intervention. Some developing countries were themselves becoming disillusioned with the results of their long campaign in GATT and the United Nations for "special and differential treatment", feeling that the limited and unreliable gains they had won through preferential tariffs unilaterally introduced by the developed countries were outweighed by their effective exclusion from influence in multilateral negotiations and their failure to bargain for permanent reductions in foreign barriers to their exports.

Virtually all governments agreed that international trade relations badly needed a renewed sense of common purpose. Beyond this point, however, there was little agreement.

Developing countries put most weight on their need to maintain and expand exports to the markets of developed countries. Although the worst of the debt crisis was to strike only in 1982, the overriding concern for many of them was already to find means of financing heavy debt service obligations to the IMF, governments and private banks. In terms of products, they focused mostly on textiles and clothing, tropical products and other agricultural goods, and non-ferrous metals, although some were also interested in the markets for manufactures such as electronic goods. In terms of trade measures, they looked for an easing of the Multifibre Arrangement (due for renewal in December 1981), for GATT safeguard rules that would not permit restrictions to be aimed at a single supplier, and for improved – if possible, preferential – treatment for their exports in foreign markets. Most of them wanted to halt the trend to bilateral trade restrictions such as "voluntary export restraints". Almost all saw no sense in giving new tasks to GATT at a time when it was having great difficulty in handling its recognized responsibilities. Finally, some developing countries still hoped for global negotiations in the United Nations, and therefore insisted that these would be the proper setting for any future multilateral negotiations on trade issues identified in GATT.

Many developed countries also saw current trade problems largely in terms of North-South relations, but from a different perspective. In their view, GATT had taken a wrong turning in the late 1950s when it had encouraged developing countries to become members without requiring them to reduce their trade barriers, and indeed had given them the right to introduce and indefinitely maintain trade restrictions in case of balance-of-payments difficulty. These errors, as they saw it, had been compounded by acceptance of the principle that in GATT negotiations developing countries should be allowed "special and differential" treatment, and in general should not themselves be asked to liberalize. The result, to these critics, was that developing countries were free riders on the GATT system, contributing nothing to the opening-up of world trade, effectively excused compliance with the GATT rules, and in practice damaging their own prospects of healthy growth by excluding competition from their economies. This situation was made even less palatable by the export success enjoyed by a few, mainly Asian developing countries, which had recently come to be classified as "newly industrializing countries" (or NICs) because of their highly competitive production of textiles, clothing, and a rapidly expanding range of other products.

These were not, however, the only considerations that in 1981 were shaping the views of developed members of GATT. They too were seeking export markets in a time of recession, and trying to restrain domestic pressures for protection against imports. The agricultural exporters among them hoped, in spite of past experience, to prise open heavily protected markets, especially in Europe and Japan, and to put some limits on the increasingly widespread use of export subsidies. Small countries, least able to defend themselves against unilateral action by the largest players in world trade, were anxious to see GATT rules properly enforced.

Japan, the third largest player in world trade, took a characteristically cautious line. Japanese sympathies and interests were not greatly different, in many respects, from those of the other major developed countries. On the other hand, it was handling its considerable trade differences with the United States and Europe mainly through bilateral agreements (Japan had never invoked GATT's dispute settlement procedures), and it would be on the defensive, with its highly protected market for foodstuffs, in any negotiation on agricultural trade.

The two largest players of all had very different attitudes.

The European Community was not particularly interested in supporting new initiatives in GATT, and had none of its own to propose. It was large and influential enough not to worry much about erosion of the GATT rules. It was intent on developing its own internal market, and on successfully integrating its own new member countries. It was conscious that any new concessions made to developing countries in general might conflict with the interests of the large group of developing countries with which it had close preferential trading relations under the Lomé Convention. And it recognized that any substantial GATT negotiation on agricultural trade would create pressure to change its painfully constructed common agricultural policy, thereby also inevitably reopening latent policy differences among its own members. Nevertheless, the Community took seriously its responsibilities as a leading trade power and a pillar of GATT, and was prepared to join fully in discussions and decisions on GATT's future.

The United States brought real enthusiasm to the prospect of revitalizing the GATT. A new Administration, under President Reagan, came to office early in 1981, eager to bring fresh ideas and energies to bear on America's relations with the rest of the world and to show a clear break with the policies of the previous Democratic Administration. Spurred by its own free-market beliefs and by the need to relieve Congressional pressures to restrict US imports, the new Administration identified an ambitious set of negotiating objectives for GATT, going far beyond its traditional focus on tariffs, or even its more recent attack on traditional non-tariff barriers to trade. The United States would now seek liberalization of world agricultural trade, a new basis for relations between developed countries and the more advanced developing countries, and an attack on barriers to investment and to trade in services.

Dunkel summed up the view from the GATT Secretariat in a speech in London in March 1981. He concluded that governments were being restrained from a substantial slippage towards protectionism only by "a kind of balance of terror": a fear that if they resorted to trade restrictions these would evoke retaliation, as well as undermining the trading system as a whole. Dunkel argued that this situation was untenable. The system could not cope with the pressures generated by rapid economic change, the debt difficulties of developing countries and other factors unless it could rely on a secure and reliable basis, which would not be achieved without "a concerted effort to establish momentum in the right direction". He added that he was "not unhopeful that such an effort will be made".

Dunkel's hopes were founded primarily on his judgement that, acute though the differences of view among the GATT member countries might be, all were acutely worried by the drift and deterioration in trade relations, and by the clear risk that the GATT itself – the rule of law in international trade – would be so undermined and bypassed that it would lose all credibility and effectiveness. He also had a more immediate and concrete reason for hope. A number of governments had told him that they would support a political-level meeting of GATT members that would allow a frank assessment of the trading system's difficulties, and launch new efforts to overcome them.

A new agenda for GATT

The first move towards a new initiative in the GATT came in June 1981. Top trade policy officials of the major trading countries met in the Consultative Group of Eighteen to discuss the implications for the world trading system of the worldwide slowdown in economic activity and the trade tensions associated with it. The officials concluded that "trade relations are beset by a number of complex and potentially disruptive problems, reflecting growing protectionist pressures", and that there was "a need for improved international cooperation to solve these problems". They agreed that it "would be useful to consider at the political level the overall condition of the trading system", and that to this end a meeting of government ministers of the GATT member countries should be held in 1982. A few days later, at the Economic Summit in Ottawa, the proposal for a GATT ministerial meeting was endorsed by the heads of state or government of the world's seven richest countries.

Unlike most intergovernmental organizations, GATT had no provision for regular political-level meetings of its member governments. GATT's annual "Session of the Contracting Parties" was attended by top officials, not ministers. Ministerial meetings were few, and had usually been associated with the start of major trade negotiations: the last such meeting, in 1973, had been held to launch the Tokyo Round. The proposal for a ministerial meeting in 1982 engendered expectations that, perhaps inevitably, could not be fulfilled.

Very quickly, deep differences of view emerged among the member governments about what the ministerial meeting should do. With some difficulty, a second meeting of the Consultative Group of Eighteen in October managed to define its purpose in general terms as providing an opportunity for the trading nations "to review the current state of the multilateral trading system, and to consider how it might be improved and made more effective". The Group agreed that "a ministerial meeting would also meet the need to review the implementation of the results of the Tokyo Round negotiations and to deal with issues presently under discussion in GATT, and to define GATT's tasks for the future". This formula managed to cover the interests both of those governments which gave priority to better application of the existing GATT rules and of those which were interested in opening up new areas of work. But its vagueness soon led to trouble.

Following the formal decision by GATT's annual session in November to hold the next session at ministerial level (with the aspirational but even vaguer statement of its purpose as being "to examine the functioning of the multilateral trading system, and to reinforce the common efforts of the contracting parties to support and improve the system for the benefit of all nations"), officials started to put together a detailed agenda for the ministers, and to explore what decisions their governments might be ready to support at the meeting. The work went forward partly in the Preparatory Committee, partly in a series of meetings of the Consultative Group of Eighteen, and partly in the existing GATT committees responsible for specific subjects in which ministers were expected to take an interest. An initial "shopping list" of issues which individual governments wished to have the meeting take up was examined, first to establish what action was proposed, and what support the proposals enjoyed, and then to fit the proposals into a broad framework that finally took shape in two distinct parts: a group of issues that called for a statement of political intent, and more detailed proposals that would establish the basis of work in GATT after the meeting. Unfortunately, no government was prepared to accept deletion of its own proposals, and the shopping list for future work grew unmanageably long.

Both the preparatory process and the ministerial meeting itself were extremely difficult: so much so, that many participants regretted that the decision to hold the meeting had ever been taken. The meeting itself, in Geneva, was on a very large scale, with some 70 ministers present, a total of 800 official delegates, and more than 400 journalists reporting events. The draft declaration and work programme forwarded to the meeting by the Preparatory Committee and the GATT Council included many unsettled points which ministers found hard to resolve. The meeting had to be prolonged over a weekend that included night sessions, emergency meetings in Geneva of the European Community's Council of Ministers and of other groups, and intensive negotiations in a small group of key delegations in Dunkel's offices at the GATT. Acute differences of view divided developed from developing countries, to an extent not experienced in the GATT before or since, and a legacy of mutual mistrust was left that was not fully dissipated for several years. The United States, which had brought to the meeting high (too high, as events showed) ambitions, achieved much less than it hoped, reinforcing the views of many Americans who were sceptical about possibilities of effective action through GATT. Agricultural exporters who had believed that the ministers might be able to halt the worldwide trend toward ever-increasing protection and subsidies for agriculture were bitterly disappointed: Australia actually walked out of the meeting. The European Community fought a bruising defensive battle from which it emerged without having to assume commitments that it had not wanted, but having attracted widespread criticism. For the first time, the world press made a GATT meeting a front-page story, and the story was one of disagreement, frustration and near-failure.

Undoubtedly, the ministerial meeting brought GATT close to serious breakdown. In many of its member countries, including the largest, influential people in government, business and the press were urging abandonment of the multilateral, cooperative and rules-based approach to trade relations represented by the GATT, and recommending that their countries should instead act alone or in company with a few like-minded others, relying on their own economic and political strength to bring about the trade policy aims they sought. Had the ministers been unable to reach agreement – an outcome that over several days seemed all too possible – severe damage would have been done to the international trading system. However, agreement was reached, and a final Ministerial Declaration was approved that, in spite of evident weaknesses, acknowledged that "the multilateral trading system, of which the General Agreement is the legal foundation, is seriously endangered", expressed determination to create "a renewed consensus in support of the GATT system", and launched cautious exploratory work on themes that in due course were to figure importantly in the Uruguay Round negotiations.

William Brock, head of the US delegation, commented not long afterwards that the ministerial meeting had achieved "the avoidance of tragedy and limited movement in the right direction". In retrospect, it can be argued that it achieved considerably more. Up to the 1982 meeting, the majority of governments and interested observers saw no need for major new initiatives in the GATT. They believed that, in spite of the difficulties brought about by international recession and the debt crisis, it would be sufficient to continue along the path defined by the results of the Tokyo Round, using the normal GATT mechanisms of consultation and dispute settlement to handle such crises as might arise. The experience of the 1982 meeting persuaded many governments and observers that this view was mistaken and that matters could not be left to continue as they were. Although only a few were as yet ready to accept that a fresh and wide-ranging round of multilateral negotiations would be desirable, most were searching, from 1983 onwards, for ways of putting international trade relations on a more secure and less divisive basis. Moreover, the GATT work programme that was the main fruit of the ministerial meeting served in many areas as an essential means of preparing future negotiations, by requiring a thorough look at existing problems and opportunities, and thereby making governments think hard about the possibility that multilateral negotiations in these areas might be to their advantage.

The Ministerial Declaration, whatever its shortcomings, required GATT to start work on a number of subjects, and to renew efforts on others. Broad undertakings to make trade policies and measures – including, by implication, existing measures – consistent with GATT principles and rules, to resist protectionist pressures, to avoid distorting or limiting international trade were seriously weakened by language that called only for "determined efforts" to make them effective. Moreover, they underlined the inability of GATT members to reach an agreement on the use of safeguard actions, even though yet another effort was made to reach an understanding, this time with an end-1983 deadline. Nevertheless, these "standstill and rollback" undertakings provided benchmarks by which the performance of governments could be judged as well as a basis on which the GATT Secretariat for the first time felt itself free to collect and publish detailed information about the trade policy actions of individual GATT members, including voluntary export restraints and other measures not covered by the GATT roles (and of which it therefore was not officially informed). In the same way, what one critic described as "predictable homilies" about attention to the problems of developing countries gave the basis for detailed examination of the trade treatment of developing countries by individual developed countries and of possibilities for encouraging exports of tropical products. Some useful, if comparatively minor, improvements were made in the GATT procedures for settling disputes: if procedural (as distinct from substantive) problems continued nevertheless to arise in reaching a prompt and satisfactory resolution of differences brought to GATT, this at least demonstrated that there was a need for more thoroughgoing overhaul of the dispute settlement rules.

In many other ways, too, the work programme established by the ministerial meeting laid foundations for the Uruguay Round. On the most hotly controversial subject of all – agriculture – the meeting launched a comprehensive examination of "all matters affecting trade, market access and competition and supply in agricultural products", with the new body established for this task charged with making recommendations for trade liberalization. This was a step forward even though the European Community insisted that it accepted no commitment to any new negotiation or obligation in relation to agricultural products. Reviews of existing non-tariff measures, of the relation between tariff levels and the degree of processing of the products protected by these tariffs ("tariff escalation"), of trade in textiles and clothing and in non-ferrous metals, forestry products and fish, and of dual-pricing practices and rules of origin were all set up with the openly declared purpose not only of fact-finding but of establishing a basis for future liberalization or other action

The United States, in particular, had pushed before and during the meeting for work to be launched in GATT on the so-called "new subjects" of services, trade in counterfeit goods, investment measures and trade in high-technology goods. It found only limited support among developed countries, and outright opposition from most developing countries. Ministers of the developing-country Group of 77 declared that GATT involvement in these subjects "would not only be detrimental to the interests of developing countries in international markets, but would hamper efforts aimed at reforming GATT in order to adapt it more closely to the needs and interests of developing countries". Neither investment nor high technology were included in the work programme. Work on services was confined for the present to an exchange of information among interested countries, with no acknowledgement that there was a role for the GATT itself in this area, and the subject of counterfeit goods was treated with hardly less caution. In no circumstances, however, would GATT members have been ready to start negotiations on services in 1982: they lacked the necessary factual knowledge, and in consequence were unable to identify what their national interests would be in such negotiations. The work begun in 1982 led to the acquisition of that knowledge, and persuaded some key countries, in addition to the United States, that services negotiations could be rewarding. The delay on counterfeit goods was also productive, since further study (and a GATT dispute linked to patent rights) persuaded the sponsors of work on this problem to widen its scope to the far larger field of the trade-related problems of intellectual property.

The benefits of this kind of hindsight were not available, however, in 1983. To most observers, the 1982 meeting had been at best a narrow escape from disastrous failure. The work programme, which for the most part required only that reports be ready for consideration at the GATT annual session of November 1984, appeared a poor substitute for the firm commitments sought in particular by the United States. Although the work programme was duly set in motion in early 1983, the tone of international trade relations was poisoned by the very difficult economic climate, and by a long series of trade-restrictive actions taken, with limited regard for the GATT rules, by the major developed countries. The year 1983 was in fact to see a quite rapid recovery from the 1982 recession, which had involved a shrinkage both in output in the industrialized countries and, for the first time since World War II, in the volume of world trade. However, the United States continued to run a massive trade deficit, reflecting its budget deficit and what was perceived as an overvalued dollar. Latin American countries were cutting imports as part of their struggle with debt service difficulties. The Multifibre Arrangement, extended in December 1981 to July 1986, was applied even more toughly than its predecessor. Responding to pressures from domestic industry, both the United States and the European Community introduced new bilateral trade restraints, aiming them particularly at Japan, but also at the newly industrializing countries, at some other developed countries, and at each other.

These dismaying trends reinforced the belief of some observers that new multilateral negotiations in GATT were needed sooner rather than later. In the United States in particular, a new GATT round was increasingly seen as a way to counter protectionist pressures that were being fed by the large US trade deficit. The US Government began to push in this direction, consulting its own business community on the issues that might be negotiated, and trying to build a political-level consensus among governments in quiet informal gatherings of trade ministers from about 25 countries, developed and developing, who met about twice a year from 1983 onwards. Dunkel, who took part in these meetings was conscious that GATT members were for the most part still not ready to contemplate new negotiations. Nevertheless, he began to make public statements that clearly pointed in that direction. In a speech in March 1983, for instance, he focused on the current GATT work programme, but acknowledged that there were real problems in international trade relations, and that "the answer to them lies in negotiation, not in further breaches of the rules which must weaken the whole trading system".

As seen from the GATT Secretariat the most striking feature of national trade policies at this time was the contradiction between, on the one hand, professed – and indeed genuine – concern to preserve and develop the multilateral system based on the GATT and, on the other, a persistent and growing tendency to undermine that system by taking restrictive action, outside the rules, in response to short-term preoccupations. The Secretariat could itself point to this contradiction, and did so in its reports and through Dunkel's own speeches and meetings with ministers. Inevitably, however, it was seen as an interested party; moreover, undue harping on the sins of its leading member countries risked damaging their trust in it, and their willingness to discuss problems openly with it. With encouragement from several governments that he consulted, Dunkel decided to introduce a new element into the discussion, by bringing together a group of independent experts to report on the problems of the trading system, and how these might be overcome. In doing so, he was influenced by past experience: four eminent economists had in 1958 helped to provide new direction to GATT's work through a report, *Trends in International Trade*. However, that report was comparatively lengthy, closely-written, and directed more to governments than to the general public. Dunkel wanted to influence governments, and to prod them to action in GATT, but he felt that this might best be achieved by asking a small group of non-governmental figures of recognized standing to look at the state of trade relations and report their findings in terms that a general audience would grasp.

Dunkel announced the formation of the group[1] at the annual GATT session in November 1983. To underline group's independence, and to avoid what he foresaw could be damaging and lengthy controversy over its membership and mandate, he sought neither permission nor financing from the GATT member governments. The seven members of the group were

---

[1]   Members were Bill Bradley (US Senator, member Senate Finance Committee), Pehr Gyllenhammar (Chairman, AB Volvo), Guy Ladreit de Lacharrière (Vice President, International Court of Justice), Fritz Leutwiler (Chairman) (Chairman, Swiss National Bank and President, Bank for International Settlements), I.G. Patel (Director, London School of Economics and former Governor of Reserve Bank of India), Mario Henrique Simonsen (Getulio Vargas Foundation and former Minister of Finance of Brazil) and Sumitro Djojohadikusumo (former Minister of Trade and Industry and Minister of Finance of Indonesia). Finance was provided from various private non-profit sources, the largest contributor being the Ford Foundation.

invited to draw on their wide experience in industry, banking, economics, law and politics "to identify the fundamental causes of the problems afflicting the international trading system and to consider how these may be overcome during the remainder of the 1980s".

Chaired by Fritz Leutwiler, head of the Swiss central bank and a leader in current international efforts to overcome the debt crisis, the group held five meetings and came up in early 1985 with a short (50-page) and unanimous report. The report argued that fundamental economic changes were taking place in the world, and that these changes were not only inevitable but to be welcomed as a motor for economic growth and development. Open international trade was a key to sustained growth – but the world market was being choked by a growing accumulation of restrictive measures, and the GATT roles were "increasingly ignored or evaded". Protectionism was not the answer. Trade restrictions acted only as brakes on each economy's ability to take advantage of new technology, and to grow. A new commitment to open trade was needed – but growth would also require the wise use of monetary and fiscal policies, and of debt and development policies.

This diagnosis was in no way controversial, although the emphasis of its members on such matters as opening the formulation of trade policies to greater public discussion, the integration of developing countries into the trading system rather than giving them trade preferences of limited value, the need for adjustment assistance for displaced workers, and the lack of clarity in GATT rules on regional trade agreements gave the report a distinctive flavour, unlike any text negotiated among governments. Most attention, however, was attracted by the group's "fifteen recommendations for specific, immediate action to meet the present crisis in the trading system" – and particularly by its support for a new round of GATT negotiations "provided they are directed toward the primary goal of strengthening the multilateral trading system and further opening world markets". Other recommendations included some that were surprisingly bold for a report by a group of this kind. One was a strong call for clearer and fairer rules for agricultural trade ("efficient agricultural producers should be given the maximum opportunity to compete"). Voluntary export restraints and other trade measures of both developed and developing countries that were inconsistent with GATT obligations should be brought into line with the rules – with a timetable and procedures to ensure that this was done. Trade in textiles and clothing should be fully subject to the ordinary rules of the GATT. Countries should be subject to regular oversight of their policies and actions. Safeguard actions against imports should not discriminate between suppliers. The group endorsed, but without enthusiasm, an examination of ways and means of expanding trade in services, and added a cautionary sentence that was evidently applicable more widely: "An attempt to extend a role-based approach to new areas of economic relations while permitting the rules for trade in goods to continue to decay would lack credibility."

In retrospect, the group's recommendations stand up well, since they accurately identified most of the issues that were to be included in the Uruguay Round, and in some cases clearly foreshadowed the results of the negotiations. There are some gaps. From the standpoint of the 1990s, it may in particular seem surprising to find no mention of environmental issues, although in this respect the Leutwiler Group was only representative of its time.

The report, published under the title *Trade Policies for a Better Future*, received wide publicity. In developed countries, at least, it was generally welcomed, although its boldest recommendations, such as that for abolition of the restrictive Multifibre Arrangement, ran into predictable opposition. In most developing countries, it was given a polite reception, precisely because of its recommendations on such matters as textiles, agriculture and voluntary export restraints. Even its scepticism on the value of trade preferences was generally received respectfully, since the group included three distinguished economists and public servants from developing countries.

In Geneva, however, the report was fated to be judged by governments according to whether they favoured new negotiations or not. By the time it appeared, in March 1985, battle lines were already largely drawn between, on one side, an increasing number of developed and developing countries who were now convinced that only a new formal round of negotiations could meet the needs of the trading system and, on the other, a group of developing countries which, under the leadership of Brazil and India, remained fiercely opposed to GATT negotiations that they feared would put them under pressure to adopt policies in which they did not believe, and would weaken rather than strengthen the GATT rules.

The decision to negotiate

The 1982 work programme had gone forward reasonably smoothly. A first deadline was missed when the officials in Geneva failed, at the end of 1983, to reach agreement on the perennial problem of safeguards. However, the issue was now much better understood and, in any case, many people doubted that it could be resolved in isolation from others. A general review of the work programme in November 1984 showed surprisingly good progress in discussions on agricultural trade and on such matters as the review of quantitative restrictions and improvement of dispute settlement arrangements. Even the discussion of trade in services had apparently been put on a more solid footing, with the GATT Secretariat and building henceforth officially involved. However, there was by this time a certain air of unreality about the work programme. In part, this was because the central commitments of 1982 to halt protectionist trends and return to GATT legality were all too clearly not being observed, in spite of an economic upturn. Equally important was the combined effect of a growing belief on the part of many governments that the work programme made sense only as preparation for a new round of trade negotiations in the GATT, and the fears of some others that such negotiations, at least on the terms that seemed likely, would not serve their national interests.

Even before the November 1982 ministerial meeting, the United States favoured a new round of GATT negotiations, although it recognized that the time was not yet ripe. Many other governments including those of some developing countries, saw that the 1982 work programme was likely to lead, in the end, to new negotiations. The gradual strengthening and broadening of support for a new round can be clearly traced through a succession of high-level meetings of government leaders. In May 1983 at Williamsburg, heads of state or government of seven major industrialized countries discussed the possibility of new GATT negotiations for the first time: the subject was to figure in the communiqués of such annual "summit" meetings for the next decade. In November, in the annual GATT session at which Dunkel announced establishment of the Leutwiler Group, Japan made the first formal reference in a GATT body to the idea of a new round. In February 1984, Brock brought together trade ministers of what came to be known as the "Quad" – Canada, the European Community (represented by its Commission), Japan and the United States – to discuss what the content of such negotiations might be. Three months later the discussions were enlarged in an informal meeting of trade ministers attended not only by the Quad but also by representatives of ten other countries, developed and developing, as well as by Dunkel and the Managing Director of the International Monetary Fund. This meeting – the first of a series of trade ministers' meetings that was to be held over the coming years – was officially to review progress with the 1982 work programme. However, many participants made clear that they were now looking to a new round of GATT negotiations. In the same month, at the Organisation for Economic Cooperation and Development (OECD) in Paris, trade and finance ministers of the developed countries put on record their belief that a new round would be of the utmost importance.

Dunkel, who had become convinced some time earlier that new negotiations were both inevitable and desirable, welcomed the trend as "an encouraging change from the defensive preoccupations" of 1982. However, in a speech in March 1984 he warned that any initiative for a new round would be "premature and counterproductive" unless based on a widely shared understanding as to the agenda and objectives of the negotiations. His anxiety was well justified. Developing countries, who already made up the great majority of the GATT membership, had yet to be convinced that a new round of negotiations would be in their interest. They made this clear at a meeting of the GATT Council in May 1984. Speaking on their behalf, the representative of Uruguay insisted that priority must be given to the 1982 work programme, and particularly to the commitments that ministers had undertaken to help developing countries. "Unless and until the work programme is fully implemented in this manner," he concluded, "any initiative such as a new round of negotiations in GATT would be lacking in credibility and devoid of relevance, particularly for developing countries."

The message was not lost on the major industrialized countries. A month later at their 1984 summit meeting in London, they chose their wording with care: they agreed to accelerate completion of the 1982 work programme and "to consult partners in the GATT with a view to decisions at an early date on the possible objectives, arrangements and timing for a new negotiating round". Nevertheless, they were increasingly determined that negotiations should be launched as soon as possible. They were attracted by the potential gains from a new GATT round: a fresh stimulus to trade and the world economy from further liberalization of trade in goods, reinforcement of trading rules that were clearly under pressure, and the opening up of new fields such as trade in services. They were driven equally by a fear that, without new negotiations, GATT would slide into impotence and irrelevance. Trade restriction and trade management had gained much ground since the end of the Tokyo Round, and threatened further advance. In the United States Congress, there was even talk of shutting off the world's largest market behind the protection of an import surcharge that could not be justified under the GATT rules. The US Administration, determined to open negotiations as a means not least of diverting congressional pressures for trade action, warned that it would, if necessary, negotiate outside GATT with "like-minded" governments.

At the annual GATT session in November 1984, the United States, with the support of the European Community, suggested that senior trade policy officials from national capitals should meet to explore the possibilities of a new round. In March 1985, the Community's members reached agreement among themselves, and issued a declaration which, although it set some conditions, including the achievement of "adequate prior international consensus", was a clear "Yes" to the idea of a new round of GATT negotiations. Early in April, ministers of the industrialized countries, meeting at OECD, agreed to propose that a Preparatory Committee of senior officials should meet in Geneva before the end of the summer, with the aim of reaching broad consensus on subjects for the coming negotiations.

The Leutwiler Group's report, injected into this situation, inevitably ran into a barrage of criticism from developing countries that were hostile to the idea of a new round. So did Dunkel, both as the instigator of the group and because he had decided that he could no longer appear to be sitting on the fence on the issue of new negotiations. Introducing the report, he told GATT Council members that he saw a decision to launch a new round as an expression of readiness to work out solutions to problems identified by the 1982 work programme. The new round, he said, "should be directed towards the primary goal of strengthening the multilateral trading system and further opening world markets."

This April 1985 meeting of the Council marked the opening of nearly a year and a half of continuous, at times bitter, and eventually decisive debate in

GATT on whether and how to launch a new round and on what the aims of the Round should be. The debate was at times procedural; at other times, it centred on the question of whether or not the Round should include negotiations on trade in services. At stake, however, were opposing views on whether new negotiations were desirable at all, and on the direction that the GATT should take in the years ahead. In the years since then, national trade policies, especially in many developing countries, have changed so much that it is difficult now to recall how deep were the disagreements that were fought out at the time. They were, however, very real.

The industrialized countries now opened a determined push for new negotiations. At the 1985 summit meeting, held in Bonn in May, the seven heads of state and government declared their strong endorsement of the OECD agreement that a new GATT round should begin as soon as possible, and added: "most of us think this should be in 1986". A few days later, the Swedish trade minister hosted an informal meeting in Stockholm for ministers from 24 countries, attended also by Dunkel. The meeting appeared to bring developed and developing countries close to agreement on a two-track approach which would result in one set of negotiations: on trade in goods within the framework of GATT, and "separate but parallel" negotiations on services. Supporters of the new Round also agreed to put forward in GATT their proposed objectives for the Round.

The June 1985 meeting of the GATT Council saw its first full debate on the possibility of a new round of negotiations. Immediately it became clear that the Stockholm meeting had not secured agreement. India, on behalf of 24 developing countries,[2] insisted that new negotiations could not take place without prior action on "confidence-building measures to restore credibility to the trading system". These should include "a firm and credible commitment, supported by appropriate legislative action where necessary", not to introduce new GATT-inconsistent restrictive trade measures and to roll back existing measures "forthwith, or through phase-out in accordance with a time-bound programme". Among numerous further conditions were, in GATT, recognition of the unsuitability of the Multifibre Arrangement to regulate trade in textiles and clothing, and an agreement on safeguard. A parallel process should also be started elsewhere "to review and reform the international financial and monetary system". Only on this basis, according to the statement, could negotiations take place. Moreover, such negotiations should focus on concerns of developing countries and confined to trade in goods, leaving aside "new themes alien to the jurisdictional competence of the General Agreement". For their part, the supporters of the new Round proposed a preparatory meeting, to be held before the end of the summer, in which issues to be taken up

---

[2]   Argentina, Bangladesh, Brazil, Burma, Cameroon, Colombia, Côte d'Ivoire, Cuba, Cyprus, Egypt, Ghana, India, Jamaica, Nicaragua, Nigeria, Pakistan, Peru, Romania, Sri Lanka, Tanzania, Trinidad and Tobago, Uruguay, Yugoslavia and Zaire.

could be discussed without commitment. The discussion ended inconclusively, but was renewed at the Council's July meeting. This time a clash could not be avoided.

All the main developed countries submitted their proposals, as agreed in Stockholm. Each government naturally highlighted its particular concerns, and the statements have continuing interest as a succinct listing of the aims pursued by these countries in the years that followed. In the context of the July Council meeting, however, their differences were less important than their similarities. All were insistent on the need for new negotiations; none posed preconditions; all either advocated negotiations on the "new subjects", including services, or at least did not state opposition; all called for a meeting of senior officials to review the agenda for the new Round.

They found important allies among developing countries. Meeting just before the July Council, foreign ministers of the Association of South-East Asian Nations (ASEAN) – at that time consisting of Indonesia, Malaysia, the Philippines, Singapore and Thailand – welcomed the prospect of a new round of negotiations, and called for preparations to start "expeditiously". Korea and Chile also backed the new Round, and made it clear that they would not oppose the inclusion of negotiations on trade in services. A number of other developing countries stated their readiness, although with some conditions, to support a meeting of senior officials to discuss the possible content and organization of a new round of negotiations. However, many of the 24 co-sponsors of the June statement by developing countries repeated their insistence that no such meeting should take place except on the basis of acceptance of the statement's conditions.

Decisions in GATT were traditionally taken by consensus – in other words, by continuing discussion of an issue until a proposed course of action found general support. Determined opposition by one or more countries could block a decision on this basis. This proved to be the situation in the Council Meeting in spite of successive efforts, spread over three days, to find a basis for agreement on a high-level meeting. A Brazilian proposal that would have allowed study of services issues only on a basis rigidly separated from negotiations on goods was found unacceptable by developed countries. Compromise proposals by Sweden and by the European Community gained quite wide support, but failed to win over the Indian-led group. Clearly, no consensus decision was possible. However, consensus was not in fact a legal requirement for GATT decisions. The rules of the General Agreement on Tariffs and Trade provided for decisions to be taken by vote, even though such votes usually were no more than formal confirmation of a decision already reached informally among GATT members. Article XXV of the Agreement, which authorized "joint action" by GATT members and had been the basis on which most earlier negotiations had been launched, permitted decisions that were supported by a two-thirds majority of votes cast, provided that this majority included more than half the GATT membership. Convinced that more than half the GATT membership in fact wanted to launch a new round of negotiations, the United States announced that since "the Council was incapable of taking a decision" it would request a meeting of GATT's highest body, the Session of Contracting Parties.

In making this apparently procedural request, the United States was in fact ensuring a crucial test of support for the new Round. A special Session called at the request of one member country needed the same support – from at least one half of the GATT membership – as a vote for joint action under Article XXV. By the end of August 1985, the necessary number of countries had agreed that a special Session should be called. From that point onwards, it was virtually certain that the new round of negotiations would take place. If any doubt remained, a Secretariat paper on "The launching and organization of trade negotiations in the GATT" spelled out the hard facts of the voting rules. The GATT contracting parties could by simple majority "decide to conduct, sponsor or support multilateral negotiations", although they could not oblige individual countries to accept new substantive obligations as a result of such negotiations. The decision to call for the special Session showed that the necessary majority support for negotiations could be mustered if necessary. In consequence, those countries which remained opposed to the Uruguay Round to the last never pushed their opposition to the point of demanding a vote, and decisions throughout the Round were always taken on the basis of consensus.

The special Session was called at the end of September and, after three days, reached agreement on 2 October that "a preparatory process on the proposed new round of multilateral trade negotiations has now been initiated". A group of senior officials, open to all GATT members, was set up to further the process and to report to the regular November GATT Session, at which "a decision will be taken on the establishment of a Preparatory Committee to prepare the basis for the launching of a new round".

Although the key trial of strength had taken place, and had yielded a clear answer, the group of developing countries that had consistently fought against negotiations on the basis sought by developed countries continued to put up a dogged resistance. The Senior Officials Group met intensively throughout most of October and November, working its way through a systematic discussion of all the issues that had been proposed for negotiation. Brazil and India, in particular, did their best to minimize the significance of the Group's work, preventing any agreed conclusions or even summary of the discussions, so that the Group could finally only transmit a full record of its meetings to the Session. The lack of recommendations from the Group meant that many questions about the aims and content of the new Round had to remain unanswered for the time being. However, the Session had no need of such recommendations to move the process forward. After another round of tough discussions, the contracting parties reached agreement on 28 November to establish a Preparatory Committee, open to all GATT members, "to determine the objectives, subject-matter, modalities for and participation in the multilateral trade negotiations", and to make recommendations by mid-July 1986 for adoption at a ministerial meeting to be held in September 1986. A separate decision on services endorsed the continued exchange of information agreed upon a year earlier, and the preparation of recommendations for the 1986 Session. Summing up the outcome of the Session, its chairman, Felipe Jaramillo of Colombia, claimed buoyantly: "We have demonstrated to that very large community whose future is bound up with the health of international trade that GATT can and will meet the challenges that face the international trading system."

Chapter II

Launching the Uruguay Round

Even though the fundamental decision to negotiate had now been made, the new Preparatory Committee set up by the GATT contracting parties in November 1985 found the going no easier than had the earlier Senior Officials Group.

In nine meetings, running from January to July 1986, the Committee discussed each of the subjects proposed for the new round of negotiations. It started with those which had been given priority by the November Session: the concept of standstill and rollback of restrictive trade measures, treatment of developing countries, and safeguards. It fixed the date and place for the ministerial meeting. Offers to host the meeting came from Canada (Montreal), the European Community (Brussels) and Uruguay (Punta del Este). It picked Uruguay, largely because of the feeling that the new Round must have clear developing-country endorsement. From April onwards, the Committee tried to define how each potential subject for negotiation should be treated in the Declaration to be adopted by ministers in Uruguay: the objectives to be sought, the problems to be tackled, and the way in which the negotiations should be conducted. Progress was extremely slow. The 24 hardliners who in summer 1985 had opposed moves toward new negotiations had now shrunk in number to ten,[3] but they continued to insist that GATT (and therefore the Preparatory Committee) could not discuss the three proposed "new subjects" – services, trade aspects of intellectual property, and trade-related investment measures – which they insisted were outside GATT's competence. Other developing countries tended to sympathize with this view, although they disagreed with the Ten in actively wanting a new round of negotiations on trade in goods, and in feeling that the intransigence of the hardliners was ill-advised. In June, the Ten co-sponsored a draft Ministerial Declaration that made no concessions on the "new subjects", and would have made launching of a new round dependent on prior commitments on a standstill and rollback of trade restrictions that

---

[3]   Argentina, Brazil, Cuba, Egypt, India, Nicaragua, Nigeria, Peru, Tanzania and Yugoslavia.

few observers felt likely to be achieved. The draft received little support, even from other developing countries."

With the July deadline for recommendations by the Preparatory Committee looming, a small group of developed countries, frustrated by the lack of progress in the Committee and by the lack of any evident desire by the Ten to move matters forward, worked together to develop their own draft Ministerial Declaration. The group's participants – representatives of the EFTA countries, Australia, Canada and New Zealand – then approached 20 developing countries which they knew wanted to see the new Round launched. A dialogue was opened between them, with the proceedings chaired alternately by the Swiss Ambassador, Pierre-Louis Girard, and by Jaramillo. These discussions, bypassing the Preparatory Committee in which progress had been blocked, became the key forum in hammering out the draft Ministerial Declaration, with an eventual total of over 40 participants meeting in the EFTA headquarters building. In the last stages, they included the three largest traders, the EC, Japan and the United States. The hardliners, whose unwillingness to cooperate had led to this temporary abandonment of the official GATT forum for negotiations, found themselves excluded. The bargaining was intense, particularly over the aims and methods to be adopted for the negotiations on services and agriculture. Even at the end of the process the text was not fully agreed among the participants: it went forward on 30 July to the Preparatory Committee incorporating compromise language worked out by Girard and Jaramillo. The following day, the Committee, accepting that it would not be able to reach agreement on a single document agreed to forward three texts to the ministerial meeting: the Swiss-Colombian draft, a modification of this text sponsored by Argentina, and a revised but essentially unchanged text from the hardliners (now reduced to nine by Argentina's defection). Most participants in the Committee stated their preferences among the three proposals. The great majority backed the Swiss-Colombian draft as the basis for ministerial discussion, although future problems were foreshadowed by the European Community's unreadiness to endorse the text, prompted essentially by French objections to the proposed commitments on negotiations on agriculture and, on the other side, by the reservations of a number of agricultural exporters who, unlike the French, felt that the same section of the draft did not go far enough.

Six days later, Dunkel sent the three texts to Enrique Iglesias, the Foreign Minister of Uruguay, who was to chair the ministerial meeting. Choosing his words with care, Dunkel noted that "a large number of members of the Committee have indicated their preference" for the Swiss-Colombian text, but that it "was not possible to reach agreed views in the Committee". For this statement, he earned a series of rebukes in formal letters from the representatives of Brazil, India and other members of the hardliners as having, in their view, departed from total evenhandedness. Unpalatable though Dunkel's comment might have been, he could not fairly be accused of any distortion of the truth: the views of the hardliners had been disowned by the majority of developing-country participants in the Committee.

Punta del Este

On 14 September 1986, the ministerial meeting opened in Punta del Este, a pleasant seaside resort on the Atlantic coast, east of the Uruguayan capital of Montevideo. In spite of the remote location, attendance was even greater than in 1982. Wonders had been worked by the Uruguayans to convert to GATT's use facilities that, earlier in the year, had seemed inadequate to the needs of a major negotiating meeting. Nevertheless, conditions for the meeting were not easy. The packed plenary meetings were held in the casino of the town's only large hotel. The critically important sessions of heads of delegations (in which each country would be represented by a single minister, accompanied by one official) took place in the hotel's night club or its dining room, neither of which bore much resemblance to a normal meeting room. Fabric-walled temporary buildings erected to house delegations proved inhospitable when the weather turned cold and stormy. But these drawbacks were offset by the energy and warmth of the hosts, and by the feeling that the participants were embarking, with the new round of negotiations, on a shared and long-delayed adventure.

During the weeks since the final meeting of the Preparatory Committee, some important developments had occurred. The Multifibre Arrangement had been extended, also on 31 July, for a further five years to 1991. This extension apparently settled the shape of the trade regime for textiles and clothing for a period that would run well beyond the new Round, and thereby reduced the sensitivity of the issue for the Punta meeting. The Americans had been extremely active, insisting to their trading partners on the need for new negotiations, including negotiations on services, and making it clear that if the GATT round was not launched, the United States would negotiate elsewhere, or bilaterally. On 13 September, in a radio address, President Reagan called for a new round that would include services, intellectual property and investment. And, in August, a striking new element in the negotiating equation had emerged: a meeting in Cairns, Australia of representatives of 14 predominantly agricultural exporting countries[4] dubbing themselves "key fair trading countries in agriculture", issued a declaration in which they pledged to work together on agricultural trade issues. Their alliance was highly significant, not just because it added a powerful new voice to the negotiations on agriculture, ensuring that this time farm trade could not be ignored in GATT talks, but

---

4   Argentina, Australia, Brazil, Canada, Chile, Colombia, Fiji, Hungary, Indonesia, Malaysia, Philippines, New Zealand, Thailand and Uruguay. Together, these countries account for about one quarter of total world exports of agricultural products.

because the Cairns Group broke clear of the traditional groupings of postwar international economic negotiations. It was composed of several high-income countries (including a member of the Quad); developing countries from Latin America (hardliner Brazil among them), Asia and the Pacific; and an East European nation. The Cairns Declaration, along with the developed-developing country cooperation that had resulted in the Swiss-Colombian proposal of July, served notice that the new Round would be different in character from the North-South confrontations that had dominated so many large international negotiations for the past 20 years.

Most of the real business of the meeting took place away from the plenary hall, either in the discussions among heads of delegations or in smaller groups. The Swiss-Colombian text, already the result of near-agreement among over 40 countries, was the almost automatic basis for negotiation, and in very large part was left unchanged. However, some major issues still had to be settled. The first to be resolved was agriculture. The Swiss-Colombian text had taken a middle position between the European Community and the Cairns Group and, in consequence, the changes made were not large: the text that emerged took care of the preoccupations of both by calling for "more discipline and predictability" and also for "greater liberalization", leaving it to the actual negotiating process to decide how the balance between these aims might come out. The "new issues" – services, intellectual property, and investment – took longer. They involved prolonged negotiation in which the United States, Brazil and India were the central participants, with the US representatives making clear that they were still ready to walk away from the proposed new Round if it did not include these issues. The principal result, which emerged from a long and difficult night meeting of heads of delegations chaired by Iglesias, was a detailed procedural agreement that ensured coverage of all three subjects, but separated them sufficiently from the traditional areas of GATT negotiations to be acceptable to Brazil, India and their allies. The agreement put services in a separate compartment of the overall negotiations. Intellectual property and investment were to be handled along with the more traditional subjects, but with an understanding that any difficulties that might arise in negotiations on the two issues, which almost all developing countries would at that time have preferred to leave off the agenda of the Round, would not be allowed to affect progress in other areas. Further negotiations were also needed in Punta del Este to settle whether or not to include in the new Round a number of subjects which individual countries were keen to pursue.

After a week of intensive negotiation, first among officials and then among ministers, the Punta del Este meeting was successfully concluded on Saturday 20 September, with the adoption of a lengthy declaration that set out the agreed aims and procedures of the coming round of negotiations. The Uruguay Round had been launched. Moreover, it had been launched, everyone seemed to agree, in highly satisfactory style: the dissidents had been won over, all the main issues of world trade would be covered, and ministers had (as the London *Financial Times* put it) "sent a signal to the world that the open trading system can be revitalized in such a way as to reinforce, not drag down, growth and stability in the world economy."

The Punta del Este Declaration

The Declaration adopted by ministers at Punta del Este is printed in full at the end of this book and its specific provisions for the negotiations on individual subjects are cited frequently in the following chapters. However, it deserves a general review because it provided the essential agreed basis on which the Uruguay Round as a whole took place.

The key to handling the subject of services was found in dividing the negotiations into two parts. Negotiations on trade in goods were placed firmly in the context of GATT, and defined in the first (and by far the longest) part of the Declaration, which was adopted by ministers acting in their capacity of contracting parties to the General Agreement. The coming negotiations on trade in services were defined in Part II of the Declaration which, although it provided for GATT procedures and practices to be applied and for the negotiations to be serviced by the GATT Secretariat, was adopted separately by ministers acting simply as representatives of their governments. On the same basis, the ministers finally adopted the Declaration as a whole, including a preamble that, for the first time in GATT's history, gave the new Round an official name – the Uruguay Round – in honour of the host country of the meeting. (Previous rounds of negotiation were never *officially* given the names by which they are more generally known – e.g. the Kennedy Round or the Tokyo Round.) They announced confidently that the negotiations "will be concluded within four years", and also agreed to meet again, when results of the negotiations had been established, to decide how they should be put into effect.

The procedural distinction between the goods and services negotiations was to be maintained throughout the Round. The goods negotiations were guided by a "Group of Negotiations on Goods", chaired first by Dunkel and later by his successor Peter Sutherland in the official capacity of Director-General of the sponsoring body, GATT. A separate "Group of Negotiations on Services" looked after services. The Uruguay Round as a whole was directed by the Trade Negotiations Committee, chaired by the Uruguayan foreign minister when meeting at ministerial level and, at official-level meetings, by Dunkel or Sutherland, who for this purpose were elected to the chairmanship in their personal capacity, to preserve the distinction between GATT and the Round as a whole. The distinction was never understood by the general public and became increasingly artificial as the passionate disagreements over the issue of services faded, and the political reality of the unity of the negotiations became obvious.

Part I of the Punta del Este Declaration, covering the negotiations on trade in goods, consists of a preamble and seven sections.

The preamble contains the basic decision to negotiate, as well as stating the determination of GATT members to halt and reverse protectionism, remove distortions to trade, preserve GATT's principles and forward its objectives, and develop a more open, viable and durable multilateral trading system. It also expresses the ministers' conviction that such action would promote growth and development, and their consciousness of the Round's relevance to problems of international finance, money and debt.

The first operative section, on the Round's objectives, reflects the considerations set out in the preamble. The negotiations are to be aimed at liberalizing and expanding world trade, to the benefit of all countries and especially developing countries, and are to include the improvement of access to markets by reducing and removing trade barriers. GATT's role is to be strengthened, its rules reinforced and given greater coverage, and its responsiveness to the evolving international economic environment improved. (A mention at this point of trade in high technology products, difficulties in commodity markets, and the debt issue served to bring into the Declaration matters on which no agreement had been reached to negotiate specifically.) The negotiations are to help strengthen the inter-relationship between trade and other economic policies affecting growth and development, and to contribute to improvement in the functioning of the international monetary system and the flow of finance and investment to developing countries.

The second section states general principles for the negotiations. They are to be transparent – an aim particularly important for the smaller countries which feared that their interests would be affected by deals reached among the larger participants. The negotiations are to be treated from start to finish as a single undertaking. This rule, on which the European Community laid particular stress, underlay the assertion oft-repeated during the Round that "nothing is agreed until everything is agreed", although it formally did not apply to the negotiations on services. Even within the goods negotiations, balanced concessions are to be sought within broad trading areas and subjects, "in order to avoid unwarranted cross-sectoral demands".

A statement of the principles that are to govern the participation of developing countries in the Round repeats, almost word for word, the relevant sections of the "enabling clause" drawn up at the end of the Tokyo Round. The next section, on "standstill and rollback", is intended to stop participants in the Round from taking trade measures to improve their negotiating position against other countries, but also represents a renewal of the pledges made in 1982. The standstill commitments require that no GATT-inconsistent trade restrictions shall be introduced, and that even GATT-consistent measures shall not go beyond a necessary minimum. Rollback calls for either phasing-out by the end of the Round all trade-restrictive or distorting measures inconsistent with GATT, or for them to be brought into conformity with the post-Uruguay Round rules, with no counterpart concessions to be asked from other participants.

The next two sections set out the specific aims for each area of the negotiations on goods. Thirteen "subjects for negotiations" are given: tariffs, non-tariff measures, tropical products, natural resource-based products, textiles and clothing, agriculture, GATT Articles, safeguards, the MTN agreements and arrangements (i.e. the "codes" negotiated in the Tokyo Round), subsidies and countervailing measures, dispute settlement, trade-related aspects of intellectual property rights (including trade in counterfeit goods), and trade-related investment measures. A fourteenth negotiating subject is added by a section on "Functioning of the GATT System".

The last two sections of Part I define participation in the negotiations on goods and organizational matters. Ministers agreed that the negotiations should be open to GATT members and provisional members, to countries which in practice were treated as if they were members and had, by April 1987, applied for membership, to countries which had already applied for membership, and to developing countries that started accession procedures by April 1987. These conditions effectively set participation in the Round at more than 100 countries even from the beginning, and permitted almost any country to take full part, except that they offered no opening to the Soviet Union, and provided specifically that non-members of GATT would have no say in decisions to change or add to the GATT rules. The organizational provisions established the Group of Negotiations on Goods and called on it to decide on detailed negotiating plans by mid-December, to set up a mechanism to monitor performance under the standstill and rollback commitments, and to establish and coordinate working groups. The Group was also given the right to decide on the inclusion of additional subjects in the Round. Finally, it was required to evaluate, at the end of the Round, the results achieved for developing countries.

The separate Part II of the Punta del Este Declaration, on services, is very brief. Like the "subject" sections of Part I, it sets out the aims of negotiations on services. It also makes clear that the negotiations form part of the Uruguay Round, are to be directed by the Group of Negotiations on Services, shall follow GATT procedures and practices, and will be serviced by the GATT Secretariat, with technical support as required from other organizations.

An essential part of the Punta del Este package was an agreed statement made by the meeting's chairman before the Declaration was adopted. This included a number of points on which no agreement had been reached, in some cases because of fundamental differences, in others simply for lack of time. African countries, in particular, had made a late proposal on their problems in the area of commodities, natural resource-based products and tropical products, and it was agreed that this proposal should be referred to the Trade Negotiations Committee. The statement acknowledged a common concern with "disequilibria" in world trade, but recognized that there was no agreement on whether the problem was one for international, rather than national, action. Other issues recorded as lacking a consensus to negotiate "at this time" included the export of hazardous substances (a concern especially of several African countries), commodity arrangements and restrictive business practices (both traditional developing-country interests but never seriously tackled in GATT), and workers' rights – a subject which the US Congress had required the American delegation to raise, but which was strongly opposed by developing and other countries.

The negotiations begin

Back in Geneva, the Trade Negotiations Committee, the Group of Negotiations on Goods, and the Group of Negotiations on Services (immediately and inevitably abbreviated to TNC, GNG and GNS, respectively) held their first meetings. Dunkel, as already noted, chaired the first two; Jaramillo chaired the services group. The most urgent business – establishment of negotiating groups for the various goods issues, and the elaboration of negotiating plans – took longer than expected and, in consequence, the Round experienced the first of many missed deadlines as 19 December 1986 went past with no agreement on the negotiating plans. However, the hold-up was not serious. After some discussion of alternative possibilities, negotiating groups were established for each of the 15 subjects identified in the Punta del Este Declaration (the 14 goods-related subjects in Part I, plus services), and provided with their marching orders in the shape of negotiating plans based on the corresponding commitments in the Declaration. The Surveillance Body was set up to keep performance under the standstill and rollback commitments under review. Chairmen were appointed for each body, for the most part drawn from senior trade officials of the Uruguay Round participants.

Starting with the Negotiating Group on Tariffs on 10 February 1987, each of the negotiating groups in turn embarked on its work.

Chapter III

The road to Montreal: 1986–88

From the launching of work in the 15 negotiating groups in February 1987, and up to mid-1988, the focus of the Uruguay Round shifted. Meetings of the Trade Negotiations Committee were rare. For the time being, the road ahead was clear and little guidance of the Round as a whole was needed. Each negotiating group began to explore how to meet the objectives set for its part of the Round by the Punta del Este Declaration and by its own negotiating plan. Each had its own specific set of tasks, but all had to cover the same initial ground, as Dunkel explained later in the year to finance ministers in Washington: "a clear definition and understanding of specific issues to be tackled, the proposals on which negotiations will be based and the negotiating techniques that may be appropriate. The task of negotiating specific agreements reaching agreed solutions should then begin."

Access to markets: tackling traditional barriers to trade

The Uruguay Round was to be the most ambitious and widest-ranging trade negotiation ever undertaken. But ambition and the inclusion of subjects new to GATT did not mean that the need for renewed efforts to reduce the traditional barriers to international trade could be ignored. Two of the fifteen negotiating groups set up under the Punta del Este Declaration were set tasks familiar to GATT negotiators for 40 years. They were required to engage in mutual bargaining to reduce tariffs (import duties) and non-tariff barriers to trade. Two more groups were established to look at possibilities of removing tariff and non-tariff restrictions affecting two specific sectors of trade: tropical products, and products based on natural resources. Together, these four groups embodied one main thrust of the Round: the drive to improve access to international markets. This effort was important in itself, but it was also important to acceptance of the results of the Round as a whole. As the Tokyo Round had shown, multilateral agreements on trade rules, however significant in their eventual effects, attract little attention or understanding from the press and public opinion: what wins public and legislative support for an international trade agreement is still its measurable effect in cutting down

29

import duties and removing quotas. US negotiators, in particular, insisted that a good market access result from the Uruguay Round was essential to Congressional approval.

All four negotiating groups were treading paths well defined in previous negotiating rounds.

Most traditional and familiar of all the Round's negotiating areas was tariffs. GATT indeed came into being as an agreement to improve market access through the reduction of tariffs, the means by which countries have traditionally restricted imports in order to protect their domestic producers. The GATT tackled tariffs by mutual bargaining among its member countries, in a series of negotiating rounds that began in 1947 and stretched down to the Tokyo Round of the 1970s. In the early years, the bargaining was mostly bilateral, between pairs of countries who would each agree on mutual reductions in the rates (usually percentage rates of the value of the imported goods) they charged on imports of particular categories of goods, and would give undertakings ("bindings") not to raise these rates subsequently without providing compensation. The benefits of this bilateral request-and-offer bargaining on dozens or hundreds of individual tariff rates were then extended to all the GATT signatories, in accordance with Article I of the GATT – the most-favoured-nation (MFN) rule which provided that each member would give all others the benefit of the best treatment that it offered on the goods of any foreign country. In later rounds, starting in the 1960s, the negotiating technique changed. An overall target or formula was set for the tariff reductions to be made, and the final negotiation was concerned with exceptions to the general rule: agreement on which tariffs would be reduced by less (sometimes more) than the target amount.

By common consent, the continuing effort in GATT to reduce and bind tariffs had been – as far as it went – a huge success. The major industrialized countries progressively slashed the average level of their import duties on manufactured products from 40% or more in the immediate postwar period to less than 5% when the Tokyo Round cuts were fully in force. This opening-up of the world's biggest markets is agreed to have been one of the main forces behind the explosive growth in international trade during the second half of the twentieth century, and a principal contributor to economic growth and the consequent rise in living standards in most countries over the same period.

But the story is not one of unalloyed success. Average tariffs indeed fell sharply, but in some sectors the cuts were small and high rates of duty remained. This was particularly true for textiles and clothing, and for agricultural products. Moreover, importing countries were usually happy to have cheap raw materials for their domestic manufacturers, but less ready to allow in finished products made from those materials. In consequence, raw-material producers found themselves facing "tariff escalation" in their export markets: a tariff structure that hit their semi-manufactures harder than their primary products, and manufactures harder still, thereby discouraging them from building export industries based on the resources that should have been a major competitive strength. As a result, primary-producing countries had taken only a marginal part in GATT tariff negotiations up to the Uruguay Round, and their own tariffs remained high and largely unbound. Developing countries hardly participated in tariff negotiations at all. Most of them were convinced that they were better off with high tariff protection. Most, too, were insistent that they should not in any case be asked to pay for trade concessions by the rich developed countries – a point of view which, whatever its economic or political justification in theory, in practice meant that they deprived themselves of any real bargaining power in negotiations.

For the Uruguay Round, each participant would approach the tariff negotiations with its own national trade interests in mind, urged on in particular by its national business community. It would be seeking to open up foreign markets for the goods it already produced or felt itself well placed to produce in the future. Moreover, it would usually be reluctant to cut its own tariffs, even if economists argued that this would help national economic growth and consumers would have welcomed lower-priced imports. Pressures from domestic producers unwilling to face greater competition, and sometimes also the fear that lower tariffs might lead to a fall in government revenues, meant that most countries would offer tariff reductions only in exchange for comparable cuts by their negotiating partners. Each participant, in any case, would also be reluctant to show its hand until the last possible moment, since disclosure might deprive it of later bargaining power and would expose it to criticism by domestic interests facing loss of protection. GATT tariff negotiations have always had something in common with poker.

Past negotiations on non-tariff measures had been an outgrowth of the efforts to cut tariffs. Many of the key rules of the General Agreement on Tariffs and Trade, originally negotiated in 1947, were concerned essentially with protecting the value of tariff reductions that had been agreed among the signatory countries by ensuring that those reductions were not subsequently eroded or that protection was not provided through other means. As tariffs were cut to lower and lower levels, these other means of protection became increasingly important. The effect of existing barriers grew more obvious as import duties ceased to be such significant obstacles to trade, and new non-tariff barriers were erected in response to protectionist pressures from domestic producers, or as incidental by-products of policies with quite different purposes, such as consumer safety.

In the immediate postwar years, by far the most important non-tariff barriers were quantitative restrictions, or quotas, usually applied to restrict imports but, occasionally, also to prevent exports. Quantitative restrictions were brought under control in two ways. First, the General Agreement broadly banned their use, subject to a number of specific exceptions. For instance, quotas could be used to restrain the total inflow of imports if a country ran into balance-of-payments difficulties, or in safeguard action to restrict imports of particular categories of goods if competing domestic industries ran into difficulties. Restrictions could also be imposed for reasons of health or national security, or to foster infant industries in developing countries. Second, in the immediate postwar years successful efforts were made in GATT and under the Marshall Plan to dismantle other restrictions left over from the Depression years of the 1930s and World War II. In spite of these efforts, a good many quotas remained, even in developed countries.

The drive to control and remove other non-tariff barriers came later. The first big multilateral agreement to deal with one type of non-tariff measure was negotiated during the Kennedy Round of the 1960s, and set rules for the use of anti-dumping measures. Bargaining on a variety of individual national non-tariff measures also took place during the Kennedy Round. Soon afterwards, GATT started to build up a systematic inventory of non-tariff measures affecting trade. (The distinction between non-tariff barriers – NTBs – and non-tariff measures – NTMs – is that the latter includes measures that distort exports as well those affecting imports.) This inventory formed the basis for much wider negotiations on NTMs in the Tokyo Round, leading to the set of multilateral agreements or codes of conduct agreed in 1979. But it also provided the basis for further bargaining, similar in character to that on tariffs, aimed at removing specific national non-tariff measures that blocked or restricted trade.

For the Uruguay Round, the negotiations on non-tariff barriers were handled on several different tracks, not all of which were directly concerned with specific measures. The negotiations on safeguards, for instance, had the aim of reinvigorating GATT rules whose decline into disuse had opened the way for introduction of "voluntary export restraints" and other important non-tariff restrictions on trade which had no justification under GATT. Logically, success in these negotiations would open the way to the disappearance of such restrictions. Similarly, the aim of most participants in the textiles and clothing negotiations was to end the Multifibre Arrangement which permitted a web of bilateral restrictions on trade. The group on trade-related investment measures (TRIMS) was to spend much time discussing whether to discipline national requirements that effectively restricted imports. In the Round's Surveillance Body, periodic efforts were made by developing countries to obtain concrete results from commitments made in Punta del Este to "roll back" progressively, without compensation, trade-restrictive or distorting measures inconsistent with the GATT rules. But there were also two tracks specifically concerned with negotiations on non-tariff measures as such. On the first track, improvement of the big multilateral codes negotiated in the Tokyo Round was assigned to negotiating groups set up for that purpose: a separate group to deal with the subsidies code of 1979, and another to negotiate on whatever changes might be sought in the remaining codes. The second track – the responsibility of the Group on Non-Tariff Measures – was to handle whatever further negotiations seemed necessary on NTMs not covered by the Tokyo Round codes, whether these turned out to be essentially a matter for bilateral bargaining (like most tariff negotiations) or lent themselves to efforts to reach new multilateral agreements.

A third market access group was set up at the insistence of a number of countries which were major producers of natural resource-based products, such as mineral ores, fish and forest products, including timber and paper. Remembering difficulties in past negotiations, they hoped that they might obtain better results, in terms of opening up export markets for these products, in a group which would focus exclusively on natural resource-based products, and which could look not only at tariffs and non-tariff measures but also at government policies which affected trade in these products.

From the first, the three groups – tariffs, non-tariff measures and natural resource-based products – were seen as closely linked to such an extent that they were given a single chairman, and often held their meetings on successive days.

A fourth negotiating group, on tropical products, was more distinct from the others. In substance, because of its product coverage, its work was to some extent tied to the agricultural negotiations. Politically, the group had a special importance because it was outstandingly the area of the Round in which developing countries, including some of the poorest among them, had a particular export interest, while developed countries generally played the part only of importers. Arising from this exceptional status, it had been agreed by ministers in Punta del Este that the tropical products negotiations should be given priority, and that their results could be brought into effect ahead of those in the rest of the Round. Nevertheless, this group too was essentially dealing with problems of market access familiar from earlier GATT negotiations.

A problem common to all the market access negotiations was that the potential value of concessions on the specific obstacles with which they were dealing would depend to a great extent on what was achieved in other areas of the Uruguay Round. The significance of tariffs on textiles and agricultural products, for example, would depend on what was done about the broader policies that essentially governed trade in these sectors. Similarly the risks involved in removing tariffs protecting sensitive sectors would be affected by what was done about the GATT rules on safeguard action, subsidies and dumping. Apart from the tropical products negotiations, which at least partially escaped the problem because of their priority status, the final bargaining stage in the market access negotiations could not begin until participants were reasonably confident of the wider trade policy regime into which a future dismantling of specific trade barriers would fit. Moreover, negotiations on general trade rules stimulate much less vigorous lobbying of governments than proposals to remove tariffs or non-tariff measures directly affecting particular industries. The toughest item-by-item bargaining on such measures has always, in consequence, happened over a short period at the very end of trade negotiations. The effect of these factors in the Uruguay Round was that the market access negotiations were to be constantly held hostage to progress elsewhere.

Tariffs

The Punta del Este Declaration called for the negotiators to "aim, by appropriate methods, to reduce or, as appropriate, eliminate tariffs including the reduction or elimination of high tariffs and tariff escalation", and added that "emphasis shall be given to the expansion of tariff concessions among all participants". This inelegant formulation sketched a number of possibilities and broad objectives, but it was noticeably lacking in precision. By implication, it required the negotiators to consider such questions as:

- Which tariffs might it be appropriate to eliminate, rather than just to reduce?
- For those tariffs which were not eliminated, could a target level of reduction be agreed?
- What level of tariff should be considered "high", and how might such tariffs be reduced or eliminated? (And how, in contrast, should low tariffs be handled?)
- How should tariff escalation be defined and identified, and what method might be appropriate for reducing it?
- If some participants had not in the past given many tariff concessions, how could they be persuaded to do so now? (Most were developing countries which did not accept that they should negotiate on a basis of reciprocity; the remainder were largely countries that would reduce and bind their tariffs only if markets for agricultural products and primary products were opened to them.)
- Could some kind of basic tariff-cutting formula be worked out that would, if applied, achieve the results sought?
- What tariffs were actually applied against imports by the participating countries? What tariff bindings had they committed themselves to in past GATT negotiations? And given that most countries' bindings were at higher rates than they actually applied, should the negotiations be concerned with the bound rates or the applied rates? A reduction of, say, two-fifths from an applied rate of 10% would result in a much lower final tariff (just 6%) than a similar cut in a GATT-bound rate of 20% (reduced to 12%). But it was the bound rates that represented a country's present obligations: was it fair that it be subject to larger cuts because it had been more liberal than required in its import policy?
- What was the value of each country's imports under each tariff heading? (This would provide a rough indication of the value of a cut in the tariff

concerned to its trading partners, in terms of the additional exports that the cut might permit.)

The negotiating group on tariffs spent most of the first two years of the Uruguay Round wrestling with questions like this. Some of the answers emerged from its meetings. Others had to await political decisions.

A key question, with which the group quickly came to grips, was whether agreement could be reached on a "formula" approach to the tariff negotiations, as used in the Kennedy and Tokyo Rounds. In the Kennedy Round, it had been decided quite early on that the objective for the industrialized countries would be to cut all tariffs by 50%, with only a bare minimum of exceptions which would have to be individually justified. For the Tokyo Round, a similar but somewhat more complicated formula had been found which had the effect of requiring larger cuts in the highest tariffs. In both cases, the formula approach cut through many problems, and meant that the negotiations focused on which exceptions to the formula should be permitted. Again in both cases, the final result had been an average cut in tariffs on manufactured goods of about one third. Obviously, if the aim of elimination of tariffs was adopted, that would simplify the negotiations still further.

On the whole, it was the smaller countries which preferred a formula approach to the negotiations. This was not surprising, since an automatic tariff-cutting procedure would help to overcome their inherent lack of bargaining power against the larger countries. The United States took the opposite view, believing that there was not much point in applying an overall cut to what were now, as a result of past negotiations, generally low tariffs (the US average rate was less than 4%, and 99% of its imports were bound). It felt that for the industrialized countries, a request-and-offer bargaining procedure, focused on individual products, would yield better results in reducing high tariffs and tariff escalation. Moreover, modern data-processing techniques would mean that the mechanics of negotiating on individual tariff lines should be more manageable than in the past. Some commentators pointed out that an unstated advantage of a non-formula approach was that sensitive sectors such as textiles might more easily escape large cuts in tariffs. Proposals from the European Community, the Nordic countries and Switzerland envisaged a "hybrid procedure", with a formula to be applied to the higher tariffs, and request-and-offer bargaining for low tariffs. Alone among developed countries, Japan argued for complete elimination of industrial tariffs by developed countries except for tariffs on mining and forestry products, on which in any case it preferred to negotiate in the group on natural resource-based products.

On bindings, the most far-reaching proposal, also put forward early in the negotiations, came from Canada which suggested that all countries should bind their entire range of tariffs. This step would require only a comparatively small advance by industrialized countries, whose tariffs on manufactures at least were already largely bound, but it implied a fairly revolutionary shift in policy by developing countries. Less ambitiously, several other developed countries, including the European Community, agreed that all industrial tariffs ought to be bound. They suggested that developing countries could appropriately contribute to the outcome of the tariff negotiations by increasing the proportion of their tariffs that were bound, even if the bindings were at comparatively high levels.

Brazil proposed that developed countries eliminate all tariffs immediately for imports from developing countries, and after ten years for imports from developed countries. For their part, developing countries would reduce and bind a substantial proportion of their import duties.

The need for a broad and reliable database on tariff rates and trade flows was generally felt. GATT already had a Tariff Study, launched several years earlier, but it included only twelve participants (one, however, was the twelve-member EC). A database had also been built up to support the technically challenging changeover from the former tariff classification system to the new Harmonized System, due to be completed by the larger countries by the beginning of 1988. An ambitious proposal was under discussion in the GATT Council for a fully computerized integrated database that would bring together detailed tariff and trade data for countries responsible for more than 90% of trade among GATT members. However, this clearly would involve technical and other problems that might take so long to overcome that it would not be available to support the negotiations.

Almost from the beginning of the negotiations, there were also disagreements about whether tariffs and product-specific non-tariff measures should be negotiated together or separately, and whether negotiations on tariffs on agricultural, tropical and natural resource-based products should take place in the tariff group or in the specialized groups for these sectors. For textiles, many countries argued that tariffs on textiles and clothing should be part of the work of the tariff group, since the textiles negotiating group was essentially concerned with what should replace the quantitative restrictions of the Multifibre Arrangement.

These issues provided the main subject-matter for the tariff group right up to the mid-term review of the Round at the end of 1988, and in some cases beyond.

On the question of whether to use a formula approach or item-by-item bargaining, the United States was almost alone in preferring the second approach, but was adamant in its position. Ideas on a possible formula approach were refined, with Switzerland (the author of the formula adopted for the Tokyo Round) suggesting a formula that would apply to all countries and would reduce even peak tariffs to a maximum of 15%. The European countries and New Zealand proposed a combination of formula and item-by-item for maximum impact. Australia argued for combining tariff and non-tariff negotiations to reduce their total "effective rate of assistance". While other countries doubted the technical practicability of the Australian proposal, there was some movement towards the view that, in the end, market access commitments might best be discussed in a single negotiation. Brazil's proposal found little support, but developing countries in general argued strongly that they should make their own decisions on what they could afford to offer in the way of reductions or bindings. To this, the reply of many developed countries was that the more advanced developing countries, at least, should join fully in the tariff reductions. On the question of basing negotiations on bound or unbound rates, the majority of countries preferred to use the bound rates, where these existed; if no rate had been bound, most but not all countries thought that negotiations should take as their starting point the rate applied in September 1986, when the Uruguay Round was launched. Finally, some countries which had recently made tariff cuts autonomously (i.e. on their own initiative, not as result of negotiation with other countries), insisted that these should be "credited" to them in the Uruguay Round negotiations. Such cuts, which had often accompanied a stabilization agreement reached with the International Monetary Fund or World Bank, became an important issue later in the negotiations, as many more developing countries and countries of Central and Eastern Europe autonomously reduced or removed trade barriers.

Lack of adequate factual information, especially from developing countries, on applied tariff levels and on the trade in each product was a matter of great concern. For a long time, no additional information was available beyond that given by the twelve participants in the Tariff Study. Only under pressure, and when some developed countries said that they were simply not prepared to negotiate with participants who had not given such information, did an increasing but still small number of developing countries begin to submit data.

By the early summer of 1988, many participants were becoming worried by the lack of progress, particularly in settling the question of whether to negotiate on the basis of a general formula or item by item. They pressed the group's chairman, Lindsay Duthie of Australia, to put forward compromise proposals. He declined, however, believing that views were still too far apart to discern possible common ground. In June, however, came an informal proposal by seven countries (Australia, Canada, Hong Kong, Hungary, Korea, New Zealand and Switzerland) which, although not accepted as it stood, gave the negotiating process a strong push forward.

The essence of the proposal was that the negotiations should apply a harmonization formula to all tariffs, and should aim at a substantial increase in the level of bindings by all participants. Perhaps more important, however, was the source of the proposal and the response it elicited. It emerged from what amounted to a reconstitution of the alliance of countries which, in the summer of 1986, had provided the decisive push towards negotiation of the aims and ground rules of the Uruguay Round. The sponsors of the paper, along with Colombia and the Nordic countries, had formed what became known (because of the Geneva hotel where they had met) as the "De la Paix Group". De la Paix Group members, unlike members of the Cairns Group, did not necessarily share even broad objectives on specific issues, but they were all dedicated to bringing the Round to a successful conclusion. From this time onwards, they were on many occasions to exert a strong and constructive influence on the progress of the Round. On this occasion, apart from creating considerable surprise, they shocked other countries into trying to formulate a generally acceptable basis for the tariff negotiations.

The most productive new idea came from the United States which, still maintaining its opposition to the use of a general tariff-cutting formula, suggested that the group should focus on reaching agreement about the ultimate results to be achieved from the tariff negotiations. A US working paper circulated in October suggested that the immediate aim might be an agreed commitment to a given percentage cut in average tariff levels over a stated period, with each participant achieving this through its own choice of "modality" (trade negotiators' jargon: "method" or "procedure" provide close equivalents), and with all countries participating fully and binding their entire tariff schedules. A focus on results, the United States argued, would recognize the political and practical needs of different parties to approach the negotiations in different ways, and permit them to pursue their individual objectives, but acknowledge the obligation of all to participate fully. Each could decide whether to use a formula or request-and-offer approach. Korea produced a somewhat similar proposal that participants agree on a "macro-target" for the negotiations.

The immediate reaction to the US proposal was unenthusiastic. The De la Paix Group, in particular, argued that it meant abandonment of the aim of abolishing tariff peaks and escalation, that a formula approach would ensure wider participation of developing countries, that a target reduction might be reached through cuts in tariffs of no interest to others, and that it was unrealistic to expect developing countries to bind all their tariffs. But others thought that a target figure offered a way out of the impasse into which the discussion on aims had strayed, and could provide the basis for a politically worthwhile agreement. This discussion effectively brought to an end the clash over whether a formula or item-by-item approach to the negotiations should be adopted: the US position was recognized as meaning that no agreement was attainable on a uniform formula approach.

The final weeks before the mid-term review of the Round at the end of 1988 were taken up by efforts to hammer out a statement of aims for the tariff negotiations that would set targets for the main elements of a final agreement and also settle other outstanding issues such as the choice of bound or unbound rates as the base for negotiations and the starting date for detailed bargaining. Successive proposals narrowed the gaps. Gradually, the more technical issues were agreed: 1 July 1989 was set as the starting point for negotiations, tariff and trade data were to be exchanged accordingly, the phasing of tariff cuts was left to be settled in the negotiations, bound MFN rates were to be used as the basis for negotiations or, if no binding existed, the unbound rate applied in

September 1986. Other agreed language repeated aims and guidelines already set for the tariff negotiations in the Punta del Este Declaration.

The ministers were left with just a few key decisions. Could a figure or other clear indication be set as a target for the tariff reductions? should the aim be to increase tariff bindings substantially, or to achieve the binding of all tariffs (and should this include agricultural tariffs)? And should developed, as well as developing, countries be given credit for autonomous liberalization?

Non-tariff measures

For non-tariff measures, the instructions provided by the Punta del Este Declaration were brief in the extreme: "Negotiations shall aim to reduce or eliminate non-tariff measures, including quantitative restrictions, without prejudice to any action to be taken in fulfilment of the rollback commitments." The second half of the sentence apparently narrowed the field to measures that were permissible under the GATT rules, since those that were not legal were supposed to be dismantled unilaterally under the rollback requirements. But this still left a very wide range of measures for possible negotiation.

In practice, the first two years of negotiations on non-tariff measures ran closely in parallel with those on tariffs. Indeed, to some extent they overlapped, since such issues as whether the group should be dealing with agricultural trade barriers came up in both sets of negotiations, and other common issues arose which led to the same proposals by governments sometimes being put to both groups.

The negotiators inherited a good deal of preliminary work that had been carried out under the 1982 work programme. Between 1983 and 1986, a working group assembled fairly full information on quantitative and other non-tariff restrictions maintained by GATT members, on the basis of notifications by the countries concerned, and it had been agreed that this information base should be kept up to date by a new GATT technical group. A separate inventory of measures affecting trade in industrial products had been established at the end of the Tokyo Round, based on reverse notifications – in other words, on information provided by countries whose exports were hampered by measures applied in the national markets concerned. The 1983-86 work had included some analysis by the Secretariat of which products were affected by the notified measures in each country, and some discussion in the working group of how negotiations on them might be undertaken. As already mentioned, the Secretariat, in a task that covered both tariffs and non-tariff measures, was engaged in studying how a computerized and integrated database might be built up that would bring together detailed information on trade barriers and matching trade flows. Soon afterwards, the GATT Council gave the go-ahead for establishment of the database.

Among the first matters discussed by the negotiating group were how existing information on individual non-tariff measures could be improved, supplemented, and perhaps reorganized. One idea considered but discarded as likely to be unproductive was that known barriers might be sorted into categories according to whether they could best be liberalized through application of a formula approach, through existing or new multilateral arrangements or through the application of a request-and-offer approach. Another potential distinction was between measures that were legal under GATT and those that were not, since the latter were supposed to be removed unilaterally. This was proposed as early as the group's first meeting, but again not adopted, partly because scrutiny of illegal measures was felt not to be the task of this group, and partly because it was felt that the work would not lead to useful results. Many countries felt that in any case the group should not try to define its subject-matter too closely, leaving it open to any country to seek reduction in whatever non-tariff barriers it felt were important obstacles to its trade. Although no decisions on these proposals were reached, the group did agree in October 1987 to update the basic information in the database, and to seek to enlarge it to all participants in the Round.

Discussion of the negotiating approach also began early. Proposals from Australia, the United States and Canada in June 1987 set out the main options. Australia suggested alternative possibilities of formula, multilateral code or item-by-item bargaining, according to the nature of the measure. The two other proposals suggested that tariffs and non-tariff measures might best be negotiated together, thus attacking all the measures affecting a particular product. This approach implied that the negotiations would be largely on an item-by-item basis. The Canadians also proposed that countries put forward, by December 1987, lists of the products in which they had an export interest. Further discussion on negotiating techniques in later meetings brought out a variety of concerns and comments. Was there a risk that an integrated approach might lead to actual increases in tariffs, if these replaced non-tariff measures? Could a formula approach be useful for cutting back quantitative restrictions and reducing fixed fees charged on imports, such as consular fees? How could the group keep a collective eye on bilateral request-and-offer negotiations? Would a central negotiating register (an EC idea) help in this? Could the Australian ideas on measurement of the effective rate of assistance to an industry, put forward also in the tariff group, be useful in assessing the value of offers?

In February 1988, a year after its first meeting, the negotiating group on non-tariff measures accepted a proposal by its chairman that participants should submit their proposals by June on which measures should be covered, and which problems should be tackled, by multilateral, formula and request-and-offer procedures respectively. Participants were also to come forward by September with any proposals they might have for the conduct of the negotiations, including specific arrangements affecting developing countries. The hope of the chairman and Secretariat was that such written proposals might help to move the negotiations away from discussion of general principles towards more productive discussion of specific problems and measures. The aim, as they saw it, should be to reach an understanding, at the mid-term ministerial meeting in Montreal at the end of the year, on procedures for the negotiations and a timetable for carrying them out.

The same meeting launched discussion on an issue that was eventually to lead to a separate Uruguay Round agreement. Indonesia asked the group to take up the subject of preshipment inspection, a subject which had already been raised outside the Round in the GATT Committee on Customs Valuation. Preshipment inspection services, increasingly used by developing countries in recent years, involve verification by private specialist companies of the quality, quantity or price of goods about to be shipped. The work is carried out in the country of export, but on behalf of the importing country, usually with the aim of preventing fraud or the illegal export of capital through overstatement of the cost of imported goods. As Indonesia pointed out, bilateral friction had arisen because such services were said to result in delays, increased costs, and arbitrary price-setting. A multilateral agreement on preshipment inspection, it suggested, would be greatly preferable to the unilateral regulation by exporting countries that otherwise seemed likely. The group agreed to take the matter up, and it featured regularly in later meetings. A second subject also destined to be covered by a separate multilateral agreement was raised in May 1988, when the group agreed to look at possible problems for trade caused by the administration of the rules of origin which are widely used by governments to decide the customs classification of imports, as well as whether they are covered by outstanding safeguard, anti-dumping or other measures.

By June, the first four proposals had been received, covering both detailed notifications of the specific non-tariff measures which countries wished to see tackled in the negotiations, and proposals on the techniques to be adopted. Of the four, three came from the largest participants in the negotiations (the European Communities, Japan and the United States) and one in the name of 15 countries of the De la Paix Group. The first three each essentially endorsed request-and-offer negotiations on most non-tariff measures; the fourth argued for a formula approach. The US preference for item-by-item bargaining was in line with its approach to tariff negotiations; the EC and Japan favoured a formula approach to tariffs, but did not believe it was practicable when dealing with the varied forms of non-tariff measures. Moreover, the EC wanted to keep the tariff and non-tariff negotiations separate, at least as long as it was unclear what approach would be adopted in sectoral negotiations, above all on agriculture. The De la Paix Group, in contrast, believed that the most effective way of improving market access was to tackle tariff and non-tariff measures together, and to use an automatic formula approach to reduce the volume – or price-restrictive effects of individual non-tariff measures. Further proposals soon followed from Australia, New Zealand, Canada and Czechoslovakia. Although wide differences continued over the approach to be used for negotiations on individual measures, views began to converge on issues that might lend themselves to multilateral agreements, with preshipment inspection and roles of origin as leading candidates, and proposals also for further agreements to provide rules for import deposit systems, fees and other import charges, and customs and consular formalities. By the end of the year, the Secretariat had produced, or was preparing, papers on all these subjects as a starting-point for possible multilateral negotiation. It was also asked by the group to sort through and classify the individual measures proposed by governments for negotiation.

The approach of the end-1988 mid-term review of the Round forced the non-tariff negotiators to seek agreement on a report and recommendations that ministers could endorse and that would provide guidelines for the remainder of the negotiations. Some of the recommendations caused little difficulty: the need for the widest possible participation and liberalization; no bargaining over the removal of measures that were inconsistent with GATT; examination of which measures might appropriately be dealt with through multilateral agreements; a target date of June 1989 to establish procedures for the negoti-ations; and several other points. But most of the De la Paix Group countries wanted commitments for non-tariff measures that would parallel those for tariffs, whereas the European Community and many developing countries did not. Australia and New Zealand held out for adoption of a formula approach. India felt the case had not yet been made to negotiate multilateral agreements on some subjects. Some countries wanted all non-tariff measures to be open to negotiation in the group, while others felt strongly that measures affecting textiles and agriculture (for example) should be taken up in the specialized groups concerned. Developed countries wanted a commitment to full participation by developing countries which Brazil and others did not feel ready to give. Brazil and others, in turn, wanted to see more proposals before deciding on negotiation procedures. And the major developed countries were not prepared to promise negotiating credit to developing countries for liberalization since the Round had begun, as long as no commitment was given that the liberalization measures would not be reversed.

In the event, although the non-tariff measures group itself could not reach agreement on what to ask of ministers, the senior officials who met in the GNG and in informal meetings chaired by Dunkel proved more flexible. For most of the disputed points, they reached tacit agreement that no decisions could be reached at this stage, and that perhaps none were really yet needed. On negotiating credit for recent liberalization, the text for ministers called ambiguously for "appropriate recognition" to be given. For the rest, the text simply left the disputed points open or even unmentioned, in the knowledge that they would almost certainly be raised again, and fought over, in the months to come.

Natural resource-based products

The Punta del Este Declaration called for "the fullest liberalization of trade in natural resource-based products, including in their processed and semi-processed forms", with the aim of reducing or eliminating tariffs and non-tariff measures, including tariff escalation.

There could be no doubt that trade in these products mattered a great deal to many countries. For a large number of developing countries, for instance, exports of ores, minerals and non-ferrous metals provided more than half their export earnings. They included several countries of Africa, whose economic resources were otherwise very limited. Among developed countries, Australia and Canada, in particular, were also still heavily dependent on exports of natural resource-based products. In the Tokyo Round, Canada had taken the lead in pressing for "sectoral" negotiations that would focus on removing barriers in defined and related groups of products, looking especially at possibilities of removing tariffs and non-tariff measures affecting the raw material concerned as well as semi-finished and finished products made from it. The approach was labelled a "complementary technique" but, even as such, it produced no results. The biggest difficulty was that negotiations on this basis did not offer, in themselves, a balance of advantage: their potential interest for producers was obvious enough, but the importing countries could see little advantage in them. One possible counterpart of real interest would have been commitments on security of supply from the exporters, a subject of burning interest at the opening of the Tokyo Round, which coincided with the first OPEC oil shock. For the exporters, however, "access to supplies" raised highly sensitive issues of sovereignty, on which they were extremely reluctant to negotiate.

In spite of the Tokyo Round experience, the exporting countries concerned continued to be interested in having negotiations focus on their special interests in natural resource-based products. At the 1982 ministerial meeting, they won agreement to an examination of problems of trade in nonferrous metals and minerals, forestry products, and fish and fisheries products, and this led to difficult discussions from 1984 onwards in a working party that looked at trade problems in each sector. The working party finally produced a set of reports on these sectoral problems, but they showed no agreement on what action might be taken. Indeed, they displayed a great deal of sensitivity about even discussing trade barriers affecting some products (paper, for example) which countries such as EC members and Sweden felt the working party was not entitled to discuss. Among the few things on which agreement emerged was that the problems identified could perhaps best be tackled in the context of a wider multilateral negotiation. However, even when such a negotiation was clearly in prospect, in the spring of 1986, discussions in the Preparatory Committee showed that many countries still doubted whether a sectoral approach to trade liberalization would work. Optimism was not enhanced by proposals that the natural resource negotiations should include efforts to stabilize commodity prices, or by disagreements on whether the issue of access to fishing grounds could be covered.

From the first meeting, in February 1987, of the separate group established to handle natural resource-based products, it became obvious that there was no agreement on what the role of the group should be, or what the negotiations could cover. For some countries, the group should itself carry forward the negotiations; for others, its task was to monitor what might be done elsewhere, and especially in the groups on tariffs, non-tariff measures and agriculture. Even within the agreed sectors of non-ferrous metals, forestry products and fish, there were wide differences over what the negotiations might cover. For some countries, the Punta del Este Declaration covered only tariffs and non-tariff barriers (and this in turn suggested to them that the real negotiations would have to take place in the market access groups concerned). Others saw the point of a special negotiating group on natural resource-based products as being precisely that it could take up other measures affecting trade in these products. Australia which, from the beginning, took a particularly ambitious line, wanted the group to focus on export and domestic subsidies which it believed were a principal obstacle to fair trading conditions. The United States wanted the negotiations to take up "double pricing": the practice of holding down the domestic price of raw or scrap materials, usually by imposing export restrictions, with the effect that processing industries gained cheap raw materials that were not available to others. Japan, Korea and other countries were accused of such restrictions on exports of non-ferrous metal. Similar practices affected other materials. Restrictions on hide and rattan exports favoured domestic producers of leather and furniture. Specially low prices for oil and natural gas could make a decisive difference to the cost of making fertilizers and petrochemicals. When it came to fish, the European Communities complained that the general introduction of national fishing zones stretching 200 miles offshore (the result of negotiations in the United Nations) had led to access rights for foreign fishing boats being tied up through bilateral treaties that paid no attention to the GATT principle of most-favoured-nation treatment.

Nor was this all. Some countries wanted to expand the product coverage of the group beyond the agreed trio of non-ferrous metals, forest products and fish to iron ore, construction materials, energy (uranium, coal, natural gas and oil) and energy-based products. Oil in particular was bound to be highly controversial. It was a strategic product of the highest importance, politically sensitive, in large part produced by countries which were not members of GATT or participants in the Round, and with trade to a great extent governed by decisions of governments. For all these reasons, it had been conspicuously left out of previous GATT negotiations. Four African countries – Cameroon, Côte d'Ivoire, Senegal and Zaire – stressed national sovereignty over natural resources, the need for special and differential treatment for developing countries and (quoting aspirations expressed in the GATT itself, in Article XXXVI) the aim of "stable, equitable and remunerative prices". Others saw the problems of trade in natural resource-based products as linked with restrictive business practices or, alternatively, with state trading and government regulation.

Discussion on these lines could and did continue through a long series of meetings, which also brought some comprehensive negotiating proposals. The most striking came from Australia, which in November 1987 proposed the elimination, over ten years, of all tariffs, non-tariff measures, export subsidies and other subsidies disruptive of trade affecting all minerals, energy products, forestry and fishery products at each stage from the raw material up to primary processing. The fact of the matter, however, was that there was little common ground between the participants. If the negotiations were to deal only with tariffs and non-tariff barriers, there seemed little point in involving the group, except in the harmless role of observer. If they were to go further, either they would trespass on the tasks of other groups (for instance, subsidies) or they would enter into subjects which many countries were simply not prepared to negotiate about in GATT, and perhaps not at all. The group never overcame these fundamental differences. Delegates made lengthy statements to one another which included proposals which many of their negotiating partners were not prepared even to discuss. There was no indication that any country was prepared to change its position. Instead, and following a line familiar the world over to bodies unable to agree on anything of substance, the group called on the Secretariat to prepare detailed studies of trade in each sector. The studies, comprehensive and thorough, were duly prepared, praised and even published, but had no discernible effect on the negotiations.

At the end of 1988, the group agreed on a report and recommendations to the mid-term review that effectively changed nothing. Participants were to "continue to pursue" their agreed original objectives, to "continue to pursue and give effect to" the agreed negotiating plan, to "continue their examination of issues brought forward", and to develop techniques to deal with specific issues and problems, to the extent that negotiating approaches developed in other groups suggested that further measures might be needed to achieve the objectives for natural resource-based products. "Effective negotiations should begin as soon as possible", with relevant trade and barrier data to be provided by the end of June 1989.

Tropical products

For tropical products, the objectives of the Uruguay Round, as set out in the Punta del Este Declaration, were almost identical to those for natural resource-based products: the "fullest liberalization", inclusion of processed and semi-processed forms of the products, and coverage of tariffs and non-tariff measures. But there was a crucial difference. Tropical products were singled out, alone among all the subjects of the Round, as being of such importance to developing countries that they should be given "special attention", including as regards the general rules on the timing of negotiations and entry into force of the results. Decoded, this agreement meant that participants were ready to move fast on tropical products, without worrying too much about the general principle that "the launching, the conduct and the implementation" of the Round should proceed as "a single undertaking".

Tropical products had regularly been given a privileged place in GATT negotiations before, but without very striking effect. Most recently, in the Tokyo Round, the sector had been declared "special and priority", and had been the subject of the earliest negotiations and the first results to be reached. However, these results had been limited. Developed countries had finally given a combination of most-favoured-nation and GSP (Generalized System of Preferences) concessions, but most were of greater symbolic than practical effect. The United States had been unwilling to make a substantial offer in the absence of significant reciprocity from developing countries, and the European Community and some other countries insisted that the problems of trade in key tropical products were too closely intertwined with those of agricultural trade for much independent liberalization to be possible. Although further reductions in tropical product barriers were agreed in the final stages of the Tokyo Round, as part of the broader dismantling of tariffs and quotas, the outcome was generally considered disappointing. Hence, as soon as discussions began after the Tokyo Round on future work in GATT, developing countries pressed for tropical products to be given a special place.

In 1981 and 1982, consultations were held among some 50 countries on trade barriers affecting six broad categories of tropical products. Developing countries pointed to difficulties they identified, including tariffs and particularly tariff escalation, quantitative restrictions, internal taxes which they believed held down consumption, and other regulatory measures. Developed countries generally argued that these measures had been much reduced compared with their earlier levels, and that the restrictions that remained were justified by such reasons as the need to take account of possible substitution between the tropical product and competing temperate agricultural products, or to maintain preferences for associated countries and territories. They also doubted whether internal taxes, for instance on coffee and cocoa, had significant trade effects.

Tropical products were an automatic choice for inclusion in the work programme established by the 1982 ministerial meeting, with priority once again indicated by the ministers' call not only for consultations but also "appropriate negotiations" on tropical products. "Appropriate" was not defined, leaving open at least two important questions: Would the coming negotiations be multilateral or bilateral? And would only the developed countries be expected to make contributions? Consultations in the next two years added to general knowledge of specific trade barriers affecting the sector, but did not provide answers to these questions. When the decision was taken to launch the Uruguay Round, with multilateral trade negotiations across the whole range of issues covered by the GATT, and other issues besides, the first question was answered: tropical products would be included, and these negotiations too would be multilateral. But there was no agreement on whether, as in the Tokyo Round, only the developed countries would contribute. Some developing countries stated their expectation that this would be so. Canada, however, told the Preparatory Committee that it would expect developing countries to contribute "in line with their level of development".

As the Uruguay Round opened, the tropical products negotiators were in the happy situation not only of being given priority, but of being well equipped to take advantage of it. The discussions over the past five years had brought a deeper understanding of the issues at stake, of the specific trade measures that the negotiations should attack, and of possible negotiating techniques, than in almost any other sector of the Round. Work got off to a quick start.

Although "tropical products" had not been strictly defined, the main focus was on seven groups of products that had been the subject of earlier consultations. These seven groups were tropical beverages (coffee, cocoa and tea, and products based on them); spices, cut flowers, tropical plants and plant products; oilseeds, vegetable oils and oilcake; tobacco, rice and tropical roots such as manioc; tropical fruits and nuts; tropical wood and rubber; and jute and other hard fibres such as sisal. On each of these, the Secretariat quickly produced a series of background studies that set out production and consumption figures, trade flows, and relevant trade measures in each of the main developed-country markets. At the same time, and starting as soon as the negotiating group's first meeting in February 1987, discussion began on how the negotiations should be carried out.

A first proposal came from the ASEAN countries, which suggested that developed countries should harmonize (i.e. bring into line with one another) their tropical products tariffs, aligning the rate for each product with the lowest rate in force in any of their markets. Less strikingly, and in parallel with arguments that were being put forward in the tariff and non-tariff groups, several developed countries stated their preference for negotiating on the basis of requests and offers, or for combining the two approaches.

In fact, an automatic formula approach to the reduction of barriers to tropical products raised considerable difficulties for some developed countries. Prominent among them was that this approach would make it hard to limit reductions affecting two particularly sensitive groups of tropical products: those which competed directly with temperate products that were protected under domestic agricultural support policies, and those which, if given easier market access, would threaten to displace suppliers in associated countries which at present enjoyed preferential status. The United States was unwilling to deal with tropical products in isolation from agriculture. The European Community was particularly awkwardly placed. It was engaged, in the agriculture negotiating group, in defending its common agricultural policy, while at the same time being asked in the tropical products negotiations to find more room in its market for products such as vegetable oils that competed directly with its own oils and fats. Even more difficult were its contractual arrangements, under the Lomé Convention, with a number of African, Caribbean and

Pacific countries (mostly former colonies) to import their bananas and other products at preferentially low tariff rates. In opening its markets for tropical products it would risk damaging the fragile economies of the Lomé countries, and throughout the negotiations – as in those on agriculture – it was clear that these countries were urging the EC negotiators not to sacrifice their interests.

In July, a widely drawn group of developing countries (Bangladesh, Colombia, Cuba, Egypt, India, Nigeria, Pakistan and Sri Lanka, joined later by Nicaragua) put forward a detailed 22-page list of the products for which they sought from developed countries "the fullest trade liberalization of tariff and all non-tariff measures affecting exports of these products, including in their semi-processed and processed forms". Not long afterwards, Cameroon, Côte d'Ivoire, Senegal and Zaire, who were also working together in the natural resource-based group, joined by Gabon, also put forward a list of the tropical products for which they sought removal of trade barriers by developed countries. Like the ASEAN countries, they suggested harmonization and binding of tariff rates at the lowest prevailing levels, but they added a call to maintain existing preferential margins in favour of African countries.

Discussion in the negotiating group showed considerable understanding for these proposals but also, on the part of the developed countries, a strong view that they should not be alone in opening up their markets for tropical products. Several of them called for "burden-sharing" (in other words, comparable efforts by all developed countries), and also for contributions by state-trading countries and by the developing countries themselves, and especially by those which were importers of tropical products.

The first offer from a major importer came in October from the European Community which, in spite of its awkward situation, was to make the running in these negotiations. It envisaged the abolition or reduction of tariffs on many unprocessed products, "significant" reductions for semi-processed products, cuts of up to 50% for finished products, elimination of most quantitative restrictions, and reduction or elimination of consumption taxes on coffee, cocoa and tea. However, the EC offer excluded agricultural products covered by its own common agricultural policy. It stressed burden sharing and reciprocity, with a call in particular for developing countries which enjoyed a dominant supply position for raw materials on world markets to reduce restrictions on exports of these products. (It will be noted that some of the issues in the tropical products negotiations were similar to those affecting natural resource-based products.) Soon afterwards, the United States came forward with its first proposals. It linked these with the proposals it was putting forward in the agriculture negotiations, on the ground that most of the tropical products under discussion were in fact agricultural. As in the agricultural group, it called for elimination of all support and protective measures affecting trade, but it was ready to accept a faster timetable for action on tropical products. For non-agricultural products, it proposed to negotiate on the basis of requests and offers. It was not, however, prepared to give concessions without reciprocity.

By the beginning of 1988, the group was ready to launch the detailed negotiations, with the aim of having results to show at the mid-term review at the end of the year, and of putting these results into effect as soon as possible thereafter. On the proposal of its chairman, Paul Leong Khee Seong of Malaysia, the group agreed in January that "indicative lists" should be submitted by participants by the end of March. The lists should cover proposed general negotiating approaches, formulae and measures to be taken, and should set out specific requests. Participants were also invited to submit "indicative offers or broad indications of possible individual contributions to a successful outcome of the negotiations". Multilateral consultations covering all seven product groups were to take place in two rounds, in May and June, with a subsequent review of their results and further negotiations as necessary. Apart from a certain ambiguity, necessary to secure agreement, about who was supposed to be making requests and offers, and the lack of agreement so far about the basis on which negotiations would take place, the procedures offered a blueprint for action that was in refreshing contrast to the absence of clear progress and purpose in most of the other Uruguay Round negotiating groups.

By the time the group met in April, 13 indicative lists had already been submitted which, since they included lists from the EC and the Nordic and ASEAN regional groups, covered over 30 countries. Some were devoted largely to proposals on tariff formulae to be applied in the negotiations and on the removal of non-tariff measures. Others, and particularly the submissions from Peru and the ASEAN, gave detailed lists of products for which liberalization by the developed countries was sought. The United States confined itself to asking developing countries a number of highly specific questions about their own trade policy measures affecting tropical products, noting that these were "a sample of the types of measures that should be the subject of negotiations" in the group. The European Community asked similar questions. Both sets of questions were received without enthusiasm by those developing countries which were resisting the idea that they should be making their own contributions to the negotiations, and several underlined that the fact they were giving responses did not mean they were prepared to negotiate on these measures.

By June, the chairman was able to report to the group that the first round of consultations had taken place, and that participants had first reviewed the specific tariff and non-tariff measures affecting each product group and then looked at how the various proposals would affect trade in each case. The discussion in the group showed that although the consultations were agreed to have helped to clarify matters, there was still much uncertainty about the basis for the negotiations and concern that the United States, in particular, was linking its offer with progress in the agricultural negotiations (which in fact were not progressing at all). Several developing countries insisted that the tropical products negotiations were not to be based on reciprocity, with India taking an especially strong line. The second round of consultations, in late June, was largely similar to the first, except that it went into more detail. A July meeting of the negotiating group showed the same misgivings as a month earlier about the continuing lack of agreement on the basis for negotiations, but accepted a new set of arrangements proposed for the autumn by the chairman. Initial offers were to be submitted by the end of September. They could be based on general, formula, product specific or country-specific approaches, and could build on the proposals and discussions in the May and June consultations. Consultations and negotiations should take place from September to early November, followed by assessment in the group of how the results measured up against the Punta del Este objectives for tropical products.

Further indicative lists flowed in during the summer, notably including offers by Japan and the Nordic countries. A September meeting of the group brought praise for some features of the Japanese offer which included tariff reductions and elimination, the removal of a range of quotas, and the prospect of abolition of commodity and sugar taxes. But there was also criticism of its exclusion of such important products as rice, bananas, palm oil and plywood, which Japan insisted would have to be dealt with in other negotiating groups. There was also a significant softening of the US position. The United States maintained its insistence on reciprocity, and on the link between agriculture and tropical products negotiations as far as concerned subsidy issues, health and sanitary regulations. However, it was now ready to negotiate earlier on tariff and non-tariff barriers affecting a list of tropical products that included those mainly produced or traded by developing countries, and was prepared to remove these barriers entirely provided others did the same.

Two stock-taking meetings of the group in November showed that the negotiations were making progress, but less than might be hoped. At the first, many developing countries expressed disappointment with the results so far, insisted that the outcome of these negotiations would influence their participation in the Uruguay Round as a whole, and said that whatever happened at the mid-term meeting in Montreal, negotiations on tropical products would have to continue afterwards. Several developed countries insisted that more rapid progress depended on a larger number of participants joining in the negotiations and being ready to liberalize their trade. A statement by Central American countries showed that they at least were ready to make contributions, though not necessarily on tropical products. By the second meeting, the tone was only slightly more cheerful. The Colombian delegate was reported as saying that "the results obtained so far are not all that satisfactory" (no delegate could ever be expected to say more in a negotiation that was still unfinished). A straw in the wind was the group's tentative acceptance of its chairman's report to the GNG. This spoke explicitly of the agreement of all participants to make contributions towards achieving the objectives of the tropical products negotiations. Although some countries were careful to make the point that their contributions would not necessarily be in the tropical products sector, the idea of reciprocity was evidently no longer simply anathema.

The tropical products negotiators went to Montreal with cautious hopes that a worthwhile deal might be struck there.

Rule-making

If the man in the street has heard of GATT (which is far from certain, even after the Uruguay Round), his knowledge is almost certainly of its market-opening efforts and its institutional aspects as "world trade watchdog", not of its rules. No doubt this is largely because rules are not inherently attractive or interesting, particularly when they deal with the minutiae of customs procedures or notification requirements, but it must also reflect the complicated way in which rights and obligations under the GATT have evolved and are stated.

Lawyers have tended to despair of GATT.

The General Agreement itself, as signed in 1947, was a treaty in the eyes of most countries, but not of all. It had been applied only provisionally, albeit over a period of nearly half a century. Because of the GATT's provisional status, certain countries had been able to maintain practices flatly contrary to some of its most important rules, and any member had been free to withdraw from it at short notice. Its Articles of Agreement had, in practical terms, been incapable of amendment so that necessary changes had to take the form of numerous interpretations or supplementary decisions applicable to all members, or of agreements which tied only their signatories.

The original GATT rules, set out in the General Agreement, were drawn up essentially to ensure that the market-opening commitments negotiated among the founding GATT members would be effective. They were modified somewhat in the early 1950s, mostly to fill gaps that were obvious when it became clear that the "temporary" GATT would not be replaced, as originally intended, by a more elaborate International Trade Organization. Thereafter, however, these basic rules were not altered, apart from the addition in the 1960s of the three articles on "Trade and Development" which constitute Part Four of the GATT. They remained unchanged not because anyone regarded them as perfect, but because change was effectively blocked by the extremely tough requirements set by the General Agreement itself for acceptance of any amendments. Instead, the rules were given meaning through understandings and decisions reached among all the member countries in the GATT Council of Representatives, the annual Session or other bodies, or they were interpreted by panels of experts in the course of settlement of trade disputes.

A second way of effectively changing the rules, circumventing the requirement that virtually all countries must approve a formal change, was developed in the Kennedy and Tokyo Rounds when tighter and broader provisions on several matters were negotiated and accepted by a comparatively small number of countries. The first such agreement, interpreting and expanding the rules on anti-dumping action set out in Article VI of the GATT, was signed at the end of the Kennedy Round in 1967. The technique was carried much further in the Tokyo Round, when nine separate agreements or codes (including a revision of the anti-dumping agreement) were negotiated with the aim of regulating various potential distortions of trade. Most of the codes were signed by all the developed countries, but by very few developing countries. The non-signatories remained bound only by the General Agreement itself.

Many governments and outside observers, looking at the difficulties of trade relations in the early 1980s, concluded that weaknesses in the GATT rules were quite largely responsible. One obvious problem concerned Article XIX of the GATT, the Agreement's chief escape clause or "safeguard" provision, designed to respond to emergencies when domestic industries could not cope with competition from imports. Views differed strongly on what was wrong with the safeguard rules – so much so, that negotiations to improve them continued without success from 1973 right up to the launching of the Uruguay Round. Manifestly, however, they did not work properly. Rather than take safeguard action in accordance with Article XIX, countries restricted trade in a variety of other ways, some not envisaged at all under GATT, others intended to deal with unfair, rather than fair, competition. These actions led to many disputes, all too often unresolved, and to a widespread perception that the GATT system itself was working badly and often unfairly.

Four separate subjects related to the GATT rules – two specific, and two general – were included in the Uruguay Round negotiations by the Punta del Este Declaration. One, inevitably, was safeguards. The second specific subject was subsidies. The subsidies code had been negotiated in the Tokyo Round but had not worked well, partly because the negotiators had been driven to use insufficiently precise language on some key points in order to obtain agreement. Some countries, especially the United States, felt that government subsidies were increasingly distorting international trade and falsifying competition. Others believed that the United States itself was distorting trade by using countervailing duties (intended to offset subsidies) as a means of harassing and excluding competition from fairly priced imports. There was clearly much to negotiate about. The third and more general subject was the remaining Tokyo Round codes. It was known that countries had a number of ideas, some more controversial than others, on how individual codes might be improved, so an opportunity was provided to raise any of these ideas in the Round. From the beginning, it was seen likely that the anti-dumping code, which raised some of the same difficulties as the subsidies code, would feature largely in these negotiations. Finally, the Punta del Este Declaration gave an opening to discuss and negotiate on the other main rules. the GATT Articles themselves.

Safeguards

The General Agreement in fact includes several safeguard provisions, allowing governments to impose trade barriers or restrictions for such reasons as balance-of-payments difficulties, economic development programmes, or unfair competition (especially from goods whose prices are abnormally low because they are being "dumped" by the producer or have benefited from government subsidy). Article XIX, however, is different. As its title ("Emergency action on imports of particular products") indicates, it exists to meet the situation of a single industry which cannot handle a buildup of fair competition from imports.

Article XIX allows bound import duties to be raised, or quantitative restrictions introduced, if an increase in imports of a particular product causes, or threatens to cause, serious injury to domestic producers of the same ("like or directly competitive") products. The increase in protection may be to the extent and for the time necessary to prevent or remedy the injury. The rules have been generally, though not universally, interpreted as requiring the increase to apply on an MFN basis: in other words, it cannot apply only to imports from a particular supplying country. Article XIX also provides that a price be paid for the safeguard action, either by offering compensation (a tariff concession on other products) or by suffering retaliation (the withdrawal of concessions by the country whose exports are affected by the action).

These apparently logical and sensible rules have not worked well. Effective when used for brief periods to meet such problems as seasonal gluts of fruit, the application of Article XIX has too often led to trade restrictions being introduced and maintained for years. Worse, importing countries have increasingly turned to the use of other forms of safeguard action, not authorized under the GATT rules, and largely escaping examination. Typically, these have taken the form of bilateral deals such as voluntary export restraints or orderly marketing arrangements (VERs and OMAs in trade policy jargon) under which the exporting country is persuaded to prevent exports of the product concerned from exceeding a certain level. These "grey-area" measures, so called because they are neither authorized nor clearly condemned by the GATT rules, proliferated from the mid-1970s onwards. Surveys by the GATT Secretariat showed that grey-area measures outnumbered Article XIX actions in a proportion of about ten to one. They were particularly widely used to limit competition in automobiles, steel, footwear and electronic products. Their chief target was Japan, along with the more advanced developing countries. Restraints of this kind are not always as unpopular with exporters as might be supposed, since the virtual certainty that there will be a market for the prescribed quantity of the restricted product permits the seller to charge abnormally high prices and so earn exceptional profits. But from the point of view of the trading system as a whole, grey-area measures undermine the authority of the GATT rules, foster trade policies that seek to manage trade relations rather than rely on market forces, penalize the most efficient producers, and raise prices for consumers.

Although grey-area measures were the main replacement for safeguard action under Article XIX, it can be argued that other trade restrictions also flourished because of the Article's shortcomings. The whole elaborate structure of bilateral restrictions on trade in textiles and clothing under the Multifibre Arrangement is a substitute for Article XIX safeguard action, so in many instances is the misuse of measures meant to counter unfairly dumped or subsidized products.

Not surprisingly, success in the negotiations on safeguards was widely regarded as central to restoring the credibility of the GATT rules as the basis of international trade.

In no other sector of the Uruguay Round were the negotiations so clearly an extension of a process already under way. The issues were clearly understood: indeed, a Secretariat report of 1979, which lists the reasons why the safeguards negotiations of the Tokyo Round failed, covers all the main problems with which the Uruguay Round negotiators were to grapple. Consultations in 1983-84 had kept the discussion up to date. The one real change brought by the Round was that it placed the safeguard negotiations in a wider context, raising hopes that the promise of a broad package of trade reforms might persuade governments to accept rule changes that would be unacceptable in isolation.

For the safeguards negotiators, therefore, the marching orders given them by the Punta del Este Declaration were entirely familiar. They were to seek an agreement, "based on the basic principles of the General Agreement", which would clarify and reinforce the agreement's disciplines and apply to all GATT members. Among the specific elements it should cover were transparency, coverage, criteria for action including the Article XIX concept of serious injury or the threat of such injury, the temporary nature of safeguard action, "degressivity" (progressive removal of the safeguard) and structural adjustment, compensation and retaliation, and the linked issues of notification, consultation, surveillance and dispute settlement.

Many of these issues were not even particularly controversial. But one was – so much so that it was not even clearly stated in the list of the Punta del Este Declaration, but buried in under the heading of "coverage", which included several other questions. This was the issue of "selectivity", or whether safeguard action should only be authorized if it applied to imports from all sources. This critical issue had prevented a safeguard agreement from being reached in earlier years, and continued to be the core question during the Uruguay Round.

The chief supporter of selectivity was the European Community, which argued that it made sense to apply restrictions only to those countries whose exports were causing disruption, and that as long as this was impossible under Article XIX, governments would prefer to take safeguard action, when necessary, through grey-area measures. The Community also pointed out that many GATT members effectively escaped Article XIX disciplines, since their lack of tariff bindings and scope to use non-tariff measures left them free to raise trade barriers at will. For many countries, however, the idea of explicitly permitting importing countries to introduce restrictions that discriminated against particular suppliers was anathema. For them, MFN treatment was the central premise on which the GATT system of rights and obligations was built, and the main protection that GATT offered, in particular, to the smaller and weaker countries. The members of the Leutwiler Group, reporting in early 1985, were among the most robust defenders of a non-discriminatory safeguard rule. They explained why: "Time and again the negotiation of voluntary export restraints with one supplier (the most 'disruptive' and therefore by definition the most competitive) has been followed by a proliferation of bilateral deals with *all* efficient suppliers who are not in a position to refuse.... It is therefore untrue that 'selective' action helps to limit the extent of disruption of trade. Moreover, the process of discrimination against the most efficient suppliers contravenes the principle of comparative advantage and maximizes the cost to the world economy of the protection granted to the inefficient." Developing countries were unanimous in opposing selectivity, but the issue cut across North-South lines, as a number of developed countries agreed with them. The United States, usually in the forefront of any negotiation, did not take a strong position on safeguards, stating only that the question was "negotiable".

Because the main issues were so well known, the negotiating group was able to get down to work quickly. Two proposals were tabled in May 1987. One was from Brazil, and the other – particularly important both because of its substance and its sponsors – from five "Pacific Rim" countries: two developed (Australia and New Zealand) and three of the most dynamic Asian developing countries (Hong Kong, Korea and Singapore). Both papers argued that Article XIX actions must continue to be taken on a non-discriminatory basis. Brazil believed that the safeguard action ought primarily to take the form of adjustment assistance to the domestic industry, and that import restrictions should be allowed only later, after a collective determination that injury was being caused by imports. Special and more favourable treatment for developing countries should be built into the new Article XIX rules. The Pacific Rim countries called for tougher criteria in establishing the link between increased imports and injury, and suggested other conditions for safeguard action such as the use of tariffs as the normal mechanism, a standard time-limit of three years, with possible extension to five years, and progressive liberalization of the measures. They also insisted on the need for structural adjustment, which should be a prerequisite for any extension of a measure; preferred compensation over retaliation; and stressed transparency and surveillance. All grey-area measures should be notified, and either brought into conformity with Article XIX or eliminated. Later proposals by Egypt, China and India took up many of the same themes, with particular emphasis on the need to avoid applying safeguard measures against exports of developing countries. Japan, whose views were in some ways close to those of the Pacific Rim countries, differed in envisaging other measures than tariffs, and was clearly opposed to Brazil's thinking on structural adjustment measures, since it believed that adjustment should basically be accomplished through the mechanism of the market.

An important early discussion in the group focused on grey-area measures. As a Swiss working paper put it, one might ask whether such measures "reflect a reprehensible contempt for the multilateral provisions, or were necessary because the General Agreement does not cover the situations that prompted them". This theme was taken up by others, who argued that simple condemnation of grey are a measures would not get rid of them. The reasons of "real economic life" that had led to them had to be discussed; as another delegate put it, they could not be removed "without considering the broader problem of structural adjustment and the political readiness of governments for economic change". "The most important objective of the negotiations on safeguards", according to the same speaker, was to "preserve and further trade liberalization". On the other hand, as the Nordic countries put it, the negotiations "should definitely not seek to adapt good rules to bad practices". In November, the United States introduced a paper that set out five options for a safeguard mechanism, ranging from strict MFN treatment (with a ban on grey-area measures) to permission to introduce selective measures without the consent of the affected country. Even this last and undesirable option, it was suggested, might, if subject to appropriate disciplines, be an improvement on the present situation. In any case, the United States saw the basic issue in the negotiations as being how to give countries adversely affected by fairly traded imports the opportunity to adjust without undermining the principles of an open and equitable trading system.

By this stage, the principal elements of the negotiation were all visible, except that there was as yet no hint of how common ground might be found on the issue of selectivity. For the rest, it was fairly clear that on each condition to be attached to safeguard action, there would have to be a search for compromise between the desire to prevent trade restrictions from being introduced or maintained without full justification and the need to remove the attraction of acting instead through grey-area measures.

During 1988, there was no substantial movement in the negotiating positions of the main participants. However, ideas were developed, and became clearer, on several subsidiary issues, which were taken up in turn. Perhaps the most important concerned the conditions which would justify safeguard action. For instance: Was it necessary that imports of the product concerned increase sharply, suddenly or unexpectedly, and must they be the essential cause of injury? What proportion of the domestic industry would have to be in trouble, how should this be measured, and should injury be determined by the national authorities or by an international body? The Pacific Rim countries argued for strict conditions, and for the exclusion of such factors as technological change and shifts in consumer tastes from the assessment. The European Community cautioned that conditions that were too difficult to fulfil would just drive governments to adopt grey-area measures. Other issues discussed included how long safeguards might be left in place and how they should be progressively dismantled; whether rights to compensation and retaliation should be retained; and rules on transparency and consultation. The coverage question also came up in its less controversial aspects, with such questions as whether safeguard action should be preceded by structural adjustment efforts or confined to tariff increases, and whether safeguard clauses for agricultural products should be negotiated separately in the Uruguay Round group for agriculture.

On selectivity, a renewed debate in the group in September 1988 showed no movement. The European Community insisted that while selectivity could be harmful, so could a too-rigid position on non-discrimination. The United States agreed that inflexible application of the MFN principle ignored reality, and suggested that limited selectivity might be allowed, subject to tougher disciplines on duration and degressivity. Developing countries, with Brazil in the forefront, said once again that selective actions against imports had no place in Article XIX.

As the mid-term review meeting of the Round approached, the safe-guards negotiators turned to drafting proposals for the ministers to adopt in Montreal. They reached agreement with no great difficulty on a set of basically procedural points, including recognition that all elements of the negotiation were so inter-related that none could be settled in isolation, and that the stage had been reached at which negotiations should start on the basis of a draft text by its chairman, Ambassador George Maciel of Brazil. However, India, with the support of several other delegations, insisted that the group's report to ministers "should reflect appropriately the strong views expressed in the group in favour of: (i) establishing non-discrimination and temporariness as the key principles which should govern a future com-prehensive understanding on safeguards; and (ii) declaring grey-area measures with selective application as measures proscribed by GATT." This proposal proved unacceptable. For the European Community and others sympathetic to selective action, such a declaration would in effect have ruled against them on the main disputed issue in the negotiations. Moreover, many countries which agreed with India's views thought that a Ministerial Declaration supporting them would scarcely be consistent with the agreement that individual elements of the negotiation could not be settled in isolation, or with the fact that discussion of the subject had not been completed. India insisted that its proposal be put to ministers, and a text drafted by it was accordingly included in the section on safeguards that went to Montreal. India's language was marked off by the square brackets that indicate lack of agreement.

Subsidies and countervailing measures

The GATT subsidy rules provided a classic example of obligations at several different levels. Some rules, laid down in articles of the General Agreement, applied to all countries. A provision in one article, made effective by a supplementary agreement, was applicable only to some countries. Finally, a full Tokyo Round code, with limited membership, had been negotiated in the 1970s. To complicate matters further, subsidies affecting agricultural products, a principal focus of discussions in the Uruguay Round, were to be discussed mainly in the negotiating group dealing specially with agriculture; subsidies to civil aircraft production were governed also by a Tokyo Round code that was not taken up in the Uruguay Round; and subsidies to the steel and coal industries, among others, were of concern to the negotiating group on natural resource-based products. Moreover, the subsidy group was required to take up not only the rules on subsidies but also those governing the application of the countervailing duties which are used by importing countries to cancel out advantages enjoyed by imports which have received subsidies from their home governments. These duties are also closely similar in nature and application to the anti-dumping duties used to offset unfair pricing by individual firms – another very sensitive subject almost certain to come up in the Round, in a different group.

The Punta del Este Declaration required that the negotiators review both the two relevant Articles of GATT and the subsidies code "with the objective of improving GATT disciplines relating to all subsidies and countervailing measures that affect international trade".

The basic GATT rules on subsidies are in Article XVI. Its first paragraph requires that GATT members who provide subsidies, including income or price support, that have the direct or indirect effect of increasing exports or reducing imports shall notify GATT, and be prepared to discuss limiting the subsidy if it seriously damages the interests of another GATT member. The remainder of the Article is devoted to export subsidies. Countries are to "seek to avoid" using subsidies on exports of primary products, but are not actually forbidden to do so: rather, they should not give a subsidy which results in the exporting country gaining "more than an equitable share of world export trade in that product". A tougher requirement, brought into effect in 1962, forbids export subsidies which reduce the sale price of a nonprimary product below its domestic sales price. However, this requirement was accepted only by developed countries and therefore did not bind developing countries. The other GATT Article concerned is Article VI, which covers both anti-dumping and countervailing duties. As far as concerns countervailing duties, this Article requires that they shall be no greater than is required to offset the subsidy granted on the manufacture, production or export of an imported product. Of central importance is the injury requirement: no countervailing (or anti-dumping) duty shall be levied unless the subsidy (or dumping) is "such as to cause or threaten material injury to an established domestic industry, or is such as to retard materially the establishment of a domestic industry".

The code on subsidies and countervailing duties signed in 1979, at the end of the Tokyo Round, was intended to strengthen the rules in Articles VI and XVI by going into much greater detail about how they should be applied. Whereas the GATT subsidy and countervail provisions together take up less than three pages of the official published text of the General Agreement, the subsidy code, set in the same type, runs to 25 pages and 40 footnotes. Anyone who attempts to summarize an agreement as long, controversial and technical as this does so at his or her peril. However, it may be said that it states some basic principles and understandings on subsidies, lays down detailed provisions and procedures for the application of countervailing duties, and establishes arrangements for regular review and for settling disputes.

On subsidies, the code frankly recognized the potential conflict which makes this such a sensitive subject for international trade relations: "subsidies are used by governments to promote important objectives of social and economic policy" but also "may cause adverse effects to the interests of other signatories". To reduce such adverse effects, it developed the disciplines on export subsidies laid down in Article XVI, partly by providing a non-exhaustive list of the kind of subsidies on non-primary products which are banned, and partly by offering some more detailed definition of such key phrases in the Article, intended to limit the effects of export subsidy competition in primary products, as "more than an equitable share of world export trade". As far as other subsidies are concerned, signatories agreed, in heavily footnoted undertakings, to "seek to avoid" causing injury to the domestic industry of another signatory, nullification or impairment of its GATT benefits, or "serious prejudice" to its interests. Later paragraphs described the objectives and nature of these subsidies in some detail, as well as the practical implications of "seeking to avoid" adverse effects on the interests of others, but stated that none of the agreed language actually created any basis for action under the GATT itself.

For developing countries, the 1979 code imposed looser disciplines, explicitly accepting that subsidies, including export subsidies, "are an integral part" of their development programmes. The other half of the code went into great detail about when countervailing duties could be justified and how they should be calculated and imposed. Again, the agreement tried to establish a delicate balance between allowing due relief to domestic producers affected by subsidized imports and preventing countervailing measures from becoming a unjustified barrier to trade. The code laid down rules on such matters as the launching of investigations (normally only on request by the affected industry), their coverage (both subsidy and injury to be considered simultaneously), opportunities to be provided to give evidence, time-limits on the investigation, consultations, the imposition and removal of provisional and definitive duties, the acceptance of undertakings to remove subsidies or to raise prices to remove the advantage of the subsidy, and the determination of whether the subsidized imports really caused injury to domestic producers. Some of the most important concepts in the code, including "serious prejudice", "material injury" and even "subsidy" were not defined, leaving much room for differing national interpretations.

The 1979 subsidies code was essentially the result of a tug-of-war between two largely conflicting interests. On one side, it reflected the concern, felt most strongly by the United States but shared in some measure by many countries, to limit what they saw as damage unfairly inflicted on their trade interests by the subsidies granted by other governments. On the other side, it was meant to respond to the belief that the threat or use of countervailing duties had too often been unfairly used, particularly by US industry, as an auxiliary means of harassing and limiting imports. Unfortunately, it failed to respond adequately to either set of worries. The United States, in particular, always felt that the code did not go far enough in limiting subsidies, and quite soon found, when it complained formally about practices which it thought were covered by the code, that other participants disagreed, and that it could not gain acceptance of its views through dispute settlement procedures. Other countries, for their part, found the new countervailing duty rules failed to end what they saw as harassment of their exports to the United States, which continued to be by far the largest user of such duties. Both sides therefore brought to the Uruguay Round negotiations on subsidies essentially the same opposed concerns that had motivated them in the Tokyo Round. The most important difference in the new negotiations was that the United States, convinced that the code had failed because its rules had concentrated on limiting the effects of subsidies, now sought to limit the use of subsidies themselves. But another difference, too, helped to push the negotiations toward a successful conclusion. Almost all governments were increasingly conscious of the burden which subsidies placed on their national budgets and taxpayers, and of the risk that any subsidy introduced to give a competitive advantage would only be matched by other countries in (as the United States put it) "a self-defeating spiral". A Uruguay Round agreement that could in effect provide a mutual disarmament treaty for subsidies would serve the interests of all.

Virtually the whole of the first 18 months of the Uruguay Round negotiations on subsidies was devoted to fundamental review of Articles VI and XVI and of the 1979 code, with the main participants bringing forward their ideas on what issues should be taken up in the negotiations. Some countries wanted to give priority to the rules on subsidies; others, predictably, were much more concerned to discipline the use of countervailing duties. Given these opposed aims, there was in fact no possibility of moving the negotiations forward unless both aspects were given equal priority, and discussed in parallel. One theme widely expressed was that a principal aim should be to seek agreement on the objectives and meaning of the present rules, rather than negotiate new ones. Thus on subsidies, the European Community argued that the group should try to resolve key questions left unanswered by the Tokyo Round. For instance: what measures are to be regarded as subsidies – only those that involve a financial charge on government (the EC and Japanese view), or also measures which in practice give a special benefit to the recipient? When are subsidies potentially trade-distorting, and hence potentially actionable? How should they be measured? On countervailing duties, Canada, Korea and the Community stressed such matters as the rules governing the launching of investigations (who, for instance, may initiate a complaint), the minimum amount or threat of injury required to justify action, and the level of duty to be imposed. Developing countries argued their need to use subsidies for economic and social purposes, to offset their particular handicaps; the United States and European Community found common ground in calling for greater subsidy discipline on the more advanced developing countries. More generally, the United States stated its belief, in the very first working paper put to the negotiating group, that both the GATT and code rules suffered from basic deficiencies: some rules were vague, others were weak, and some "drew distinctions between permitted and prohibited subsidy practices that appear to have little basis in sound economic policy". "The subsidies code," it commented, "has become a source of conflict, rather than an instrument for conciliation and the objective arbitration of differences between contracting parties."

By mid-1988, the discussions had thrown up a formidable list of issues on which one or more participants wished to negotiate. A Secretariat listing, regularly amended to reflect the progress of debate, by May 1988 included, on subsidies themselves, "Principles and approaches" (eight separate points), "Definitions and concepts related to subsidies" (eleven points), "Disciplines on subsidies" (at least 14 points), and "Measurement of the amount of a counter-vailable subsidy" (just one point, but fundamental). On countervailing duties, the Secretariat listed similarly numerous points under the headings "Determination of the existence of material injury", "Definition of sale", "Initiation and conduct of countervailing duty investigations", "Imposition and duration of countervailing measures", and two other topics. Another ten points reflected differing views on the rules that should apply concerning developing countries and on dispute settlement.

Underlying this long list of issues was still the basic difference among the negotiating countries over whether the principal aim should be to ban some subsidies, and restrict the use of others, or to tighten the rules on countervailing action to prevent their abuse. Nevertheless, progress was being made in the search for a framework within which the participants might be able to negotiate effective commitments. The GATT and Tokyo Round rules had concentrated on trade effects in specific cases, apart from the prohibition of export subsidies by developed countries on non-primary products. If the negotiators could come to some agreement that certain kinds of subsidy always, or never, distorted trade, this would surely clear away a great deal of disagreement and misunderstanding, leaving only a middle category of potentially harmful subsidies for definition and examination, and at the same time reducing the scope for the application of countervailing duties. In the Secretariat listing, this idea was to be found in the suggested distinction between "prohibited", "actionable" and "non-actionable" subsidies.

This three-category classification was not a new idea. The United States had even put it forward in the Tokyo Round, but had subsequently had misgivings about it, mainly because of doubts whether any subsidy could always be considered harmless. The European Community had proposed the "non-actionable" category in June 1987, and Colombia put forward all three categories in November of the same year. By February 1988, the concept had been fully developed in a paper by Switzerland. This argued that the categories of subsidies identified by the existing GATT rules were not logically linked to the legal action that could be taken on them, and that it would be far clearer if some subsidies could be identified as prohibited, with a presumption that their use caused injury to others. Of the remaining two categories, one would correspond with existing GATT practice in being regarded as potentially damaging, but with action allowed only if material injury was shown to be caused or threatened, and the other would consist of subsidies which would be declared non-actionable. This third category might include both subsidies very unlikely to harm third parties (such as those to local public transport) and ("more importantly") structural adjustment measures which "need to be tolerated for the sake of the cure and must not be countervailed even in case of injury".

These ideas were not fully accepted, but the three-category concept proved critical to developing a balanced approach to the Uruguay Round subsidy negotiations. In October of 1988, the chairman of the group, Michael Cartland (who was Hong Kong's representative at GATT), put to the participants an informal note which summarized the main issues raised in discussions, and offered a framework within which they could be further discussed. The framework, essentially built around the three categories, provided the basis on which the negotiating group succeeded in working out agreed recommendations for approval at the mid-term review meeting in Montreal. The recommendations solved no substantive issues, but they provided a flexible, logical and quite detailed framework into which proposals and negotiations on all the issues which governments wished to take up could easily fit. Inevitably, the framework, with its combination of prohibited ("red"), undecided ("amber") and authorized ("green") categories, quickly became known as the "traffic light" approach.

For prohibited (red) subsidies, the framework called for their identification, and for agreement on what remedies could be used against them. For the amber category, the subsidies that were not prohibited but might be acted against, the main issues were automatically those of most concern to countries seeking clearer rules on the use of countervailing duties. This was the longest section of the framework, listing such issues as the conditions under which the subsidy might be actionable (its nature, its trade effects in the importing and subsidizing countries' markets and elsewhere) and the rules on countervailing action itself (who would be eligible to petition for relief, how investigations should be initiated and pursued, how measures should be imposed, how long they should last, and so on). For non-countervailable (green) subsidies the main concern would be to set the conditions for inclusion in the category. More generally, the negotiators were also to consider special and differential treatment for developing countries, notification and surveillance, and dispute settlement. It was a formidable list, but at least the group had found a common approach to what was generally recognized as one of the most difficult and divisive subjects in the whole Round.

The Tokyo Round codes

Nine "MTN Agreements and Arrangements" were negotiated in the Tokyo Round (whose official name was the Multilateral Trade Negotiations, or MTN). The Punta del Este agreement called for them to be improved, clarified or expanded, "as appropriate". Negotiations on one agreement – subsidies and countervailing duties – were entrusted to a separate group, as described in the previous section of this chapter. The remainder were the responsibility of a separate MTN Agreements and Arrangements group. In practice, three Tokyo Round "sectoral agreements" were never raised in the Round. Two of these, the arrangements on dairy products and meat, were concerned purely with agricultural products and would thus have been discussed, if at all, in the agriculture group. In fact, they were not: their limited aims meant that no one wished to negotiate about them. The third was the 1979 Agreement on Trade in Civil Aircraft, which had been signed mainly by developed countries and provided that they would charge no import duties on aircraft and parts, and would observe certain subsidy disciplines. The latter provisions proved highly controversial, and intermittent fierce disputes between the United States and European Community over subsidies, especially to the Airbus aircraft built by a multinational European consortium, provided a counterpoint and irritant to the Uruguay Round. Again, however, there was no suggestion that the code itself be reviewed in the Round. There remained five codes which, to a greater or lesser extent, were to be the subject of negotiations. These were, in the apparently logic-free order in which GATT published them in 1979, the agreements on technical barriers to trade (the "standards code"), government procurement, customs valuation, import licensing, and dumping (the "anti-dumping code").

When the negotiations opened, however, it was not clear which agreements would be taken up, nor what changes would be sought. At the first meetings of the group, in early 1987, the main discussion of substance concerned the role of the codes in general. Their signatories defended them as an effort by certain countries to develop their cooperation, and to make the multilateral trading system more stable and open, by taking on extra obligations beyond those laid down in the General Agreement itself. The codes, they said, had in general worked well, and had strengthened international defences against non-tariff barriers to trade. Some improvements were no doubt possible, and wider membership would be welcome, but they saw no need for wholesale renegotiation. Non-signatories, which in practice meant developing countries, were less convinced that the supposed advantages of the codes outweighed their disadvantages. Like many academic observers, they feared that the codes threatened the unity and integrity of the trading system, with important trade problems discussed and settled among a comparatively small group of countries, and different trade rules applying to members and non-members. Although a 1979 decision of the GATT member countries had declared that the codes could not deprive non-signatories of their GATT rights, including that of MFN treatment, experience led some non-signatories to be less sure that the codes had not undermined their rights. In particular, the United States had taken a strong line against subsidized exports of some non-signatories, subjecting them to countervailing duties without giving them the benefit of the subsidy code's requirement that duties only be imposed if the imports caused injury to US industry. For both sides in the discussion, an obvious conclusion was that more developing countries should, if possible, sign the codes. Widely varying explanations of why they had not done so were put forward. The codes, it was suggested, gave insufficient special and differential treatment to developing countries. Some codes were of no interest to them, or included rules that were unclear or inflexible. Others could restrict developing countries' policy choices, undermine their revenues, or put excessive burdens on their frail administration.

A second set of general questions taken up immediately in the group appeared purely procedural, but in fact had both substance and sensitivity. At Punta del Este, it had been agreed that all participants in the Round could take part in all negotiations. Negotiations on the codes, however, were unique in that some participants had already assumed the obligations under discussion, while others had not. Moreover, each code had its own standing committee, and some of these had been discussing possible improvements in the codes they supervised. The committees might well be better qualified than the negotiating group to assess some of the more technical problems, but there was a risk that if they tried to do so, non-signatories would effectively be excluded from negotiations. In practice, initial discussions were generally pursued in both the code committee and the negotiating group, with transparency maintained by fairly elaborate reporting from one to the other and by the attendance of many of the expert delegates in both groups. Later on, serious negotiation was largely in the Uruguay Round negotiating group, or in specialized sub-groups established by it. The exception was the negotiations on government procurement which, in consequence, were considered to fall outside the Round.

Although these general issues took up most of the early meetings of the group, proposals on individual codes were introduced as early as the very first meeting. The United States called for negotiations on the import licensing and standards agreements, other delegations expressed dissatisfaction with both the anti-dumping and subsidy agreements, and a discussion took place on whether proposed negotiations to broaden the scope of the government procurement agreement should take place in the code committee or the group. By the second meeting, Korea had produced a detailed proposal for negotiations on the anti-dumping agreement, and Colombia a proposal to examine how an article of the subsidy agreement was being applied to developing countries. A stream of further proposals, some highly specific, others less so, followed throughout 1987 and into 1988 and were discussed in the group. Japan, the European Community, India, the Nordic countries and the United States wanted changes in the standards code, or to have the code's provisions clarified. India and Korea made proposals on government procurement; India also sought an important change in the customs valuation agreement. On import licensing, the United States produced detailed ideas on improving and widening the code, and the European Community also had proposals. For the anti-dumping code, which from the first attracted a great deal of attention, Japan, India, Korea and the Nordic countries all put forward early proposals which were followed, in late 1987 and early 1988 respectively, by calls from the United States and European Community for major amendments. These direct proposals to the negotiating group were supplemented by reports on discussions in the code committees, in each of which the signatories had reviewed issues which might be taken up in the Round.

This flood of proposals for negotiations on a large number of highly technical and varied matters was difficult for the group to handle. In part, the solution was to have the Secretariat, which had already produced a series of briefing notes on the content and history of individual codes, assemble and regularly revise working papers which kept systematic track of the proposals put forward for changes to particular provisions of the codes. From 1988 onwards, the group also devoted each meeting primarily to a small number of codes, the choice being decided well in advance so that each could be discussed thoroughly, and experts on a given subject could participate. Later, this problem was eased as it became clear that negotiations on some codes would touch on only one or two issues (usually involving problems encountered by developing countries as non-signatories or potential signatories), and the more complex discussions were entrusted to sub-groups which became the real forum for negotiations. But in the period up to the mid-term review, the negotiators and their chairman (Chulsu Kim of the Republic of Korea, a senior trade official who later became his country's Minister of Trade, Industry and Energy) had to grapple with an extraordinarily large number of issues which were only gradually defined.

By the end of 1988, the picture had become much clearer. The most substantial issues facing the negotiators were – in descending order of controversy – the anti-dumping, standards and licensing codes. For customs valuation and government procurement, the problems were far narrower in scope, as was the single issue raised in this group concerning the subsidy code.

Anti-dumping

The anti-dumping provisions in the GATT itself (Article VI) and in the Tokyo Round code (Agreement on Implementation of Article VI) have much in common with the GATT and code provisions on countervailing duties. The obvious difference is that countervailing duties are meant to offset government subsidies, whereas the purpose of anti-dumping duties is to provide a defence against unfair pricing practices of private companies. Because the GATT is an agreement among governments, it can include disciplines for subsidies themselves, as well as for the action that may be taken against them. It cannot prevent companies from dumping: it can only prescribe how governments should act against goods that are dumped. Nevertheless, the reasons for acting against subsidies and dumping are very similar, and the technical issues that arise are much the same.

The technical similarities are so close that GATT's Article VI covers both anti-dumping and countervailing duties. As far as dumping is concerned, Article VI straightforwardly condemns it. Dumping is defined as the introduction of a product of one country into the commerce of another at "less than its normal value", if it causes or threatens material injury to an established industry or "materially retards the establishment of a domestic industry". A selling price is "less than normal value" if it is lower than the normal selling price in the market of the country it is exported from; or (if this domestic price is unavailable) is lower than the normal price in other export markets; or lower than the production cost plus a reasonable margin for costs and profit. If both dumping and injury are established, anti-dumping duties may be imposed up to a level that offsets the margin of dumping.

The anti-dumping code negotiated in the Tokyo Round (itself an amended version of an earlier Kennedy Round agreement) spells out in greater detail how governments are to go about satisfying themselves that both sets of conditions (dumping and injury) in Article VI have been met. The code covers such matters as the detailed questions that may need to be asked in determining that a product is actually being sold below normal value (is the product the same as sold in the home market? What profit margin should be allowed? What allowance should be made for the effects of local taxation on selling prices?) and that it is causing or threatening injury (have imports increased? Have they been the cause of depressed market prices? Who says so?). It also governs how investigations of supposed injurious dumping shall be launched and carried out, who can give evidence, whether and how anti-dumping action should be halted if the supplier agrees to raise its prices or cease selling, and how and for how long anti-dumping duties should be applied. All these considerations are very similar to those which arise for the countervailing duties applied to offset subsidies, and indeed the main reason for revising the existing anti-dumping code in the Tokyo Round had been to bring it into line with the rules in the new subsidies code. The code was supervised by a permanent committee made up of representatives of its signatories. The committee examined the legislation and practice of each country, and sought agreement on technical problems with the code as these arose.

Even more important than the technical similarities between the two codes were the similarities in how they were viewed by governments, traders and the public. For all concerned, subsidies and dumping, and the countervailing and anti-dumping duties imposed to cancel them out, had emerged, by the time the Uruguay Round began, as a serious trade problem. An earlier section of this chapter has already discussed the negotiations on subsidies. Dumping was seen in a very similar light (indeed, the general public seldom distinguished between subsidies and dumping at all). For one side, dumping was the classic example of unfair trade, in which suppliers drove prices down to uneconomic levels, selling goods at a loss and "targeting" vulnerable domestic suppliers to put them out of business. From the foreign suppliers' side, anti-dumping action itself was often seen as an unfair means of preventing fair competition. As they saw it, domestic producers unable to match more efficient foreign suppliers' prices or products often sought to launch anti-dumping procedures to discourage and choke off imports. If successful, the suppliers' efforts to develop their sales in that market would be frustrated by anti-dumping duties or by being forced to raise prices to uncompetitive levels or to impose restraints on exports. Such success was made more likely if, as many believed, some governments interpreted the GATT rules in ways that were biased towards producing a finding of dumping and injury. Even if unsuccessful, anti-dumping cases all too often involved trade disruption and heavy legal costs. And, as in the case of subsidies, anti-dumping issues were among the most divisive disputes brought to GATT, both before and during the Uruguay Round.

There was, however, one important difference between the negotiations on subsidies and on dumping. In the subsidy negotiations, the United States stood almost alone, as the most fervent opponent of subsidies and overwhelmingly the world's largest user of countervailing duties. In the negotiations on the anti-dumping code, the United States was less isolated. The European Community was another major user of anti-dumping duties, and blamed for practices similar to those of which the United States was accused. Moreover, a large number of other countries, including developing countries such as Mexico which had recently liberalized their trade policies, had equipped themselves with rules and duties designed to combat dumping.

The negotiations on the anti-dumping code began on a deceptively calm note; indeed, it was not until much later that they emerged as one of the most difficult and divisive issues of the entire Round. Right from the beginning, however, a clear division was evident between the fundamental aims of those countries whose exports were most commonly exposed to anti-dumping action, and those which took such action. The first group wanted the anti-dumping rules to be as tight and explicit as possible, allowing the minimum of discretion to the authorities administering them, and providing maximum transparency. The points they raised were in general those which had already come up in the Anti-dumping Committee during the early 1980s, as experience was gained of the strengths and weaknesses of the code. The second group wanted to retain and even expand their discretion to meet what they saw as much-changed patterns of international trade, in which new practices were being used by companies to get around the present rules of the anti-dumping code and thereby cause injury to domestic industry. Their proposals tended to be the most radical and controversial.

From the side of exporting countries, Korea was the first to put forward detailed ideas, proposing negotiations on more than a dozen highly specific points in the code. These covered such matters as the concept of "like product", practices followed in determining what a "normal value" for a product should be, the question of whether dumped exports by several small suppliers could be "cumulated" to establish that, taken together, they caused injury, and the possibility of setting limits to the duration of anti-dumping measures through a "sunset clause". These proposals, made as early as May 1987, in fact covered a large proportion of the objections raised to the code and to its predecessor and, in several instances, paralleled proposals made to improve the subsidy code. With support from a number of other countries, Korea complained that a number of code signatories had national anti-dumping laws which contained provisions inconsistent with the anti-dumping code, or which were applied in an arbitrary manner.

Another substantial proposal from the exporters' side came in September from Japan. This proposal not only raised many of the same issues as Korea but also, in effect, attempted to forestall some of the key developments which the major users of anti-dumping action were keen to take further. One such trend, Japan pointed out, was "a move towards imposing anti-dumping duty on parts or components of products subject to anti-dumping duty under the assumption that those parts or components are imported in such forms to circumvent the said duty". The most recent such move, although Japan did not say so, had come only three months earlier, when the European Community introduced new anti-dumping regulations which provided for "anti-circumvention" action. Much was to be heard of this issue in the coming negotiations. A second new development, Japan pointed out, was the concept of "input dumping", under which it was suggested that anti-dumping duties could be imposed on products which, although not themselves dumped, incorporated dumped parts or materials. This question had already been discussed in the code committee, largely at the initiative of the United States. Another issue raised by Japan was the danger that products might be found dumped when in fact their lower price in an export market, compared with their earlier price in the home market, might simply reflect advances in production technology.

A further proposal to take up issues already discussed in the code committee was put forward by the Nordic countries. They also suggested that the whole idea of dumping, judged on the basis of export prices being lower than the domestic price of a product, might not make much sense in modern circumstances. Export prices, they believed, were usually governed by competitive pressures in the export market concerned. If domestic suppliers cut their prices, the foreign supplier had to follow or lose market share; yet if the result was that he charged less than his domestic price, he was open to anti-dumping charges.

The first proposals from the side of the United States and the European Community came somewhat later, in December 1987 and March 1988 respectively. The United States called for the negotiations "to improve existing remedies and disciplines with respect to injurious dumping". It was worried by "practices that seem to defeat the intent of the code to address effectively injurious dumping". These included "recidivist" (repeat) dumping by some companies that appeared to regard anti-dumping duties as simply a part of doing business. A solution, not at present permitted by the code, might be to impose severe penalties on repeated dumping. Similarly, "certain diversionary practices", such as "input dumping", could at present be used to evade anti-dumping orders on those products capable of being exported in a different form. The United States also proposed to change the definition of "domestic industry" (important in establishing the right to initiate a complaint against dumping) to cover primary agricultural producers when their production was the main input to a processed agricultural product threatened by dumping. (The rejection of a recent GATT complaint had turned on this point.) For its part, the European Community called for the code to be adapted "to new realities", notably by incorporating into it the principles of its own new anti-circumvention laws. The Community's concern was that the defences provided by its anti-dumping duties were being evaded by companies which either imported the component parts of the product affected by the duty, and then simply put them together in so-called "screwdriver plants", or carried out similar assembly in a third country before shipping the product to the Community. Action against these practices was made more difficult because they were often carried out by companies which were legally distinct, although in practice closely related. Less defensively, the Community also proposed other changes to the code, including adoption of its own practice of an automatic "sunset clause" under which anti-dumping measures would lapse after five years unless shown to be still needed.

Both the American and Community proposals were discussed in meetings of the negotiating group in June and October 1988, along with further, more detailed, ideas from Japan which covered several of the same subjects, though from a different viewpoint. As far as concerned incorporating a sunset clause into the code, along with other points discussed in the code committee, there was a great deal of support. But many countries were strongly opposed to the extension of the code to cover screwdriver plants in the importing country, third-country assembly, and input dumping. The discussion was coloured by developments elsewhere in GATT: Japan had just launched a GATT complaint against the Community following imposition of anti-dumping duties on electronic typewriters and scales assembled at Japanese-owned plants in the United Kingdom and France. It was to win the case in 1990, precisely on the ground that the Community's anti-circumvention regulations were contrary to the existing GATT rules. Japan saw the regulations as an effort to force local content requirements on the new overseas plants its investors were building in the Community and elsewhere. Many developing countries saw the Community regulations as a breach of the Punta del Este standstill undertaking not to introduce new restrictions on trade. In the negotiating group, Japan, Korea, Hong Kong, Singapore and the Nordic countries argued that the EC proposals would unjustifiably broaden the anti-dumping code. The US suggestion that repeated dumping should be penalized was opposed on the grounds that such dumping was not likely to cause injury and that anti-dumping duties were supposed to correct abnormal prices, not impose penalties.

Both these meetings gave an opportunity for governments to state their general approach to the negotiations on the anti-dumping code. Encouragingly, they showed a widespread readiness to make a good many technical improvements which had been identified as desirable in the negotiating group and in the code committee. However, they also showed once again the gulf in objectives between the countries whose exporters were most often at risk of anti-dumping action and the United States, the European Community and the few other regular users of anti-dumping regulations. As yet, the negotiations had not really been engaged, although Korea proposed some new language for the anti-dumping code just before the break for the mid-erm review. The coming bargaining, when it began, was expected to be difficult. No one, however, foresaw just how difficult it would turn out to be.

Standards

The agreement on technical barriers to trade – familiarly known as the "standards code" or, in the jargon of the officials concerned, "TBT" – was perhaps the most successful of the Tokyo Round agreements. It filled a gap in the trading system's defences against non-tariff barriers, had functioned smoothly and cooperatively, and had attracted nearly 40 signatories, including a fairly large number of developing countries. Not surprisingly, experience had shown that it could be improved in a number of technical respects. More substantially, the United States and the European Community, as well as some other signatories, had ideas on how its scope might be widened or its rules made more effective. Most of the proposals that were to come forward in the Uruguay Round had already been aired in the committee which oversaw the operation of the standards code, and had been systematically reviewed in the months before the Punta del Este meeting. Some in fact might have been negotiated within the committee, had the Round not been launched. The Round, however, gave a political push to negotiations and a forum in which major changes to the code itself could be considered. It offered the opportunity to negotiate directly with developing countries that were not signatories and, by placing the discussions in a much wider context, made it possible to develop a package agreement on standards that might require greater efforts by some countries than others.

The Tokyo Round standards code was drawn up to ensure that international trade would not be unnecessarily hampered by technical regulations and standards drawn up to protect health, safety and the environment, to prevent fraud, or for other reasons. The need for such regulations and standards is universally accepted. They can however easily operate in ways that discriminate against imports, particularly if the standards are different from those used in other countries, are enforced through testing or certification requirements which imports cannot easily meet, or are insufficiently publicized. The 1979 code encouraged signatories to use internationally agreed standards, where these existed; required them to inform one another about their preparation, adoption and application of standards, and to consult on this when necessary. It called for testing and certifying bodies to avoid discrimination against imports and, as far as possible, to recognize each other's tests and certificates. An elaborate set of procedures for notification and consultation, making use of the GATT Secretariat, a standing committee and "enquiry points" in each government, ensured that the rules worked in practice.

The proposals made by governments in the negotiating group, as well as in the code committee, showed that no one wanted to change these essential features of the standards agreement. What some countries sought was, in terms of the analysis developed in the code committee, further improvement, clarification or expansion of the agreement. Virtually all the proposals came forward very quickly, both separately from the governments concerned and in a September 1987 listing forwarded to the group by the chairman of the code committee. Later proposals from delegations, in 1988 and 1989, spelled out these ideas in terms of drafting, but in general contained no surprises. In consequence, the standards negotiations moved forward smoothly and (as far as governments were concerned) uncontroversially, in the strongest possible contrast to the battle in the same negotiating group over the anti-dumping code. At the very end of the Uruguay Round, environmental activists criticized the standards code as a potential obstacle to action to protect the environment, and minor alterations were made to it in response, but the code was never an issue that seriously divided the negotiators themselves.

Under the heading of "improvement", there were two major proposals: one from the European Community for negotiation of a " Code of Good Practice" for non-governmental standardizing bodies, and another put forward by the United States for better transparency about bilateral and regional work and agreements on standards. Under "clarification", the United States sought a clear understanding of whether the agreement covered standards governing processes and production methods. Under "expansion", the European Community was concerned to bring standardizing bodies at the local (sub-central) level within the scope of the main obligations of the code. Other proposals came from India, the Nordic countries and Japan, and were generally concerned with one or another aspect of improving the flow of information about national standards activities and with giving better opportunities for other governments to comment on them.

Essentially, the 1979 code was concerned with setting obligations that would apply between the central governments which signed it. To a large extent, this was sufficient to meet the code's purposes. However, in some countries, standards activities are carried out by non-governmental bodies, or by local governments. This is particularly the case in the United States, but also in some other countries, particularly those with federal structures which leave many important regulatory functions to "second-tier" governments such as those of the American states or Canadian provinces. The 1979 code provided only that the signatory governments should "take such reasonable measures as may be available to them". The Community's proposal for a Code of Good Practice sought to get round this problem, as far as non-governmental standardizing bodies were concerned, by translating the main obligations under the code – national and most-favoured-nation treatment, the use of international standards and transparency – into operational guide-lines that would be submitted to these bodies for acceptance. The Community also proposed to extend the reach of the code more effectively by making central governments more responsible for whether local governments carried out the code's requirements. The concerns of the US were in the other direction: it worried that American producers might be put at a dis-advantage by standards agreements reached between other governments, and particularly by regional organizations such as are particularly active in Europe. It argued that outsiders could be left in the dark about proposals for new standards or certification systems, with the result that they were unable to comment until too late on proposals which might be biased against their interests, or give a competitive advantage to producers of the countries concerned, or compromise the setting of international standards. The United States proposed to overcome these problems mainly by requiring greater information to be given on bilateral and regional standards activities ("transparency"), and by allowing outsiders to comment in good time before proposed new standards were introduced. India added a further proposal on transparency that would cover standards adopted voluntarily by national producers since it believed that these could, in practice, have the same kind of trade-hampering effect as compulsory standards.

The US proposal to clarify whether the code covered processes and production methods was highly technical in character and potentially important in practice. In general, the code was concerned with rules that lay down what characteristics a product must have, setting for instance the performance it shall deliver, its size or its safety. The code was not concerned with rules about how the product was manufactured or grown, although its dispute settlement rules could be invoked if process or production requirements were believed to be used as a means of avoiding obligations under the code. Three recent and somewhat inconclusive disputes had arisen between the United States and the European Community which turned on production and processing requirements. In each case, the United States complained about EC regulations affecting the production or preparation of chicken or beef meat. One illustrates particularly clearly why this issue was to be of interest to non-governmental activists: it concerned a regulation that banned the use of growth hormones for beef cattle. Whether the ban was scientifically justified was highly controversial. It was introduced primarily because of consumer concern about the health effects of the hormones, and it effectively closed the European market to a large proportion of US beef exports. This particular dispute happened to concern an agricultural product, but it has a wider significance. Increasingly, environmental campaigners have been concerned with the damage that can be done to the environment by production processes that involve, for instance, atmospheric pollution or the introduction of chemicals into farming. In moving towards international rules that would regulate standards for production and processing methods in order to avoid creating barriers to trade, the negotiators were taking the GATT in a direction that risked an eventual confrontation with the "Greens".

These were the main issues raised in the early discussions on the standards code. Most of the remainder were concerned with improving transparency in the applications of the code and the setting of national standards. While countries showed varying degrees of enthusiasm for the proposals, none were so controversial as to be rejected out of hand. Accordingly, there was no difficulty in simply reporting to ministers in Montreal the stage reached in the negotiations, with the expectation that serious drafting would begin in 1989.

Import licensing

When governments put quantitative restrictions on imports or (more rarely) exports, some form of mechanism will be needed to administer the restrictions. Usually, traders will have to seek a license which authorizes the customs authorities to let the goods concerned enter or leave the country. The licensing procedures will cover such matters as the information to be provided, and penalties for misinformation. From the point of view of the trader, the most important features of the procedures are likely to be how long he must wait for approval, how complicated the application requirements are, whether the timing and other conditions of the license in practice make trade practicable and worthwhile, and whether he is treated on the same basis as other applicants: if he is not, the quota may be exhausted without his being able to obtain a share in it. Licences may also be used by governments simply as a means of keeping track of trade flows; in this case authorization to import or export is given automatically, but delays and administrative hassle can still be a problem.

The Agreement on Import Licensing Procedures negotiated in 1979 was intended to ensure that the necessary administrative tool of licensing does not itself become a trade policy measure, and in particular does not hamper or distort trade. The agreement's provisions require that import licensing procedures be applied neutrally and fairly, and seek to make these procedures as simple as possible, with adequate notice of requirements and time-limits for processing applications. Probably the least controversial of all the Tokyo Round codes, and certainly among the shortest, it had functioned quite well, and had attracted a reasonably large number of signatories, although few developing countries had thought it worthwhile to join. By the time the Uruguay Round began, experience had shown that its provisions could be tightened up, particularly by making some of them rather more specific. Proposals for possible changes were under discussion in the committee which administered the code. As in the case of the standards code, these proposals were initially developed in both the committee and the negotiating group, a procedure which in practice worked without difficulty since the same experts were for the most part present in both groups.

Throughout the negotiations on the licensing code, the main source of ideas and driving force for change was the United States, and the history of these negotiations is essentially that of the introduction and refinement of the US proposals until they became generally acceptable. The United States itself explained its aims most clearly in a statement in March 1988. The proliferation of licensing systems was, it said, an increasing problem in the world trading system. Although it acknowledged the value of automatic import licensing for various purposes, and accepted that non-automatic licensing could be used legitimately to administer measures adopted under relevant GATT provisions, its central idea was to limit the use of licensing.

As early as the first meeting of the negotiating group, both the United States and the European Community proposed improvements to the licensing agreement. Each followed up their initial statements by circulating written proposals which formed the basis of most discussion of the agreement in the first two years of the Round. The US proposals were far-reaching. Their most controversial element was the suggestion that the negotiating group should examine ways of limiting licensing, for example by putting time limits or phase-out requirements on the use of licences, or restricting the proportion of tariff headings or of total trade for which licences might be required. Because quantitative restrictions and import licences were so closely related, the United States proposed that the code should set guidelines for notifying and justifying the administration of such restrictions. (The code required signatories to respond to questions about their licensing requirements, but did not call for them to be notified.) The United States also proposed review and dispute settlement procedures, as well as a general clarification of guidelines for licensing practices, and adoption into the code of tighter provisions on time-limits and other matters on which the code committee had reached agreement early in 1987. The European Community's proposals were less ambitious, their most controversial element being a call to extend the code's coverage to export restrictions.

Intermittent discussion at meetings of the negotiating group during 1987 and 1988 showed that many of the United States' ideas, in particular, were widely supported. However, its proposals on limiting the use of licensing were criticized on the ground that this would, in effect, amount also to limiting recourse to restrictive measures which were specifically authorized under various GATT Articles. Any such alteration in the balance of rights and obligations under the GATT would, it was said, go far beyond the group's negotiating authority. The EC proposal to extend the code to cover export licensing was criticized on much the same grounds. For its part, the US maintained that the group had the authority to negotiate an expansion of the licensing code's scope.

Customs valuation

For customs valuation, the question was whether one particular and important rule could be applied in such a way that developing countries would find it more attractive to accept the code. The issue for them was whether, in signing the code, they could retain what they regarded as essential weapons against fraud by importers.

Customs valuation procedures can seriously distort trade, because they determine the impact that import duties and other charges will have on a particular shipment. Duties and charges are almost always *ad valorem* (related to the value of the goods). If the customs authorities do not accept the importer's declared value, and charge duties on a higher value, the duties collected will be proportionately higher. Valuation can be difficult. Customs officials may be justified in setting higher values if they suspect fraud or find error. When, as is often the case, the shipper and importer are related companies, there can be room for legitimate disagreement on how costs are allocated, and thus for claiming different valuations. The provisions on valuation in Article VII of the GATT were supplemented by the Tokyo Round valuation code, which established a presumption that valuation should be based on the price actually paid (the "transaction value") for the imported goods. Alternative methods of valuation were set out in a prescribed hierarchy, to be used only if the earlier methods could not be applied.

Developing countries were reluctant to accept the presumption that they should use the transaction value, because they believed that importers frequently undervalued their shipments, so as to reduce the duties payable, or overvalued them, with the collusion of the shippers, as a means of illegally moving money out of the country. For most developing countries, customs duties provided a very important share of total government revenues, and undervaluation, the more common practice, was therefore a serious threat to their incomes. India, as part of a broader effort to adapt the Tokyo Round codes so that more developing countries would find membership worthwhile, proposed in November 1987 that when customs administrations suspected fraud (usually because the declared price of imported goods was out of line with other shipments of the same products) they should be able to shift the burden of proof that the goods were priced correctly from the customs authorities to the importer. Many developed countries were initially reluctant to accept the proposal. They felt the code had worked well in its present form, and they saw the rule which normally required acceptance of the transaction value as an important defence for traders against arbitrary action by customs authorities. Some, moreover, felt that the code already gave customs officials the authority they needed. However, they remained ready to discuss the proposal, particularly because India did not insist on an actual amendment of the code, and a number of developing countries said that they might well sign the code if a satisfactory decision could be reached.

Government procurement

Fewer countries had signed the government procurement agreement than any other code, and all but three of its signatories were developed countries. Essentially the code provided a set of rules under which signatories opened up to traders of other signatories the possibility of bidding for purchasing contracts of various government-owned bodies. The bodies and purchasing sectors covered were specified in negotiated lists. Because purchases by governments for their own use are effectively not covered by the GATT rules, the code signatories were free to extend its privileges only to one another. In theory, there was no reason why negotiations on the substance of the code and its coverage could not have taken place as part of the Uruguay Round. In fact, they did not. Far-reaching negotiations to expand the coverage of the 1979 code took place during the period of the Round, and a final agreement was to be reached and actually signed in Marrakesh. These negotiations, however, were separate from the Round, and had actually started earlier. They took place essentially among the signatories of the code, in a working group set up by the code committee, with just one other country (Korea) involved. One reason they were kept separate was that they included negotiations on services as well as goods, and thereby mixed two elements that were supposedly kept rigidly apart under the ground-rules of the Uruguay Round. Within the Round, in the negotiating group on the codes, discussion was limited essentially to the question of how membership in the government procurement code might be made more attractive to developing countries.

As in the case of customs valuation, the issue was raised in September 1987 by India. Pointing out that only one of the four developing countries that had taken part in the Tokyo Round negotiations on government procurement had finally signed the code, India proposed that the code's special provisions for developing countries should be reinforced to attract more of them to join it. India was particularly critical of the effective veto over new accessions which the code gave each existing signatory by requiring that all signatories approve terms of accession, which included the list of government bodies ("entities") whose purchases the candidate country proposed to open up to foreign suppliers. In December 1987, further detailed proposals aimed at helping developing countries to join were put forward by Korea which had a natural interest in trying to ease the path of its own accession. Korea wanted developing countries to be able to accede with a limited entity offer, provided they undertook to expand their entity lists gradually later on. Among its other proposals, also with the aim of making accession easier, were changes in tendering procedures and information requirements. These proposals were not discussed at any length in the period before the Montreal meeting, although Korea put them into the form of specific texts late in 1988.

Subsidies

On subsidies, Colombia suggested in June 1987 that the negotiating group examine how signatories of the code were applying its Article 14.5. This provision calls on developing-country signatories "to endeavour to enter into a commitment to reduce or eliminate export subsidies when the use of such export subsidies is inconsistent with its competitive and development needs". Colombia's target was clearly the United States, which some developing countries felt had been using the provision as a means of pushing them to undertake commitments for which they were not ready. However, other members of the group were reluctant to take up the issue, mainly because they felt it belonged in the separate negotiating group on subsidies. Colombia did not pursue it further.

GATT Articles

"Participants shall review GATT Articles, provisions and disciplines as requested by interested contracting parties, and, as appropriate, undertake negotiations."

As this brief instruction in the Punta del Este Declaration suggests, the negotiations on GATT Articles were envisaged essentially as a means of handling whatever residual issues on the GATT rules might later be identified as being worth attention. Several countries were quick to point out that the negotiating group set up for the task had no mandate to embark on any wholesale renegotiation of the GATT. Moreover, there was a quite widespread feeling that all major issues for the Round had been spelled out elsewhere in the Declaration. Several, such as safeguards, subsidies and dispute settlement, were concerned essentially with the working of individual articles. The implication, as some saw it, was that nothing very novel, important or difficult ought to come up in the GATT Articles group. To a great extent, this proved to be the case. But there were exceptions, one of which was to arouse great controversy.

Early meetings of the negotiating group brought forward a long list of proposals that particular articles be taken up for study and possible negotiations. In each case, there was a comparatively brief discussion which served to show what problems the proposer felt were encountered in the operation of the GATT rule concerned, and to what extent other governments agreed or disagreed with the diagnosis. Most important, this initial discussion usually gave a fairly clear indication of whether the proposals made were likely to be negotiable, in the sense that governments could see a possible shared interest in working for an agreement that would respond to the concerns raised. It quickly became obvious that the proposals ranged from basically technical improvements, with which few were likely to disagree, to changes that would be accepted by some countries only with deep reluctance, or not at all. Altogether, the proposals made during the first year of the Round covered 12 of the General Agreement's 38 articles, as well as the Protocol of Provisional Application by which the whole of the GATT was actually put into force. This initial phase, during which the Secretariat provided background papers that set out, for most of the articles raised, their essential provisions and how they had been applied in practice, lasted until November 1987. The negotiating group then began reviewing each proposal in greater detail in order to establish if negotiations would be appropriate and, if so, on what basis. On the technical questions, the discussion advanced quite rapidly, no doubt because matters of political principle or major economic interest were not involved, and there were no cross-linkages to other issues in the Round. Negotiations on the more difficult matters moved much more slowly, in parallel with the major issues dealt with in other groups.

So many unrelated issues were raised that at one stage the possibility was discussed of effectively breaking up the GATT Articles group by spreading its work over a number of sub-groups. Although this was not done, each meeting of the group in practice had to take up a series of distinct questions, varying widely in significance, difficulty and degree of progress. Because of this diversity, any attempt to provide an essentially chronological account of the GATT Articles negotiations as a whole would be confusing and largely pointless. Instead, the following account looks in turn at work in the first two years of the Round on each of the issues discussed, taking them as far as possible in the numerical order of the articles concerned. As none of questions raised had reached a point, by the end of 1988, at which decisions or guidance by ministers was needed, the work of the GATT Articles group was not an issue at the mid-term meeting in Montreal.

Schedules of concessions

On a numerical basis, Article II of the GATT was the first to be raised, on an essentially technical proposal made by New Zealand. This Article, "Schedules of Concessions", is basic to the original and classic market-opening function of the GATT. It sets out the requirements and implications of the lists in which each GATT participant specifies the precise tariff commitments it has undertaken as a result of negotiations with other members. For each product covered, these lists ("schedules") in principle provide its trading partners with a definitive statement of the maximum protection which their exports of that product will face in its market. New Zealand made the point that paragraph 1(b) of the Article, which sets out the basic requirement that "ordinary customs duties" shall not be higher than specified in the schedules, in fact left a loophole for higher charges to be imposed. This was because it failed to cover some other duties or charges borne only by imports. Even to the extent that these other charges were in fact bound, they were not necessarily shown in the schedules, so that traders could not easily learn what trade barriers they faced. New Zealand's proposal that "ordinary customs duties" be defined in a way that would close the loophole, and that the full coverage of bindings be shown in the schedules, was well received.

Balance-of-payments provisions

The next issue in numerical order was by contrast extremely controversial. It concerned the GATT Articles which permit countries in balance-of-payments difficulties to introduce trade restrictions at higher levels than those bound in their schedules. In fact, there are four relevant Articles: XII, XIV, XV, and XVIII. Of these, XII and XVIII are of primary importance, the first setting out the basic ground-rules for using trade restrictions when in balance-of-payments difficulties, and the second (in its section B) offering an easier set of provisions that are available only to developing countries. In practice, although Article XII had been important in the earlier years of GATT, developed countries had almost ceased to use it. On the rare occasions that it was invoked, this was generally in response to a sudden crisis, and the country concerned usually disinvoked it, removing the additional protection within a matter of months. Article XVIII:B was used quite differently. It was invoked by many developing countries, including some of the largest and most active in GATT such as Brazil, Egypt, India, Korea and Pakistan, and it permitted them to maintain strict and far-reaching limitations on imports which in some cases had been in force for many years. In the Tokyo Round, agreement had been reached on a number of additional principles and rules. These included recognition that "restrictive trade measures are in general an inefficient means to maintain or restore balance-of-payments equilibrium" and introduced quite detailed procedures for regular justification and examination of such measures in GATT. But the agreement essentially did nothing to curtail the ability of countries to resort to Articles XII or XVIII:B to reduce imports. As early as

May 1987, the United States signalled its intention to try to change the situation.

The United States argued that the international monetary situation has changed profoundly since the GATT balance-of-payments articles were written. With the introduction of floating exchange rates. and with various forms of assistance available through the International Monetary Fund countries should now be able to adjust their balance-of-payments situation without resorting to trade restrictions. Yet Article XVIII:B, in particular, was cast in terms which allowed developing countries to maintain import restrictions on a virtually permanent basis. (According to a later US analysis, 19 developing countries had made use of Article XVIII:B over the previous 23 years but only four had ceased to invoke it.) Moreover, some countries, it said, were using XVIII:B selectively, so as to protect particular industries rather than the country's balance-of-payments as a whole. In doing so, they were by-passing other GATT rules (XVIII:C and D) which permit developing countries to withdraw concessions and introduce protection "infant industries" but which require that they offer compensation for doing so. The procedures for GATT examinations of balance-of-payments measures were also not working as well as they should.

The United States – soon joined by Canada – was raising extremely sensitive issues, on which many developed and developing countries held diametrically opposed views. For the United States, Canada and (though openly acknowledged) some other developed countries, the exception to usual GATT rules provided by Article XVIII:B permitted the developing countries which invoked it to escape fundamental obligations of member in the international trading system. As they saw it, these countries were riders on the system, enjoying its benefits but giving nothing in return. On the other side, many or even most developing countries held views at least equally strong. They saw Article XVIII:B's recognition of their right to maintain restrictions to protect the balance-of-payments as their principal defence against having their efforts to develop their economies derailed by unwanted and unnecessary imports. They believed that developing countries for many reasons laboured at a disadvantage in international trade, with own economies weak and beset by difficulties that almost always include chronic balance-of-payments problems, and with the richer countries far better equipped economically and inexcusably protectionist in their treatment of developing-country products. Article XVIII:B was one of the few GATT rules which gave them the special and differential treatment which they believed should be more generally available. For many of these countries, resistance to any weakening of their Article XVIII:B rights quickly became their chief priority in the GATT Articles negotiations: at least one told other negotiators privately that this was an issue as sensitive for it as any in the entire Uruguay Round. Not surprisingly, the group could not agree on whether to take up the balance-of-payments articles as a subject for negotiation, although a way out of the confrontation was at least suggested by a European Community proposal which took a more conciliatory line than the United States and Canada, and also suggested that the time had come at which developed countries no longer needed the protection of Article XII.

State trading

Far less controversial was a suggestion that the group look at the precise requirements and effectiveness of Article XVII, on state-trading enterprises. This issue was initially raised by Chile in the very first written proposal to the negotiating group. (Later, the United States also made proposals on it.) Import monopolies, government-owned or otherwise, are obviously in a strong position to distort trade by favouring particular suppliers, restricting quantities imported, or setting high retail prices. The main thrust of Article XVII is to ensure that government-owned enterprises, or those which enjoy a special status or privileges granted by the government, do not provide a means of escaping GATT rules of non-discrimination in trade which governments are bound to respect in the measures they apply to private companies. The requirements of the Article do not apply to imports by state-trading enterprises of goods for use by governments themselves. However, many such enterprises have been given responsibility for handling trade in particular commodities: in several countries, for instance, imports and retail sales of alcoholic beverages are reserved exclusively or in part to state enterprises. Disputes had arisen over the exact coverage of the Article, and its notification provisions were the worst-observed of any under the General Agreement. Chile and the United States felt that the rules on state-trading enterprises needed to be strengthened, particularly in order to make clearer which enterprises were covered and what the non-discrimination obligations implied.

Although there was sympathy with the Chilean and US proposals, most countries were much readier to tighten up definitions and notification procedures than to undertake any major overhaul of the Article. They were frankly unwilling to follow up a further US suggestion that the Article's requirements might have some bearing on countertrade (barter). Countertrade, used particularly by developing and Eastern European countries short of convertible currencies, was at the time attracting a great deal of attention and some extravagant estimates of its use. India, however, pointed out that countertrade had been specifically excluded from the subject-matter of the Round as part of a package decision under which restrictive business practices, a subject of interest to it, had also been left out.

Security exceptions

Article XXI of the General Agreement overrides all others in recognizing what has been described as the first duty of any state: to protect national security. Nothing in the agreement shall prevent a member from taking any action necessary to protect these interests, notably "in time of war or other emergency in international relations". (The other exceptions concern fissionable materials, the arms trade, and actions under United Nations obligations for maintenance of peace and security.) In November 1987 Nicaragua called for an examination of Article XXI. Nicaragua claimed that the trade embargo maintained against it by the United States, and justified by the latter as a security matter, was an essentially political measure of a kind that should only be taken in conformity with obligations such as resolutions of the UN Security Council. It also complained that in practice it had been unable to exercise its rights under the dispute procedures of the GATT. Later, both it and Argentina, which had been subjected to a broader trade embargo in the early 1980s at the time of the South Atlantic conflict, proposed that the GATT security exceptions be defined more tightly. Other participants, however, were not ready to take up the proposals, believing that the issue was too politically sensitive for successful negotiation, and that in any case no country would give up the right to be judge of its own security interests.

Regional agreements

Japan, which in general initiated few proposals in the Uruguay Round, came forward in September 1987 with a call to strengthen the rules governing regional trade agreements in Article XXIV. India made a further proposal two months later. This Article was originally regarded as a minor exception to the general rules of the GATT. In GATT's early years, the most significant exceptions to trade on an MFN basis consisted of long-established arrangements such as the Commonwealth Preferences involving Britain and its present or former dependencies. Regional arrangements were few and small, with the Benelux agreement between Belgium, the Netherlands and Luxembourg probably the most significant. From 1958 onwards, however, Article XXIV's significance grew enormously. By the time the Uruguay Round opened, it had already provided the GATT basis for the establishment of the European Economic Community, the European Free Trade Association (EFTA), and a large number of other arrangements by which these countries, along with many others, dismantled trade barriers among themselves while maintaining tariffs and other restrictions against non-members. Moreover, the trend towards regional integration appeared to be accelerating, with a free trade agreement between Canada and the United States only the most striking of many proposals under discussion.

Article XXIV's rules are complicated, not least because they have to cover two technically different forms of free trade agreement – the customs union and the free trade area. Their main purpose, however, is quite straightforward: to ensure that countries which form such arrangements, and thereby inevitably introduce discrimination against non-members, provide adequate compensation for any damage done and move to genuinely free trade among themselves. To this end, they include a number of detailed requirements. Customs unions, which are distinguished from free trade areas in that their member countries all charge the same rates of import duty on imports from non-members, are required to set these duties and other regulations at a level not higher or more restrictive on the whole than the overall level ("general incidence") of the individual members before the grouping was formed, and to compensate for increases. Free trade areas, which use rules of origin to identify products that qualify for the duty-free treatment, must not allow these to become a trade obstacle in themselves. To qualify as either a customs union or free trade area, members must remove duties and other restrictions affecting "substantially all" the trade among them. Other rules require that detailed plans and schedules showing how the members will move to free trade be provided, and that these be examined in GATT to confirm that they are in accordance with its rules.

These rules had given rise to difficulty, to such an extent that only a handful of some 70 regional trading arrangements examined over the years had been explicitly recognized as meeting the requirements of Article XXIV. Japan and India, which were among the few big countries not already or prospectively involved in regional trading arrangements, had good reason to want the rules clarified and tightened up, especially to make certain that new agreements did not raise barriers to imports from non-members. They found their main allies among countries such as Australia, New Zealand and Korea, which feared they would be at a disadvantage in a world of trading blocs. On the defensive were the European countries, and to a lesser extent the very large number of other participants in the negotiations who were either linked with the European regional agreements or contemplating regional agreements of their own.

Japan's proposals included an obligation on members of new agreements to share on an MFN basis a part of the concessions agreed; better consultation with GATT before and after agreements were reached; a firm time limit on "interim agreements", to ensure that members moved to genuinely free trade; a clear-cut definition of "general incidence"; and explicit recognition that a new customs union could claim no negotiating credit ("reverse compensation") if that general incidence were actually lower than before. India raised many of the same points, and added others. One concerned a critically important issue that had bedevilled many GATT Article XXIV reviews. How, it asked, should the term "substantially all trade" be interpreted if the agreement excluded agriculture, or if only one group of countries eliminated the trade restrictions? The exclusion of agriculture had been a feature of agreements involving the EFTA countries, and the European Community had claimed free trade area status for agreements in which its developing-country partners made no tariff reductions.

India also raised a question on a quite different aspect of Article XXIV, likely to strike a much stronger chord of sympathy from the European Community. This concerned paragraph 12 of the Article, which calls on each GATT member to "take such reasonable measures as may be available to it" to ensure that GATT provisions are observed by regional and local governments.

As noted earlier in this chapter, the Community felt that GATT obligations were tilted in favour of federal states whose second-level governments could too easily distort trade by granting subsidies, setting technical standards, or taking other measures. India asked that the negotiators clarify whether Article XXIV:12 limited the applicability of other provisions of GATT, or merely limited the obligation of federal states to see that the provisions were applied.

Although the issues raised under Article XXIV were less sensitive than those on the GATT balance-of-payments rules, discussions in the negotiating group were not easy. No agreement to negotiate on Article XXIV had been reached by the time of the Montreal ministerial meeting.

Waivers

Article XXV of the General Agreement provides the basic authority to the member countries to act together to further the Agreement's purposes: it is in fact the basis on which the successive negotiating rounds have been launched. Paragraph 5 of the Article is the waiver provision which allows individual countries to be relieved of particular GATT obligations provided this is approved by a vote in which the proposal must win a two-thirds majority, with that majority including at least half of all GATT members. Apart from the voting provisions, Article XXV:5 is unspecific about the conditions for waivers. Experience, and in particular the continued existence of a far-reaching waiver granted over 30 years earlier to the United States to maintain import restrictions on some agricultural products had led many countries to believe that waivers should only be granted on strict conditions, and above all for a limited period. One of the first proposals to the negotiating group, in May 1987, was a European Community call to draw up waiver rules in order "to prevent the perpetuation of, or to forestall, virtually permanent privileged situations".

De facto status under the GATT

When a country joins the GATT, its acceptance normally also covers any dependent territories it may have. The GATT rules on accession, in Article XXVI, stated that if these territories later became independent, as happened in the postwar years (and especially the 1960s) with many former colonies, they could themselves join GATT without formalities, provided they accepted whatever tariff commitments had been assumed on their behalf by the country previously responsible for them. In practice, many newly independent countries opted for *de facto* status, an in-between arrangement which was intended to allow them time to decide whether they wished to become full GATT members or not. *De facto* countries were treated as if they are GATT members, on the assumption that they gave GATT treatment in return to the member countries. However, until recently large numbers of the *de facto* countries retained that status for many years. There was no kind of check on whether they were in fact recognizing any obligations towards GATT members, or were maintaining tariff commitments. The United States proposed that paragraph 5 of Article XXVI be reviewed in order to make it easier to know what commitments a *de facto* country had assumed, and in particular to establish a schedule of commitments for it. The proposal was not however taken up by the negotiating group. Whatever its merits at the time, it has since been overtaken by events: from 1990 onwards, most of the *de facto* countries joined the GATT, and there is no *de facto* status under the new trade rules that have emerged from the Uruguay Round.

Renegotiation of tariff concessions

Most of the preceding proposals were discussed only briefly in the period leading up to the mid-term review of the Uruguay Round. One, however, was examined in great detail, and the shape of a possible agreement was already beginning to emerge by the end of 1988. This was the highly technical question of the negotiating rights of other GATT members when a country seeks to raise tariffs that it has bound at a particular level in a previous negotiation. The issue was important. These rules determine, for example, whether a country is able to claim compensation for export markets put at risk when a new member of a customs union raises some tariffs to align them with those of the other members.

The rules on renegotiation of tariff concessions are laid down in Article XXVIII. Paragraph 1 of the Article requires that a country wishing to raise bound tariffs negotiate appropriate compensation, normally by lowering other tariffs, with the country with which it originally negotiated the binding, and also with a country which has a "principal supplying interest". A supplier is recognized as having a principal supplying interest if it holds, or recently held, a bigger share of the market for the product concerned than that of the country which originally negotiated the concession.

In practice, the greater weight in world trade of the larger countries means that they tend to be the principal suppliers, and thus have been the only countries which can usually claim negotiating rights when someone has sought to raise bound tariffs. The effect has been that small suppliers have no say in the matter, even if the exports threatened by an increase in tariffs are relatively much more important to them than they are to the principal supplier. If the compensatory tariff reductions secured by the principal supplier turn out to be on products they do not export, their trade can suffer seriously with no offsetting advantages. Developing countries, particularly likely to be small suppliers, have seen the rule as one example of how the trading system gives inadequate attention to their problems.

The potential injustice of the principal supplier rule had been recognized in a note to the Article which allows a second principal supplier to be recognized if the tariff being renegotiated affects "a major part of its total exports". This provision had never been invoked, perhaps because it was insufficiently clear. In May 1987, the Republic of Korea suggested that it be defined in terms of the ratio of the value of the affected exports to the total exports of the country concerned. Korea's proposal was followed by others from Argentina, Canada, Japan, New Zealand, Peru and Switzerland, each of which tried to define the significance of a particular trade flow to the exporting country concerned by measuring it against that country's gross national product, its population, its total exports of the product, or its share of total exports from that sector of the economy. Throughout the negotiation the moral case for strengthening the negotiating position of small supplier was widely recognized, but the discussion was complicated by fears of introducing complications, distortions and legal uncertainty into future tariff negotiations. The larger countries, which would have to yield ground to other suppliers if the rules were changed, also argued that their present position reflected not only their greater economic strength but also the fact that they had participated most fully in past tariff negotiations.

In the early autumn of 1988, the chairman of the group, John Weeks (Canadian ambassador to GATT) circulated an informal paper which brought together the issues raised on Article XXVIII. Just before the Montreal meeting in November, the De la Paix Group put forward a comprehensive joint proposal. Most notably, it proposed a new negotiating right to be based on "the highest ratio of exports of the affected product to the market concerned to its total exports". The De la Paix proposal came too late for action in Montreal, but it was to prove afterwards to be the basis for agreement.

Non-application of the GATT

A country cannot be forced to maintain GATT relations with another. Provided it so declares when it, or the other country concerned, signs the General Agreement, it can regard the rights and obligations of the GATT as simply not applying in its relations with that country. The rules concerned are in a short article, Article XXXV, which in earlier years of the GATT was quite frequently invoked by countries which did not wish to have trade relations with another country (usually because it disapproved of it politically or was afraid of its competitive power). Article XXXV, however, made this right of non-application conditional on the two countries concerned not having entered into tariff negotiations with one another. The United States, in a proposal in November 1987, suggested that this condition be eased so that countries could explore with one another the scope for negotiations without at that stage having to decide whether or not to invoke the right of non-application. The proposal was not discussed further until after Montreal.

The "grandfather clause"

The remaining provision raised in the GATT Articles group before Montreal was the Protocol of Provisional Application. This agreement had a key and somewhat peculiar place in GATT. Strictly, the GATT itself was never brought formally into effect. Instead, because it was expected in 1947 that it would soon be covered by the more elaborate rules of the International Trade

Organization which was then under negotiation, the GATT was made effective "provisionally". As part of this arrangement, signatory countries could maintain some measures inconsistent with Part II of the GATT (broadly, the provisions dealing with national treatment and non-tariff measures), provided legislation in force at that time required that they do so. Forty years later, some practices were still covered by this "grandfather clause". Although it was not entirely clear how many of them remained, or what their significance was, they included the important Jones Act which excludes foreign-built ships from trading between United States ports. The Protocol also gave the GATT an impermanent status unique among international agreements of its importance, with no formal organizational structure, and subject to denunciation by any member at just 60 days' notice.

Two separate issues were raised concerning the Protocol of Provisional Application. One, by the European Community, was the imbalance which the grandfather clause introduced, in its view, into GATT relations. Some countries were permitted by it to maintain measures which contravened rules in Part II of the General Agreement; others were not. As a first step towards acting to correct the imbalance, the Community called for greater information about the extent to which countries were maintaining such measures. The second question, more far-reaching, was whether anything could be done to get rid of the Protocol altogether, and put the GATT on a more solid basis.

Past errors revisited: a new look at textiles and agriculture

Food, clothing and shelter. Of the three basic necessities of life, the third is by its nature unlikely ever to feature largely in international trade. The first two, however, each account for large shares in total trade. Neither can be reckoned among the successes of past efforts to open up world markets. Both were inevitably on the core agenda for the Uruguay Round, but it was far from clear what level of ambition would be adopted for the coming negotiations, or how likely it was that ambitions could be achieved.

Agriculture was barely touched by successive rounds of negotiations in GATT to reduce trade barriers. While tariffs and other obstacles to the movement of manufactures were whittled away, trade in agricultural goods was governed by special exceptions to the GATT rules – some general, some granted to particular member countries – and was increasingly hampered or distorted by complex systems of import restrictions and export subsidies put in place in the majority of industrialized countries. Typically, these system secured higher living standards for the more efficient among the protected farmers, and slowed to some extent the inexorable shift of the workforce out of agriculture. But these gains were bought at a heavy national cost in government subsidies, high prices for consumers, unwanted surplus production and overall distortion of the national economy. Moreover, the import barriers and subsidized exports of the surpluses to third markets denied trading opportunities and earnings to countries with comparative advantage in agricultural production. In trade relations, this situation was reflected in constant disputes in GATT over agricultural trade issues. Although the share of agriculture in world trade sank from one half to only one tenth over the 40 years from 1948, agriculture continued to account for about half of all disputes brought to GATT.

Trade in textiles and clothing had also been largely removed from the influence of the GATT rules. Textiles and clothing manufacture has classically been the first step in industrialization, and international competition has always been keenest in textile products based on low-wage and low-technology mass production. Today, developing countries are among the most competitive producers, and textiles and clothing account for a large proportion of their total exports of manufactures. The barriers these exports face in many markets, and above all in industrialized countries, are seen by developing countries both as a serious obstacle to their economic growth and as evidence that the importing countries are reluctant to apply the GATT rules of liberal trade when it does not suit them to do so. Yet the importers too face serious difficulties. Their own textiles and clothing industries tend to employ large numbers of low-paid workers, often in places where little alternative work is available. Protection over many years, starting with restrictions on imports from Japan over half a century ago, has made these industries even less capable of facing outside competition. From the 1960s onwards, the whole sector of international trade in textiles and clothing became increasingly a tolerated and official exception to the normal GATT rules, and especially to the rule of non-discrimination among GATT members. GATT itself, the international guardian of liberal trading practices, was made the agent of protection and managed trade through restrictive multilateral agreements that were negotiated, first, to regulate trade in cotton textile and then, from 1974 onwards, to bring trade in virtually all kinds of textile and clothing within a web of restrictions applied by most developed countries against developing-country exporters.

Both the agricultural and textiles sectors had regularly featured in past GATT negotiating rounds, but always with disappointing results. The Uruguay Round was to be the first serious attempt to turn back the protectionist tide that had been running for more than a generation in these highly sensitive sectors. Not surprisingly, the effort aroused great passions and put severe pressures on the negotiators.

Textiles and clothing

International trade in textiles and clothing is affected, like other sectors of trade, by import duties (tariffs) that protect domestic markets, and by the usual panoply of non-tariff actions that countries can take under the GATT rules to protect themselves against unfair trade or to safeguard threatened domestic industries. Tariff barriers, in particular, tend to be higher in the textiles and clothing sector than for other goods because they have regularly been made an exception in GATT tariff-cutting rounds, and subjected to below-average cuts.

But for exporters of low-cost textiles and clothing – which overwhelmingly now means developing countries – the most important factor in international trade policy has since 1974 been the Arrangement Regarding International Trade in Textiles, universally known as the Multifibre Arrangement or MFA. To understand the Uruguay Round negotiations on textiles and clothing, a brief description of the MFA is necessary. Readers should be warned that the Arrangement and its history are complex, and that the account given of it here is necessarily oversimplified.

The Multifibre Arrangement, originally negotiated in GATT in 1973 to run for four years, and regularly renewed thereafter, was introduced to bring order into a chaotic situation in which bilateral, unsupervised and sometimes secret restrictive agreements restraining trade in textiles were proliferating, and were also encouraging the spread of similar action, outside the GATT rules, into other sectors of trade. The MFA at least brought these controls on trade in textiles and clothing within an agreed and predictable framework, even though it permitted arrangements that, in the words of an Indian statement, "transgressed the basic principles and rules of GATT in letter and spirit".

Fundamentally, the Arrangement constituted a bargain under which governments attempted to reconcile two objectives: on the one side "the expansion of trade, the reduction of barriers to such trade and the progressive liberalization of world trade in textile products" and on the other "the orderly and equitable development of this trade and the avoidance of disruptive effects in individual markets and on individual lines of production in both importing and exporting countries." To these ends, the MFA provided a multilateral umbrella under which governments could introduce restraints usually under bilaterally negotiated agreements, on imports of textiles and clothing which threatened to disrupt their domestic industries. Whereas the GATT allowed only safeguard actions that were applied equally against imports from all sources, and provided for compensation for the trade damage done, the MFA specifically permitted restrictions that affected only one supplying country. No compensation was provided for. However, the MFA's rules required that the restrictions be gradually eased, in principle by enlarging quotas by 6% annually, and all bilateral agreements and other actions taken under the Arrangement were subject to close supervision by a standing Textiles Surveillance Body.

The number of signatories to the MFA varied over the years. However, it always included the main participants in world trade in textiles, even though their number fell well short of the total GATT membership or of the total participation in the Uruguay Round. It also included an important nonmember of GATT – China. Restrictions under the MFA were applied by most of the major industrialized importers, including in particular the United States and the European Community, as well as Canada and several other European countries. The exporters affected were all developing countries. They tended to fall into three groups: highly competitive East Asian producers who were compensated to some extent for the strict MFA quota restrictions by the higher prices that they could charge for artificially scarce supplies; a second group of important suppliers, including Brazil, India and Pakistan, who were originally helped by the guaranteed markets promised by MFA quotas, but later felt competitive enough to do better if markets were fully open to them; and a fairly large number of smaller suppliers who were less competitive and whose textile and clothing industries were probably favoured by receiving a reserved share of developed-country markets through quotas under the MFA. The three groups had significantly different interests in the Uruguay Round, not only because of their varying attitudes to the MFA, but also because some were much less dependent on textiles exports than others and were therefore concerned also with pursuing goals in other areas of the negotiations.

For the industrialized countries which, as importers, made use of the MFA to restrict imports of textiles and clothing this concern with other objectives of the Uruguay Round was an even more important factor. However large, sensitive and vociferous their textiles industries might be, they had diversified economies, and a broad range of export interests. Some of those interests could be met only if developing countries agreed to support initiatives elsewhere in the negotiations – for instance, services, or intellectual property. Moreover, even in the textiles and clothing sector, many of the same countries that restricted imports through the MFA had some export interests to pursue, particularly for higher-value clothing. (The European Community, for instance, was a big exporter of textiles, with a strong interest in the US market.) Finally, governments of the industrialized countries knew what their textiles industries were reluctant to acknowledge: the MFA could not be maintained forever. It had been introduced in 1974 "for the next few years" and renewal had been increasingly difficult. It was inconsistent with their own declared economic philosophy and it set a damaging example for other sectors of trade.

By the time ministers met in Punta del Este, agreement had been reached on the negotiating objective to be set for textiles and clothing: "to formulate modalities that would permit the eventual integration of this sector into GATT on the basis of strengthened GATT rules and disciplines, thereby also contributing to the objective of further liberalization". But this objective, agreed fairly easily at a time when the MFA had just been renewed until 1991, was highly ambiguous. "To formulate modalities" – in nonbureaucratic language, to work out how trade in textiles and clothing might eventually be brought back under the normal GATT rules – was not the same as actually abolishing the MFA. To draw up a tentative plan is one thing; to decide when (and even whether) to execute it is another. Moreover, what were the "strengthened rules and disciplines" to be, and would they be negotiated in the same group, or elsewhere, as part of the Uruguay Round package?

The negotiating plan adopted in Geneva for textiles and clothing did not resolve these ambiguities. Similar to the plans adopted for most other sectors of the Round, it simply called for preparatory work, followed by an examination of "techniques and modalities", and then negotiations "aimed at achieving the Negotiating Objective".

The group got off to a slow start. A first meeting in February 1987 decided to put together basic information, bringing up to date a GATT Secretariat study of world textiles trade that had been completed in 1984, and collecting data on MFA restrictions, statistics and developments in textiles markets. The meeting also saw the entry into the negotiations of a new element, the International Textiles and Clothing Bureau (ITCB), a body which brought together some 20 developing countries, exporters of textiles and clothing. The ITCB was to act as a coordinator of the views of these countries throughout the Uruguay Round, playing a role in some ways similar to that of the Cairns Group for the agricultural exporters. From July 1987 its officers were on hand in the negotiating group's meetings.

By December, after four formal meetings devoted to study of the basic facts, the group moved to the second stage of its work: the examination of "techniques and modalities in the light of proposals made by participants".

The next twelve months, up to the mid-term ministerial review in Montreal, were devoted to a still-tentative discussion of the broad shape of the possible outcome of the negotiations, with no meeting of minds as yet on what that outcome should be. Pakistan introduced a proposal for a four-phase programme to bring the textiles and clothing sector back under the GATT rules. The first phase would remove non-clothing products from MFA coverage, and also remove "low prices" as a possible justification for MFA restrictions; the second would further limit the criteria that could be invoked for restrictions; the third would allow restrictions only with the approval of a monitoring body; and the fourth would move to eliminate restrictions on clothing. The ITCB countries then made their first proposal, also envisaging a staged move to abolition of the MFA but progressing partly through a freeze and then reduction and removal of MFA restrictions and partly through narrowing the grounds on which restrictions could be justified. From the importers' side, both the European Community and Canada made proposals. The EC proposed "a common diagnosis of the problem", stressing that liberalization would require strengthening of all GATT rules and disciplines, and a general opening of markets. This emphasis on non-MFA issues was rejected by developing countries, which insisted that such matters were for negotiation elsewhere in the Round. Canada outlined a number of options for liberalization, covering ways of phasing out the MFA over an agreed period, combined with other commitments, including the reduction of tariffs and (an important element in the eventual result of the negotiations) a special safeguard provision to allow selective action during the phase-out.

By now, the Montreal mid-term review was approaching, and all negotiating groups were supposed to agree on recommendations that could be put forward for ministers to consider and decide on. The textiles and clothing group was one of those which failed to do so: in spite of much time spent working on its report, the draft recommendations it sent forward to Montreal were full of bracketed language indicating the continuing lack of agreement about what the negotiations were really seeking to achieve.

Agriculture

Preparation for the agricultural negotiations of the Uruguay Round had been careful and thorough, but also very difficult. The interests at stake were large. The national policies that governed trade in agriculture had been formulated with little regard for any international rules or guidelines. The objectives of the main participants often seemed diametrically opposed. At the ministerial meetings of 1982 and 1984, and again in the final preparations for Punta del Este, disagreements over agriculture had threatened to block progress in the wider effort to open world markets and bring the international trading system up to date. Similar difficulties were to arise throughout the Uruguay Round itself.

For agriculture, more than for any other issue except perhaps services, the foundations for the Uruguay Round were laid by the work programme launched by ministers in 1982. The Committee on Trade in Agriculture spent two years systematically examining "all matters affecting trade, market access and competition and supply in agricultural products", and in 1984, in accordance with its mandate, put forward recommendations on how trade in agricultural products might be liberalized. Chaired by Aart De Zeeuw, a senior Dutch trade official, the Committee studied the policies of 41 individual countries and of the European Community, and built up a body of knowledge in particular about the array of non-tariff measures by which GATT members regulated imports and exports of agricultural goods. The Committee also studied the GATT rules affecting trade in agriculture, especially those on subsidies, as well as the various exceptions under which some GATT members had been granted the right to maintain measures that would otherwise not have been permitted by the rules. In 1984 this work led to recommendations, accepted by the annual session of GATT members, aimed at establishing conditions "under which substantially all measures affecting agriculture will be brought under more operationally effective GATT rules and disciplines". The recommendations foresaw action on four fronts: better access to markets; "greater discipline" in export competition; clearer definition of how the GATT rules on quantitative restrictions and subsidies should limit the trade effects of agricultural policies; and more effective special treatment under GATT for developing countries. During 1985 and the first half of 1986, the Committee developed what was in fact a blueprint for negotiations: specific proposals on how the objectives of it 1984 recommendations might be met. By the time work began on the Punta del Este Declaration, the ingredients of the coming negotiations on agriculture were fairly clear. Work in GATT (and among the developed countries in the OECD in Paris) had yielded detailed knowledge of agricultural policies in force throughout the world, the reasons why these policies were maintained, and their impact both on farmers' incomes and on trade flows. There was also fairly broad agreement about the likely effects of possible changes in these policies. The Punta del Este Declaration supplied the ingredient still missing for negotiations – an agreed set of goals that built upon the recommendations of 1984.

An obvious result of all this earlier work, as well as of the sensitivity of the issue, was that the Punta del Este Declaration was more specific and detailed on agriculture than on any other subject for negotiation. Whereas textiles and some other subjects were each dealt with in a single sentence, three paragraphs were devoted to agriculture. They set the scene for a much wider negotiation than had ever before been attempted on a global scale for agriculture. Ministers agreed in recognizing "an urgent need to bring more discipline and predictability to world agricultural trade by correcting and preventing restrictions and distortions including those related to structural surpluses so as to reduce the uncertainty, imbalances and instability in world agricultural markets". The coming negotiations should "aim to achieve greater liberalization of trade in agriculture and bring all measures affecting import access and export competition under strengthened and more operationally effective rules". These objectives would be pursued by improving market access, particularly through reduction of import barriers, by "improving the competitive environment" through greater discipline on the use of subsidies and other measures, and by minimizing the adverse effects on trade in agriculture of sanitary and phytosanitary regulations and barriers (that is, measures to protect food safety, as well as animal and plant health). A special negotiating group would be set up for agriculture, and should base itself on the work done since 1982.

The new negotiating group, chaired like its predecessor by De Zeeuw, thus started work with the benefit of a thorough knowledge of the basis problems of agricultural trade and with unusually detailed and bold marching orders from ministers. Shared knowledge and a known mandate, however, did not add up to shared objectives. The concerns and aims of the participants differed greatly.

The chief sponsor of ambitious negotiations on agriculture was the United States: highly competitive as a producer of cereals, meat and a wide range of other agricultural products, yet also restricting (with the help of a special GATT waiver dating from 1955) imports of dairy products, sugar, peanuts and cotton. The United States made heavy use of export subsidies, especially for grains, but insisted that it did so only to meet the subsidy practices of others. It was strongly supported by the newly formed Cairns Group, the self-styled "fair trading countries", which were each major players in world trade in one or more agricultural commodities, collectively accounted for about a quarter of world exports of agricultural products, and brought together in a common effort both developed and developing countries. Canada, a member of the Group, shared its ambition to liberalize trade in most agricultural products, but wished to maintain protection for its dairy farmers.

Most of the Western European countries, Japan, Korea and a large number of the smaller developing countries were broadly on the defensive throughout the Uruguay Round negotiations on agriculture. The European Community was especially concerned to defend its common agricultural policy (CAP). This maintained high prices for EC farmers – and consumers – by a complex mechanism whose key element was a system of border adjustments: variable import levies that imposed duties on most agricultural imports – enough to raise their price to that of European producers – and "export restrictions" that provided sufficient subsidies to agricultural exports to make them competitive on world markets. However, the Community was not entirely on the defensive. It had very large agricultural export interests, including some that did not depend on subsidy; it was in any case beginning to contemplate CAP reform, not least in order to restrain its soaring budgetary cost and persistent tendency to generate surpluses; and it shared the general desire to reduce to a minimum hindrances to trade caused by regulations on food safety and animal and plant health protection. Moreover, the EC, as much as any other participant in the Round, had an interest in easing the differences among GATT members over agricultural trade that were poisoning international trade relations as a whole. Of the remaining Western European countries, most had only limited export interests in agriculture, but maintained restrictions on imports designed to protect high-cost domestic producers, often for social or environmental reasons. Japan, although the world's largest food importer, kept strict limits on imports of a number of agricultural products, and maintained a total embargo on imports of rice, pleading a need for secure supplies of its staple food and for support to it rural economy. Korea followed similar agricultural trade policies.

Among developing countries, there was a wide range of views. Some, as fully competitive producers, were enthusiastic members of the Cairns Group, while others had only limited interests at stake and were to play little part in the negotiations. But two other groups, with overlapping membership, were both on the defensive. One comprised countries which enjoyed preferential access to the EC markets for agricultural products, and feared the loss of those markets if more competitive producers were allowed equal access. The other consisted of what became known as the "net food-importing countries", a largely African group that relied heavily on imports of grain and other products to feed their populations. They feared that an international agreement to cut export subsidies would result in higher and, for them, unaffordable world prices.

These aims and concerns led the countries participating in the Round to lean generally towards one or other of two basic approaches in the agricultural negotiations. The United States and the Cairns Group sought to liberalize trade by getting rid of import restrictions, subsidies and other trade distortions, and to overhaul the relevant GATT rules to prevent distortions from being reintroduced. Other countries gave higher priority to non-economic factors. The European Community, in particular, emphasized the need for more balanced and stable world markets. It had finally accepted the Punta del Este terms of reference for the agricultural negotiations because they called not only for "increasing discipline" on the use of subsidies, "including the phased reduction of their negative effects", but also for "dealing with their causes".

Initially, the negotiating group's work focused on fact-finding, putting together data from the earlier Committee on Trade in Agriculture and from other sources, and reviewing the issues for negotiation. The group also embarked on an important technical study, aimed at reaching agreement on a common measure of the total assistance given by governments to farmers through the very varied forms of import restriction, domestic price support and export subsidies. Two slightly different measures were studied: the Producer Subsidy Equivalent (PSE), developed in the OECD, and a more narrowly drawn Aggregate Measure of Support (AMS) that could exclude support that did not significantly affect trade. Whichever measure could be agreed on would be important later as a common denominator for negotiating reductions in trade-distorting support policies. Purely technical judgements on how best to calculate the PSE or AMS, or over the reliability of data, could have a huge eventual effect on the results of the negotiations.

Starting in July 1987, the main participants began to lay out their ideas on how the Punta del Este mandate should be fulfilled. Immediately, the enormous differences between their views became obvious.

The first proposal, from the United States, called for "complete phaseout over ten years of all agricultural subsidies which directly or indirectly affect trade", including a freeze and phase-out of subsidized exports. Import barriers should also be phased out over the same period. The first step in achieving these objectives would be to establish each country's AMS, bringing in all forms of market price support (import quotas, variable levies, tariffs, export subsidies and credits, etc.), income support (deficiency payments, acreage payments, etc.) and other forms of support such as subsidized insurance, fuel and fertilizer, and marketing programmes. Only direct payments not linked to production and marketing, and "bona fide" foreign and domestic aid programmes, would be excluded from the AMS. All agriculture commodities, food, beverages, forest products and fish and fish products would be covered. The second step would be to agree on policy changes that would reduce support, as measured by the AMS, to zero over ten years.

The United States had made no secret of its aim of getting rid of all export subsidies, but almost all other countries were surprised by the sweeping nature of its proposals. Even the Cairns Group did not go so far. Its proposal, introduced at GATT by the Australian Prime Minister Bob Hawke, put stress instead on the desirability of combining "early action to give relief and a reform programme that will take us progressively from these massively distorted agricultural markets to a point where all subsidies and other government support measures having an effect on agricultural trade are no longer permitted and domestic markets are open to effective competition from imports".

Many other participants reacted more strongly. They were not prepared to go nearly as far as the Americans were proposing. Several pointed out that the US was suggesting freer trade in agriculture than had been achieved either for manufactures or services. Outside the GATT meeting rooms, some were more outspoken, suggesting that the US proposals were primarily for domestic consumption, and not to be taken seriously, and that until the United States showed greater realism, there was no point (and, indeed, serious danger) in negotiation. Justified or not, this reaction helps to explain why negotiations on agriculture in the Uruguay Round were engaged so slowly.

First proposals by other participants in the group were much more cautious, although there was quite wide sympathy with the idea of seeking some kind of freeze on the use of export subsidies, and early efforts to stop the apparently relentless build up of surpluses. Japan – which itself was not a significant agricultural exporter – was prepared to support the elimination of export subsidies, because it felt that the crisis in international trade in agricultural products was basically caused by a combination of over-production and export competition. However, it rejected most of the other US proposals. Agriculture, it insisted, had specific characteristics which meant that it must be treated differently from other sectors. Constraints on land resources, the need for stable food supplies and demands for environmental protection required that "the rule of market forces should be modified". This meant that the United States proposal was "too ambitious". Japan also saw serious flaws in the proposal to measure agricultural protection through a single AMS. Proposals by the Nordic countries and Switzerland, although less forthright in rejecting the goals suggested by the United States, echoed Japan's emphasis on the "specificity" of agriculture. The Nordics agreed on the objective of more liberal agricultural trade, and that market signals should play a larger part in determining the allocation of resources in agriculture, but insisted that the requirements of food security "and other aspects relating to the biological nature of the production process" had to be taken into account. Switzerland, which shared with Japan a high reliance on imported food and low exports of its own products, leaned towards "a system that would combine the maintenance of national agricultural policies based on support for agriculture and the minimization of the effects of such policies on international trade in agricultural policies".

The European Community put forward its own proposals for the agricultural negotiations in October. They were less specific than those of the United States, and far less radical, but they contained a number of important concepts. Along with the US proposals, they defined many of the key elements that went into the final Uruguay Round bargain, although the Community's position was to evolve in parallel with its own internal agricultural reforms.

The central problem, the Community argued, was the imbalance of supply and demand. The immediate need was to bring production under control. Once achieved, this would permit "a significant, balanced reduction in import barriers" and the establishment of "sound conditions for competition". As a starting point, the Community proposed emergency measures, valid for one year, to stabilize markets for cereals, sugar and dairy products. This emergency action would be followed up by phased longer-term measures to reduce support to agriculture. Each country should decide for itself how the agreed reductions in support should be put into effect. At some point, it would be necessary to compensate for the effects of reduced production support by instead providing support to farm incomes. Such income support would have to take a form that did not affect production, and this approach – the "decoupling" of support from production – would need to be worked out more precisely "to make sure that what is thrown out of the window does not come back in through the door". Once major markets had been stabilized, binding commitments on the levels of protection for agriculture could be negotiated. The Community insisted, however, that it was not prepared to leave agriculture entirely to the play of market forces, without support and aid. Moreover, it raised a concern of which much more would be heard: it wanted protection to be "re-balanced". The Community had long maintained that its market was being distorted by some tariff concessions made in past GATT negotiations, when it had undertaken not to impose tariffs in future on imports of some apparently minor products that could be used as substitutes for cereals in feeding livestock. One such cereal substitute was corn gluten, a by-product of maize processing. The Community had come to regret the concession, since unrestrained and very large imports, largely from the United States, had undercut EC suppliers of cattlefeed, with expensive knock-on effects on prices and production of cereals and livestock. Finally, the Community reminded other countries that it would accept an agricultural agreement only as part of a satisfactory outcome to the whole of the Uruguay Round.

In other proposals, the ASEAN countries lined up with the Cairns Group, while a number of developing countries – particularly the net importers – put forward their concerns.

No real progress was made on any of these broad proposals for agricultural reform during the next year. Each was further explained, and discussed in the group. But there was no meeting of minds.

The most fruitful work of the negotiating group was on technical matters. The concept of the AMS was explored and refined, with all major participants contributing constructive ideas. A technical group was established to carry the work forward on the basis of information from governments on the support given to agriculture in each country. Another important development was the United States' idea of "tariffication" whereby the total effect of whatever barriers were maintained by a country against imports of a particular product would be calculated and expressed in terms of the level of import duty that would be required to have the same restrictive effect. The attraction of this approach was that, if it could be successfully worked out, it would allow conversion of the wide variety of agricultural import restrictions to equivalent tariffs that could be then be subjected to the familiar GATT processes of bargaining, reduction and binding.

Work was also launched on one aspect of agricultural liberalization on which most countries saw eye to eye: the need to keep to a minimum the effects on trade of government actions taken to ensure the safety of food and the protection of animal and plant health. The aims sought, and the problems involved, were closely related to those covered by the Tokyo Round code on technical barriers to trade (the "standards code") on which, as described earlier, negotiations were taking place in a separate group. A working group on sanitary and phytosanitary regulations and barriers was set up for the purpose in September 1988, and thereafter this sector, at least, of the negotiations on agriculture was to move ahead quickly.

From mid-1988 onwards, several countries began to push for decisions by ministers at the mid-term review meeting in Montreal. The Cairns Group proposed a "framework" approach for agriculture. This would combine an immediate freeze by the developed countries on their trade-distorting support and subsidy actions, as well as specific cuts in support during the next two years, with decisions on long-term objectives and methods for the reduction of agricultural support and the liberalization of trade. The Cairns proposal had a mixed reception, as was to be expected. Countries tended to be doubtful either about the idea of short-term action (because of fears that the measures taken might prove inconsistent with longer-term market-oriented reform) or about decisions for the longer term (because they opposed sweeping long-term liberalization), and some countries disliked both. Several governments maintained that decisions on long-term policies were in any case not required until the end of the negotiations. A number of developing countries also pressed for decisions at Montreal, and for early easing of market barriers in developed countries.

Given these wide differences of view, the negotiating group did not try to produce agreed recommendations for the ministers to consider in Montreal. Instead, it was left to De Zeeuw to send his own report at the end of November to the Group of Negotiations on Goods. However, the content of the report had been discussed in the group, so that the ideas it put forward were known to have considerable support. The agricultural negotiations, he concluded now needed decisions that would define "in operational terms" the general direction and procedures to be followed in their final phases. He asked for ministerial endorsement in Montreal of a framework approach to achieving the Punta del Este objectives. This approach, set out in some detail, would combine long-term efforts to establish a fair and market-oriented agricultural trading system, a short-term freeze (and initial cut) in agricultural support and protection, and work on sanitary and phytosanitary regulations. De Zeeuw's report pointed clearly to the main decisions that were needed. For the long term, he asked that ministers agree to initiate reform through commitments on support and protection and a strengthened GATT regime. They would need to decide "whether the ultimate goal should be the elimination *or* the substantial reduction of trade-distortive support and protection" and whether this goal should be sought through negotiations on specific policies and measures or through commitments on an AMS, or both. For the short-term, he asked for a freeze commitment and for an initial cut in support, whose size in percentage terms the ministers were asked to set.

De Zeeuw's report in fact provided all the elements for ministerial decision on how the Uruguay Round negotiations on agriculture should go forward. The question was whether government views had yet evolved sufficiently to allow those decisions to be taken.

The new subjects

All GATT negotiations up to the Uruguay Round were concerned only with trade in goods. During GATT's first 15 years, up to the Kennedy Round of the 1960s, the member governments were bargaining almost exclusively about the reduction and binding of import duties, along with the removal of quantitative restrictions. Later came the drive to reduce other non-tariff distortions of trade, particularly through the Tokyo Round codes. As already described, these continuing tasks were taken up again in the Uruguay Round, and although individual countries varied in their objectives and enthusiasm for negotiations on particular subjects, they were fully agreed that these were issues appropriate for a GATT negotiation. For the three so-called "new subjects" included in the Punta del Este mandate for the Uruguay Round, however, there was no such unity of view. Even though agreement had been reached to negotiate on trade in services, on trade-related aspects of intellectual property rights, and on trade-related investment measures, that agreement had been conceded by many countries only with deep reluctance, and only after securing tightly limiting conditions on the negotiating mandate and on the way in which the negotiations would be handled. All three subjects were seen as bearing on issues that had, up to now, largely been considered as matters of internal policy and national sovereignty; they also tended to range developed against developing countries. The negotiations were clearly going to be tough, and there was no certainty that they would lead to substantial results.

The issue of whether GATT should negotiate on services had dominated preparations for the Uruguay Round. In the early 1980s, the United States was almost alone in advocating such negotiations. Later, it succeeded in persuading other developed countries that they too had an interest in negotiating to open up markets for their services suppliers. A dialogue was launched among them on the problems and possible scope of services negotiations. Hostility by many developing countries to any initiative in this area was such that GATT Secretariat officials were unable to take part in the meetings, and the GATT premises could not be used for the purpose. From 1984 onwards, some developing countries decided that the potential of services negotiations deserved closer study, and the informal dialogue gained official recognition. Only at Punta del Este, however, was a formula worked out to allow services to be included in the Uruguay Round: the negotiations would be kept fully separate from those on goods and would not be under the auspices of GATT. This vigorous and at times ill-tempered disagreement on whether and how to negotiate reflected, in fact, a shared view that trade in services was going to be increasingly important in national economic development and in international relations. The value of world trade in services, although not easily measurable, was agreed to be growing extremely fast and already equal to about one quarter of the value of trade in goods.

A huge attraction for the developed countries was that international trade in services consisted largely of the activities at which they were best, and which drew on some of their greatest assets: banking and insurance, management know-how, shipping and air transport, advanced communications and other technology. They argued that they could not accept open competition in their markets for products such as textiles and clothing, for which developing countries had important competitive advantages over them, unless they were allowed to exercise in world markets their competitive advantage for services. They also insisted that trade in goods was to an increasing extent linked with the supply of services, so that rules and disciplines for services were needed to ensure the strength of the international trading system as a whole.

Developing countries generally felt themselves to be at a disadvantage in the area of services except, possibly, as suppliers of manpower. It was fairly clear that the movement of labour, closely linked with the politically sensitive issue of national immigration policies, was not a promising area for negotiations. Moreover, although developing countries were increasingly being converted to belief in market forces as the best means of achieving rapid economic growth, not all of them were convinced that the GATT approach was appropriate for trade in services. To a great extent, they accepted inclusion of trade in services in the Uruguay Round only because this was a price they had to pay for negotiations on other matters of importance to them, and because they preferred multilaterally agreed rules to the almost certain alternative prospect of unilateral action by major countries to force open their markets.

As a subject for GATT negotiation, intellectual property raised many of the same difficulties. Know-how and brand names belong overwhelmingly to the richest and most developed countries, and in particular to large corporations that arouse strong and often hostile emotions in developing countries. For years, international debate on intellectual property issues had been conducted in terms of demands that the kind of knowledge protected by patents, copyright and trademarks, far from being given additional protection, should be made available either free or on highly favourable terms to developing countries. This discussion of "transfer of technology" had led nowhere, but it required an extraordinary shift in the terms of debate to expect productive negotiations to reinforce the position of owners of intellectual property.

Against this, however, several factors helped to move negotiations along. One was the high priority given to the issue by developed countries, particularly by the United States. As in the case of services, developed countries saw their strength in the development of technology as a central competitive advantage on which they would need to be able to rely in the future, not least if they were being challenged by developing countries in areas of trade where they were at a competitive disadvantage. All participants in the Round soon became aware that an agreement on TRIPS ("trade-related aspects of intellectual property rights") was, whether they liked it or not, an essential element for any final package. A second factor, which applied also to the services and investment negotiations, was that the debate was not entirely a North-South matter. Developed countries had concerns about one another's policies, and wished to negotiate on them, and some developing countries had intellectual property interests they wished to protect, just as they saw opportunities to export services or to invest in other countries.

A further factor was recognition that governments could not condone simple theft. Definitions of theft could vary, and could be diametrically opposed when it came to such matters as the denial of patent protection to biological discoveries. But there was widespread readiness to act against counterfeiting of brand-name products, as a matter of morality and of consumer protection, and earlier work in GATT had shown that there was scope for action in this area that need not go beyond the traditional kinds of international cooperation on trade matters. A fourth factor was the evident risk that, as in the case of services, international agreement on new rules to protect intellectual property rights might be the only alternative to facing unilateral action by major countries to enforce their own view of what constituted proper protection of intellectual property. Finally, both the autonomous moves by developing countries to adopt open-market economies and their increasing need to attract foreign investment encouraged a new approach to intellectual property rights. In the period after the Montreal mid-term review, these factors all helped the negotiations on TRIPS to move further and faster than anyone expected.

Trade-related investment measures, the third of the new subjects, was included in the agenda of the Uruguay Round only in the final bargaining in Punta del Este. Unlike services, for which the mandate emerged from several years of heated and detailed preparatory discussion, or intellectual property, where there was at least some experience of negotiating about trade in counterfeit goods, negotiations on investment measures were launched with little prior discussion in GATT, and for many countries virtually without warning. In 1981, the United States had circulated a discussion paper to the Consultative Group of Eighteen which identified ten major types of performance requirements, focusing in particular on requirements to export or to use substitutes for imports, and suggested that they violated at least four GATT Articles. In the 1985 and 1986 discussions that preceded the launching of the new Round it had proposed that negotiations should seek to control and reduce "government investment measures which divert investment flows or distort trade flows", in the light of "the specific Articles of the GATT, as well as its overall objectives". No work, however, had been done, and the Punta del Este mandate tied any negotiations that might take place closely to trade-related measures and to specific GATT provisions.

Even with these restrictions, this third "new subject" was yet another which divided the negotiating countries largely on North-South lines, with the same developed-country concerns to build on their competitive strengths; the same developing-country fears of conceding control over a key area of national economic sovereignty; and the same misgivings, in particular, about a potential loss of bargaining power in future dealings with foreign corporations. Of the three subjects, trade-related investment measures or TRIMS – as it quickly came to be called – was from the beginning the one which seemed to offer the smallest potential for a mutually interesting agreement. Ominously for the future, it was also the subject that appeared to arouse the least excitement and commitment even among the countries that had sought negotiations on it. In the United States in particular, powerful industry lobbies, critical to eventual acceptance of the outcome of the Uruguay Round, maintained unremitting pressure for substantial agreements on services and intellectual property. They never showed comparable interest in the negotiations on trade-related investment measures.

Services

The informal discussions in GATT in the early 1980s had helped to establish a broad understanding of the make-up and problems of international trade in services. Thirteen studies submitted by developed countries after 1982 showed the scale and diversity of services in national economies and in international trade, the surging growth of the sector as a whole, the complexity of its structure and of the regulations imposed on it, and the serious gaps in knowledge of just how large it was. From 1985 onwards, GATT discussion of services was effectively legitimized by decision of the November 1984 annual session, and broadened by the addition of developing countries to the exchange of information and ideas. It was at this time that the United States, supported by the United Kingdom, called for negotiation of a framework of rules for trade in services comparable to the GATT rules for trade in goods, and identified a number of the basic GATT principles, such as market access, transparency and national treatment, as being applicable also to services. However, it was not until the launching of the Uruguay Round in September 1986 that agreement was reached to negotiation services. Up to that point, developing countries which had resisted negotiations refused to enter into discussion of how international rules might be developed for the sector, and of how trade in services might be liberalized.

Because these issues, fundamental to any negotiation on services, were effectively being discussed for the first time, the new Uruguay Round "Group of Negotiations on Services" (GNS for short) initially had to spend a great deal of time on them and on other basic questions. With some major developing-country participants still most unenthusiastic about services negotiations, and fearful that they would become linked with negotiations on goods, the GNS made very slow progress during the first two years of the Uruguay Round.

The Punta del Este Declaration stated that the negotiations should "aim to establish a multilateral framework of principles and rules for trade in services, including elaboration of possible disciplines for individual sectors". The framework's purpose was to be the expansion of trade in services "under conditions of transparency and progressive liberalization and as a means of promoting economic growth of all trading partners and the development of developing countries". It was to respect the policy objectives of national laws and regulations applying to services, and take into account the work of relevant international organizations.

With these ultimate objectives in mind, the GNS agreed that it had to tackle five initial tasks: (i) look at problems of definition and statistics; (ii) examine broad concepts on which principles and rules for trade in services might be based, including disciplines that might be appropriate for particular service sectors; (iii) consider how wide the coverage of the services framework ought to be; (iv) survey what disciplines and arrangements already affected trade in services; and (v) look at the measures and practices that helped or hindered the growth of trade in services and which might be candidates for rules on transparency and liberalization. These tasks were in principle to be treated as equally important, although in practice there was little agreement over the amount of attention each deserved.

Definitions and statistics of trade in services were obviously desirable, but some countries put much more weight on their importance than others. Statistics on trade in services are far less complete and reliable than those for trade in goods, mainly because goods can fairly easily be identified and valued as they cross frontiers, whereas services (once memorably defined as things you cannot drop on your foot) are harder to identify, and in any case do not always take the simple form of a direct export from a producing country to an importing consumer. An important example is tourism, where the consumer comes to the service, the reverse of the normal procedure with goods. The GNS spent considerable time reviewing statistical questions and building up a database, but recognized that there was little chance that services statistics would improve greatly in the near future. Whether this mattered much was disputed: those who thought it did matter argued that reliable statistics would be essential in order to judge the balance of advantage when negotiations reached the stage of bargaining. Similarly, it was in general the same countries that wanted a clear definition of trade in services, on the ground that in its absence, no firm view would be possible of how widely the rules and principles of the proposed multilateral framework would apply.

The definition issue was concerned not with the different sectors into which services trade can be divided (for instance, tourism and tele-communications), but with the ways in which services can be delivered. A multilateral framework for services could be limited to those services which are straightforwardly sent across borders in the same way as goods, or could be extended to services that are bought by the foreign consumer in the providing country (tourism being the leading example), or supplied in conjunction with the establishment of offices in the consuming country, or require the movement of personnel. Banking and consulting services, for example, often entail physical presence in the country buying the service. These are classic forms of international service trade, but they raise much more sensitive issues in political and regulatory terms than traditional trade measures such as customs duties. Moreover, developing countries quickly established a link between possible rights of establishment and the movement of labour, and suggested that a balanced negotiation would require that concessions by themselves on establishment be linked with greater readiness by others to admit workers from their countries. These definitions were also to have a practical importance in the later stages of the services negotiations, when liberalization offers were classified in terms of their "modes of supply".

The whole question of statistics and definitions was complicated by the fact that, quite apart from its substantial aspects, it was helpful to those countries which wanted to do as little as possible in the services negotiations, and to maintain a clear distinction between services and the GATT-based negotiations on goods. These countries tended to argue that more progress was needed on statistics and definitions before bargaining could begin, and that the GATT Secretariat needed the expert support of other organizations in order to develop the missing information. The same countries were reluctant, in the early stages of the Round, to authorize the Secretariat to produce any documentation other than (exhaustive) reports on the meetings of the GNS.

The discussion of concepts on which principles and rules for trade in services might be based was more substantial, and in due course was to lead directly into the negotiation of the multilateral framework that eventually became the General Agreement on Trade in Services. For most countries, an obvious starting point was the principles of the GATT, even if these might need to be defined rather differently when applied to services. In the broadest terms, this suggested such concepts as mutual advantage, international competition, progressive liberalization and – heavily stressed by developing countries – the promotion of economic growth and development. This aim, they felt, might not necessarily be best served by such concepts as international competition and liberalization in the area of services. More specifically, the GATT example suggested the concepts of transparency in regulations and practices affecting trade in services, national treatment of foreign service suppliers (i.e. that they be treated no less favourably than domestic suppliers), and most-favoured-nation treatment (non-discrimination among foreign suppliers).

Discussion in the GNS during 1987 explored the practical implications of each of these concepts, helped by papers from Canada, Australia, Japan, Mexico and others. On transparency, for example, it considered the kind of requirements for notification of national rules and practices affecting service sectors that might be incorporated into a services framework agreement. On both national treatment and non-discrimination, there were differences right from the beginning of the negotiations. National treatment, some countries believed, might be more difficult to apply to services than to goods. On the other hand, it was recognized that a preference given to national service suppliers over foreign suppliers might well be much more important, in restricting international trade in services, than border measures of the kind that affect trade in goods. Non-discrimination was for some countries a principle that should be fundamental and unconditional in any services agreement; others thought this might not be practicable, not least because they believed that their legislatures would not be ready to open up their services markets to countries which did not offer similar openings in return. While many developing countries felt that all these concepts would need to be applied differently to them, given their overriding development objectives, some developed countries argued that those objectives were likely to be best served by allowing greater competition into trade in services.

The possible coverage of a services agreement, the third initial task facing the GNS, was obviously a key issue. Should the agreement cover all services, or should some sectors be left out? Many countries wanted universal coverage, not least because they believed that this would result in an agreement that covered everyone's interests, and therefore allow a balance of advantage to be achieved. But there were strong arguments also on the other side: arguments that foreshadowed later difficulties in the service negotiations which were to shape the final outcome, and even result in marked shifts in position by some countries which initially favoured universal coverage.

There were at least three basic reasons why countries had doubts about the inclusion of specific service sectors. Some sectors were seen as special for reasons similar to those which have traditionally affected GATT negotiations on goods. Just as agriculture and textiles have enjoyed longstanding protection in many countries, service sectors such as shipping in the United States, film-making in Western Europe and banking in India have been given help and protection against foreign competition, and can count on the support of vocal lobbies. Some sectors have characteristics that are recognized as needing close oversight by governments: financial services such as banking and insurance are obvious examples, in which "prudential" considerations will require that they be regulated to prevent fraud or reckless behaviour. A third possible reason to exclude a sector might be that it is already governed by an international agreement that seems adequate.

From an early stage, it became obvious that there could be a halfway house between inclusion and exclusion of a sector, through negotiation of a special agreement for that sector which would add to, or subtract from, the general rules to be included in the framework agreement for services. This was to be another key element in the outcome of the Round. The negotiators also discussed the possibility of reaching limited-membership agreements for some sectors. An agreement of this kind, Switzerland suggested, might apply initially among a few countries (perhaps as few as two) that were ready to liberalize that sector, but with membership remaining open to another country prepared to offer a similar commitment. In the event, nothing came of this idea of "optional most-favoured-nation treatment".

One obvious question – and the fourth agreed issue for the GNS – was whether existing arrangements and institutions already provided, for some service sectors, the kind of disciplines or liberalization that the Uruguay Round was seeking to achieve. In general, agreements affecting a single sector ("horizontal" agreements) exist to further technical cooperation rather than to liberalize trade. However, the group discussed with three organizations – the International Civil Aviation Organization, the International Telecommunications Union, and the United Nations Conference on Trade and Development (which is responsible for the "Liner Code" affecting maritime services) – the way in which their sectoral agreements function. One conclusion quickly reached was that although national treatment and transparency were important elements in these agreements, MFN treatment was not: agreements on air services, in particular, typically take the form of tightly drawn bilateral deals based on strict reciprocity. A broader conclusion reached by many countries in the GNS was that, even in the sector concerned, there was scope for liberalization in the Uruguay Round. On the other hand, those developing countries most reluctant to bring service within GATT valued these discussions with other international organization both as distancing the negotiations a little from GATT and its principles, an as showing – particularly in the case of civil aviation – that an alternative to full-blown multilateral regime for services could be (as the chief India delegate at the time later pointed out) "a very thin layer of multilateralism giving as large a scope as possible for bilateral negotiations to settle the issues to the satisfaction of both parties".

The fifth and final initial task of the GNS was to look at measures and practices that help or hinder trade in services. In doing so, the negotiations were taking their first collective look at the specific trade barriers and distortions on which they would be called to bargain later in the Round. The United States was the first to come forward, in mid-1987, with extracts from the inventory of barriers to trade in services that it had begun to build up on the basis of information provided by US private business. However, the examination of individual barriers was not taken far, since most countries were clearly not yet ready for it.

In late 1987 and early 1988, several countries individually set out their ideas on the shape and content of a framework agreement for service. In doing so, they sparked disagreement in the GNS between those countries which felt the general discussion of broad concepts had gone as far as was useful, and which wished to move on to concrete negotiation; and a small group of developing countries which believed that basic issues had not yet been fully explored. The first group was to express increasing frustration at lack of pro- gress throughout 1988. Countries in the second group, whose views were set out with particular eloquence by Brazil, complained that they were being rushed into negotiations on issues that were not adequately understood, and with an inappropriately exclusive focus on trade liberalization. As they saw it, the GNS was, in effect, trying to run not only before it had learned to walk, but also before it had determined whether running was even a desirable objective.

The first comprehensive proposal, in October 1987, came from the United States, which called on the GNS to concentrate its efforts on the proposed multilateral framework of principles and rules for services, so as to reach an early agreement that would allow the greatest possible scope for subsequent negotiation on individual sector agreements. The main elements of the US proposal are worth setting out at some length, since this statement by the main sponsor of the services negotiations brought out many issues that were to govern the negotiations throughout most of the Uruguay Round.

As "general considerations", the United States proposed that the framework be designed to achieve progressive liberalization of a wide range of sectors in as many countries as possible, and that it should recognize the sovereign right of every country to regulate its services industries, dealing only with measures that restrict the access and operations of foreign service suppliers. It should ensure against measures that restrict or distort trade, and include agreement not to introduce new restrictive measures against foreign service suppliers. It should also apply to the greatest extent possible to existing measures. In the US view, progressive and time-phased liberalization of world services markets would benefit all countries. The framework should apply both to the cross-border movement of services and to the establishment of foreign branches and subsidiaries to deliver services in the host country. It should provide a point of reference for the negotiation of individual sector agreements, with additional rules appropriate to each sector.

The US proposal endorsed national treatment as a fundamental element for the framework agreement, and also gave great weight to transparency. But it was sceptical about non-discrimination. Some countries, it anticipated, would not sign even the framework agreement, and in this case should have no right to its benefits. Others would not be able to apply the obligations of the framework agreement to some sectors. This situation might be handled by allowing signatories to take some exceptions to the agreement's provisions, but permitting other countries not to apply (to "non-apply", in the jargon) the agreement to those who made excessive use of exceptions. The United States believed that the framework agreement should also discipline monopoly service suppliers, prohibit export subsidies to service suppliers as well as domestic subsidies that could injure foreign suppliers, and provide rules on the licensing of professional service suppliers and on consultation and dispute settlement.

This comprehensive US proposal was followed by others, less detailed but on somewhat similar lines, from the Nordic countries and the European Community. The Nordics, no doubt reflecting the experience of smaller countries with limited individual bargaining power, put more weight than the United States on non-discrimination. They envisaged achieving this through sectoral agreements that, under the umbrella of the framework agreement, would be somewhat similar to the Tokyo Round codes in applying only to those who signed them. The EC focused on broad concepts for the framework agreement, with its core seen as being based on a balance between seeking "a major expansion of trade in services, thereby boosting growth in the world economy, while respecting the policy objectives which have led to international and national regulation of services and promoting the development of developing countries".

All these ideas were elaborated during 1988, with further contributions from both developed and developing countries that served to clarify options and concerns. By the end of the year no less than 35 separate negotiating proposals had been tabled in the GNS since the beginning of the Round. For its part, the Secretariat prepared, and revised at intervals, a "glossary of terms and inventory of concepts" which in practice amounted to a running record of the ideas put forward in the group, in discussions as well as in documents, that might become elements in a future framework agreement on services. Optimistic observers, and the GATT Secretariat's carefully balanced publications, could fairly point to an immense amount of fact-finding and concept-shaping that would certainly prove valuable when serious bargaining on services began. Less charitable Round-watchers, delegates of the countries most eager to see substantial results on services, and representatives of the service industries themselves, noted that the halfway point in the Uruguay Round was arriving without even one text actually under negotiation, and with detailed bargaining on specific market-opening commitments postponed until, first, a framework agreement, and second, whole group of sectoral agreements could be negotiated.

One consequence of slow progress was that the GNS had not, by the autumn of 1988, reached a point at which differences of view among its members were actually obstructing its work. Since no real breakthroughs were required, it was not necessary to ask ministers meeting in Montreal to make difficult choices. The report by the GNS for the mid-term review was a straightforward account of its discussions over the preceding two years, showing where ideas tended to converge or diverge, and outlining the alternative approaches and principles suggested for the framework agreement and for the sectoral coverage of the negotiations. The Group also put forward a draft decision for ministers on the continuation of the negotiations which included a fairly large number of open points ("square brackets"), none of which, however, seemed likely to give great difficulty.

TRIPS

The Punta del Este Declaration set separate goals for negotiations on intellectual property issues and on counterfeiting. For intellectual property questions in general, the negotiators were required to "clarify GATT provisions and elaborate as appropriate new rules and disciplines" in order to reduce distortions and impediments to international trade. This apparent restriction of whatever negotiations were found "appropriate" to purely trade matters was qualified, crucially as it turned out, by the requirement to take into account "the need to promote effective and adequate protection of intellectual property rights", as well as by the less controversial need "to ensure that measures and procedures to enforce intellectual property rights do not themselves become barriers to legitimate trade". For trade in counterfeit goods, the aim was "to develop a multilateral framework of principles, rules and disciplines". Reflecting the continuing belief of many developing countries that GATT was not the proper place to discuss most issues of intellectual property, the TRIPS negotiations were agreed to be without prejudice to action that might be taken on the same issues in the World Intellectual Property Organization (WIPO) or elsewhere.

The mention of WIPO, an organization whose origins dated back a century, was a reminder that multilateral negotiations on intellectual property issues have a very long history, and have resulted in a large number of agreements that, for many years, have laid down rules to govern different aspects of protection for intellectual property. In particular, two WIPO administered agreements, each dating from the early 1880s, embody centrally important rules for two of the most important areas of intellectual property. The Paris Convention is concerned with the protection of industrial property, particularly through patents and trademarks. The Berne Convention provides the main international rules on copyright, with other rules incorporated in the Universal Copyright Convention (administered by UNESCO) and the Rome Convention (which concerns protection of performers, broadcasters, and producers of sound recordings). Regional agreements on intellectual property protection include the European Patent Convention. The central purpose of these agreements is to give foreigners the same protection for their intellectual property in the signatory countries a is given to nationals of those countries and to specify some minimum standards of protection. These agreements, however, do not add up to a single coherent pattern of worldwide protection for intellectual property. Not all countries have signed them; they differ in the level of detail they go into in specifying protection; and they leave to governments (particularly in the area of patents) considerable choice on what protection should be given. Moreover, some aspects of intellectual property are not clearly covered by them. In general, they do not deal with the question of how the rights the envisage are to be enforced, leaving this to the national authorities concerned. These issues were to be central to the TRIPS negotiations.

The negotiations were extremely difficult throughout the first two years of the Uruguay Round. A great deal of useful work was accomplished in identifying and clarifying issues and views on what was a completely new subject for many negotiators. However, a fundamental cleavage of views made impossible even tentative consensus on what a TRIPS agreement should seek to achieve.

On the surface, this discord took the form of different interpretation of the Punta del Este mandate for the negotiations on intellectual property issues. The United States and, to varying degrees, other developed countries interpreted the mandate as an invitation to negotiate better protection for intellectual property. Developing countries accepted that the group was committed to negotiate on how to discourage trade in counterfeit goods, but otherwise to look only at intellectual property issues directly connected with trade.

Underlying these positions was a deep difference in attitudes to the protection of intellectual property that had bedevilled earlier multilateral negotiations in UNCTAD and WIPO over the previous decade. Developed countries, and particularly the most industrialized among them, saw intellectual property, the fruit of the creative capacity and intellectual effort of the individual citizens and companies, as the legitimate basis for these individuals and companies to earn trading advantage. Such advantage could not be exercised unless the intellectual property concerned – industrial inventions and discoveries, designs and texts, broadcasts and recordings, trademark and names showing origin – was given protection against use by others. They also argued that in the absence of such protection, and the promise of later reward, research and development which led to inventions and new products of value to all would simply not take place. The latter argument was stated with particular force as a reason to protect the intellectual property of pharmaceutical manufacturers and producers of other goods which take a great deal of money and time to develop, to earn government approval, and to bring to market. Developing countries had a different perspective. They did not, in general, dispute the case for patent and copyright protection. But their individual citizens and companies had little intellectual property of their own to protect, and they did not see reason to give support to international standards of protection that would require them to pay large sums to use technology they needed or which might even deny them access to that technology. Once again, pharmaceuticals and high-technology products were cited as a particularly compelling case, but this time as examples of necessities for national health and development to which access ought not to be restricted by high prices enforced through excessive protection of intellectual property.

Negotiations began with the most interested participants stating their concerns. Developed countries argued that intellectual property rights were frequently given inadequate protection, and that even these rights tended to be ineffectively enforced. The United States, which from the beginning took the strongest line, gave notice that it would be putting forward proposals to improve both protection and enforcement. The Americans also proposed, without success, that governments should sign immediately the draft code on measures against trade in counterfeit goods that had been negotiated among the Quad countries and circulated in GATT in 1982. Other developed countries adopted a more cautious approach. They did not take a position on whether improved standards of protection should actually be negotiated in the TRIPS group, and they put greater weight on the need for intellectual property rights and their enforcement not to create barriers to legitimate trade. Nevertheless they too were clearly ready to have the group negotiate across a very wide range of issues that were new to GATT. Developing countries were concerned to limit discussion to issues clearly related to trade, to prevent protection of intellectual property from providing a pretext for blocking or distorting trade, and to win recognition that differing national priorities, reflecting levels of development and social concerns, meant that governments could legitimately differ also in the protection they were prepared to give to intellectual property. Some, with Brazil and India in the forefront, also insisted that the group in any case had no mandate to negotiate on the actual norms or standards of protection to be given, since this was the job of WIPO.

By late 1987, views and issues had begun to crystallize, and it was becoming easier to see that the group faced about half a dozen broad sets of problems: the enforcement of intellectual property rights; the rights themselves; the use of those rights by others than their holders; dispute settlement; the existing GATT rules; and whether negotiations on these problems could be undertaken within the Uruguay Round.

Enforcement issues were perhaps most generally accepted as being a legitimate concern for the Round, partly because they included the treatment of goods crossing national frontiers, and partly because they were not being dealt with elsewhere. The draft counterfeit agreement was largely concerned with provisions to stop international trade in goods bearing false trademarks. Developed-country participants in the negotiations wanted similar action taken to stop imports and exports of goods which infringed intellectual property rights in other ways. An example was goods which, rather than bearing counterfeit trademarks, actually stole the copyright-protected content of products belonging to others: the leading example was the flourishing "pirate" trade in audio and video cassettes offering unauthorized copies of musical performances and movies. Another aspect of border enforcement that was not a North-South issue was dissatisfaction with a provision of US law (Section 337 of the Tariff Act), which was felt to discriminate against imported goods in the defences allowed if American competitors claimed that these infringed their patent or other intellectual property rights. Enforcement problems also included the lack of action within national frontiers to protect intellectual property rights, as for instance when a blind eye was turned on production of pirate cassettes, or non-deterrent fines were imposed on offenders.

Most controversial of all was the question whether the TRIPS group should involve itself in the substance of intellectual property rights. This was the area in which developing countries, in particular, claimed that harmonized international standards would often be inappropriate to their social and development needs and that in any case WIPO and other specialized organizations were the proper place to discuss them. Developed countries were unconvinced by these arguments. In particular, they objected to the limits imposed by many developing countries on patent protection for pharma-ceuticals and other chemicals, including short patent terms and in some cases no patent protection at all, the compulsory grant of licences to local firms, and requirements to manufacture locally as a condition for receiving a patent. A further patent issue was lack of protection for advanced technologies such as integrated circuits and biotechnology. Yet another was the basic United States rule, different from that of other countries, that gave priority in recognizing patent eligibility according to the date of the invention when it was made in the United States, but which still based the priority of applications for foreign inventions only on the date when the application was filed. There were concerns of substance also on copyright questions, such as the rights (technically known as "neighbouring rights") of producers, performers and broadcasting organizations, rather than authors, to initiate action against pirates. A long-standing European concern was to strengthen the protection given to the names of wines, spirits and other products such as cheeses which were strictly protected in their own countries but not in others. This problem of "appellations of origin" was particularly obvious in the case of regional wine names such as "champagne", "burgundy" and "sherry", which were used as generic or semi-generic terms in the United States, Australia and some other countries.

The question of use of existing intellectual property rights by others than the right-holders was linked to the issue known as "transfer of technology". As already mentioned, this question of whether developing countries should have easy access to patented or otherwise protected knowledge had already been fought over, without result, in other organizations such as UNCTAD. In the TRIPS negotiations, the focus was narrower: the main areas of concern were to control abusive, anti-competitive practices in the contractual licensing of intellectual property rights and to ensure that compulsory licences – the use of a patented product or process without authorization by the patent holder – would be allowed only in carefully defined circumstances, and against compensation.

Dispute settlement was a very live issue. Existing international agreements on intellectual property did not provide practical means for one government to seek redress if another failed to live up to its commitments. From the point of view of developed countries, a major attraction of negotiating an intellectual property agreement in GATT was that it would make available the GATT dispute settlement procedures, which were themselves to be improved in the Uruguay Round. Developing countries had mixed views on this possibility. Multilateral dispute settlement procedures offered in principle an attractive alternative to suffering unilateral judgements and measures, particularly under the "Section 301" provisions of US trade law, but that attraction would be diminished if its price was that a country found in GATT to be at fault on an intellectual property matter might in consequence face the loss of market access rights for its goods that it enjoyed under GATT. This issue of "cross-retaliation", or more strictly "cross-compensation", was one which simmered on in the TRIPS (and services) discussions, but came to the boil mainly in another area of the Uruguay Round, the negotiations on dispute settlement rules.

Review in the TRIPS group showed that few of the GATT rules had much bearing on intellectual property problems. The main exception was paragraph (d) of Article XX, the GATT Article which states general exceptions to the other GATT rules. Permitted measures under XX(d) include those necessary for "the protection of patents, trademarks and copyrights, and the prevention of deceptive practices". No GATT rules, however, provided explicit require-ments for enforcement of intellectual property rights, nor for establishing such rights. Given this situation, developed countries, in general, argued that new rules and disciplines were needed, while developing countries could contend that the absence of relevant rules simply showed that the problems raised were outside GATT's competence.

The final question – what the Punta del Este mandate did or did not permit the TRIPS group to do – was, as already discussed, essentially pro-cedural. Participants reluctant to enter into negotiations used it as a means of preventing discussion of more substantive matters. The qualification by the words "as appropriate" of the mandate's call for negotiations on "new rules and disciplines" made it possible for both advocates and opponents of negotiations to claim that their view was justified. As it turned out, there was a strong parallel between the use of this procedural argument and similar efforts to block the opening of the Uruguay Round itself in 1985. The argument was effective in preventing the opening of substantive negotiations in the TRIPS group, but it gradually became clear that its continued use risked driving the negotiations elsewhere, leaving its users isolated.

Into this situation, in which the participating governments had learned of each others' concerns but differed profoundly on what should be done about them, the United States injected an ambitious proposal in October 1987. The group, it said, should negotiate a comprehensive GATT agreement on intellectual property matters that would cover minimum standards for protection and enforcement in national law of patents, trade marks, copyright, trade secrets and the layout design of semiconductors. The agreement should also provide for dispute settlement procedures in GATT that would allow withdrawal of GATT benefits (cross-retaliation) if a government did not meet its obligations. In effect, the United States was providing radical answers to virtually all of the main questions facing the TRIPS group. Not surprisingly, its ideas met strong initial opposition from most developing countries who reiterated their much more limited view of the negotiating group's mandate. Developed countries gave it a warmer welcome although, with the exception of Japan, their own ideas were less far-reaching, and also tended to put more weight on countering trade obstacles created by procedures to enforce intellectual property rights. They also differed on whether GATT should itself set minimum standards ("norms") for protection. The European Community, in particular, made it clear that it had not yet made up its mind on this point.

Meetings and new documents over the following months, up to the summer of 1988, brought more detail to the proposals, contributions from other developed countries, a clearer view of where differences lay even among the more ambitious ideas, and greater depth of knowledge to the discussions. In July 1988, the European Community joined those supporting the negotiation of minimum standards, and put particular weight on protection of "appellations of origin". But there was little shift in the views of developing countries, most of whom continued to argue vigorously that the GATT was not the place to negotiate norms of protection, except on the question of trade in counterfeit goods, which they insisted was distinct from the other TRIPS issues. Only Korea and the ASEAN countries hinted, mainly by abstaining from attacking the EC and other developed-country proposals openly, that their views were evolving, and that they might in the end be ready to join in substantive negotiations.

As the mid-term review approached, the TRIPS group was faced, like others, with the need to formulate a text that ministers could endorse in Montreal as a basis for completing the negotiations. One alternative would have been to agree on a text that left the main controversial issues open, hoping that later substantive negotiations would overcome these differences and lead to an agreement that everyone could accept. This approach was to be adopted by some other negotiating groups whose work had not in any case advanced far enough for differences of view to have fully crystallized. The opposite alternative would be to seize on the mid-term review as the opportunity to force decisions on the critical issues, and above all on the question of whether the TRIPS mandate would allow the negotiation of a GATT agreement including standards. However, this approach appeared dangerous. On one side, there was no sign that many of the leading developing countries were ready to negotiate a wide-ranging agreement on intellectual property. On the other, if the Americans gave too high a priority to TRIPS, blockage at Montreal on the issue could threaten the future of the Uruguay Round as a whole. The United

States, however, underlined its seriousness of purpose by putting forward for discussion, in a meeting otherwise largely devoted to preparations for Montreal, a more fully developed version of its 1987 proposal for a GATT intellectual property agreement that would cover standards, enforcement, dispute settlement, and the application to intellectual property protection of such GATT principles as national treatment and transparency.

Differences came to a head in mid-November 1988 when the negotiators disagreed completely on a text proposed for Montreal by the group's chairman, Lars Anell (Sweden's ambassador to GATT). Anell's text would have had ministers endorse negotiation of "appropriate and effective multilateral rules and disciplines ... on the content and limits of international rights and obligations regarding the trade aspects of protection and enforcement of intellectual property rights." It called for detailed work on the applicability of basic GATT principles, on commitments to enforce intellectual property rights, on "the specification of reference points regarding the availability, scope and use" of such rights, and on dispute settlement. It also called for negotiation of an agreement on trade in counterfeit goods, and referred to the need to facilitate the flow of technology and to provide transitional arrangements and technical cooperation for developing countries. For the United States, the text did not go far enough. For many developing countries it went much too far, and they proposed amendments to it that would have flatly asserted that neither the negotiating group nor GATT itself could deal with substantive matters of intellectual property rights, and that further work should be restricted to the narrower issues which they accepted were covered by the Punta del Este mandate.

No progress was achieved either in this meeting or in informal efforts over the remaining days before ministers met in Montreal. On the contrary, three separate further proposals were put forward as alternatives to Anell's text, and all four texts went forward together to Montreal, each enclosed within the square brackets which in such documents indicate lack of agreement. Alternative "A" to the chairman's text gave the view of Brazil, the hardest-line opponent of the US approach. It specifically excluded work on intellectual property standards, insisting that such work was the task of other organizations. Alternative "B" gave the US view: ministers should endorse negotiations on an intellectual property agreement to cover standards, border and internal enforcement measures, dispute settlement, and GATT principles. The form of the agreement should be decided when its substance had been settled: the door was thus apparently left open to the TRIPS agreement being a code, rather than applicable to all GATT members. Alternative "C", from Switzerland, amended the chairman's text in the direction of developed-country views, changing Anell's calls for "detailed work" on key issues and for "the specification of reference points" to a firm requirement to negotiate and to reach commitments in GATT to protect and enforce intellectual property rights through "existing or new norms and standards".

To use one of Dunkel's favourite images, TRIPS was going to be one of the hardest nuts to crack in the mid-term review.

TRIMS

The TRIMS negotiations were to be among the most frustrating and least productive of the Uruguay Round. Given that most developing countries had not wanted to negotiate on trade-related investment measures, and were wholly on the defensive, and that the developed countries regarded the issue as secondary and had little leverage to force progress, this outcome was almost inevitable. Moreover, the brief Punta del Este mandate for the TRIMS negotiations offered generous opportunities, quickly seized, for different interpretations and procedural delay.

The mandate required that "following an examination of the operation of GATT Articles related to the trade restrictive and distorting effects of investment measures, negotiations should elaborate, as appropriate, further provisions that may be necessary to avoid such adverse effects on trade". The negotiators had no difficulty in agreeing that their initial task was thus to identify investment measures that restricted or distorted trade, and to examine the operation of the relevant GATT Articles. However, right from the beginning it was clear that some countries, led by the United States, would be seeking a broad agreement, extending over most incentives and controls facing foreign direct investment; that other developed countries were interested primarily in controlling a few clearly trade-related measures; that the majority of developing countries would concede nothing unless they had to; and that some of these developing countries would try to avoid any discussion of substance at all.

As might be expected, the developed countries took the initiative, with four papers suggesting which measures and Articles should be taken up. The United States and (to a lesser extent) Japan suggested a wide range of measures and Articles. The European Communities and the Nordic countries were more selective. The papers provided the basis for lengthy discussion throughout meetings of the TRIMS group in 1987, in which the nature of each type of TRIM, and the relevance of the GATT Articles cited, were explored. But there was little sign of any consensus emerging either on what real problems might exist or what might be done about them. In meetings in 1988, the scope of the discussion broadened somewhat, but still with no meeting of minds.

From the beginning, there was little doubt that two types of TRIM – local content requirements and export performance requirements – were pre-eminently measures which affected trade and were legitimate subjects for discussion, if not necessarily for action. Both were also widely used. Local content requirements demand that a product incorporate materials or components supplied from the domestic market, and thus by definition exclude the use of imports. Export performance requirements generally set a minimum proportion of output that must be sold abroad, thus potentially taking a share of foreign markets away from suppliers in other countries. In both cases, the obvious assumption is that in the absence of the requirement, normal competitive pressures would have led the investor to behave differently, incorporating a higher proportion of imported materials or selling a larger share of output on the domestic market.

Beyond these two TRIMS there were some obscurities arising from what appeared to be varying definitions of what were essentially similar practices, but the real differences of view concerned whether the investment measures cited were trade-related or not. The longest list of candidates was presented by the United States. The list covered 13 different types of requirements which, separately or in combination, the US regarded as artificially reducing imports, inducing or increasing exports, or reducing exports, and therefore qualifying as "trade-related". The list is worth giving because it is the most comprehensive from any source, all others being essentially pared-down alternatives to the US proposal. In alphabetical order, it consists of domestic sales requirements, exchange restrictions, export requirements, investment incentives, licensing requirements, local content requirements, local equity requirements, manufacturing limitations, manufacturing requirements, product mandating requirements, remittance restrictions, technology transfer requirements and trade-balancing requirements.

Many of the TRIMS cited by the United States were unarguably trade-related, and some were so similar in their effects to the two leading TRIMS as to be little more than variants on them. Trade-balancing requirements, for instance, which usually take the form of authorizing imports only in proportion to the value of exports by the same firm, have import-restricting effects comparable to those of domestic content rules. But the US list included many other incentives and restrictions affecting foreign investment, such as restrictions on the proportion of equity in an investment that can be held by foreigners, or requirements on the transfer of technology. Most developed countries did not try to spread the net of the negotiations so wide, and virtually all developing countries – even those which traditionally favoured and welcomed foreign investment – were strongly opposed to doing so. The Japanese came closest to the US position. The European Communities and the Nordic countries preferred to focus on domestic content and export performance requirements, along with those TRIMS which were essentially variants upon them.

When it came to identifying relevant GATT Articles, the list was almost equally long but, again, there were two which stood out. No less than 18 Articles were cited in the negotiating group. Some were said to prohibit various forms of TRIMS, directly or indirectly. Others – for example Article XVIII:C on support to industry in developing countries – were cited in support of TRIMS. Yet others, such as the dispute settlement rules of the GATT, were claimed to be adequate to handle any problems that might arise. Articles III and XI were however most obviously relevant. Paragraph 4 of Article III requires that imports into one GATT member country from another be treated as favourably as products of the importing country in requirements covering, among other things, their purchase and use. Paragraph 5 of the same Article forbids any internal regulation on "the mixture, processing or use of products in specified amounts or proportions which requires, directly or indirectly, that any specified amount or proportion of any product which is the subject of the regulation must be supplied from domestic sources". On the face of it, these provisions seemed to forbid TRIMS which set domestic content requirements. Moreover, almost the only dispute case relevant to TRIMS which had ever come up in GATT had turned on just this point. Canada had lost to the United States in 1984 over a US complaint that the Canadian Foreign Investment Review Act (FIRA) was requiring investors to purchase goods of Canadian origin, contrary to Article III:4, although that decision explicitly recognized that the arguments upheld against Canada might not apply against developing countries. Article XI forbids both import or export restrictions, although it is tempered by exceptions stated both in the Article itself and elsewhere in the GATT. Another Article that needed serious consideration was VI, on anti-dumping and countervailing duties, which was arguably relevant if export performance requirements or similar rules forced producers to sell abroad, even at unprofitable prices. Others were Article XVII, on the behaviour of state-trading enterprises, and Article X, which calls for publication of rules on imports and exports, including their "processing, mixing or other use".

In discussion of the GATT Articles, there were several strands of difficulty. One was that countries disagreed on what the present rules required. The FIRA decision was not a great deal of help because it did not cover developing countries. Moreover, domestic content and export performance requirements were so widely used that it could be argued that the GATT rules were in this respect effectively dead. A further problem was while developing countries, in particular, saw no reason even to discuss matters not covered by the present GATT Articles, developed countries generally approached the issue from the other end: to a greater or lesser extent, they wanted to bring TRIMS under international discipline and, if the present GATT rules were inadequate to the task, they were ready to negotiate new rules. Even if the United States was more ambitious in this respect than other developed countries, they too disliked export performance requirements, which GATT rules did not seem to prohibit. (Australia, an exception among developed countries in these negotiations, aligned itself with developing countries as a user and vigorous defender of TRIMS.)

The TRIMS negotiating plan required that the group start by looking at the operation of GATT Articles "relevant to the trade restrictive and distorting effects of investment measures", and only thereafter move on to "elaborate, as appropriate, further provisions" to avoid such effects. It was easy in these circumstances for countries which did not want new disciplines on TRIMS to insist that the group had not fulfilled the initial requirements. They called for deeper studies of the operation of the Articles, and more convincing demonstration that TRIMS actually restricted or distorted trade. At the same time, they argued the case for using TRIMS as one of the few means available to them to counter restrictive business practices by the multinational corporations that account for much international investment.

Early in 1988, the group's chairman (Tomohiko Kobayashi, a senior Japanese diplomat and economic specialist) invited delegations to come forward with more defined ideas on what should be the subject-matter for actual negotiations. Although India, backed by some other developing countries, protested that this invitation was "forcing the pace", the result was quite useful in narrowing down the discussion and calming some fears. The European Community suggested, on the basis of apparent trade effects, that negotiations could concentrate on eight types of TRIM out of the 13 identified. Japan focused on means of distinguishing between TRIMS that were covered by present GATT rules and those that were not. The United States proposed that basic GATT concepts be applied to the use of TRIMS, and mentioned not only most-favoured-nation and national treatment but also prohibition in some cases, and provision for transparency, dispute settlement, and the needs of developing countries. The US proposals, in particular, clearly reflected the view that, even if the Punta del Este mandate called for the negotiations to focus on the trade effects of TRIMS, these effects could not be brought under control without imposing some disciplines on TRIMS themselves. Most developing countries continued to argue that negotiations should focus on the harmful trade effects, if any, of TRIMS, rather than on introducing new rules to govern investment measures. However, they were somewhat reassured that all three sets of proposals recognized that development needs would justify some exceptions to any new disciplines, and that such disciplines should not impinge any further than necessary on countries' sovereign rights to set national policies on investment.

As the Montreal mid-term review approached, it could not be said that there had been any great meeting of minds in the TRIMS negotiations. However, the subject was effectively a brand new one for GATT, and the discussions had clarified the issues and the objectives of the participants. The time had not yet come for critical decisions. Without much difficulty, the group agreed to recommend to ministers a list of four "elements" to be integrated into the future negotiations on TRIMS. The list amounted to little more than recognition of the main themes of the discussion so far: identification of the harmful effects of TRIMS that were or might be covered by GATT Articles; identification of similar effects not covered by GATT but within the group's mandate; development considerations; and means of overcoming the adverse trade effects identified including, as appropriate, new provisions to deal with effects not adequately covered by the present rules.

Institutions

Removal of trade barriers and distortions can open up markets, creating opportunities for trade and growth. Agreement on rules to govern national trade policies can go far to ensure that everyone has a fair chance to make the best of market-opening. A very large proportion of the time, effort and political attention devoted to the Uruguay Round negotiations was directed to these two broad objectives. Even in combination, however, market opening and rule-making alone do not add up to an effective and enduring international trading system. Over 40 years of trade relations under the rules of the GATT have shown that effective institutions are needed too: to help settle disputes, to monitor developments, to decide when changing circumstances require new negotiations or policies, and generally to keep the system effective and running smoothly.

The crucially distinguishing characteristic of GATT, it has often been said, is that it is a contract among governments. There will always be room for disputes over contractual rights and obligations and, under a complex agreement such as GATT, as the years pass and trade relations and trade flows alter, conflicts will inevitably arise from time to time. While disputes between two countries can often be settled by mutual agreement, the help and impartial judgement of others will sometimes be needed. Without some form of central arrangement for settling trade disputes, there is always a risk that they may lead to economic conflict and soured political relations. Powerful countries will be tempted to ignore the complaints of the weak. Another danger is that if two or three governments involved in a particular dispute are allowed to decide how rules agreed on and accepted by many countries are to be interpreted, there can be no guarantee that their interpretation will respond to the interests of other members. Differing interpretations undermine the predictability of the rules, and bring uncertainty into trade relations. If rules are actually ignored, the effect is even worse: the rules concerned become worthless, and the credibility of the whole system of rights and obligations is undermined.

On the whole, the GATT dispute settlement provisions and procedures have worked well over the years. Innumerable problems have been settled or eased by direct consultation between the countries concerned, the complainant exercising its GATT right under Article XXII to "sympathetic consideration" by its trading partner of what it has to say. A far smaller number of disputes have defied bilateral resolution and have been brought to the attention of the GATT membership as a whole by the countries which believe themselves injured, using the provisions of Article XXIII. This Article permits a GATT member which considers that benefits due to it under the General Agreement are being "nullified or impaired" to appeal to the collective membership to investigate the matter and make recommendations. The practice grew up of using panels of experts, most often composed of three trade officials from countries not involved in the dispute, to investigate complaints and reach conclusions and recommendations. The GATT Council of Representatives would then decide whether to adopt the report, and thereby to put its conclusions into effect. Over the life of GATT, up to the launching of the Uruguay Round, roughly 120 disputes were brought to GATT under Article XXIII, and about 70 led to establishment of a panel. The great majority were satisfactorily settled in this way.

During the 1970s, and even more in the 1980s, governments made increasing use of panels, a trend that could be interpreted either as a vote of confidence in the dispute settlement system or, less optimistically, as evidence of rising tensions in international trade relations. Whichever interpretation was right, the need to make the system work effectively was obvious. Unfortunately, there was strong evidence that it was under strain. In spite of improvements introduced at the end of the Tokyo Round, the procedures could easily be slowed or even derailed, particularly because at almost every stage the consent of the parties to the dispute was required in order to move forward. Occasionally, requests for panels were blocked; in other cases, the establishment or work of panels was delayed; and when reports reached the Council, the adoption of some of them was blocked by the country held to be at fault. Even if accepted, recommendations were sometimes carried out after long delay, or not at all.

Some of these events could be understood, if not condoned. Countries sometimes argued that panels had simply been wrong in their findings, or that the GATT rules in question were in need of renegotiation. Delays were not always the fault of the parties. Clearly, major shifts in the national policies under fire in some dispute cases were more likely to be achieved through negotiated agreements than through disputed panel decisions: indeed, some such decisions, especially on agricultural matters, had played a big part in persuading governments to launch the Uruguay Round. Nevertheless, there was a very widespread feeling that dispute settlement was not working as well as it should. Whatever their disagreements over particular disputes and, in spite of quite widely differing conceptions of how the system should operate, all GATT members valued the dispute settlement procedures. Both as a means of defending their interests in specific disputes, and as a broad guarantee of their existing rights and of the value of the new commitments they were hoping to negotiate in the Uruguay Round, they were prepared to look for ways of making dispute settlement work better.

A similar common interest underlay the negotiations to strengthen the institutional structure of the GATT system. Indeed, dispute settlement and the group of issues lumped together as "the functioning of the GATT system" were closely linked. Just as liberalization and a set of rules are of limited value unless one can be sure that they will be maintained and enforced, a living and far-reaching set of relationships such as the GATT establishes must be continuously watched over, maintained and adapted to changing circumstances. At Punta del Este it was agreed that these needs called for development of understandings and arrangements under three headings: better monitoring of trade policies; improvement of the effectiveness and decision-making of the GATT as an institution, including the involvement of ministers; and increasing GATT's contribution to the coherence of global economic policies by strengthening its links with international organizations responsible for monetary and financial matters.

Better monitoring or surveillance, the first of the three aims, had been discussed from the Tokyo Round onwards, was generally supported, and had been strongly endorsed in 1985 by the Leutwiler Group, which had put forward some quite detailed ideas of its own. Since the beginning of the 1980s, the GATT Council had held twice-yearly special meetings to discuss trends in international trade policies and, from 1983 onwards, the Secretariat's supporting documentation for these meetings had begun to track changes in national policies in detail, including information on bilateral trade restraints. However, there was no GATT equivalent, for trade policy, of the separate reviews of national economic policies as a whole carried out by such organizations as the IMF and OECD. As for the institutional aspects of GATT, they had grown up haphazardly, in response to evolving needs and, although not quite as impermanent and ramshackle as some commentators suggested, were certainly somewhat extraordinary for an agency with such responsibilities. Formally, GATT was an agreement, not an organization, and thus had no members: when its signatories ("contracting parties") acted together, their collective role had to be indicated by the bizarre convention of referring to them in capitals as "CONTRACTING PARTIES". Some governments felt it needed a more effective governing body than its unwieldy Council of Representatives. Meetings at ministerial level were rare and irregular (so much so that, as was seen in 1982, excessive expectations were attached to them when they occurred), and routine political guidance was lacking. The GATT's paid staff, the Director-General and Secretariat, were nominally employed by a phantom agency, the Interim Commission for the International Trade Organization, which had lost its purpose nearly 40 years earlier and now existed solely as a channel for the payment of salaries and other budgetary expenses.

The issue of relationships with the monetary and financial organizations had been raised because many countries felt that international trade, monetary and debt policies discussed and pursued through GATT, the International Monetary Fund and the World Bank were sometimes at cross purposes. The prime example in 1986 was the debt crisis that had engulfed many developing countries, particularly in Latin America. The crisis originated in a combination of sharply increased oil prices, ill-judged national policies and excessive lending by American and European banks. It had been made worse, however, by trade restrictions in industrialized countries that reduced the export earnings of developing countries, bringing privation to their peoples and stunting investment in their economies and, incidentally (because so much of their export earnings had to be spent on debt service), greatly reducing their ability to buy goods from the developed countries.

Dispute settlement and "FOGS" (the unfortunate but inevitable abbreviation bestowed on the Functioning of the GATT System group) shared one further, and happy, characteristic. Even though governments differed, sometimes quite strongly, on how stronger dispute settlement procedures and a better-functioning system should be achieved, they were agreed on the broad objectives. Whereas in most other areas of the Uruguay Round the negotiations were between one group of countries which wanted concessions, and another group which would give ground only in exchange for concessions elsewhere, in these institutional negotiating groups there was to a great extent a sense of common purpose. This had two helpful practical consequences. First, proposals from national delegations often had much in common, reducing to a minimum both acrimony and the need for prolonged negotiations. Second, in these circumstances, the essential requirement that both chairman and Secretariat observe strict neutrality between contending views was a much less constraining element than in most of the other negotiating groups, and they were thus able to add thrust to the proceedings on many occasions by putting forward their own ideas and papers. A final element in these negotiations was that many of the issues under discussion had already been studied in detail during the period since the 1982 ministerial meeting. The stage was thus set for rapid advance.

A final common factor between the two negotiating groups was that, in recognition of the cross-connections between many of the issues before them, they were given two co-chairmen. One, Julio Lacarte-Múro of Uruguay, was given primary responsibility for dispute settlement. At the time Uruguay's ambassador to GATT, he had a depth of knowledge and experience that was unparalleled in either national delegations or the Secretariat, since it stretched back almost 40 years, including service with the initial, minuscule, ICITO/ GATT Secretariat. His counterpart, primarily chairing the group on the functioning of the GATT system, was another veteran of international economic negotiations, Julius Katz of the United States. Katz was to drive his group forward at a remarkable pace until after the mid-term review, when his appointment as Deputy US Trade Representative made it necessary for him to give up his chairmanship. Thereafter, Lacarte chaired the two groups, a conjunction which proved particularly valuable near the end of the Round when institutional issues arose that cut across the central mandates of both.

Dispute settlement

The Punta del Este mandate for the dispute settlement negotiations reflected a difference of view on whether difficulties experienced with GATT panels in recent years were principally the fault of the procedures, or of the rules they were trying to enforce. The negotiating group was to aim "to improve and strengthen the rules and the procedures of the dispute settlement process", yet in the same breath the mandate recognized "the contribution that would be made by more effective and enforceable GATT rules and disciplines". In fact, there was much to be said for both views. As Alan Oxley, Australia's Geneva negotiator in the first half of the Round, has put it, "attempts to finesse different views and objectives in designing rules have often postponed interpretative difficulties and stored up trouble for later". Unresolved disputes in the early 1980s too often grew out of "constructive ambiguity" (Oxley's phrase again) used by the Tokyo Round negotiators in the effort to reach an agreement. The real test for some Uruguay Round agreements will probably come only when they too become the basis of complaints that will show whether they rest on similar ambiguities. But at the same time, problems encountered in some dispute cases suggested that the dispute rules and procedures themselves needed improvement.

No doubt because of the thorough discussion on dispute settlement before the Round began, a large number of countries were ready to put forward ideas and proposals as soon as the negotiating group got down to work. Mexico, New Zealand, the United States, Jamaica and Japan all made written proposals at or before the first substantive meeting of the group in mid-1987 and, by the end of the year, Switzerland, the Nordic countries, Australia, Canada, Nicaragua, Argentina, Hungary and Korea had also submitted formal documents for consideration. This was in strong contrast to the experience of most of the other Uruguay Round negotiating groups which spent 1987, and in many cases 1988 as well, trying to arrive at even a common assessment of the problems they faced before being in a position to consider possible solutions.

As far as procedures were concerned, there was a great deal of common ground, particularly as regards ideas on speeding up the establishment and work of panels. While certain countries took the lead in crystallizing ideas, and in putting them formally to the negotiating group, support for many of them was so widespread that there is little point in attributing authorship or constructive criticism to any particular country. By the autumn of 1987, the group's chairman, Julio Lacarte, was able to conclude that delegates were close to agreement on many of these procedural proposals. Among the main ideas which enjoyed broad support were that requests for panels should include a summary of the complaint and proposed terms of reference, that panels should be established no later than the second Council meeting after the request was made, and that terms of reference should normally follow a standard format. The negotiators also broadly agreed that if panel membership could not be promptly decided, the choice of members should be left to the Director-General, that standard time-limits should be established for each stage of the panel procedures, that any objections to panel reports should be stated within one month, and that the reports should be approved within two months. Other points widely supported were that time-limits should be set for acting on panel recommendations, and that there should be follow-up examinations to see how panel reports were being put into effect. Some other proposals aroused greater doubts but could not really be called controversial. These included the American suggestion that public confidence in panel judgements would be greater if panellists were mostly drawn from non-governmental sources; the desire of some countries to strengthen the position of third parties with an interest in essentially bilateral differences; and interest in the possibility of voluntary resort to an independent arbitrator to settle some disputes. Other ideas which were to bear fruit at the very end of the Round included holding meetings of the GATT Council which would be devoted entirely to dispute questions, especially to surveillance of countries' compliance with panel recommendations, and seeking means of ending the fragmentation of dispute settlement arrangements under GATT that had arisen because of the separate procedures established under various Tokyo Round codes.

While most participants could find common ground in seeking to improve these procedural matters, there was a point beyond which views on the role of dispute settlement in GATT, and therefore on appropriate aims for the negotiations, diverged sharply.

Some countries, led by the United States but supported by Canada and others, saw the task of dispute settlement as being to establish right and wrong: to deliver a legal judgement with which the losing party ought obviously to comply. The GATT system, viewed in this light, had some extraordinary features which seriously undermined any claim to be a fair court of law. In effect, a country accused of wrongdoing in a GATT dispute was not only the defendant but also shared fully in the tasks of the "court" (the Council), and actually had a blocking voice in launching the judicial proceedings (establishment of the panel), and in judgement (acceptance of the panel's findings and recommendations). Nor were the procedures very effective in securing compliance with the rulings of a panel, even if these were endorsed by the Council. Justified or not, the much-criticized "Section 301" powers given by law to the President of the United States to take trade action against unfair behaviour by other countries were partly inspired by the American desire to provide enforcement powers missing from the GATT system.

Other countries, however, with the European Community and Japan prominent among them, saw dispute settlement under Article XXIII as essentially an extension of the conciliation process under Article XXII, with the aim less to reach legal judgements than to overcome a particular trade problem. From this point of view, it made perfectly good sense for the parties to a dispute to reach a bilateral settlement while a panel was already sitting, without necessarily telling others the basis on which agreement was reached, or to treat the letter of the GATT rules as a secondary consideration if those directly concerned believed that acting differently would make better sense for practical economic, social or political reasons. Moreover, since the interpretation of GATT law was the collective task of the member countries, the parties to the dispute had, as they saw it, a right to share in deciding how the law applied in particular circumstances.

These fundamental differences of view led to further proposals to the nego-tiating group that were far more controversial than the essentially procedural improvements previously discussed. Inevitably, they centred on the questions of whether the "losing" government in a panel case could be prevented from blocking adoption of the panel's unfavourable report, and could be forced to comply promptly with its recommendations. One proposal to this end was that Council decisions on whether to adopt panel reports should be based on "consensus minus two": in other words, on an agreement from which the two parties to the dispute would be excluded. This proposal was backed by Argentina, Australia, New Zealand and others. However, it was open to objection on two sides: it offended against the argument that all member countries should have a say in interpreting the trade laws which bound them, and (as the United States pointed out) it would leave open the possibility that a sympathetic "surrogate" delegation could block a decision on behalf of the excluded losing government. Hungary put forward a possible solution, later backed by the European Community: the Council should split its decision on each panel report into two parts, with all countries participating in a first decision on whether to accept the legal judgement of the panel members; and with a second decision, excluding the parties to the dispute, on the recommendations of the panel for settling the dispute itself.

There were further proposals too. The United States and others wanted to make Council decisions binding on the parties to the dispute. Japan believed this would work only if the parties formed part of the consensus for adoption. Nicaragua proposed that when a panel found that a developing country was the injured party in a dispute, the Council should have the task of recommending appropriate compensation or other measures. Korea believed use should be made of conciliation by the Director-General, breathing life into procedures that had been negotiated in 1966, but scarcely used. Mexico and Hungary called for third parties to have a greater say in the settlement of bilateral disputes which might touch their interests.

In March 1988, Brazil put forward formal proposals to give more favourable treatment in dispute settlement cases to developing countries, arguing that their limited power of retaliation, as well as Part IV of the GATT and earlier decisions in their favour, required that they be provided with "a higher level of equity". Brazil, one of the countries which saw the dispute settlement as a means of conciliation rather than judicial decision, put much weight on transparent and multilateral procedures as a means of improving the international trading environment which – as it pointedly put it – "has been suffering from direct and dissimulated violations of GATT rules in the field of the so-called 'grey areas' where there are rare possibilities of resorting to dispute settlement procedures". Similar proposals were put by Peru. Some developed countries argued, in reply, that any strengthening of the dispute settlement procedures, and thus of the rule of law in international trade relations, must in itself be to the advantage of developing countries and the other smaller trading powers.

A final and highly controversial demand was put forward by the European Community, backed by many other countries, and aimed squarely at the

United States and its Section 301 powers. Reform of the GATT dispute settlement procedures, it said, must include an explicit ban on any country taking unilateral action to redress what it judged to be the trade wrongs of others. Satisfactory multilateral arrangements for settling disputes would leave no excuse for any country to take the law into its own hands. Moreover, the Community maintained, all countries should bring their domestic legislation into line with this commitment to act only in accordance with the multilateral procedures.

By early 1988, it had become clear to all participants in the dispute settlement negotiations that the proposals put forward fell into two distinct categories: those for essentially procedural improvements to the existing arrangements, and those which would involve fundamental change. Proposals in the first group enjoyed very broad support, and were also quite straightforward. The second group did not, and moreover would need substantial negotiation to be brought to a stage at which final decisions could be taken. A further point was that some countries, doubtful about making bold changes in the existing rules, argued that procedural improvements might prove sufficient, and therefore ought to be tried first. The stage was thus set for drawing up an initial set of proposals for improvements to the GATT dispute settlement procedures to be put to ministers for decision at the mid-term review of the Round at the end of 1988.

In April 1988, at the negotiating group's request, the Secretariat put together an informal and unnumbered paper, distributed only to those directly involved in the negotiations (in GATT jargon, a "non-paper"), which set out what it judged to be the most important convergences and divergences of views. This approach meant that the non-paper effectively distinguished between the two groups of proposals: those suitable for early action, and those which would need further negotiation. Among the latter, as the Secretariat saw it, were the proposals for specific differential and more favourable treatment for developing countries, the idea of Council meetings devoted to dispute settlement, whether panel interpretations of GATT rules should be regarded as setting legal precedents, and the question of whether the rules on Council adoption of reports should be changed by splitting legal interpretation from recommendations or by excluding parties to the dispute from the decision process.

Based on the Secretariat paper, which was later modified to get rid of the distinction between convergent and divergent views and to leave out proposals which had no current chance of approval, the negotiating group began informal consultations to construct a first package of improvements to the dispute settlement arrangements. In June, a comprehensive and detailed proposal was put forward in the name of Mexico, which in spite of having joined GATT only weeks before the Punta del Este meeting had quickly established itself as a leading participant in the Round and in GATT activities in general. The Mexican paper covered the whole dispute settlement process, starting with consultation. If consultations brought no satisfactory adjustment within 30 days, Article XXIII would come into play, but with the option of mediation in which the Director-General or Chairman of the Council could play a part or, if the parties so agreed, of arbitration. The Mexican proposal included the idea of frequent Council meetings in "dispute settlement mode" to conduct consultations, establish panels, monitor proceedings and oversee compliance with panel conclusions. Other proposals covered the establishment, composition, terms of reference and timetable of work of panels. No change was proposed in the rules for adoption of panel reports by the Council, except that parties to the dispute would "be free to join in the consensus or not". Numerous provisions called for special attention to the needs of developing countries involved in disputes. Even though some of its elements were still controversial, the Mexican paper was well received and became a further key element in consultations. Mexico held discussions with a number of countries and put forward a revised text in October, the most obvious change being to drop the idea – whose time had evidently not yet come – of Council meetings in "dispute settlement mode".

Meanwhile Canada, which was to be very active throughout the Uruguay Round negotiations on all institutional questions, also consulted with a number of like-minded countries. They produced their own proposals in early October. To a great extent, this paper, presented by 14 countries, covered the same ground as the Mexican text. It added a political commitment to abide by the dispute settlement rules and avoid unilateral measures inconsistent with GATT, provided tight deadlines for the various stages of the panel process, and (while keeping the consensus rule for adoption of reports) proposed that "parties to a dispute shall not block a consensus to adopt a panel report". The paper also included a long section on implementation of reports which went into considerable detail about the circumstances in which an injured party could, if the offending measure were not removed within a reasonable time, be authorized to suspend obligations toward the offending country.

The October 1988 meeting of the negotiating group discussed both the Mexican and group papers, and decided to authorize Lacarte to produce a chairman's text, drawing on both, which could be recommended to ministers at the mid-term review meeting as a package of improvements to the GATT settlement rules and procedures that could be put into effect immediately on a trial basis. Lacarte's draft was discussed and revised during November. By 22 November, when the GNG's report to ministers on the negotiations on goods issues as a whole was issued, there was a complete text on dispute settlement, but several issues remained open. These included three matters of particular importance: whether domestic legislation and actions to settle disputes should be in full conformity with GATT and the dispute settlement procedures; a provision that the whole dispute settlement process should last no more than 15 months; and the question of what role the parties to a dispute should play in the Council decision on a panel report. The first point was essentially aimed at the United States, with the European Community as the moving spirit but with wide backing. Disagreement on the second was essentially a matter of differing judgements as to the realism of a rigid 15-month limit. The third, on the adoption of reports, was critically important but not yet ripe for any solution that would represent major change from the existing rule of consensus.

Consultations continued right up to the ministerial meeting, and resulted in settlement of the outstanding points. The final package provided for a long list of improvements in the dispute settlement process, none dramatic, but together adding up already to a greater achievement than had been possible in the Tokyo Round. They included time-limits for consultations, the possibility of conciliation and of arbitration as an alternative to panel proceedings, consistency of bilateral and arbitration settlements with GATT, establishment of a panel at latest by the second Council meeting after it was requested, standard terms of reference, explicit time-limits for the various stages of a panel's work, legal advice for developing countries involved in disputes, and an overall 15-month limit "unless agreed to by the parties" for the whole process from the opening of consultations to the Council decision on the panel report.

This interim agreement on dispute settlement did not resolve the two most controversial issues. The Community's desired language on conformity of domestic legislation was not included. Council adoption of panel reports was still to be by consensus, even though the text said that "the delaying of the process of dispute settlement shall be avoided". Both questions would have to be faced again in the second half of the Round.

Functioning of the GATT system

The FOGS group got off to a rapid start, with its first meeting in April 1987 providing an opportunity for many countries to describe their basic approach to the group's three subjects of improved monitoring of trade policies, more effective organization of the GATT, and greater coherence of international economic policies. Key themes emerged almost immediately that were to dominate negotiations in the group throughout much of the Round.

Many of the ingredients for these negotiations could be found in the first working paper put to the group: an Australian set of proposals which drew on the ideas for improving transparency and public understanding of trade policies put forward two years earlier in the Leutwiler Group's report on *Trade Policies for a Better Future*. Essentially, the proposal aimed at building on the improved GATT monitoring of national trade policies that had been gradually developed since the end of the Tokyo Round. The Leutwiler report had given first place among its proposals to the idea that each country should assess systematically the likely protective effects of any trade measure before introducing it and had, in fact, cited as exemplary Australia's own arrangements for doing so. The first Australian proposal was that all GATT members be invited to make an annual assessment of the protective effect of their policies, uniting for the purpose all the notifications they were required to make under various GATT provisions and applying to them some simple measurement techniques. The reports by each country would be brought together and reviewed in annual special sessions of the GATT Council. The second proposal, again drawn from the Leutwiler Group (which in this respect had been inspired by the example of the OECD) was that the policies of some of the larger GATT members should be reviewed, in rotation, by a number of other countries, on behalf of the Council, and on the basis of a Secretariat report.

There was immediate interest in these ideas, but also some hesitation. Developing countries had mixed views on increased surveillance. They did not welcome the prospect of additional examinations of their policies in GATT, yet at the same time they felt that a broad-based obligation to expose trade policies to general scrutiny would give greater balance to GATT. Many of them were under regular surveillance in the Balance-of-Payments Committee, while no such close review was maintained over the policies of the larger developed countries. The United States and European Community, by contrast, had misgivings of their own. The US delegate argued that in practice the major developed countries' policies were under continuous scrutiny in the Council, while developing countries escaped most GATT obligations; the European Community was fearful that the proposed reviews would turn into some kind of hostile assessment by tribunal that would tend to displace the careful and objective procedures for dispute settlement.

The Australians also produced the first formal proposals on the second element in the FOGS mandate: improvement of "the overall effectiveness and decision-making of the GATT as an institution". Their suggestions concentrated on how to increase ministerial participation in the work of GATT and, on this subject too, they succeeded in sparking the essential elements of the continuing later debate. Their basic diagnosis was widely shared: GATT needed the policy-level perspective that could only be provided by the more active and regular involvement of ministers. This, the Australians suggested, would encourage greater conformity with the GATT rules, provide stimulus to resolve deadlocks in GATT (especially on dispute settlement issues), and offer a mechanism for permanent negotiation on trade problems, thus reducing the existing GATT tendency to allow such problems to build up until only a very large multilateral negotiating round offered a way of overcoming them. Apart from more frequent ministerial-level GATT sessions, the Australians saw need for a permanent ministerial steering group on the lines of the existing limited but representative official level Consultative Group of Eighteen.

Most countries saw merit in having the annual GATT sessions take place at ministerial level from time to time, although the European Community and Japan feared that ministerial meetings could too easily become a devalued routine. The idea of a limited-membership group was far less welcome. The Consultative Group of Eighteen was felt to have performed disappointingly in recent years (a fertile source of ideas during the Tokyo Round, it was in fact to play no part in the Uruguay Round); it was variously felt to be too large to be effective or too small to be representative. Some countries, however, suggested that a limited ministerial group firmly tied to GATT would be preferable to the twice-yearly informal meetings of trade ministers which were currently taking place with no generally accepted mandate and with obvious gaps in representation. Others replied that, even if excluded from the present informal meetings, they could at least ignore them: they did not wish to find themselves still on the outside of a restricted ministerial group which had been granted legitimacy within GATT.

In retrospect, this early discussion on the institutional part of the FOGS mandate was remarkably narrow in scope. Certainly, the Punta del Este agreement specifically mentioned the issue of ministerial involvement, but "the overall effectiveness and decision-making of the GATT" was potentially a much bigger subject for negotiation than any country acknowledged at this stage. Not until three years after the agreement was reached did informal discussion begin on major alterations in the institutional structure of the multilateral trading system. Formal proposals for change came even later. Only one national proposal, from Canada in July 1987, mentioned in a throwaway last sentence that "it might be useful also" to examine proposals to establish an international trade organisation. At that time, not even Canada suggested any follow-up of this suggestion. A little later, in January 1988, the Nordic countries proposed that the Director-General should be given more explicit powers, and that thought be given to how the general GATT rule of decision-making by consensus could be made to work more smoothly. Again, delegations were not ready to discuss these matters (and in the first case, the Secretariat was fearful that any attempt to define the Director-General's powers would result in a negotiated text that left him with less discretion and powers of initiative than he already in practice possessed).

Little was also said by the negotiators, initially, about their ill-defined task of increasing GATT's contribution to "greater coherence in global economic policy-making". A discussion began on how GATT might cooperate more closely with the major international financial institutions, the International Monetary Fund and World Bank. The European Community made clear its main concern in this area: the disruptive effect on trade, as it saw it, of exchange rate instability – an assessment with which the United States, at least, profoundly disagreed.

Subsequent meetings expanded and developed ideas on all these. By far the most substantial negotiations took place on the issue of surveillance, with Katz pushing the group forward at a pace which some developing countries and a few other delegations, anxious that all negotiations should advance at roughly the same rate, found uncomfortable. Progress was also helped by the fact that the Secretariat had been developing its own ideas on the subject during 1986 and 1987, and found its thinking close to that of Katz. Japan, the United States and Korea also produced papers with largely convergent ideas on how regular trade policy reviews might be introduced into GATT. In September 1987,

Katz held informal consultations with delegations, and outlined his ideas on a possible GATT mechanism for review of national policies. His tentative proposals were generally welcomed, although some countries were concerned that the new mechanism should not blur what they saw as a fundamental distinction between the enforcement of GATT legal obligations on the one hand, and on the other, the aim of applying "peer pressure" to governments to encourage them to follow open and sensible trade policies. Katz followed up this meeting with a "chairman's discussion paper", developed jointly by him and the Secretariat, which suggested that the trade policies of all GATT member countries should be reviewed periodically. Basic information would be provided by annual reports which each country would make according to an agreed format that would include policy objectives and approaches, recent and impending measures, and relevant statistics. A three- or five-year cycle of individual country reviews would allow each GATT member to be covered in turn. The individual reviews would be carried out, preferably in the capital of the country concerned, by a body composed of a small number of government representatives with trade policy experience. They would base their work on a paper and suggested questions prepared by the Secretariat, and would submit a report to a supervisory body (possibly the GATT Council). This would give the opportunity for the all the trading partners of the country concerned to comment on the report, which would then be made public.

A meeting of the FOGS group in November showed broad support for the basic thrust of the chairman's paper. There was virtually unanimous agreement that a regular programme of trade policy reviews would be valuable, and most countries agreed that all GATT members should be covered. However, many felt that a "core" group (which Japan had suggested might be defined as the 30 countries with the largest shares in world trade) should be reviewed more often than the rest. Although some developing countries argued for exemption of those who were already consulting with GATT because they maintained trade restrictions to protect their balance-of-payments, others accepted that the proposed reviews would serve a different purpose and ought to apply to all. Views differed on the role of the Secretariat, with some countries seeing it only as a compiler of factual material and a postbox for government questions.

Many developing countries were reluctant to accept that review teams should visit capitals. In part, this reflected their belief that review teams should be "open-ended", allowing any interested country to join in, and that this would be impracticable unless the reviews took place at GATT headquarters. More fundamentally, visits to capitals, as well as a prominent Secretariat role in the reviews, aroused the extreme sensitivity of some countries about any arrangement that might be interpreted as putting governments under the tutelage of an international organization. This was the period, it must be remembered, of the debt crisis. The indebted countries were unable to borrow from governments and banks the very large sums they needed unless they first reached agreement with the International Monetary Fund on the economic policies they would follow. The pain and social unrest caused by rigorous policies, and the humiliation felt in being driven to adopt them, were associated in the public mind with the arrival of teams of international officials. No country felt this more strongly than Brazil.

Ideas evolved quickly. At the group's next meeting, in February, it became obvious that participants were already close to agreement on some key elements of the review mechanism: full coverage of the GATT membership, but with more frequent reviews of a core group consisting of the developed countries, as well as the larger traders among the developing countries; reviews to be conducted by an open-ended group of countries (very possibly the Council) in Geneva; the reviews to be based on material provided both by governments and the Secretariat. The Secretariat was asked to produce proposals on the format for country reports, and a tentative estimate of costs. By the following meeting, in March, the group was working on further revision of the chairman's paper, and on a first draft of the reporting format. These texts were to evolve over the following months, but the evolution was continuous and, although disagreements on specific points had to be overcome, there were at no time competing proposals for the review mechanism as a whole.

Most of the discussion revolved around a very few questions. Many countries wanted assurance that their trade policies would not be put on trial, and that the examinations would not become general reviews of national economic policy. Developing countries, who found in India a particularly effective voice on this point, also wanted the reviews to take account of difficulties they faced in their export markets. There was concern over how to handle reviews of the European Community, to ensure that trade measures taken by its individual member countries were covered. Differing views on how often the major countries should be reviewed, and whether the least developed countries and those consulting for balance-of-payments reasons should be covered, came close to cancelling out one another, with the result that the chairman's own middle-of-the-road proposals survived effectively intact, crystallizing quite early in a "2-4-6" formula (the Quad group to be reviewed every two years; the next 16 countries in trading magnitude every four; and the rest, every six). There was agreement that, in addition to the national reviews, the GATT Council should continue to review, probably once a year, the evolution of trade policies of the member countries as a whole.

The sharpest differences pitted Indian views, supported by Brazil and many other developing countries, against two related elements of the chairman's proposals. India envisaged the Secretariat report for each review as being a factual paper, with comments and judgements reserved to the country under review; the chairman gave the Secretariat a much more independent role. (Katz thought that leaving out independent analysis from the Secretariat would be "leaving the goats to mind the cabbages": most developed countries agreed.) Similarly, India was opposed to having Secretariat teams visit capitals ahead of reviews, while the chairman and others saw this as an essential part of the preparations.

These discussions moved in parallel with those on other aspects of the FOGS group's mandate. Under the same broad heading of improved surveillance of trade policies, there were some further, but inconclusive, exchanges on national ("domestic") arrangements for trade policy review, and on improved notification procedures. Almost all governments were prepared to express benevolence towards domestic surveillance, but the matter was clearly one on which individual countries should be free to make their own decisions. The dry subject of notifications was also not one to stir passions, but was important to achieving the basic aim of greater transparency in trade policies. Many GATT Articles, as well as the Tokyo Round codes, required govern-ments to make regular notifications of trade policy actions, as well as of changes in national policies and regulations. Some requirements were quite scrupu-lously observed, usually because the notifications were regularly examined; others were neglected. There were complaints that certain requirements were a waste of time, or effectively duplicated calls for information already provided. Inevitably, more notification requirements would emerge from the Uruguay Round. The United States found wide sympathy for its call for a broad review of notifications, and establishment of a central registry in GATT that would clearly show how governments were living up to their obligations to notify, and what information was available.

On broader institutional questions, successive meetings of the negotiating group brought a crystallization of the views on ministerial involvement which had been evident from the start. As far as concerned more frequent ministerial meetings of the whole GATT membership, the few initial hesitations were soon overcome. Only the minor question of whether two years or three would be the appropriate interval between ministerial sessions remained unsettled. The idea of a limited-membership group at ministerial level, however, aroused much more passion. It was strongly disliked by most developing countries, including some large enough to be fairly certain of membership, not least because they saw it as creating a GATT counterpart to the UN Security Council which would in practice undermine the existing legal equality of members under the General Agreement. On the other side, it was endorsed by many of the developed countries. The United States went so far as to describe it as a "steering group"; others, while expecting it to provide intellectual guidance and political impetus, insisted that it would have no formal role in the work of GATT.

Support for strengthening cooperation between GATT and other international organizations came most strongly from Canada, which suggested joint meetings of trade and finance ministers, participation of GATT Secretariat officials in IMF and World Bank missions, and study of the possibility of giving credit in GATT negotiations for trade liberalization under-taken by developing countries as part of economic reform programmes negotiated with the IMF or the Bank. The Nordic countries argued on similar lines, and stressed the need to ensure that Fund and Bank policy advice was consistent with the GATT rules. The European Community returned to a basic theme, already familiar from the 1982 ministerial meeting and subsequent occasions, by asking for study, with Fund and Bank input, of the relationship between such matters as the debt problem, US trade deficits, exchange-rate fluctuations, and current problems in international trade relations. The United States favoured closer GATT cooperation with the two Bretton Woods organizations, but not the EC proposals. Many developing countries were interested in the idea of obtaining negotiating credit for Fund- or Bank-sponsored trade liberalization, and were sympathetic to the EC's efforts to force discussion of the links between problems of international trade and finance. Mexico was a particularly fertile source of ideas in this respect. But the developing countries were reluctant to see GATT drawn into the development of IMF or Bank programmes, not least because of fears that this would lead to addition of still further, GATT-related, obligations to the conditions they were already required to accept in return for IMF and Bank financing. As an internal Secretariat note recorded, underlying much of the discussion was a clear difference of viewpoint between those countries which wanted to have GATT exert influence on the financial institutions and those who, on the contrary, would like to see the Fund and Bank exert greater influence on GATT

By mid-1988, it was becoming clear that a good chance existed of reaching agreement on a trade policy review mechanism at the mid-term meeting of ministers in December, and that there should also be no difficulty in agreeing also to hold some future GATT sessions at ministerial level. From this point onwards, most other issues in the FOGS group were set aside, although the European Community remained insistent that ministers should recognize the links between trade and financial issues in their mid-term statement, and developing countries were anxious to avoid any endorsement of proposals for a restricted ministerial-level group. Canada proposed that the Director-General of GATT report, jointly with the heads of the IMF and World Bank, on how the three institutions might work more closely together. This essentially procedural idea sparked differences, mainly because developing countries did not want a joint report and thought that other agencies should also be covered, but it served to postpone substantial discussion.

On the trade policy review mechanism, the most difficult issues in the negotiations turned on the role to be played by the Secretariat. India put forward a paper on behalf of developing countries that denied any need for review teams to visit capitals, and defined the documentation to come from the Secretariat as "a factual background note". While the second point was implicitly abandoned during the negotiations, the first was not. Brazil, even more than India, was not prepared to concede the right of the Secretariat to visit capitals in connection with reviews, and was also anxious that no country consulting with GATT over balance-of-payments restrictions should be placed in "double jeopardy" by also undergoing a trade policy review within a period shorter than, it suggested, 24 months. One new element in the negotiations was provided by the Nordic countries, who proposed that each review be introduced in the Council by "discussants" from other countries who could focus on issues of special importance. This proposal neatly bridged the difference between Katz's original proposal of a small review team of government officials and the emerging consensus on use of the GATT Council as the review body. It received only tepid support at first, but was incorporated later into the proposals put to ministers.

Although the introduction of trade policy reviews was clearly the main proposal to be put to ministers, many countries demanded that the mid-term review should give attention to all the FOGS issues, and should put any action taken into the broader context of developments in the world economy as a whole. In September, the European Community put forward a text which it proposed as a definition of the role of GATT in promoting global policy coherence. While this text became the basis for a preamble to the mid-term FOGS decisions, it also became the battleground for new disagreements since the EC perspective, particularly on the effect of exchange rate fluctuations (and notably an undervalued US dollar) on world trade, differed greatly from that of the United States.

In October, the De la Paix Group made an important contribution to reaching wider agreement by putting forward a single text that included a preamble based on the EC proposal; a draft decision that would put the trade policy reviews into effect immediately on a provisional basis; a further draft decision to hold ministerial-level GATT sessions every two years; a proposal to look further at the possibility of a smaller ministerial group; and to ask Dunkel to explore with the heads of the IMF and World Bank the ways in which their organizations and the GATT might strengthen their relationships. This became the basis for negotiations that reached their peak in late November, just before the GNG mid-term report was put into final form. Some issues were settled, including most of the text on the trade policy review mechanism, and a draft decision to ask Dunkel to report by September 1989 on possibilities of cooperation with the IMF and World Bank. For the trade policy reviews, a formula was found to ease Brazilian concerns on "double jeopardy", but there remained the issue of Secretariat visits to capitals. Strong opposition continued to any commitment to look further into the possibility of establishing a small ministerial consultative group; and the whole diagnosis of the interlinkages between trade, finance and debt in the long preamble remained highly controversial.

Steering the Round

The main focus of the Round during these first two years was the negotiating groups themselves. In most of the groups, work was still at the stage of setting out national proposals and exploring their implications. For some groups, this continued right up to the mid-term meeting in Montreal. They had no major problems to overcome, and no need for guidance or intervention from a higher level. Some others, as the meeting approached, had to take increasingly difficult decisions as part of the process of hammering out both final and procedural agreements to be put to ministers. These decisions were influenced by an extraordinary variety of meetings and pressures, formal and informal, that grew in number and intensity as the Round progressed.

Within the formal structures of the Round, the apex and chief guiding influence was the Trade Negotiations Committee, chaired in its non-ministerial sessions by Arthur Dunkel. Dunkel called TNC meetings infrequently, often six months or more apart, so that they served principally as carefully prepared set-piece occasions for stock-taking, for deciding on changes of course, or for setting new deadlines for the negotiations. Immediately below the TNC were three bodies: the Group of Negotiations on Goods (the GNG), the Group of Negotiations on Services (the GNS), and the Surveillance Body. The three differed greatly in their character and tasks.

The GNS was a straightforward negotiating body, comparable in nature with the 14 negotiating groups that dealt with trade in goods. The GNG, on the other hand, had no function except to oversee those 14 groups, a task which essentially duplicated that of the TNC. The GNG and GNS each reported to the TNC. This careful separation of responsibility for goods and services, conceived in Punta del Este as the instrument that would ensure that the GATT and non-GATT aspects of the negotiations were kept clearly apart, fulfilled that purpose reasonably well, at least until the closing stages of the Round. However, the GNG itself was all too obviously superfluous. Its early meetings were devoted to broad-ranging reviews of progress in the various goods negotiating groups; but when these were promptly followed by meetings of the TNC (with largely the same attendance and even the same chairman) delegations found themselves with little to add, except on developments in services. Gradually the GNG meetings became no more than a brief formality, and the main discussion took place in the TNC.

The Surveillance Body had the task of seeing that countries participating in the Round lived up to the "standstill and rollback" commitments they had made in Punta del Este. Its regular meetings were chaired by Madan Mathur, one of Dunkel's two deputies, and served mainly to review notifications in which governments drew attention to moves they had made to liberalize trade, or complained about the trade-restrictive actions of others. Complaints tended to predominate. The rollback commitments in the Punta del Este Declaration, by which developing countries had set particular store, called for the phase-out of trade restrictive or distorting measures inconsistent with the GATT, and stipulated that no GATT concessions were to be requested for their elimination. However, the commitment called only for action not later than the formal completion of the Round, and even this requirement was conditioned by mention of possible arrangements that might be reached as part of the Round. Everyone knew that these "arrangements", if they could be agreed to in the context of the negotiations on safeguards and other issues, would be the key to removal of GATT-inconsistent measures. The standstill commitments were a more urgent concern. Governments had pledged not to take restrictive measures inconsistent with GATT, not to take GATT-consistent measures stronger than necessary, and not to take any trade measures to improve its negotiating position. The last point was important to everyone: disarmament negotiations are hardly possible if the negotiators are at the same time building up their weapon stocks. Moreover, the meetings of the Surveillance Body provided a useful extra forum, in addition to the normal organs of GATT, in which to hold up to public view and condemnation the trade transgressions of others.

These formal meetings of the Uruguay Round bodies were only a small fraction of the gatherings in Geneva and worldwide by which governments sought to guide the progress of the Round, and others sought to influence it.

An essential element in the Round itself was the so-called "green-room" meetings chaired by Dunkel and held in his small private conference room. (The name came from the olive-green fabric panels that covered the end walls: the predominant colour of the room was in fact off-white.) These brought together the heads of the main delegations concerned about a particular issue. The attendance varied according to the subject, but typically would involve 20 to 30 delegates, and a handful of the senior Secretariat officials involved. Sessions were generally held late in the day, and on many occasions ran far into the night. Dunkel used them for frank and off-the-record exchanges on any subject of importance, the aim sometimes being simply to get a first reaction to ideas he or a delegation might wish to air, sometimes to reach agreement on practical matters such as scheduling of meetings, and sometimes (and most importantly) to face disagreements openly and try to negotiate solutions to them. Repeatedly and throughout the Round, green-room sessions served to hammer out solutions to some of the most difficult problems that arose in the negotiating groups. Even when they failed to find solutions, the meetings served the essential purpose of alerting capitals to the existence of serious difficulties that would require hard decisions, probably at political level. The same green-room technique was to be adopted quite successfully at the ministerial meeting in Montreal, and less successfully in Brussels.

Dunkel travelled widely, visiting the capitals of all the countries active in the Round, explaining current issues to responsible ministers, learning their concerns first-hand, and speaking to many public and private audiences and to the local press. On some occasions his task was simply to give an objective view of where the negotiations stood; on others, he sought to establish the precise positions of governments on disputed issues, with the aim of helping to broker solutions in Geneva. To a lesser extent, his deputies and other senior members of the Secretariat performed similar roles throughout the Round.

Many other meetings, official and unofficial, acknowledged and secret, contributed to the process of steering the Round. Inside the GATT building, developing countries held regular informal meetings which allowed them to compare assessments of progress and to keep the smaller delegations, which found it difficult to be represented in all negotiating meetings, abreast of what was happening. The Latin American countries and the members of ASEAN discussed their positions regularly. EFTA members and particularly the Nordic countries which – like the ASEANs – generally spoke through a single negotiator in each group, met at least weekly. The member countries of the European Community "coordinated" their views before all meetings to settle the line the Commission representative would take. Every Friday the "Article 113 Committee" (named after the Treaty of Rome Article that prescribes a common external trade policy) would bring together in Brussels the Geneva-based EC representatives and national and Commission trade policy officials.

Nor was this all. The periodic ministerial-level meetings of the Quad (the Community, represented by its Commission, the United States, Canada and Japan) and of the Cairns Group of agricultural exporters were supplemented by meetings of the same countries' Geneva ambassadors. The De la Paix Group, essentially the countries that had drawn up the breakthrough draft text for Punta del Este, found common ground in spite of widely varying national concerns in their shared desire to keep the negotiations moving forward. Similarly, work in several of the negotiating groups was supported by informal meetings of "Friends": delegates who wanted to see progress on the subject concerned who discussed current issues and, on occasion, prepared draft proposals that subsequently were put forward in the name of one or more of the participating countries. These "Friends" meetings were to become increasingly important when formal negotiations in some of the groups were hindered or blocked.

At the political level, the Uruguay Round was always on the agenda of meetings of economic and trade ministers, although it became a leading issue only after the Montreal meeting showed that the negotiations threatened (or promised, according to one's point of view) to force changes in long-established major policies. Communiqués of the annual economic summit meetings of the most industrialized countries, of the OECD Ministerial Council, the ministerial committees of the IMF and World Bank, and of innumerable other meetings of regional groupings around the world recorded agreements to push the negotiations forward or to pursue particular objectives. Resolutions of the United Nations and its constituent agencies echoed the views expressed in Geneva. On the whole, these Ministerial Declarations provided signals of political-level attention and concerns, but seldom had much visible impact on the negotiations. Indeed, the repeated failure of annual pledges by the Summit participants to accelerate and complete the negotiations became obvious to all, and the subject of much press ridicule.

The press itself, and public opinion, was to be an important influence on the Round. The Kennedy and Tokyo Rounds had been news, and even on occasion made the front pages of the more serious papers, but there was no precedent in GATT negotiations for the continuous and often intense interest shown by the media in the progress of the Uruguay Round. This interest, already evident in the coverage of the 1982 and 1986 ministerial meetings, grew throughout the Round as it became clear that important national policies, and the futures of identifiable jobs and industries, were at stake. At the mid-term meeting in Montreal the number of registered journalists topped 600, and this figure was to be far exceeded two years later in Brussels. Equally important, the media continued to follow developments closely between the big meetings. So, increasingly, did a number of non-governmental pressure groups, although most of these raised their voices only in the final stages of the Round. The academic community held numerous conferences and published papers which helped to stimulate and further debate, particularly in Europe, North America and India.

The first full expression of this worldwide concern about where the negotiations were heading, and what they implied for international relations, economic growth, development and the future of particular industries and jobs, came with the mid-term review meeting of ministers of the participating countries in Montreal in December 1988.

Chapter IV

The mid-term review

Lack of sufficient high-level political attention and guidance, it was widely thought, had been a main reason why the Tokyo Round of the 1970s dragged on so long. At Punta del Este, ministers resolved not to make the same mistake in the Uruguay Round. They agreed that the guiding body of the Round, the Trade Negotiations Committee, should meet "as appropriate" at ministerial level. With the negotiations expected to last four years, and the initial year or two likely to be largely taken up with studies and proposals, it seemed probable that the intended halfway point in the Round would be a good moment to bring ministers together again. By early 1987, the United States was suggesting that it might be possible to reap an "early harvest" of interim results from the Round, and that this could appropriately be sought through a mid-term ministerial review. Many countries doubted whether a significant early harvest could be achieved. As far as they were concerned, the Round was a whole: they were not going to allow it to move forward in some areas, if others in which they were more interested were left behind. However, they were prepared to see if interim results could be achieved, and in any case they accepted that a mid-term review of progress could be useful. Discussion of the proposal went forward in Geneva, and in February 1988 the TNC took the formal decision to meet at ministerial level in Montreal in the following December.

Preparatory discussion in Geneva, as well as political direction provided by a summit meeting of the seven largest industrial powers in Venice in July and by meetings of the informal group of trade ministers in Germany and Pakistan all helped to define the issues to be covered in Montreal. The detail was spelled out in reports from each of the 14 negotiating groups concerned with trade in goods, consolidated in November into a single report by the GNG, and in a separate report from the negotiating group on services. Much of both reports was devoted to an account of meetings held, and views expressed. What mattered, however, was the long list of recommendations and issues on which ministers were asked to decide.

By the time that ministers assembled in Montreal, in early December, a package of possible decisions was shaping up, helped by a virtually nonstop week of green-room sessions in Geneva in which each negotiating group's report was subjected to a concerted effort to reduce differences and offer clear recommendations. In three areas, negotiations had advanced to a point where substantive decisions – a true "early harvest" – seemed possible. These were tropical products, dispute settlement, and two institutional issues – trade policy reviews and future ministerial meetings.

Of the other negotiating subjects (including some that were highly contentious), most either required no high-level attention at this stage, or needed only decisions on which agreement appeared close. Six of the 15 negotiating groups had indeed been able to reach full agreement on their reports, which had accordingly been adopted by the GNG, and needed no ministerial action beyond endorsement. These were Non-Tariff Measures, Natural Resource-Based Products, GATT Articles, MTN Agreements and Arrangements, Subsidies and Countervailing Measures, and TRIMS.

Half a dozen of the remaining negotiating subjects, however, were clearly approaching a moment of truth: they required fundamental and often difficult decisions that would in large part govern the eventual results of the Uruguay Round. In particular, the United States and the Cairns Group were looking for clearer definition of the long-term aims of the agricultural negotiations, as well as an agreement on short-term policies. Developed countries in general wanted a commitment to negotiate on standards of protection for intellectual property and their enforcement. Developing countries were looking for early results on tropical products and for concrete pledges on key issues in the negotiations on textiles and clothing. Beyond these specific concerns, the outcome of the Montreal meeting was seen as a possible indication of prospects not only for the Round itself, but also for international cooperation in response to a worldwide slowdown in economic growth, and strong protectionist pressures.

Montreal

With these large interests at stake, underlined by a pre-meeting exchange of strongly opposed statements on agricultural objectives from the US and EC, the Montreal meeting attracted support and press attention on a scale never before experienced in trade negotiations. More than 1,000 delegates, including over 90 government ministers, crammed the cavernous plenary meeting hall of Montreal's Palais des Congrès for the opening session, addressed by the Canadian Prime Minister, Brian Mulroney. Over 600 journalists were present to report on the proceedings.

The meeting also saw the first big agricultural demonstration of the Round as Canadian dairy farmers, joined by contingents of farmers from Europe and elsewhere, staged a large protest parade through the streets near the meeting hall, marking their anxiety that delegates would bargain away their livelihood. Later in the Uruguay Round, the farmers' demonstrations grew larger. (In Europe and East Asia they sometimes degenerated into riot.) In due course other issues, too, such as the feared effects of the intellectual property negotiations on the price of medicines and seeds, and of trade liberalization and tougher dispute settlement rules on protection of the environment, were to agitate public opinion and lead to protest meetings and demonstrations in several countries. But the farmers' demonstration in Montreal was the first that caught the public eye, and was an indication that the negotiations, far-reaching in their potential impact on long-protected industries and on domestic as well as international policies, were indeed touching highly sensitive interests.

While ministers of each participating country set out their concerns in policy statements to the huge plenary meeting, negotiators got down to work on the issues that remained unsettled. Initially groups of delegates from a dozen or fewer countries most interested in a particular issue would meet under the chairmanship of a senior official and, with Secretariat help, try to clear away minor issues, define clearly those remaining choices that they could not themselves agree on, and produce recommendations for ministerial action. Although most of the people concerned were the same officials who had been negotiating in Geneva, progress was easier because time pressure forced quick reactions to new ideas, more senior officials from capitals joined in, and ministers were available to give guidance. The results of these discussions were then brought to larger negotiating groups, presided over by ministers, which worked on the same principle as the Geneva green-room meetings. The key unresolved issues were faced openly. Countries which still could not agree explained their difficulties; other countries would put forward suggestions for reconciling the different views; these suggestions, and proposals by the ministers chairing the meetings would be discussed privately, sometimes after the delegations concerned had consulted their governments. Some of the most difficult issues were brought to an informal TNC group, chaired by Dunkel.

Working this way, the Montreal meetings soon made useful progress, reaching agreement over three days on five of the nine negotiating subjects on which substantive ministerial decisions were needed.

First, the expected early harvest was gathered in, in the shape of agreements on tropical products, dispute settlement, and the two institutional questions.

The tropical products negotiators had been reasonably confident that they could produce results in Montreal, but much less sure that the liberalization would be substantial. Developed countries were reluctant to act unless they were certain that all of them would contribute, and were holding out for some show of reciprocity from developing countries. Some developing countries were prepared to contemplate making offers but wanted reassurance that these would earn a worthwhile response. The chairman and Secretariat responded by organizing what became known as "dark room" meetings, in which the negotiators met and discussed, speaking personally and without commitment, the offers their governments might be ready to make. Meeting in Montreal over the weekend before ministers arrived, they succeeded in developing understandings which opened the door for serious negotiation. The breakthrough came with the consent by key developing countries that they too would contribute. Non-stop negotiation among officials of a large group of countries began. At three o'clock in the morning of the second day of the meeting, a package was agreed on, just in time for ministers to vaunt their countries' offers in speeches to the plenary session, and for the press to be able to report that the meeting was already bringing results in the shape of the first market-opening agreement – indeed, by a few hours, the very first agreement of any kind – to emerge from the Uruguay Round.

The package was more substantial than expected – much bigger than that achieved in the Tokyo Round, and also more significant since it represented the result of a genuine negotiation rather than a gesture by the richer countries. All the developed countries contributed, mostly with the promise of tariff cuts to be brought into effect as soon as possible and, in most cases, by mid-1989. Among developing countries (some of which had taken the decision to contribute only in the last hours of the negotiation) Brazil, the Central American countries, Colombia, Malaysia, Mexico, the Philippines and Thailand also agreed to reduce barriers to imports of tropical products. Later, other countries were to join them. The concessions affected products in all seven of the groups that the tropical products negotiators had been working on, and were estimated to affect about $20 billion out of total world trade in tropical products of some $70 billion.

Beyond the concrete value of the tropical products agreement as a stimulus to the trade of some of the world's poorest countries was its effect on the Uruguay Round itself. Both developed and developing countries were thereafter to feel greater confidence in one another's seriousness of purpose. Developed countries had made a real early effort in the Round, and fulfilled their promise to give priority to a major concern of developing countries. Developing countries had shown the developed countries that they were prepared to be true partners in the negotiations – not just supplicants; at the same time, they learned that their bargaining power in negotiations would be greatly increased if they were ready to make offers as well as requests.

The dispute settlement text had been essentially settled before the meeting opened. Of the three significant issues outstanding in the GNG's report, one (the 15-month overall limit for handling dispute cases) had been fully resolved. The remaining two, concerning domestic legislation inconsistent with GATT (an EC point aimed at the Americans) and the vexed question of what role parties to a dispute should play in decisions on panel reports, were left unanswered – but both were earmarked for attention in the second half of the negotiations.

The FOGS negotiators spent most of their time painfully hammering out mutually acceptable language for the statement on relationships between trade, finance and debt, with the most difficult discussion concerned, as always, with the question of exchange rates. Eventually the European Community and the United States were helped to find language they could live with. As with most such drafting exercises designed to cloak policy differences, the effort was disproportionate to the results. The text was fated to be forgotten as soon as ministers had agreed to it. There was already agreement to hold ministerial-level GATT sessions every two years. The question of a possible restricted ministerial group was dealt with for the moment by simply deleting any mention of the matter. Most outstanding issues on the trade policy reviews were resolved, but no solution could be found on what to say about visits by Secretariat review teams to capitals. For Brazil, this was an issue of the utmost sensitivity, and neither official or ministerial-level consultations proved capable of settling it. An elegant solution was found by Dunkel in a late-night green-room session: he expressed confidence that GATT member countries would in practice be glad to welcome Secretariat teams, and proposed that the ministerial decision be silent on the question. (Later events were to confirm his judgement. Once the trade policy reviews began, all the countries under review, including Brazil, proved ready to welcome Secretariat visits. The issue had not been whether visits should be made, but whether they were to be imposed on governments.) This cleared the way for provisional introduction of the trade policy review mechanism in 1989, leaving to the FOGS group the task of reaching agreement, when negotiations resumed, on the detailed format of review reports.

There was more good news, even if the agreements reached were less definitive, from the groups negotiating on tariffs and services. Breakthrough for the tariff negotiators came when they agreed to aim at "a target amount for overall reductions at least as ambitious as that achieved by the formula participants in the Tokyo Round". With this objective set – implying an average cut of some 30% – the other outstanding issues for the tariff nego-tiations were quickly agreed to: the aim on bindings was set as simply "a substantial increase", with negotiating credit to be given for such bindings and also for liberalization measures adopted (by implication, by all countries) since June 1986. On services, agreement was achieved on the elements and timetable for the remaining negotiations, and on a list of concepts, principles and rules that could be applied to the multilateral framework that was intended to be the centrepiece of the results in this area of the Round.

These solid achievements, however, were not enough to ensure success in Montreal. On four subjects – agriculture, textiles and clothing, safeguards and TRIPS – there was no breakthrough. On three of the four, agreement might perhaps have been reached, given more time. Agriculture, however, defied solution, and brought the Montreal meeting to an abrupt and premature end.

The difficulty with the agricultural negotiations was quite simple: the two largest participants were not ready to shift from their respective, and incompatible, positions. The United States continued to insist on full liberalization of agricultural trade over ten years; the European Community was prepared to contemplate only limited and gradual reduction in support to agriculture. Green-room meetings during the first two days in Montreal brought only a sterile repetition of known views. Under pressure from the other participants, the US and EC finally began to seek common ground, but soon failed in the attempt: governments on neither side had yet reached the point of accepting that their original goals could not be maintained. It became obvious that there was no hope that a way forward would be found before ministers left Montreal.

The outcome was dramatic. Whereas the reaction of the EC, US and some others to the situation was to suggest that ministers approve the useful package of results achieved in most other areas of the negotiations, and instruct their negotiators to go back to work on agricultural questions in Geneva, this approach was flatly rejected by the five Latin American members of the Cairns Group. They insisted that until there was agreement on agriculture, they would accept no agreement at all.

The immediate effect of this stand by the Latin Americans was to bring the negotiations in Montreal to a halt: GATT required consensus to reach agreements, and their refusal to go on meant that consensus would be impossible. The longer-term effect was still more important, for two reasons. First, it was made absolutely clear that the Uruguay Round was likely to differ from all previous GATT rounds in that minimal results on agriculture would be unacceptable. For the first time, there were countries that could and would veto agreements, however attractive they might be, unless corresponding progress was made on liberalizing agricultural trade. Second, and perhaps even more surprising, the blockage at Montreal was brought about by some of the smaller participants in the Round. For once, the pace and direction of international trade negotiations was not being dictated by the United States or the European Community.

With the blockage on agriculture, discussion in Montreal on the three other unresolved subjects also came to a halt. Textiles and clothing, safeguards and TRIPS joined agriculture as issues on which ministers had not reached even provisional agreement, and which would have to be settled before the Uruguay Round as a whole could be re-started.

No real progress had been made in Montreal on textiles and clothing. The much-bracketed set of draft recommendations was the subject of intense and lengthy negotiations, but no results had been achieved by the time the meeting was broken off because of the impasse on agriculture. On safeguards, the situation was essentially the same. India's proposed paragraph on selectivity and grey-area measures, which if left unchanged would have essentially settled the core issue of the safeguards negotiations against the strong views of the European Community, was discussed but left unaltered.

Negotiations on intellectual property made some headway in Montreal, but there were no breakthroughs. For the first time, a number of developing countries showed readiness to negotiate on standards. However, India, Brazil and some others insisted that any such negotiations must recognize public interest objectives, including health, development and the availability of technology – arguments which could be used, as the United States and others saw it, to deny protection to pharmaceuticals and other key products. Moreover, the same developing countries wanted any substantive intellectual property negotiations to take place outside GATT itself, perhaps on the model of the services negotiations. Night negotiating sessions produced a draft text by the ministerial chairman of the group, essentially based on the chairman's text forwarded from Geneva, but this was found unacceptable by India. Continuing discussions were halted when the agricultural negotiations broke down.

Faced with the blockage on agriculture, and with substantive agreement in Montreal therefore clearly impossible, ministers agreed that the Uruguay Round as a whole should be effectively suspended for four months to give time to seek agreement on the subjects still outstanding while avoiding the loss of the real progress achieved on other issues. A formal closing session of the Montreal meeting on 9 December decided that the Trade Negotiations Committee should meet again in the first week of April 1989 at the level of senior officials and that the results achieved in Montreal should be put "on hold" until then. Meanwhile Dunkel was to conduct consultations on agriculture, textiles and clothing, safeguards and TRIPS. The April meeting of the TNC should then review the position reached on the entire Uruguay Round package.

The negotiations were back in the hands of the officials, and no further meeting of the TNC at ministerial level was to take place until the end of 1990, the scheduled end of the Round. Montreal had shown the way forward on some issues, but it had also exposed enormous difficulties for the future. And before the Round could progress further, breakthroughs were needed on the four outstanding subjects.

Completing the mid-term review

Back in Geneva, all efforts were focused on reaching agreement on the four blocked issues. The discussions were entirely informal. None of the Uruguay Round negotiating groups met, and although a few delegates exchanged ideas on one or other of the eleven subjects agreed to in Montreal, they could make no real progress as long as many of their colleagues were under strict orders not to resume negotiations until the roadblock on agriculture had been cleared away.

The roadblock was removed, although not without difficulty. The key lay in recognition by the US and EC that they could not continue to camp on their existing positions. Each had to give some ground on general principles. The United States (which perhaps gained some flexibility as a new administration under President Bush took office) accepted that it could not obtain endorsement of its previously sought explicit target of removal of all trade-distorting supports to agriculture. The European Community could no longer avoid some broad commitment to liberalization if it were not to wreck the Round. Other countries, too, had to shift their positions and accept objectives for the negotiations that implied, for some, important and painful later changes in domestic agricultural policies and, for others, a reduction in their ambitions for freer world markets. No one, however, had to make specific commitments at this stage, although all would from now on be committed to negotiating in good faith to achieve objectives which were more precisely defined than in the Punta del Este Declaration and which, in comparison with what previous multilateral trade negotiations had achieved, were highly ambitious.

The April 1989 text, reflecting the more realistic US and EC positions, was based on De Zeeuw's report of the previous November. The "framework" approach originally put forward by the Cairns Group, and picked up by De Zeeuw, now gained general endorsement. For the long term, the objective of the agricultural negotiations was agreed to be "to establish a fair and market-oriented agricultural trading system", with a reform process that would involve "substantial progressive reductions in agricultural support and protection sustained over an agreed period of time, resulting in correcting and preventing restrictions and distortions in world agricultural markets". This should be achieved through negotiations that could involve commitments on specific measures and policies, or on an aggregate measure of support (AMS), or a combination of the two approaches. "Strengthened and more operationally effective GATT rules and disciplines" should cover "all measures affecting directly or indirectly import access and export competition". Detailed proposals should be made by participants by December 1989. For the short term, developed countries agreed not to increase support and protection of agriculture beyond present levels, and said that they actually intended to reduce such support and protection in 1990. All participants also agreed on a work programme for the less controversial subject of keeping to a minimum trade barriers caused by regulations to protect food safety and plant and animal health.

The agricultural agreement also covered other concerns voiced in the pre-Montreal negotiations. Developing countries were assured that special and differential treatment for them was an integral part of the negotiations, that help to agricultural and rural development was an acknowledged element in their development programmes, and that ways of meeting the possible problems of net food-importing countries would have to be worked out. The concerns of Japan, Korea, Switzerland and other countries about food security, the survival of farming in mountain areas and other issues were similarly acknowledged.

As later developments were to show, the April 1989 agreement was open to a wide range of interpretations. Most countries pronounced themselves satisfied because they felt that their original positions were still protected, even if their views had not been fully accepted by their negotiating partners. The major participants each declared their own success, the United States and European Community, in particular, maintaining that their respective aims of eventual abolition of all trade distortions and preservation of the common agricultural policy were still intact, and the Cairns Group expressing satisfaction at its own considerable role in bringing about agreement. The most important single outcome of the agreement was that it allowed resumption of the Round with agriculture still established as a principal element in the negotiations. As far as the agricultural negotiations themselves were concerned, its main value probably lay in the acceptance that a final deal would have to cover all the main means by which governments affect international trade in agricultural products: border measures (tariffs and non-tariffs barriers) that affect access to markets, support given to domestic agriculture, subsidies to exports, and rules and regulations on food safety and plant and animal health.

Although most public attention focused on the agreement reached on agriculture as opening the way to the decisive second half of the Uruguay Round, the agreements reached on the negotiations on textiles and clothing, safeguards, and TRIPS were also important, both in themselves and in completing the mid-term review.

For textiles and clothing, Dunkel's approach was to replace the text on which agreement had proved impossible in Montreal with a new draft whose main elements brought together recognition of the importance of this trade for many countries (particularly for developing countries), recognition also that this was a key sector of the Round and should contribute to trade liberalization, a commitment to begin substantive negotiations, and agreement on major points to be taken into account. This approach yielded results, although only after intense negotiations. The resulting text, which became one of the component decisions of the completed mid-term review, called for agreement to be reached within the time-frame of the Round on modalities for integration of the textiles and clothing sector into GATT "in accordance with the negotiating objective", and specified that these modalities should include the progressive phase-out of MFA restrictions and other restrictions inconsistent with GATT, over a period starting after the end of the Uruguay Round. The decision also stated that the least-developed countries should be given special treatment, and that participants should, to provide a positive climate for the negotiations, "endeavour to improve the trade situation paving the way for the integration of the textiles and clothing sector into GATT".

The way forward for the safeguards negotiations was unblocked by consultations and negotiations which resulted in replacement of India's draft text, which would have straightforwardly outlawed all selective action and grey-area measures, by ministerial endorsement of what were by implication closely similar objectives. The new language called for "a comprehensive agreement on safeguards based on the basic principles of the General Agreement which would aim to re-establish multilateral control over safeguards, *inter alia*, by eliminating measures which escape its control".

The consultations on trade-related intellectual property (TRIPS) issues amounted to a fairly direct continuation of the incomplete discussions in

Montreal, helped both by some further evolution in national positions during the intervening weeks and by the all-important opening on agriculture. The outcome was an agreement on future work that built both on the original proposal by the Geneva chairman, Anell, and on the text that had been under negotiation in Montreal. Its biggest advance was the agreement at last that the Uruguay Round should include negotiations on "the provision of adequate standards and principles" on the availability, scope and use of intellectual property rights. Negotiations were to cover the applicability of the basic principles of the GATT and of relevant intellectual property agreements, as well as the provision of "effective and appropriate" means of enforcement and "effective and expeditious" procedures for multilateral dispute settlement. All these were central planks of the proposals made by the United States and other developed countries. But the agreement also left aside until the end of the Round the institutional arrangements that would put a final TRIPS agreement into force. Moreover, it provided explicitly that concerns about the underlying public policy objectives of national systems of intellectual property protection should be considered in the negotiations, and by implication discouraged unilateral action in intellectual property disputes by calling for stronger commitments to resolve such disputes through multilateral procedures.

With agreement on the four issues that had been left unsettled in Montreal, the way was open to resume the Uruguay Round negotiations as a whole. On 8 April, senior officials meeting in the TNC adopted, in the name of their ministers, not only the four new agreements but the whole remaining package that had been put "on hold" in Montreal. The agreement, published the same day, meant that all 15 of the Uruguay Round negotiating groups had a fresh set of instructions and a clear time schedule. Moreover, it meant that the first concrete results of the Round could be put into force. Four days later, the GATT Council approved, provisionally and until the end of the Round, the new Trade Policy Review Mechanism, the decision to hold regular ministerial-level GATT meetings, and the interim package of improvements to the GATT dispute settlement arrangements. No ministerial meetings were in fact held during the Round, but the trade policy reviews rapidly became a major feature of GATT's regular work, and the new dispute settlement provisions helped in handling a large number of panel cases that arose in the next years.

Dunkel undoubtedly spoke for everyone when he declared after the TNC meeting that "this outcome is good for the Uruguay Round, good for the participants and, above all, good for the multilateral trading system". The mood, however, was one of intense relief rather than exhilaration. The mid-term review had permanently altered the atmosphere of the Round. Four months of the allotted time for the negotiations had been lost, and from now onwards the negotiators would be struggling to beat the clock. The early harvest had been possible only in areas of the negotiations which were comparatively non-controversial, where all participants saw gains for themselves, either in terms of foreign policy (for concessions given on tropical products) or in institutional strengthening of the multilateral trading system of which they all were members. The remaining agreements were helpful in pushing the negotiations forward. Some represented solid progress, in the sense that they defined the negotiating objectives more clearly, and perhaps even set goals more ambitious than those of Punta del Este. But others were essentially procedural. They did not in themselves commit governments to change important policies. The fact that they had nevertheless been so hard to reach made it clear that the final stages of the Round would be very difficult. Rightly, and perhaps even more prophetically than she knew, US Trade Representative Carla Hills warned a Congressional committee a few days after the mid-term agreement was reached that "there is a very long way to go in this process, and the tough part lies ahead".

Chapter V

Second half: 1989–90

With adoption of the mid-term package in April 1989, the focus of the Uruguay Round returned once again to work in the 15 specialized negotiating groups. For the time being, at least, each had its own instructions and timetable, and some had the benefit of breakthrough agreements which enabled them to overcome obstacles that had held up work in 1988. In these circumstances, the Round initially needed little steering, although the Trade Negotiations Community continued to meet at roughly four-month intervals, preceded by meetings of the Surveillance Body and the GNG, and – as always – there were innumerable meetings of heads of delegations in Geneva to discuss problems of both organization and substance.

Periodic meetings of the TNC gave governments the chance to put on record their assessment of overall progress in the Round and of issues in the individual negotiating groups. This in turn gave an opportunity to keep the press and public up to date. The TNC meetings also provided the occasion to reach and record understandings about the broad timetable for the negotiations.

On Dunkel's proposal (itself worked out in informal meetings with the most active delegations in the green room) the TNC agreed in its July 1989 meeting – the first since the Round re-started after the mid-term agreement – a three-phase scenario for the remaining negotiations. The first phase, to the end of 1989, would permit governments to complete the definition of their national positions, table them in each group, and build the elements of compromise proposals. During the second phase, to July/August 1990, the negotiators were to build bridges between these proposals and reach broad agreement in every group. The final phase, running to the end of the year, would be "devoted to polishing the agreements and preparing the necessary legal instruments for final adoption". The same meeting took the decision to hold the final meeting of the Round at ministerial level in Brussels; the date was later fixed as the first week of December 1990. Dunkel told the press that the decision could be read as "a political commitment to end the Round on time".

By December 1989, at its next meeting, the TNC was able to note with satisfaction that most national positions had indeed been tabled, and to conclude that in spite of some specific problems "the scene was now set for the major effort necessary to secure a substantial result in every area in the next eleven months". Four months later, in April 1990, a note of concern was creeping into the TNC's discussions: the second phase was not going according to plan. Dunkel, stressing the encouraging elements in the picture, noted "a very strong collective plea in favour of multilateralism", a clear desire on the part of participants to keep to the ambitious objectives of the Round, a general perception that dramatic changes in the political and economic map of the world had made a strong multilateral trading system more indispensable than ever, and a consequent increase in the relevance of the Uruguay Round. However, it was very difficult, he said, to identify areas of real convergence on substantive issues in the different negotiating areas. This would have been a source of serious worry had it not been balanced by statements indicating readiness to negotiate. The July deadline, he concluded, was crucial for the success of the Round because if it was not possible by then to draw up "the profile of a package", the "rendezvous of Brussels will be in great jeopardy".

It was not until the TNC meeting in late July 1990, with barely four months of the Round left to run, that concern about the lack of progress and decisions in the Round became acute. Shortly before, at the Houston Summit meeting of the world's seven most powerful industrialized countries, their leaders had declared the Uruguay Round to have "the highest priority on the international economic agenda", and had stated their "determination to take the difficult political decisions necessary". Ahead of the meeting, the chairmen of each of the 15 negotiating groups forwarded to Dunkel what was meant to be the promised "profile of results". But many of these profiles were, as Dunkel pointed out, only "a compendium of positions, rather than draft agreements". He acknowledged that they had forced negotiators to focus on concrete options, on issues that needed to be resolved and "perhaps" on potential meeting points. If they had not done more, it was for two reasons: negotiators had not been given new instructions on the adjustment in positions needed to reconcile divergent interests, and linkages between and among negotiating subjects were being used negatively, with negotiators "largely playing hide-and-seek with one another and not revealing their hand".

The outcome of this meeting was agreement on "a radically changed and more urgent approach" to the negotiations, with each negotiating group called on to produce by the first week of October a single text that would identify clearly any points remaining outstanding. From the following week, Dunkel said, "we will have to consider that we are *de facto* in Brussels". Senior officials would have to be in Geneva from then on, with full power to negotiate and conclude agreement. The focus would be on the TNC, which would direct the negotiations with support wherever necessary from the negotiating groups.

Speaking to finance and development ministers in September, at the meeting of the World Bank-IMF Development Committee in Washington, Dunkel told them that the negotiations were now in their crucial closing phase, sketched what was at stake in each area, and called for determination and commitment to achieve success. He did not hint at the possibility of failure. Ministers endorsed his statement, but in the communiqué of the sister Interim Committee they acknowledged that the preparations for the Brussels meeting were not going according to plan: they spoke of "deep concern over delays" and "differences yet to be resolved on several issues that are crucial to an overall agreement".

The rest of this chapter traces the negotiations in each of the 15 groups between the mid-term review and the Brussels meeting. In retrospect, it is easy to see that the negotiations lagged from the first, and that by mid-1990 time was so short, and views on fundamental and interlinked questions so far apart, that the risk of failure in Brussels was already very great. The concern expressed by ministers in Washington in September 1990 was fully justified. It is equally easy, however, to forget that the Uruguay Round went forward, over the entire period from 1986 onwards, in an atmosphere in which the possibility of failure was never even suggested by anyone in a position of authority. Meetings throughout the world, formal and informal, of heads of state, government ministers, officials and professional and pressure groups regularly and increasingly gave prominent place in their discussions (or at least, in their communiqués) to the trade negotiations which were grinding forwards in Geneva, and pledged support to their completion. The difficulties were known, but the need for success, and the political will to achieve it, seemed so strong that even cynical officials who had seen innumerable international initiatives run into the sand did not seriously contemplate the Round's failure. Even if they had witnessed failures in the past, most had also seen surprising successes achieved once their political masters, armed with full powers of decision, were brought face to face with an inescapable need to act.

Throughout this whole period, in frequent speeches and interviews, Dunkel tried to make both business audiences and the general public aware of what the Uruguay Round negotiations were seeking to achieve, as well as the impact their success could have. (Deliberately, he did not at this time raise the possibility of failure, or discuss its possible consequences.) In a typical speech to a conference of European and American journalists in the United States in May 1989, just after completion of the mid-term review, he suggested that the real challenge of the Round was "how good and efficient a multilateral system we want, and to what extent governments and, more particularly, businessmen are prepared to put up with second best". With a very short space of time remaining until the autumn of 1990, when the Round "must and will" end, the negotiating groups were, he pointed out, committed to achieve substantial trade liberalization, to reinforce competition in world trade, to delve into national policies on such matters as enforcement of intellectual property rights which had previously been seen only in a domestic perspective, to achieve long-term fundamental reform of agricultural trade, to take major decisions on the international trade rules, and especially to put in place a "comprehensive and credible" safeguard system, and to create a whole new framework of rules for trade in services. Commenting on the extraordinarily wide participation in the negotiation as "one of its most attractive and necessary features", he added that "we must ensure that every participant comes out of the Uruguay Round with solid benefits". All too prophetically, he emphasized that "the industrial countries have fundamental responsibilities in ensuring the success of the Round".

Later, the focus of the Round would shift to clashes at the highest levels of international and domestic policy. But these did not emerge clearly for another 18 months, when they were to prove decisive in Brussels. In the meantime, and after the traumas of the mid-term review, the action of the Round returned in the spring of 1989 to the small and multiple stages of the negotiating groups.

Market access

Four market access groups continued to meet, and each had its fresh instructions from ministers. But two were from now onwards largely on the sidelines, even though this was not publicly acknowledged. The negotiating group on natural resource-based products was unable to live up to its description: not enough countries, and particularly not enough of the largest participants in the Round, were prepared to negotiate on non-ferrous metals, forestry products, fish or other product sectors in isolation from the main tariff and non-tariff bargaining. The group's remaining meetings were to show its impotence. As for tropical products, the group's meetings in 1989 and 1990 reflected its early success. Most countries had given all they were prepared to give ahead of the final Uruguay Round package, particularly on tropical agricultural products which competed with those of temperate regions. All too clearly, the agricultural negotiations were going to be a fight to the finish, and as long as the outcome of that fight was in doubt, no importer was prepared to make commitments that might reduce its room to manoeuvre in the final bargaining.

Tariffs

Montreal had set an overall target for the tariff negotiations: "at the minimum, the tariff reduction achieved by the formula participants in the Tokyo Round", which meant an average cut of just over one third. It also provided for tariff bindings to be "substantially widened to provide greater security and predictability in international trade", and for negotiating credit to be given for bindings and any liberalization that countries had adopted since 1 June 1986. Developing countries would take part on the basis of the general principles for the negotiations, including those giving them special treatment. Actual negotiation should start on 1 July 1989. The target figure was helpful, but left unresolved the question of the negotiating technique to be used. The decision on bindings, combined with that on developing countries, implied that the

Round should lead to a striking advance on the earlier situation in which the more industrialized among the developed countries had bound virtually all their tariffs on industrial products, while the rest of the world had very few bindings indeed and could raise tariff barriers against imports at will, without offering compensation. It also promised countries accepting bindings that this would not go unrewarded, even if the tariff rates they actually applied against imports were not greatly reduced. These decisions meant that developing countries were expected to make a much more substantial contribution to the tariff negotiations than in the past, but that they would get credit for the large cuts in protection which many of them had recently made, usually as part of broader economic reforms – provided they were prepared to make these cuts permanent.

For the Secretariat, the most immediately worrying issues were the lack of a negotiating technique, the fact that the product coverage of the tariff negotiations was still undefined, and the lack of data from almost all the developing countries which could now be expected to take an unprecedented active part in the negotiations. As far as techniques were concerned, the Secretariat came to the early conclusion that the United States was not going to budge from its position that it would negotiate with others only on the time-honoured basis of requests and offers. Delegations and the press continued to speculate that the US position would change, but it was the Secretariat's assessment that proved right. "Product coverage" was in fact code for "Are we talking about tariff reductions on agricultural products?" – a question which the Secretariat rightly judged would remain unanswered until the negotiations on agriculture were essentially settled, which meant only towards the end of the Round. This was to be one among several factors that delayed real bargaining on market access until the final weeks of the Round.

The problem of missing data was a serious one for all active participants in the tariff negotiations. In the absence of full information from a country on what tariffs it was applying at present and what amount of trade it carried on under each tariff heading, no clear view could be formed of the value of whatever tariff reduction offer it might make. The problem was of very direct concern to the Secretariat itself, since it was responsible for the complex and largely computer-based task of putting trade and tariff data received from governments on a comparable basis, circulating each set of national data to all those others who had provided comparable information, and (later on) recording, analyzing and circulating the tariff offers and requests. The Secretariat also had the task of advising many developing countries, at their request, on preparing their own data and interpreting the information received from others. From summer of 1989 onwards, there was a gradual improvement in the availability of information, but the highly technical task of processing and analyzing it was a constant and increasingly heavy task for a Secretariat team of data-processing and tariff experts right up to the end of the Round. Of the 26,000 pages which embodied the final Uruguay Round agreements signed at Marrakesh, some 22,000 were the detailed national schedules, largely devoted to setting out many thousands of future tariff rates, which emerged from the negotiations on tariffs and other market access issues.

The debate on the negotiating technique to be adopted was taken up by the tariff group once again in its first post-Montreal meeting, and was soon nourished by formal proposals from the European Community, Japan and (somewhat later) Canada. The EC proposed to link negotiations on tariffs and non-tariff measures. It argued for a basically formula approach. Developed countries, and the more advanced developing countries, would cut all tariff rates now over 40% to a maximum of 20%, and would reduce lower rates by between 21% and 50%. Most other developing countries should accept a ceiling of 35% on their tariff rates, with further reductions to be negotiated on a request-and-offer basis. Least-developed countries would give what they could. Japan dropped its earlier proposal for tariff elimination, and proposed that a reduction formula that would yield an average 33% cut be combined with request-and-offer negotiations. The Canadian proposal, addressed to all the market access groups, was for a general approach that would reduce tariffs now over 30% by about 38%, and cut mid-level tariffs by 32%; any resulting tariffs that were 3% or less would be eliminated altogether, and various simplifications would be introduced.

All three of these proposals attracted considerable support. Criticism came mainly from developing countries, with doubts expressed in particular about the basis on which countries might be categorized as relatively advanced, as required by the EC proposal, and on which the poorest countries might be asked to contribute. Tanzania, always among the most outspoken, made a formal statement declaring that it was in no economic position to make any contribution.

For many participants, the main task, following the EC, Japanese and Canadian proposals, was to combine them and so provide the needed general formula for the negotiations. But if three of the Quad participants, the acknowledged key players of the Round, were on the same track, the fourth was not. Although the United States gradually moved to acceptance that other participants could draw up their tariff offers on the basis of a formula if they so desired, it insisted that it would itself negotiate only item by item, dealing with relevant tariff and non-tariff measures at the same time. Moreover, it effectively closed off discussion by putting detailed product-specific request lists to each of its main trading partners, starting in July 1989 with the developed countries, and submitting further lists from October onwards.

In February 1990, after months of fruitless discussion, the negotiators at last accepted an outcome which Australia had presciently suggested as long ago as the previous summer. They accepted that each participant could follow its own approach, although all would be expected to meet their Montreal targets. Offers should be put forward immediately, by mid-March, and assessed from April onwards, taking account of what each country was offering in other negotiating groups. This would be followed by requests for specific adjustments in offers, signalling the opening of detailed and largely bilateral bargaining.

By early April, all the developed countries had made tariff reduction proposals. The offers differed widely. The European Community, the EFTA countries, Japan, Korea and (in reaction to the others) Canada made no offer on agricultural products, on the grounds that this was a matter for negotiation in the agricultural group. In contrast, the United States offered to remove entirely its tariffs on all agricultural items, reflecting the proposals it was putting forward in that group. For industrial products, the EC proposed formula reductions, without exceptions, that would bring its maximum tariff down to 20% and its average tariff down from nearly 5½% to just under 4%. The EFTA countries, generally believed to be aiming to align their tariffs broadly with that of the EC, made similar offers. Canada, Japan and Austria offered to cut tariffs according to the Canadian formula, and Australia and New Zealand also made far-reaching offers. For its part, the United States extended its offer of zero tariffs beyond agricultural products to cover steel, non-ferrous metals, paper products, pharmaceuticals, construction equipment, some furniture and toys and dolls; in a supplementary offer later in the year it was to offer zero tariffs also on beer, distilled spirits and some electronic equipment. These initial "zero for zero" offers, so called because they were conditional on others also abolishing tariffs on the same items, had no immediate impact, but helped to define the sectors on which the most ambitious bargaining was to take place towards the end of the Round. For other industrial tariffs, the United States made no offer, but invited requests that could be met within its negotiating authority to agree to cuts of up to 50%.

Initial offers by developing countries were slow to come. It was not until July that virtually all the more important traders among them had submitted their proposals. They varied considerably. Argentina, Korea, Mexico and Turkey, for example, made quite ambitious offers, whereas proposals by many others were much more limited and consisted mainly of the offer to bind some tariffs at maximum levels – often higher than those currently charged.

For many countries, and especially the smaller and developing countries, there was little incentive to put their negotiating cards on the table in the market access groups as long as so many of the key elements in the bargaining were unknown. Developing countries had their own particular concerns – their desire to have past liberalization fully recognized, and their belief that they should not in any case be expected to make very substantial contributions. But there was also reluctance to come forward as long as the largest players were not making measurable offers in key sectors. Of all the proposals on the table by July, the Secretariat observed, about half contained no offers on agricultural products (which by definition included a large proportion of tropical products). For textiles, footwear and many other industrial products, the United States proposed only an "offer to negotiate". Yet at the same time, the failure of the developing countries to offer the kind of reductions and bindings for which the developed countries were looking made the latter, in turn, unready to offer further concessions; indeed, they were reported, in bilateral discussions, to be threatening to withdraw some of the offers now on the table. This deadlock was compounded by the more general reluctance to get into definitive bargaining on tariffs and specific non-tariff barriers, as long as the outcome of negotiations elsewhere in the Round, and especially on such ground rules as those governing safeguard and anti-dumping action, remained in doubt.

An informal meeting of trade ministers in April, in Mexico, gave what was seen as a potential boost to the market access negotiations by agreeing to send negotiating teams to Geneva for intensive bilateral talks. A large number of bilateral meetings took place in June and July, but were (according to an internal Secretariat assessment) "absolutely disappointing": they were limited to explanation of national positions, and no specific item-by-item bargaining took place. This was the background against which Dunkel, at the TNC meeting in late July, called on all participants to improve the quality of their market access offers and complete the process of tabling offers by 15 October. Nevertheless, further bilateral meetings in September brought little change in the situation. In the middle of the month, the four market access groups held a joint meeting to ensure that whatever concessions were put forward in one group or the other would be taken into account in overall judgement of what each country was offering. Many participants acknowledged that the negotiations were behindhand and that bilateral negotiations must be speeded up. Shortly afterwards, Lindsay Duthie, chairman of three of the four groups, warned that "many of the participants are still falling short of the level of ambition set by ministers at Montreal – in both qualitative and quantitative terms". He saw real danger that, unless offers were improved by 15 October (the deadline for specific tariff proposals), others would "claw back" some offers already on the table. He was also concerned that no guidelines had yet been set for putting into force whatever concessions might finally be agreed on.

In the remaining weeks before the Brussels meeting, some progress was made. By November, about 50 participants (the EC, as always, counted as one) had made proposals. Innumerable bilateral discussions had been held, as well as six review and assessment meetings by the negotiating groups. A draft Uruguay Round protocol governing non-tariff measures as well as tariffs was worked out, prescribing 1 January 1992 as the starting date for reductions which would be carried out in equal annual instalments. The period over which the tariff cuts would be made had not been decided: some countries argued for eight years (as for the Tokyo Round), others preferred five years. More importantly, however, major problems remained on the substance of the tariff liberalization to be undertaken. Each country's offer was still conditional on a satisfactory response to its requests to its negotiating partners; many offers fell short of the Montreal targets; developed countries were generally dissatisfied with the contributions from developing countries, and especially with what they regarded as an inadequate level of bindings; and there was no agreement yet, in spite of technical proposals made by several developing countries, on how credit might be given for bindings or for autonomous liberalization. In spite of all this, the tariff negotiators, along with the other participants in the market access groups, went to Brussels with the agreed objective of concluding their negotiations by the end of the one-week meeting.

Non-tariff measures

To a great extent, the negotiations on non-tariff measures moved in parallel with those on tariffs. The link was natural, to the extent that a country seeking access for a particular product to a foreign market would be interested in reducing all obstacles placed in its way. Tariffs and non-tariff measures can be interchangeable, and similar considerations arise in negotiations on both: the need for transparency, for some security against re-introduction of the measure, for agreement on whether credit will be given for earlier liberalization, and for a timetable for carrying out the agreed liberalization. Moreover, the insistence of the United States, the largest participant in the Round, on item-by-item bargaining, and on dealing with tariffs and non-tariff measures together, had the practical effect of merging much of the substance and calendar of the two negotiations.

In July 1989, the chairman of the non-tariff measures group put forward proposals on how the remaining negotiations should be conducted. The proposals were not in fact adopted then, because Brazil was unwilling to accept a commitment to negotiate at a time when it was under threat of unilateral action against its exports by the United States who, in turn, stated that it would not accept negotiating rules that did not apply to all participants. (This was one of the clearest of the many occasions on which outside events, in this case the threat of action against Brazil, India and Japan under Section 301 of the US Trade Act, impinged on the Round.) However, many countries, including the European Community, stated that they would be guided by the proposals, and these were finally adopted in February 1990. They made it clear that the group's work would henceforth be on two tracks: negotiations to draw up new multilateral rules on those measures for which this approach might be agreed, and bargaining for the removal or modification of particular national measures. On the first track, the group was to examine subjects suggested as suitable candidates for new rules. For the negotiations on specific measures, the possibility of applying formula-based approaches was retained, but the agreement consisted largely of detailed provisions for request-and-offer negotiations, with a deadline of end-March 1990 set for submission of initial request lists, and the responding initial offers by mid-May at the latest. "Appropriate recognition" should be given for liberalization measures already adopted, and the group would examine proposals aimed at ensuring that concessions were not subsequently nullified or impaired.

In fact, numerous proposals had been put forward for the negotiations before the mid-term review, and had been summarized and classified by the Secretariat. A revision of the Secretariat list issued in April 1989, when the negotiations resumed, showed clearly where most countries' interests lay. Only Australia, New Zealand and Turkey had suggested that a formula approach might be appropriate for some categories of measures. In the absence of greater support, and with US refusal to negotiate on tariffs on a formula basis, there was no chance that the approach would be adopted. The same three countries, along with Czechoslovakia and Poland, were interested in the possibility of negotiating multilateral rules to cover the use of a wide variety of non-tariff measures, including such matters as customs formalities, marking requirements and import taxes. Only one issue, preshipment inspections, was agreed by the European Community, Japan and the United States to be an appropriate subject for new multilateral rules. Japan and the United States were both interested in negotiating on rules of origin, and the EC and Japan shared an interest in rules for import taxes, partly because the United States had not yet acted on a relevant panel decision that had gone against it on "customs user fees". As it turned out, just two subjects were finally taken up: preshipment inspection and rules of origin. Significantly, the great bulk of the Secretariat note was concerned with specific national non-tariff measures for which countries proposed request-and-offer negotiations.

Although all the work of the non-tariff measure group went forward simultaneously, clarity demands that its different elements be described separately.

The negotiations on preshipment inspection had the potential to produce a North-South clash, but fortunately did not do so. Typically, these services were used by developing countries, but carried out by private companies in the developed countries. From the point of view of the developing countries which used them – Indonesia was the largest, but African countries accounted for a large proportion of their customers – they were a valuable tool, especially for countries in balance-of-payments difficulties or those which relied on customs duties for a significant part of government revenue. Such inspections helped prevent fraud and the illegal export of capital, and compensated for weaknesses in the importing countries' own administrations. From the point of view of the exporting countries, the inspection companies were an irritant on their own doorsteps, blamed for causing delays to export shipments, second-guessing contractual prices and other conditions, disclosing confidential information and adding to exporters' costs. Two countries, Germany and the United States, decided to take action, and began to develop their own national rules and legislation to regulate the activities of these companies.

In GATT, complaints about preshipment inspection had first been raised officially in 1984, when the European Community objected to aspects of its use by Nigeria. The subject had been pursued in the Committee on Customs Valuation, because of claims that companies were not following valuation rules.

It was not raised during preparations for the Uruguay Round, and was brought up only after a GATT Council meeting in 1987 when several governments concluded that pre-inspection problems would probably best be handled as part of the larger negotiation. Discussion on the non-tariff measures group began with an Indonesian statement in July 1988, but got seriously under way only after May 1989, when Zaire, supported by other user countries, argued that preshipment served important and legitimate interests of developing countries. It felt that a code of practice drawn up by an association of the companies concerned should make multilateral rules unnecessary. This view was challenged by the United States and backed by several other countries including some developing-country exporters. They doubted whether the code of practice would meet their concerns, and also wanted a mechanism to settle differences that might arise over decisions on valuation or other matters taken by preshipment inspection companies. Among user countries, there was a gradual shift of view over the following months, probably reflecting their realization that multilaterally agreed rules which they had helped to draw up would be preferable to differing rules unilaterally developed by the exporting countries, and easily imposed by these countries because the inspections took place on their territory. The change was signalled in a statement by Zaire in November 1989 accepting the idea of a GATT instrument that would establish disciplines for preshipment inspection but safeguard the right of developing countries to use it. Acceptance of this twin aim by all concerned made it possible to negotiate constructively.

Negotiations were effectively launched by the group's decision in February 1990 to have the Secretariat draw up, and discuss with delegations, a paper recording the points so far put forward for possible inclusion in an agreement. This was followed by a further Secretariat text that brought out points of agreement and disagreement. By July, the elements of an agreement were taking shape, with draft provisions setting out how inspection companies should be used, and how they should carry out their work, on the basis of rules to govern the behaviour of the user, the exporting countries, and the companies themselves. There were however still a large number of detailed questions open, covering such matters as the appropriate time limits for the preshipment inspection companies to complete their inspections and take decisions, the confidentiality of contractual information, the basis on which companies might legitimately request that prices be changed, the official status to be given to the companies by exporting governments, and the structure and terms of reference of an independent review mechanism to settle disputes.

By October, negotiations had advanced sufficiently to allow their chairman, Peter Williams of the GATT Secretariat, to circulate a draft text that had only three main points unsettled. Of these, the most difficult concerned the key issue of the grounds on which an inspection company could reject a contract price agreed between the importer and exporter. The crucial difference concerned whether the agreed price could be checked against that of similar goods exported to a different country: importers saw this as necessary to avoid overcharging; exporters (principally the United States and the Nordic countries) felt this was beyond the legitimate role of pre-inspection: as they saw it, it should not be to pass judgement on whether profit margins or contractually agreed prices were high, but to ensure that goods were not being invoiced fraudulently to evade customs duties and/or foreign exchange restrictions. The other points at issue, as the draft agreement went to Brussels in December 1990, concerned the action to be taken when an independent panel had ruled on a dispute, and the relationship between the agreement and national laws. Agreement in principle had already been given by the International Chamber of Commerce and the International Federation of Inspection Agencies, representing exporters and inspection companies respectively, to administer the arrangements for settling disputes.

The negotiations on rules of origin followed similar lines, although there was greater disagreement over whether they were needed at all, and what they should cover. Rules of origin are essentially a necessary tool for the application of trade measures to particular products. By defining which countries are the source of particular internationally traded goods, they help also to define the treatment which they should be given when they are imported. For example, their origin may qualify them for reduced or zero import duties (because they come from a developing country granted generalized preferential treatment, or from a partner in a free trade area or customs union) or may on the contrary identify them as subject to penalty anti-dumping or countervailing duties, or as being excluded altogether from entry because they do not fall within quantitative limits under a safeguard action or for other reasons. Traditionally, a country of origin has been recognized on the basis that a product has been wholly produced there, or has undergone substantial transformation there. (Transformation may be measured in terms of the percentage of value added or of the specific manufacturing or processing operation undergone, or of the processing having been such as to move the product from one customs classification category to another.) The whole subject has become increasingly complex with the worldwide trend to carry out successive steps in production in different countries, and with the growing importance of preferential trade agreements.

Ideally, all countries would use the same bases to determine origin, and thereby avoid differences that add to the difficulty and uncertainty faced by businessmen engaged in international trade. Standardization or harmonization of rules would also reduce the temptation to governments to use rules of origin as a barrier to trade in their own right. Since the Harmonized System for tariff classification was developed by the intergovernmental body concerned, the Customs Cooperation Council (CCC) – now the WCO (World Customs Organization) – and successfully introduced worldwide after 1988, the possibility of also harmonizing rules of origin has seemed attainable and attractive. It was clear that this would be a highly technical task, and in any case could not be fitted easily into the framework or time limits of the Uruguay Round. On the other hand, rules of origin had a broader trade policy significance which, to some countries, seemed appropriate for discussion in GATT.

In June 1989, Japan, with US support, called for establishment of harmonized rules of origin, as well as a mechanism for notification, consultation and dispute settlement. The European Community and the EFTA countries were initially reluctant to take up the subject because they thought it better suited to the more technical CCC. They also believed that the discussion should be confined to rules governing trade on an MFN basis, leaving aside the rules of origin used by preferential arrangements such as their own. During the autumn of 1989, Hong Kong, the United States, Japan and the European Community all put forward proposals. The United States was particularly keen, and the European Community least so, to see an early start on negotiations to harmonize rules of origin. Gradually, the proposal for harmonization, agreed to be a desirable long-term objective, was separated from the idea that it would be useful to define in the trade policy setting of the Uruguay Round negotiations some basic guidelines to govern the use of such rules. Among these guidelines, it was suggested, should be requirements that rules of origin ensure non-discrimination, transparency, fairness, objectivity and predictability, and that they should be simple, and provide for notification, consultation and dispute settlement. In February 1990 agreement was reached that the group should seek to define such policy principles to govern the application of rules of origin. There was however no agreement on whether the principles should cover rules for preferential arrangements, or the precise objective of the negotiations, the role that the CCC should have in them, or the desirability of making special arrangements for dispute settlement.

An informal drafting group on rules of origin, chaired by the Secretariat, met from May onwards, and a first draft agreement emerged in July. Further work during the autumn resulted in a gradual narrowing of the remaining differences. Well before the draft agreement went to ministers in Brussels, two central questions had been answered: there was agreement to embark after the Uruguay Round on a three-year work programme, in cooperation with the CCC, to harmonize rules of origin; and there was agreement that in the meantime some general principles for application of such rules would be useful. Among the few undecided points, the most important was whether the principles should apply to rules used under preferential agreements.

The request-and-offer negotiations on non-tariff measures also took place mainly from February 1990 onwards, and as the year went on became increasingly indistinguishable from the tariff negotiations already described. They lagged behind schedule. Whereas requests were supposed to have been submitted by end-March, only eleven had been received by April, 25 by May, and 34 by July. The offer situation was strikingly worse: although initial offers should have been in by mid-May, there were only five on the table by July. The pace of work speeded up in the autumn, as the negotiations were effectively combined with those on tariffs, and the shared date of 15 October was set for all offers to be in. But delays continued. The United States and the European Community failed to meet the deadline; other countries saw no reason to show their hands as long as their leading trading partners did not do so. The EC initial offer came only on 23 October, and the US followed on 29 October, barely a month before the supposedly final Brussels meeting would open.

Offers of this kind cannot be meaningfully summarized since they consist of large numbers of very specific proposals, each usually of interest only to a few supplying countries, often not even known at this stage to other countries, and always conditional on what would be offered in response. Comparison is even harder if the offers are not on the same basis. The EC offer consisted of long lists of products, defined in terms of their Harmonized System nomenclature, for which the Community was prepared, in response to requests made by other countries, to lift non-tariff measures such as quantitative restrictions. The most significant aspect of the EC list was what it left out: it did not cover agricultural products or measures related to the work in other negotiating groups. The United States, which had put over 15,000 requests covering both tariffs and non-tariff measures to 36 countries, in response made a complex initial offer, again covering both tariffs and non-tariff measures, that included the elimination or modification of measures affecting agriculture, voluntary restraint arrangements on steel, government procurement and standards. In its case, the obvious criticism to be made, by those few people who had both seen the US offers and had time to assess them, was that many of these offers were unlikely ever to become reality since they were conditional on agricultural liberalization that the European Community and others would not accept.

Essentially, the Uruguay Round negotiations on tariffs and specific non-tariff measures came together during the autumn of 1990 as a single effort to arrive at the highest possible degree of liberalization of both kinds of market access barrier. The merger was signalled by the draft Uruguay Round Protocol sent to ministers in Brussels, which covered both tariffs and non-tariff barriers. The commentary which accompanied it promised that, for both, negotiators would be holding intensive bilateral negotiations with the aim of completing them by the end of the Brussels meeting.

Natural resource-based products

In theory, the negotiating group on natural resource-based products continued to have a life and purpose of its own in the period between Montreal and Brussels. In fact, it was largely going through the motions of independence. To the extent that it found matter for discussion distinct from the work going on in the tariff and non-tariff measure groups, this largely took the form of fresh attempts to raise and pursue ideas that had already, before Montreal, been shown to have little or no chance of being generally acceptable. Thus the United States and Australia both urged negotiations on energy-related products (Australia's interest was mainly in reducing other countries' subsidies to coal producers). Australia also more generally pressed for negotiations to achieve an overall reduction of one third in the level of barriers affecting trade in natural resource-based products. There were continuing differences over whether actual negotiations should take place in the group, and whether, if they did not, negotiations on fish should be combined with those on agriculture.

In terms of procedures and meetings, the group remained active to the end of 1990. It agreed on negotiating procedures in March 1990, with provision for countries to make specific proposals to the group, and also to notify requests or offers made in other groups. It held meetings both on its own, and jointly with the other market access groups. In November, it assessed the contributions that were on offer for natural resource-based products from 34 participants. As far as specific liberalization efforts were concerned, the action was taking place elsewhere – essentially in the tariff and non-tariff measure groups and in the groups working on new disciplines on subsidies and other matters. The draft agreement that went to Brussels contained no separate text on natural resource-based products.

In substance, however, important negotiations on an essentially sectoral basis were to continue right up to the end of the Round, and to bear useful fruit. These included the so-called zero-for-zero negotiations, broached by the United States in 1990 in the context of the tariff group, but pursued energetically only in the final months of the Round. While most of the product sectors covered were manufactures, both non-ferrous metals and forestry products were included. For natural resource-based products, the success of the Round has to be assessed in terms of the liberalization commitments finally accepted by the participating countries, not by the early eclipse of the body officially in charge of negotiations on them.

Tropical products

The fate of the negotiating group on tropical products was very similar to that of the group on natural resource-based products, just described. There was an important difference, in that the group's negotiations had already produced the liberalization package agreed to in Montreal. But the parallels were considerable: both groups continued to meet, and to hear ambitious proposals; both adopted negotiating plans and timetables for 1990; both reviewed the tariff and non-tariff requests and offers that affected the products for which they had responsibility; and, in practice, both languished because the real negotiations were taking place elsewhere. For tropical products, there was an additional factor: prospects for liberalization were largely bound up with what could be decided for agriculture as a whole, and the agricultural negotiations were effectively deadlocked.

There was no separate draft or package on tropical products in the texts that went to ministers in Brussels. It was assumed that whatever results might be achieved, including confirmation of the interim package agreed to in the mid-term review, would be folded into the schedules of specific tariff and non-tariff concessions attached to the Uruguay Round Protocol, or covered by the agreements to be reached on agriculture and other subjects.

Rule-making

For all four of the negotiating groups concerned with the GATT rules, the mid-term review had essentially been no more than an occasion for stock-taking. Three of the groups – subsidies, MTN codes and GATT Articles – had reached agreement in Geneva on what they would ask ministers to say. In the fourth group, safeguards, India and some other developing countries had tried to force an early decision on critical questions, but had not really succeeded. The time had now come for real negotiation.

Safeguards

The mid-term decisions called on the chairman of the safeguards negotiations to draw up a draft text of a comprehensive agreement on which negotiations could begin in June 1989, and also invited participants to put forward their own texts and proposals. By June, the negotiating group had before it both a chairman's text, drawn up by Maciel with help from the Secretariat and input from delegations, and proposals from the United States and European Community. From this point onwards, the safeguards negotiations were seriously engaged.

The US proposal was essentially a revision of its ideas of the previous year. The five options for a safeguard regime previously envisaged were now pared down to three: non-selective, but recognizing that a continuation of grey-area measures would then be probable; normally non-selective, but allowing selective action subject to conditions that would be a disincentive to acting in this way; and non-selective or selective, with consent of the exporting country required in the latter case. This third option, the United States pointed out, would give the greatest flexibility and therefore be least likely to be accompanied by continuation of grey-area measures. But it emphasized that it had not made a choice of its own among the three options. Other features of the US proposal were that safeguard action might take the form of a tariff increase of up to 50 percentage points or a quota restriction based on recent trade, that the maximum period should be eight years (or five years for a selective action), with progressive easing of the safeguard action, that compensation or retaliation should be allowed, and that there should be a standing safeguards committee.

The European Community's proposal was of great significance because it introduced the concept which was to offer a way out of the black-and-white confrontation over selectivity. The Community believed that tariff increases would often be the most appropriate form of safeguard measure. However, it suggested that quantitative restrictions, normally to be set reflecting recent and traditional trade flows, could be adjusted to "take into account the extent to which the pattern of imports has contributed to overall injury, so that quotas could be modulated when necessary to keep imports from certain sources within the limits set by the need to absorb injury". The paper suggested a distinction between short-term safeguards, effective for perhaps three years at most, and long-term action which would be permitted only if an adjustment process were undertaken. It also proposed that safeguard actions consistent with the new rules should not be subject to compensation or retaliation. For the rest, it endorsed an injury definition that was clear and required a causal link to competing imports, gradual dismantling of whatever safeguard measures were chosen, and a permanent surveillance committee.

Both papers were heavily criticized at the time for envisaging selective action, and for other reasons – notably what some delegations saw as a US failure to recognize that Article XIX was only intended to regulate safeguard actions taken against fair competition. However, the Community's idea of "quota modulation", which would combine action against all significant suppliers with some variation in the intensity of restriction, was to be particularly important later.

Maciel introduced his draft safeguards agreement with becoming modesty as a synthesis of proposals already made by participants, formally or informally, "a framework and a general structure to which a lot of flesh will be added by future discussions", and a simple basis for negotiation. In fact, it was a great deal more, for it brought together many elements that were to find their way into the final agreement. This was immediately recognized by the negotiators. Reviewing it together for the first time in September 1989, they gave it a warm welcome (unlike some chairman's drafts introduced in other groups) and, although criticizing some points, accepted it as the basis for their future work.

Maciel's draft took up the Community's idea that there should be an initial time limit for safeguard measures, with any extension requiring justification and adjustment measures for the industry concerned. (His proposal left deliberate blanks for all time periods.) Beyond the maximum period for a safeguard measure, there would be a period in which no further measure could be applied. Measures would be permitted only when there had been an unforeseen, sharp and substantial increase in imports of a product, and this increase was causing or imminently threatening serious injury, determined on the basis of listed criteria, to competing domestic producers. Measures should be applied to products from all sources, but (a careful footnote suggested) "the negotiating group should examine the possibility of exceptions to be applied in special situations (e.g. serious injury caused by sudden increase in imports from a very limited number of suppliers), which would permit the application of selective measures on a mutually agreed basis, subject to adequate guarantees for all exporting countries and stricter disciplines and surveillance in order to prevent abuse". No compensation or retaliation would be due unless the measure did not conform with the rules, or was extended. Tariffs would be the preferred measure, but quotas could be used. Safeguard measures should not be applied against imports from least-developed countries, or developing countries with a minimal share in the market. A standing safeguards committee would oversee the use of safeguards and the phase-out of grey-area measures.

Virtually all the remaining meetings of the safeguards negotiating group over the following year (1990) were devoted to discussing and refining this draft agreement. Although its wording underwent considerable change, the alterations in substance as the draft went through numerous successive editions, formal and informal, were quite small. Positions on secondary issues moved gradually closer. On the key question of selectivity, there was much discussion of how a limited option might be introduced, suitably hedged about with restrictive conditions, and possibly using the Community's idea of "quota modulation". The Community itself put forward a detailed proposal on how selectivity might work, envisaging a sequence of interim and final measures and the possibility of retaliation by the affected country. Most countries, however, continued to see any concession to the concept of selectivity as unacceptably risky – and as long as this was the case, nothing else could be agreed.

At the TNC meeting in July, when Dunkel reviewed the situation reached in each negotiating group, he singled out selectivity as the most critical safeguards issue, and said pointedly that "it seems to me that the onus is on delegations proposing the selective application of safeguard measures to demonstrate that this would strengthen the GATT system and to specify the exceptional circumstances which would in their view justify selective action". The Community in effect responded to this challenge in September, when it insisted that it was not seeking selectivity, which was a cornerstone of GATT, but rather "a limited specific option which would be neither arbitrary nor discriminatory and would be based on an objective assessment of injury". Many delegations, however, professed inability to detect a difference between the Community's "option" and selectivity.

The draft safeguards text that went to Brussels still reflected this deep difference on selectivity, which had become bound up with two other issues: the treatment to be given to grey-area measures, and how safeguard measures should be applied to developing countries. In its Brussels version, the Maciel draft text was accompanied by a commentary that pointed to seven questions that still required an answer. Should selective action be allowed in exceptional circumstances and subject to specific conditions? Should the right to retaliation be waived in certain circumstances, as an incentive to act within the rules of Article XIX? Should grey-area measures be phased out or brought into conformity with the agreement, and if so, how? Should adjustment assistance be adopted as a form of safeguard measure (and if so, should such assistance be recognized as an exception to subsidy disciplines)? What special treatment could be given to developing and least-developed countries? And finally, what should be the length of the various time-periods envisaged, and should safeguards introduced for one member of a customs union be applied against imports from other members? To the first, and most crucial, question, the

ASEAN countries, India and Pakistan gave a prompt answer in the last TNC at official level at the end of November: they were not prepared to accept selectivity.

Subsidies

The mid-term agreement had endorsed the subsidy group's proposed framework for the negotiations. This set out a list of issues to be taken up, mainly in the context of the so-called traffic light approach which would seek to sort subsidies into prohibited (red), actionable (amber) and non-actionable (green) categories and prescribe how they should be handled. The framework was recognized to be flexible, and was accepted as committing no one to any particular outcome. The United States, for one, had made very clear a few months earlier that it had "grave reservations" about the practicability of identifying subsidies as green. Further progress, ministers had agreed, would require specific drafting proposals. For the subsidy negotiators, the year 1989 was devoted to working systematically through the long list of issues set out in the framework. The discussion was helped forward by detailed written proposals from many countries which offered their suggested answers to questions raised by the framework.

Most countries agreed that export subsidies were the leading candidates for inclusion in the "red" or prohibited category. Export subsidies on non-primary products by developed countries were already banned. The United States argued strongly that primary products should be covered as well. It also sought expansion of the prohibited list to include subsidies linked to domestic content or production performance, or given to companies mainly engaged in exporting, and proposed that domestic subsidies, too, should be banned if they exceeded a stated proportion of a company's sales. Australia took a similar line on primary products, and suggested that subsidies that exceeded a set ceiling should also be banned. The European Community (which was insistent throughout these negotiations that agricultural subsidies were a matter only for the agricultural negotiating group) wanted to exempt some primary products from the red list; Canada wanted them all covered. Japan agreed with the United States on the banning of domestic subsidies contingent on use of domestic over imported goods or upon production performance. (It may be noted here that such subsidies are closely related in purpose and effect to trade-related investment measures, which were under discussion in a separate negotiating group.) Canada, Japan, the Nordic countries and Switzerland wanted to turn the 1979 code's "illustrative list" of export subsidies into a definitive banned list; other countries thought this would be a mistake, given (as Australia put it) "the ingenuity of governments in devising new subsidy programmes". India argued the need of developing countries to maintain some export subsidies and, along with Korea, opposed any outright prohibition of domestic subsidies. There was a wide range of views on what action should be allowed against prohibited subsidies, if these were used. Some countries thought countervailing duties should be automatically authorized; others thought that injury to the domestic industry ought still to be demonstrated; yet others believed that the proper course would be to make a complaint, and use the dispute settlement procedures.

At the opposite end of the subsidy spectrum, the group tried to define guidelines under which subsidies could be categorized as "green", or exempt from countervailing action. Canada, Japan and others believed that subsidies that were generally available (such as government services to industry as a whole) should be exempt. Other suggestions for exemption covered specific subsidies with social or economic policy objectives, such as those given to help structural adjustment, regional development and research and development (Canada and Japan); domestic subsidy programmes directed to environmental protection (Switzerland); domestic subsidies without negative trade effects (the European Community); and *de minimis* subsidies (subsidies that did not exceed an agreed minimum level). A technical attraction of the *de minimis* principle was that it could be adjusted, with a higher level permitted for developing countries. The United States continued to be very doubtful that a green or exempt category of subsidies could be justified, particularly since money could so easily be switched from one kind of subsidy to another, but was prepared to consider exemption for such purposes as adjustment assistance and basic aid to infrastructure, as well as *de minimis* subsidies. But it was cautious about accepting the harmlessness of subsidies to research and development, particularly if the subsidies were large, or directed to technologies that would not be made publicly available.

For the in-between, or "amber", category of what the mid-term agreement called "non-prohibited but countervailable or otherwise actionable subsidies", there was a wide range of ideas on how they should be handled. One big difference of opinion, with the United States and Australia on one side and most other countries opposed to them, concerned the long-standing issue of what constituted a subsidy. Most countries saw a subsidy as involving a "charge on the public account". The United States and Australia wanted the concept of "subsidy" to be extended to cover other measures that gave benefits to their recipients: for example, measures that restricted exports of particular inputs, with the effect of making those inputs available more cheaply to domestic producers in the country concerned than to producers elsewhere. The majority view remained that a subsidy had to involve a transfer of funds from public sources to the recipient, either through direct subsidy or a concession on taxation otherwise due, and that any wider definition could open the door to the subsidy rules being used as a general purpose mechanism for trying to solve all problems in international trade and to offset any government measures in support of its traders. On almost all other issues affecting the amber category of subsidies, too, the line-up tended to isolate the United States on one side, seeking clearer but often also broader grounds for countervailing action, with other participants trying to define strict rules that would limit opportunities for their exporters to be harassed by countervailing cases brought without proper evidence that their products were subsidized or causing damage.

A number of different themes were raised in the discussion on how to handle actionable subsidies. The United States, predictably, took the toughest line: domestic industries were entitled to relief from subsidized imports, and the rules should ensure that they could get it. It proposed a large number of detailed changes in the rules to ensure that countervailing duty proceedings would give participants "whether they be foreign or domestic" the opportunity to make their case, that decisions of investigating authorities would be clear and based on the facts and the law, and that procedures would be transparent. The subsidies code's provisions should be supplemented by new rules to prevent circumvention of duties (as, for instance, when imported parts or components found to be subsidized were instead imported already incorporated into finished products of which they formed a major part). The United States also called for additional factors to be considered in determining that a domestic industry was suffering, or threatened with, injury. In contrast, most other participants wanted to tighten the present code's definitions so as to limit the scope for countervailing action. They were insistent that subsidized imports must be shown to be causing or threatening injury before action was taken. Some countries believed that suppliers with a small share of the market could be disregarded as a source of injury; others insisted that the cumulative effect of several such suppliers could be to cause injury. Past experience of unresolved disputes over who could legitimately complain of injury from subsidized imports led to proposals that key terms in the code, such as "domestic industry", and "major proportion" be tied down more precisely, if possible with quantitative definitions. Most countries wanted a "sunset clause", to ensure that countervailing duties were not maintained indefinitely without evidence that they were still needed. Some argued that the public interest might indeed sometimes be served by allowing subsidized imports to continue, and that this factor should be given appropriate weight. There was strong opposition to US ideas on new rules against circumvention. The Nordic countries suggested that compensation should be payable when a government initiated or pursued "manifestly unfounded" countervailing investigations.

Another set of problems discussed concerned the effects of subsidies given by regional governments within a country. The regional problem was raised by the European Community, which here and elsewhere in the Uruguay Round negotiations was particularly concerned that rules should bind not only central governments but also, in federal states such as the United States and Canada, the governments of provinces, states and other sub-federal units which had re-sources and powers that in other countries are reserved to central governments. The Community argued that subsidies by a regional or local government were no different in their effect from central government subsidies and should, if they had effects on international trade, be disciplined in the same way. The group also discussed whether the subsidy rules should be changed to counter the effects of a country's domestic subsidies in hampering exports by other countries to its market, or to offset subsidized competition in third markets. No one could doubt that trade was in practice affected by subsidies in both cases: many recent disputes had been prompted by the difficulty of competing against products which were said to enjoy subsidies in their domestic markets and in the markets of third countries. There was no agreement, however, on what remedial action could be taken. Most participants rejected the idea that countervailing action by the government of an injured exporter would be appropriate: from their point of view this would amount to unilateral action, and the proper course would be to bring a complaint to the GATT body responsible for the subsidy rules.

A further main theme of the subsidy discussions was the treatment to be given to developing countries. In general, developing countries defended their continuing right and need to use subsidies to offset their difficulties and encourage their economic development. In the subsidy discussion as a whole, they naturally favoured arguments that would tend to give them maximum freedom to use subsidies and to reduce the danger that their exports would be subject to countervailing duties. Thus, for instance, India argued that subsidies to reduce a country's international freight costs to generally prevailing market rates should be regarded as "green", while Brazil supported the most stringent possible rules on the initiation of countervailing duty investigations, tight definition of key requirements such as the support of the domestic industry and evidence of injury, and *de minimis* exemptions and non-cumulation of the shares of small suppliers. Developing countries also argued for special treatment, as regards both their use of subsidies and their status in counter-vailing duty actions. They did not accept that export subsidies, when used by them, should be forbidden, and they suggested that *de minimis* levels should be set higher for imports from them than from developed countries. They argued that in any case they lacked the financial resources to inflict injury or serious prejudice on other countries. The least-developed countries, represented here as in many other negotiating groups by Bangladesh, insisted that their needs were so great, and their likely impact on trade so small, that they should be exempted altogether from constraints on the use of subsidies and from liability to countervailing action. The response of developed countries to these claims was fairly uniform. The position of the least-developed countries, as well as of other countries with very low *per capita* incomes, met a great deal of under-standing. For the remaining developing countries, there was less sympathy. The United States and the European Community, in particular, believed that the more advanced countries, and especially industries in developing countries which were internationally competitive, should not escape the disciplines of the normal GATT rules, even if they would have to be given some extra time to bring their practices into line.

By the beginning of 1990, the subsidies negotiating group had covered most of the issues set out in the mid-term framework agreement, had heard proposals from many interested countries, and had been able to form some idea of the support available for each proposal. With the final ministerial meeting in Brussels scheduled for the end of the year, the time for serious negotiation was approaching. At a meeting of the group in February, its chairman, Michael Cartland, undertook to put forward a single draft text as a basis for bringing work to a conclusion. He promised to address all issues but warned that, even though there were still wide divergences among participants, he would attempt to produce a single text, without alternatives. At the group's request, he held back his draft until some remaining issues had been further discussed. During the next three months, he and the Secretariat developed a text which was circulated informally in May and taken up, largely in informal consultations, from June onwards.

Cartland's draft closely followed the structure of the mid-term framework. He proposed a classification of subsidies on the basis of their propensity to distort trade as prohibited, actionable or non-actionable, and also included provisions on countervailing measures, institutions, notification and surveillance, the treatment of developing countries, transitional measures and dispute settlement. Cartland's prohibited list included the export subsidies listed in the 1979 code, as well as subsidies contingent on using domestic rather than imported goods. Signatories would be able to take countermeasures against such subsidies. Actionable subsidies would involve a financial contribution, or income and price support, given by the government to specific enterprises. A country would be justified in taking countervailing measures if an actionable subsidy caused injury to its domestic industry, nullified or impaired its GATT rights, or seriously prejudiced (as measured by the rate of subsidy and the development of exports) its trade and production interests. Non-actionable subsidies would be those generally available, as well as specific programmes for regional development, research and development, protection of the environment, and employment adjustment. Specific programmes would have to be time-limited, degressive and notified to a new Subsidies Committee. Cartland's proposals on countervailing action were extremely detailed. They included the concept of *de minimis* subsidies or imports, but left for negotiation the level at which this should be set. There were other important blanks too: the figure at which complainants could be accepted as indeed representing a major proportion of the domestic industry, the criteria to be used in calculating the amount of a subsidy, and all the provisions to be inserted on developing countries. The draft provided, as the United States had proposed, for action against circumvention of countervailing duties, but for the present mainly displayed blanks to be filled in later on what that action might be.

The Cartland draft proved sufficiently acceptable to be used as the basis for negotiation, although early meetings brought proposals for additions as well as changes. These covered the increasingly pressing problem of how to treat subsidy measures used by former centrally planned countries transforming themselves to market economies, as well as some of the proposals raised in earlier meetings but not included by Cartland because he did not believe they enjoyed sufficient support. With modest changes, the chairman's proposal went to the July 1990 TNC meeting where Dunkel's commentary stated no more than the obvious: early progress on the basis of Cartland's text was necessary, and a solution would have to provide for better disciplines both for subsidies and countervailing duties. In September, Cartland put forward a further redraft, explaining that the text could hardly be rebalanced until some open issues had been resolved. To help in settling these issues, he circulated a set of papers that attempted to provide identifying definitions for subsidies to be regarded as "green", or non-actionable, and that also included a proposal on "quantitative disciplines" and a long draft article on criteria for calculating the amount of a subsidy.

The final weeks of negotiations before the Brussels meeting saw some progress, but also a sharpening of differences. The United States delegation, which was operating under the instructions given to it by Congress in the Trade Act of 1988, called for prohibition of a range of specific domestic subsidies, including grants to cover operating losses, direct forgiveness of debt and loans, guarantees and equity capital provided at less than the government's costs. "Such particularly egregious practices," it suggested, would best be disciplined through quantitative rules, and added that without such improvements to the subsidy rules "we cannot even consider proposals which would make certain domestic subsidies non-actionable". This late proposal – it came barely two months before the four-year negotiations were due to end – met strong criticism, notably from the European Community, which did not accept that such domestic subsidies were necessarily trade-distorting, and from developing countries which regarded them as valuable instruments of government policy. Cartland redrafted his text in November, but could not of course meet all concerns: as he observed in one meeting "in most cases, proposals coming from various participants simply cancelled themselves out". This situation continued to the end. At the group's last meeting, some delegations said they were ready to support the latest text, but many others insisted on putting on record proposals for further changes in the latest draft, ranging from points of detail to more fundamental issues. As Cartland commented, the suggested amendments "had already been proposed by some and rejected by some others on several occasions". He concluded that possibilities for progress at the technical working level had been exhausted, and that remaining difficulties could only be dealt with at political level.

Cartland's November draft, therefore, went forward to ministers as part of the main text for Brussels. The accompanying commentary suggested that the major political problems outstanding concerned precisely the tradeoff the United States had suggested in its November proposal: on the one hand, the level of disciplines to be accepted on domestic subsidies through quantitative thresholds which, if exceeded, would establish that serious prejudice was being caused; and on the other, acceptance of a green category of non-actionable subsidies.

The Tokyo Round codes

In Montreal, ministers had not needed to take any decisions on the negotiations on the Tokyo Round agreements. The mid-term agreement simply endorsed the draft text drawn up in the "MTN Agreements" negotiating group, acknowledging that the agreements clarified and elaborated some very important issues in international trading relations, that their improvement where appropriate would help the stability and predictability of trade, and that the unity and consistency of the trading system would be improved if more developing countries were encouraged to join them. Negotiations were to be vigorously pursued, and to this end participants were encouraged to come forward soon with specific texts.

As before, the anti-dumping, standards and licensing codes made up the core of negotiations in the group, with the remaining issues essentially secondary. During 1989, the negotiating group worked on all these subjects, with the emphasis increasingly on discussion and negotiation on specific texts put forward by individual delegations. From early in 1990 onwards, negotiations on individual codes quite largely shifted into informal groups, which could focus on the complexities of a single topic and make good use of experts in the subject concerned. Each informal group reported at intervals to the main negotiating group.

GATT has often made use of informal groups, and the Uruguay Round was no exception. Experience has shown that once negotiators have become fully aware of the aims and difficulties of all participants, the best way forward may be to exchange ideas and look at possible solutions off the record, avoiding further formal statements that in practice tend only to make positions more rigid. The risk of such groups is that if they leave out any active participant in the negotiations, they lose credibility, infuriate those excluded and may, in consequence, find their recommendations not generally acceptable. While such "lack of transparency" was frequently criticized in earlier negotiations, it was less of a problem in the Uruguay Round, except when critical negotiations appeared to be taking place among even smaller groups of countries such as the Quad.

Anti-dumping

Renewal of discussions on the anti-dumping code showed no narrowing in the gap which yawned between the diametrically opposed positions of the main supplying and importing countries. The suppliers, among which Asian participants were most vocal and active, continued to argue that the anti-dumping rules were being stretched and abused to achieve results that had never been intended, thereby hampering fair trade. They sought stricter provisions on both when and how governments could take anti-dumping action. The importers – principally the United States and the European Community – insisted that their domestic producers were being injured by unfair dumping practices, and that the remedies provided by the code were inadequate. They wanted new rules, in particular, to counter circumvention of anti-dumping action, to deal with "surges" in imports just before such action was taken, and to punish repeated dumping. Each side strongly disliked most of the other's proposals.

The anti-dumping negotiations provide a classic example of a story in which it is hard to see the wood for the trees: the detail tends to obscure the broad picture. To a great extent, the substance of the negotiations, as of the anti-dumping code itself, was made up of discussion of highly technical and apparently minor points, far too numerous to be covered in the present account. In anti-dumping actions, however, success or failure may well turn on technical matters. If, for example, the fact of dumping can be established on the basis of a very few sales at a low price, a complaint is more likely to be accepted as justified than if the rules require judgement to be based on a weighted average of prices over a certain period and in more than one region of a country. The acceptability of statistical sampling techniques to learn the views of an industry, by putting questions to a comparatively small number of companies, or the rules on how lack of response to such questions should be interpreted, may strongly influence whether a fragmented domestic industry is ruled to be suffering from dumping. Rules on what volume of sales shall be judged negligible, and what margin of dumping shall be considered minimal, can be as important to decisions on who shall be hit by anti-dumping duties as they are in the application of countervailing duties. Inevitably, therefore, the anti-dumping negotiations were quite largely taken up with such matters.

During 1989, the negotiating group worked its way systematically through a Secretariat list of all the specific points raised in the first two years of the negotiations, at the same time discussing a series of proposals put forward by several delegations.

Japan and Hong Kong came first. Both wanted stricter anti-dumping rules to prevent governments from acting against what was, they insisted, normal price competition. Both called especially for more precise calculation of supposed margins of dumping. Japan was particularly concerned that "constructed" valuations, in which assumptions have to be made about such matters as profit margins, should be governed by tighter rules. For instance, United States legislation governing constructed valuations assumed that prices of non-dumped goods should include an 8% margin of profit, a figure which other countries thought unduly high: this assumption, they said, could lead almost automatically to judgements that lower-priced goods were being dumped. Hong Kong argued that anti-dumping rules should give weight to the needs of industries and consumers who used the imported goods. It also called for amendments to give more precise definitions of key terms in the code such as "negligible" and "domestic industry", in the latter case specifically rejecting a

US proposal to widen the definition. In October and November, Singapore and Korea made further proposals, on much the same lines. These were welcomed by other exporters but attacked by the European Community as one-sided.

In November it was the turn of the United States to put comprehensive proposals for amendments to the code to meet its well-known concerns: circumvention, including the use of screwdriver assembly plants, input dumping, and repeat dumping. Predictably, these were supported by the European Community but opposed by Hong Kong, Korea and Singapore as attacks on normal business practices.

By this point, it was clear what each participant in the negotiations wanted, and how, in terms of amendments to the code, each proposed to achieve what it sought. A compromise package agreement, however, still seemed possible. As a necessary step towards establishing that package, the group's chairman, Chulsu Kim, prepared a quite lengthy outline headed "Objectives and principles of rules on anti-dumping practices". His paper systematically covered all the subject headings of the anti-dumping negotiations, ranging from how dumping and injury should be established through investigations, the application of anti-dumping measures and the questions of circumvention and repeated dumping, to dispute settlement procedures and the treatment of least-developed countries. This was used to guide a structured discussion in meetings at the beginning of 1990, exploring each issue in turn. Many participants felt the discussion went quite well. Even if, as Dunkel said in April of the Round as a whole, it was hard to identify areas of real convergence over substantive issues, the anti-dumping negotiations were not yet identified as the major problem which they later were seen to be. At the GNG and TNC meetings in April, which set the target of outline agreements by July for each subject of negotiation, anti-dumping was absent from the list of particular concerns mentioned by participants.

Any illusions that an easy compromise might emerge were soon dispelled, however, when an informal negotiating group charged with clarifying positions got down to work in the spring. In May it reported to its parent group that discussions had been held on how to determine the existence of dumping, material injury and circumvention, and that it was aiming to produce comprehensive proposals on revision of the code by the end of June. A month later, it had worked its way through further discussions on circumvention, material injury, investigation procedures, and anti-dumping measures. But the outcome was not happy. Early in July, Charles Carlisle, acting chairman of the informal group, submitted on his own responsibility a draft text to revise the anti-dumping code in which he suggested "possible solutions to problems, taking into account fairness, workability and the degree of consensus in the group". The draft contained no brackets, but was of course designed only to be a starting-point for detailed negotiations. Carlisle, a Deputy Director-General of GATT, included language that reflected US and EC views on circumvention by allowing dumping action against products assembled by screwdriver plants, or in a third country. Although he also suggested many changes reflecting proposals of other countries, including tighter rules on the definition of an industry, "constructed" values, *de minimis* dumping and a sunset clause, these proposals were not regarded by most of the exporting interests as balancing what he had suggested on circumvention. At a tense meeting of the negotiating group shortly before the GNG and TNC were to hold their critical summer review of preparations for the final stage of the Round, developing countries rejected the Carlisle draft as unbalanced and, therefore, an unacceptable basis for subsequent negotiations. They were not appeased being told by the Americans and the Community that they, too, found some of Carlisle's proposals difficult to accept.

Carlisle tried again in August, with a second draft which this time, more cautiously, included alternative (bracketed) proposals to reflect all the views expressed on his first text. In terms of advancing the negotiations, it was clearly a step backward from the first version, but he had little choice in view of the reception the earlier draft had received. Once again, however, his proposals were heavily criticized, and this time virtually all countries joined in the criticism, particularly because they did not see how they could negotiate effectively on a text with so many open issues. They acknowledged that it could be a working tool, but not in itself a basis for negotiations. Dunkel, concluding that criticism so fierce was unfair to the individuals concerned and could put at risk the ability of the Secretariat to fulfil its centrally important role of honest broker, decided that Carlisle and other senior officials should not be asked again to take responsibility for drafts on such sensitive negotiating subjects.

From this point onwards, the anti-dumping negotiations before Brussels took place generally in limited groups concerned with particular issues. The largest, including some 14 delegations (with Carlisle present but making no drafting proposals) continued to work up to the end of October. At this point, the negotiations broke down. Agreement on anti-circumvention measures was as far away as ever, and other issues also remained unresolved. At the level of the negotiating group, nothing constructive could be done, although it provided the setting in September for a strong complaint by Hong Kong, backed by Japan, that both the Community and the United States were applying external pressure on the negotiations, contrary to the Punta del Este standstill undertakings, by introducing new anti-dumping regulations that amounted to unilateral re-interpretation of their GATT rights.

The blockage was immediately discussed in a meeting limited to ambassadors of the main interested countries, chaired by Dunkel. In a technique used to try to overcome difficulties on other issues, delegations of four countries not associated with extreme points of view on dumping were asked to come up with suggested compromise texts. New Zealand was given the hardest task: to suggest a compromise or basis for negotiation on the central issues. Three other countries (Australia, Mexico and Switzerland) were asked to offer solutions to the large number of secondary questions. At an informal TNC meeting on 5 November, Dunkel listed 15 unresolved issues on the anti-dumping code, but reported that intensive negotiations would continue. These were not, however, to succeed. Proposals by the four delegations were combined in a single text that would have given some limited possibility of action against circumvention, as well as modest changes in rules defining dumping and injury. Brief discussions took place; a redraft of the proposals was produced on 15 November. This new text was rejected by the United States and the European Community, and viewed without enthusiasm by other countries. A final version a week later was found unacceptable by both the United States and the Asian exporters.

The draft text sent to ministers in Brussels as "a first approximation" to the results of the Uruguay Round thus included no text at all on the anti-dumping code. All it provided was a list of questions which, as the commentary put it, required political decisions to overcome continuing basic differences. What changes, it asked, were needed in the way dumping margins were calculated (it cited three specific aspects)? What changes were needed in the establishment of material injury, especially in the case of small margins of dumping and small import quantities? What anti-circumvention provisions were needed?

Looking back to the beginning of the negotiations, it was all too obvious that differences between the opposing views on anti-dumping staked out at that time were still entirely unresolved.

Standards

The negotiations on standards had moved forward smoothly and with minimum controversy up to the Montreal meeting. They continued on the same track when they resumed in May 1989, although given only secondary priority in view of the much more severe problems which the negotiating group faced on anti-dumping. Earlier proposals were refined by the countries that had put them forward, and in some cases were put by them into the form of draft texts for negotiation. New Zealand came up with its own version of how the code could give clear recognition to standards for processes and production methods, differing from the United States not only in its approach to drafting, but giving such standards a warmer endorsement. From the middle of 1989 onwards, an informal group discussed all the proposals with the aim of developing negotiating texts. This led in May 1990 to circulation of a "synoptic table" which put the proposals for changes alongside the text of the existing code and thereby defined the work still to be done. By July, negotiations had been carried to a point at which, for standards at least, Dunkel's call for a "profile" of the results that might be achieved in the Round had clearly been met. A good deal of further work was still needed, and the list of issues not fully resolved included most of the main proposals, such as the Code of Good Practice for non-governmental bodies and the extension of the agreement to processes and production methods. Nevertheless, the standards negotiations were fully on track.

Further informal meetings in September and October resolved most of the remaining points. The United States was persuaded only reluctantly to accept the European Community proposal for a Code of Good Practice, having first unsuccessfully suggested that non-governmental bodies should be required only to maintain transparency in their work, rather than report (as the EC proposal required) explicitly on what it was doing. Agreement on this Code was helped by a proposal from the International Organization for Standardization (ISO) that it should cooperate in defining what was good practice. ISO, whose membership includes both governmental and non-governmental standards bodies, had cooperated closely with GATT on the operation of the Tokyo Round code, and its support for the Code of Good Conduct made it possible for the negotiators to reach an agreement which channelled the reporting procedures through it. By the end of October the negotiating group was able to adopt a draft revised code on technical barriers to trade that had some gaps, but was clearly within striking distance of overall agreement. The sole important issue outstanding concerned the obligations of "second-level" governments. A compromise was still needed between those who thought that the new code, like the old, should require that central governments simply do their best to make local governments comply with the rules on standards and testing, and those who wanted it to put the central authorities under an obligation to ensure compliance.

Import licensing

Discussions up to Montreal had shown broad support for some tightening-up of the rules of the import licensing code, and interest – combined with some misgivings – in American ideas on making the code more operational, particularly in order to limit the use of licensing in general. The United States returned to these ideas at the group's first meeting after the mid-term review, but with some change of emphasis. Its main objectives, apart from the detailed improvements which virtually all delegations favoured, were now stated as being a direct link, in terms of scope, duration and trade effect, between the licensing procedure and the measure it was meant to administer; a requirement that licensing be used only for measures consistent with the GATT; and strengthening of notification, review and dispute settlement provisions. Stated like this, the United States was no longer open to the earlier criticism that it was trying, through the "back door" of the licensing code, to limit GATT rights to impose quantitative restrictions on trade. For its part, the European Community did not pursue its earlier proposal to extend the code to export licensing.

At the chairman's urging, the United States produced a comprehensive proposal, co-sponsored by Hong Kong, in September 1989. It took the form of a re-draft of the existing code; the fact that Hong Kong also stood behind it suggested that it would have wide appeal. This was confirmed at a meeting of the group in October, although some countries were concerned that the code's coverage would be expanded by some suggested provisions, such as a requirement that the licensing committee look at the GATT consistency of restrictions covered by the licenses. In response, the United States and Hong Kong produced a revised proposal in November which went far towards easing these worries. From this point onwards, it was fairly certain that an agreement on licensing would be reached and that, in the absence of other proposals, it would be based on the US-Hong Kong draft. From February 1990 onwards, the real negotiation took place in a Secretariat-chaired informal group which reported regularly to the main group. There were no dramatic breakthroughs: none were needed. Instead, there was a gradual narrowing of differences and growing optimism about the outcome. Successive revisions of the draft agreement were made, and the process culminated in late October with agreement in principle on a text with no disputed language at all. The only discord concerned India's desire, in which it had no support, to make acceptance of the agreement conditional on work being undertaken after the Uruguay Round on possible extension of the code to cover export licensing.

The revised licensing agreement that went to ministers in Brussels was not changed in its essentials from the Tokyo Round text, nor was it extended in coverage to the extent that the United States had initially sought. Nevertheless, its teeth had been sharpened. Non-automatic licensing procedures – those used to administer restrictions – were required in future to be limited in their coverage and duration to those of the restrictions themselves, and all new or revised procedures were to be notified. Imprecise obligations in the original code, such as that which specified that the time taken for licensing procedures should be "as short as possible", or that "the minimum number possible" of administrative bodies should need to be approached were replaced with firm numbers and deadlines. Only in one respect – the extent to which the agreement would attract support from developing countries – was it unclear what the licensing negotiations had achieved. At the very least, as a fully negotiated agreement it was a shining exception to the general rule followed by most of the texts that went to Brussels. In fact, no substantive changes were subsequently made in the agreement. For import licensing, this was the end of the Uruguay Round negotiations.

Customs valuation

The proposal to give customs authorities stronger powers to deal with suspected fraud in the valuation of imports was taken up again in October 1989, but serious negotiations began only in the spring of 1990. Before Brussels, the only proposal focusing on prevention of under-valuation came from India. In November 1989, Brazil put forward a paper which not only backed India but argued further that overvaluation of imports was an important channel for illegal capital flight. Discussion in the group showed that not all countries were yet convinced that action was needed, apart from technical assistance to help developing countries in applying the code. However, several developing countries stated that a change on the lines suggested by India could be decisive in persuading them to sign the code. This led to informal discussions among customs experts aimed at meeting the Indian and Brazilian concerns. In March 1990, Kenya, on behalf of the large number of East African countries that were members of the Preferential Trade Area (PTA), made a further proposal to counter under-valuation by giving developing-country customs authorities a permanent right to set minimum values and to add on to transaction values discounts given to some importing agents and distributors. There was considerable reluctance to go along with this proposal. Many code signatories felt it would reintroduce practices which the code had been meant to stamp out, and also create two tiers of membership.

By July, a draft ministerial decision had been worked out in the negotiations to meet the Indian and Brazilian concerns. It gave customs ad-ministrations which had "reason to doubt the truth or accuracy of the declared value" the right to call for further information and, if still unsatisfied, to move from the transaction value to the other valuation methods of the code. Essentially unchanged, the text was included in the Brussels ministerial document, but with a warning attached: several developed countries made it clear that they expected the decision to lead to increased participation of developing countries in the code. The Kenyan-PTA proposal was also mentioned in the Brussels document, but referred to the code committee for "sympathetic consideration" of individual requests. In substance, this was the end of the negotiation on customs valuation. The most important change later in the Round was to be made indirectly, when the decision to make most codes applicable to all members of the successor organization to GATT effectively resolved the issue of developing-country acceptance.

Government procurement

Government procurement also raised no great difficulties. The first substantial development after Montreal was the introduction in July 1989 of proposals by the European Community that envisaged a transitional status for possible new members of the code. These very tentative proposals, which reflected discussions in the code committee, would have established limited rights and obligations with the aim of allowing, in effect, a period of trial membership. At the beginning of 1990, Korea reverted to its proposal, made just before Montreal, for a gradual build-up of commitments by new developing-country signatories. The proposals by Korea and the Community, together with the original 1987 proposal by India, were discussed in meetings of the negotiating group and in informal consultations, but were finally abandoned in October in the face of (in the words of the group's chairman) a "lack of necessary interest shown by other participants". The final outcome was the negotiation, in informal discussions held after the final meeting of the negotiating group, of a brief draft agreement which would "invite" the code committee to endorse a number of "clarifications" about accession procedures to the code. While the text did not offer a solution to the key problem originally identified by India – the effective veto over accession available to any existing signatory because of the consensus requirement for decisions – it explicitly noted that any signatory could invoke a code provision that would make the code inapplicable between itself and the new arrival. The text was included by agreement in the Brussels document for ministers, and was thereafter to survive effectively unchanged in the final outcome of the Round. As noted in an earlier chapter, the far more important agreement to expand the coverage of the government procurement agreement itself, which was to be signed at Marrakesh in April 1994, was negotiated outside the Uruguay Round.

GATT Articles

For the negotiating group on GATT Articles, the Montreal meeting brought only one new element to its work: a call to bring forward specific proposals as soon as possible, and preferably not later than the end of 1989. Ten separate subjects had been discussed in 1987 and 1988. Two of these (security exceptions, raised by Nicaragua and Argentina, and *de facto* status, raised by the United States) were dropped because no others wished to negotiate on them. Of the remaining eight subjects, seven were taken up again in the group when the Round got under way, and negotiations went forward constructively. Agreements on the three most technical, and least controversial, articles – schedules, state trading and tariff renegotiations – were reached in the summer and autumn of 1990. Draft texts on the other four subjects were drawn up as part of the final drive to complete preparations for the Brussels meeting. On one issue, the balance-of-payments provisions of the GATT, no agreement could be reached even to engage in negotiations.

As in the first stage of the negotiations, the lack of any linkage between the issues discussed by the GATT Articles group means that the negotiations on each are best considered separately. The following account looks at them in the order just mentioned: the three that were resolved first, the four that were settled just before the Brussels meeting, and the one that defied solution.

Schedules

New Zealand had made the original proposal that GATT tariff schedules should be made more informative and secure, and give a more realistic picture of each country's true level of protection, by the inclusion of full information on bound duties and charges other than customs duties. Its ideas had been widely welcomed, apart from some legal concerns. In June 1989, it put forward a detailed proposal which was reviewed in detail over the following months, with the help of Secretariat notes on legal points which helped to lay the earlier concerns to rest. In October, the Secretariat was asked to prepare a draft decision setting out a number of alternatives, and in December the group reached tentative agreement, subject to two reservations. When these had both been lifted, in June 1990, the text was sent to the GNG. It was the first agreement on an improvement in the GATT rules to emerge from the Uruguay Round, and the first post-Montreal agreement of any kind.

Earlier, in October 1989, the United States made a further proposal which also concerned Article II. Prompted by ideas circulating in the US Congress and widely supported there, the proposal was that countries should be permitted to levy a small and uniform import fee that would fund trade-adjustment programmes for such purposes as worker training, job search and relocation. The fee would not exceed 0.15%. The United States argued that an advantage of the proposal was that workers helped by programmes financed by the fee would recognize the benefits of international trade, and protectionist pressures would be weakened. Other countries were not convinced, among other reasons because they felt that the proposal would not be effective in achieving its purpose, and because it would be a move in the wrong direction in a negotiation that aimed to reduce trade barriers. The United States continued to press the proposal until mid-1990, abandoning it finally because of lack of support.

State trading

Discussion before the mid-term meeting on Article XVII, on state-trading enterprises, had shown that many countries were interested in improving the operation of the Article, but not in changing its substance. Both the European Community and the United States made formal proposals which were first considered in October 1989. The Community called for notification requirements to be tightened up, for counter-notification procedures that would allow discussion of the activities of enterprises that were affecting international trade, and for a mechanism to permit review of the notifications. The United States proposed that a working party should clarify definitions of state-trading enterprises and review notifications; and that the activities of all these enterprises, including marketing boards, should be recognized as being subject to GATT disciplines such as the requirement to give national treatment to imported products. Initial reactions by other countries showed that all these ideas were important, enjoyed wide support, and were sufficiently close to one another that they could be largely combined. In March 1990, at the group's request, the Secretariat circulated the first draft for a decision on Article XVII. This was discussed and repeatedly revised in informal meetings over the next four months, with agreement reached in July. The final agreement provided for the first time a working definition of state-trading enterprises, the key elements being their possession of exclusive or special rights or privileges through which their purchases or sales could influence the level or direction of imports or exports. This definition in turn made it clear, again for the first time, what enterprises were subject to notification. The agreement also set up arrangements for review of notifications and counter-notifications: none had existed before.

Renegotiation of tariff concessions

The third technical issue concerned the right under Article XXVIII to be recognized as a principal supplier, and thus to seek compensation if a country raised a bound duty. Negotiations were effectively launched by a joint proposal in November 1989 by ten medium-sized developed and developing countries. This included a new attempt to define criteria that would give principal supplier rights to the country which, although its exports of the product concerned were not the largest to the market of the country raising the duty, was the most seriously affected by the increase. The solution suggested – to give such rights to the country for which exports of the product to that market represented the highest proportion of its total exports – proved finally acceptable, although much drafting and redrafting was required before a final agreement could be reached in October 1990. The same ten-country proposal also covered several other issues, including the difficult question of how compensation could be calculated when tariffs were raised on a newly introduced product whose export prospects could not be fairly estimated from past trade flows. This issue had come up in practice, when the European Community raised tariffs on imports of digital cassette recorders, a new product of which Japan was the main supplier. The agreement reached provided guidelines that would allow the compensation due in such cases to be estimated on the basis of future growth prospects.

Regional agreements

Up to the mid-term meeting, there had been little discussion of Article XXIV, dealing with customs unions and free trade areas. Japan and India had proposed tightening up the Article's rules, especially those on the compensation of non-members for loss of markets and on the trade coverage which such agreements should have in order to qualify as permitted exceptions to the general GATT rules of non-discrimination. India also proposed a clearer state-ment of the responsibility of central governments for the GATT-conformity of actions by lower-level government authorities, a matter covered by paragraph 12 of Article XXIV. No agreement had been reached before Montreal to negotiate on these matters, and they were not considered in 1989, although Japan circulated new proposals in December. These included the idea of special procedures, separate from the main GATT dispute settlement arrangements, to assess and permit compensation for damage caused by regional agreements to the trade of nonmembers.

When Article XXIV was taken up again, in the spring of 1990, some countries strongly opposed Japan's proposals for new mechanisms, partly on the ground that the trade policy reviews just introduced into GATT would give opportunities for surveillance of regional trading groups. However, there was support for an effort to clarify the present rules. The Secretariat was asked to prepare a paper on the issues raised. When this appeared, in May, it included draft texts to show how the Japanese proposals, as well as some from Australia and Canada, might be translated into a legal agreement. The European Community promptly criticized it as going too far, lacking balance, and seeming to suggest that regional agreements were inherently suspect rather than having very positive effects on trade. Detailed discussion of the paper nevertheless followed, and came close in substance, if not in name, to real negotiation.

At the same time, the Community itself came forward with a proposal designed (as its spokesman explained) "to ensure that Article XXIV:12 should not operate as an escape clause exempting some contracting parties from certain of their GATT obligations". Its central point was a call to affirm the full responsibility of GATT members for measures taken by their regional or local governments or authorities.

In July, the group agreed that the chairman could report to the TNC that there was support for negotiations on Article XXIV. Detailed informal discussions followed in September on which an interim Secretariat note reported that although they had not resolved longstanding disagreements, "they certainly gave no reason to despair about the possibility of reaching a useful, even if modest, agreement which might help to reduce future disputes". This was exactly what was in fact to emerge from the negotiations. An "understanding on the interpretation of Article XXIV" took shape, first as a proposal put together by the chairman and Secretariat and then, following negotiations in September and October, as a formal text which Weekes presented to the negotiating group.

The draft understanding's main features were a set of guidelines for the critically important calculation of the level of duties before and after a customs union is formed; a more precise statement of the obligations (in Article XXIV:6) of group members to compensate non-members for duty increases; a requirement that any transitional arrangements for the movement to free trade be clearly stated, and normally last no more than ten years; and acknowledgement that any matters arising from Article XXIV arrangements can be submitted to the GATT dispute settlement procedures. Nothing was said about trade coverage, apart from a reference in the text's preamble to the "diminished contribution" to world trade of agreements that exclude "any major sector of trade". On paragraph 12, the draft affirmed that each country "is fully responsible" for observance of all GATT provisions, and "shall take such reasonable measures as may be available to it" to ensure observance by regional and local governments and authorities.

Australia, Canada, Japan, Mexico the United States and others accepted the chairman's proposal. The European Community did not, mainly because it wanted the provisions on Article XXIV:6 changed to give fuller credit in compensation negotiations for any tariff reductions made by group members, but also because it was dissatisfied with the text on Article XXIV:12. India and Yugoslavia also withheld support, but for different reasons: India because it found the whole text disappointingly weak, and Yugoslavia (a federal state) because it did not like the provisions on XXIV:12. In consequence, the Weekes text sent to ministers in Brussels was still only a draft understanding, complete in form but by no means agreed to.

Waivers

The European Community had called in 1987 for an overhaul of the GATT waiver provisions in paragraph 5 of Article XXV. It followed this up with a detailed proposal in February 1990. The Community wanted time limits to be set for all waivers, abolition of the exceptionally permitted measures when their economic justification no longer existed, annual reviews, and a continuing right of resort to dispute settlement even though a waiver had been granted. None of these points was particularly controversial: they reflected lessons learned from experience. However, the Community also proposed that all existing waivers should be terminated, or replaced by waivers governed by the new rules. The effect of this proposal, if accepted, would have been to withdraw the open-ended approval given in 1955 to very important agricultural trade restrictions maintained by the United States. These restrictions were not sacrosanct: the United States had said it was willing to negotiate their removal as part of the wider Uruguay Round negotiations on agriculture. On the other hand, they would be given up only in exchange for trade concessions by the Community and others.

The solution was to negotiate an agreement on Article XXV that included essentially all the elements of the Community proposal, but to leave open the date on which existing waivers would be terminated. This approach allowed a text to be drawn up and agreed to on the understanding that the fate of the US waiver would depend on what happened in the agricultural negotiations. The actual negotiations took place early in 1990, without difficulty, and the draft agreement went to ministers in Brussels complete except for the missing date. The text was carried forward without substantial change during the concluding period of the Round. In its final form, however, it is distinguished by effectively appearing twice in the final Uruguay Round package: once to govern the treatment of waivers under the GATT, and a second time as the rules for waivers under the new World Trade Organization.

Non-application of the GATT

The United States returned in the early summer of 1990 to its proposal to review Article XXXV on the non-application of the GATT between particular member countries. As the US delegate pointed out, the existing rule meant that if two countries began tariff negotiations, both lost the option to refuse subsequently to apply the GATT to one another, however unsatisfactory the results of the negotiations might be. This rule might, he suggested, have made sense in a multilateral tariff-cutting enterprise, "given the web of negotiations that eventually produced final offers", but did not in the context of a bilateral tariff negotiation with a country seeking to join GATT, in which there were normally no reciprocal concessions. The United States felt that a GATT member should be able to request concessions from a would-be member, negotiate with it and, if agreement could not be reached, invoke Article XXXV.

Most countries agreed that a change in the rule would encourage members to negotiate with applicant countries, although some fears were expressed that the proposal could weaken the applicant's bargaining power.

A formal US proposal, made in August, aimed to achieve its purpose by defining "discussions ... prior to or pursuant to the establishment of a GATT schedule of concessions" as not constituting "tariff negotiations" within the meaning of Article XXXV. This ingenious piece of sophistry was dropped in the text finally sent to Brussels which simply stated that a member and an acceding government could negotiate without prejudice to their right to invoke Article XXXV against one another. Although some countries maintained reservations on the text, it was not subsequently changed, and formed part of the final Uruguay Round package.

The "grandfather clause"

The remaining GATT provision on which an agreement was reached before Brussels was the "grandfather clause" in the Protocol of Provisional Application. This clause (paragraph 1b of the Protocol) allowed the continuance of some GATT-inconsistent national legislation which pre-dated the GATT itself, and was effectively a waiver for the legislation. The Community proposed in February 1990 that this derogation be phased out by setting a terminal date after which any measures covered by it would become subject to challenge under the dispute settlement process. The arguments in favour of the move were essentially the same as for the Community's proposal on the GATT waiver provisions in Article XXV. An additional advantage, because it was not clear exactly what legislation was actually covered by the Protocol of Provisional Application, was that the change would also serve the broad Uruguay Round objective of bringing greater transparency to the international trading system.

Most countries agreed with the general objective of the proposal, although it was always obvious that the United States would need to seek some other legal cover under GATT for its restrictions on foreign shipping under the Jones Act, which for domestic political reasons were not negotiable. However, another concern also had to be cleared out of the way. Some countries suggested that the objective should be broadened, to get rid of all specific derogations from the GATT, including those contained in the agreements under which some countries had been admitted to membership. This proposal was taken as being aimed at countries such as Switzerland, whose admission protocol allowed it to maintain restrictions on agricultural products. Switzerland replied firmly that it and others had paid in their accession negotiations for whatever special treatment was granted by their membership protocols, and had an inalienable right to maintain it. The point was not further pursued.

The final result of the 1990 negotiations was an agreed text which provided that the grandfather exemption under the Protocol of Provisional Application should expire at a date which was for the present left open.

Balance-of-payments articles

As early as June 1988, an internal Secretariat note warned Dunkel that no agreement to change the substance of the four balance-of-payments articles of the GATT seemed likely to emerge from the Uruguay Round, and that the most far-reaching prospective outcome was probably an agreement to improve disciplines and procedures, perhaps on time-limits and adjustment requirements. This judgement was based on the extremely hostile reception that developing countries had given to US and Canadian proposals for radical reform, and their only slightly warmer response to EC ideas which would improve surveillance and procedures for consultation, but leave basic rights under Article XVIII intact. Events in the two years after the Montreal meeting suggested that the Secretariat's forecast was, if anything, too optimistic about the prospect of a significant result.

In November 1989 the Americans and Canadians put their earlier views into concrete form in a joint proposal which called for general tightening up of the GATT balance-of-payments exceptions "to establish a more sustainable balance" between the right to impose trade restrictions when in serious payments trouble and "the obligations of all parties to pursue policies which contribute to the viability of the GATT system as a whole". They argued that the lasting solution to external imbalances was not trade restrictions but a combination of exchange-rate adjustment and policy reforms (including trade liberalization). This being so, action under the balance-of-payments articles should be allowed only in accordance with agreed guidelines. As a starting point, the payments imbalance must be serious, and a responsible effort must be made to restore equilibrium. Both these points would be subject to the judgement of the IMF. Any trade measures taken would be subject to a series of conditions, including a time-limit on the measures, a programme for phasing them out, and coverage of substantially all products (to prevent disguised sectoral protection). The country concerned was to consult promptly and more frequently with the Balance-of-Payments Committee. Any deviations from the guidelines, unless explicitly approved by the Committee, would permit other countries to seek redress through the GATT dispute settlement procedures for damage done to their trade, with the onus on the restricting country to show that its measures are justified.

The reaction of developing countries was totally negative. Most of them concluded from the paper that it would be dangerous to get into any negotiation at all on the balance-of-payments articles. Given this atti-tude, they were not prepared to look seriously even at a much less aggressive set of proposals which the European Community put forward in February 1990. The Community concentrated on making the balance-of-payments consultations more effective, and on establishing a preference for trade measures that affected the price rather than the quantity of imports. Moreover, it proposed to ease access to the Article XVIII:C provisions to help infant industries, and to further restrict developed-country use of restrictions under Article XII.

By June 1990, the Americans and Canadians had recognized that their earlier proposals were not negotiable, and moved to a position fairly close to that of the Community, although still calling for time limits for the removal of restrictions and not offering anything for infant industries. This was still not enough, however, to persuade developing countries to negotiate on the subject. In July, when the Trade Negotiations Committee was struggling to establish a "profile" of the results of the Round, John Weekes, chairman of the negotiating group, reported that progress would be possible only if participants could decide whether or not they would negotiate. Dunkel held "green-room" consultations, but failed to find a basis on which negotiations might be launched. The effort continued into the autumn, when Weekes spent much time in a fruitless effort to develop a list of points that might be included in an agreement on the balance-of-payments rules. In the end, all that went to Brussels, the supposedly final meeting of the Round, was a bleak little note to ministers which reads (in full), "It has not yet been decided whether or not to engage in negotiations on this subject."

Textiles and clothing

The mid-term agreement transformed the negotiations on textiles and clothing. The major ambiguities of the original mandate from Punta del Este had been cleared up. The central goal was now to get rid of the Multifibre Arrangement, and of other GATT-inconsistent trade restrictions affecting the sector, over a fixed time period starting at the end of the Uruguay Round. The task of the negotiators was to decide how this should be done and whether other issues had also to be dealt with in the group.

In successive meetings of the negotiating group during 1989, leading participants brought forward their proposals. Initially, the proposals essentially put flesh on the bones of the ideas that had been introduced and discussed before the mid-term review. But as ideas were further refined, in response to the reactions of others, the main lines of convergence and divergence began to emerge quite clearly.

First to come forward, in June, was the ITCB group of developing countries. It focused on the elimination of MFA restrictions, for which it identified several possible approaches. One, it suggested, could be to remove successively from restriction products based on different fibres, starting with cotton, then moving on to wool and man-made fibres. A second might focus on liberalizing according to supplier, beginning with the least-developed countries. A third idea, which was to bear some fruit, was to distinguish among the degrees of textile processing, moving from tops (combed wool, ready for spinning) to yarn and on through fabrics, made-up textiles and garments. Another possibility would be to start by liberalizing specific products first, such as handloom products and children's clothing. The ITCB also raised other issues that were to be given much attention over the next year and more. It wanted restrictions removed from products which importers did not produce domestically, as well as from imports of products made-up from materials originating in the importing country. This "outward processing" had become very important to some countries, especially to Caribbean producers exporting for the US market. In addition, the ITCB wanted to see the end of two concepts widely used in applying MFA restrictions: that of "minimum viable production", invoked by some of the smaller importing countries; and aggregate and group limits on imports, central to bilateral agreements negotiated by the United States.

The European Community put forward the first detailed ideas from the importing side. The Community backed a staged and progressive phase-out of the MFA, with mechanisms to monitor progress; and a transitional safeguard provision, on lines similar to that of the MFA, to avoid market disruption during the liberalization process. These ideas were all to prove important. However, the Community insisted on the equal importance of strengthening the general GATT rules and disciplines affecting trade in textiles and clothing, particularly on the need for all countries to open their markets. These proposals were highly controversial, since exporters maintained that such issues were matters for discussion, if at all, elsewhere in the Round; but they too were to be reflected in the final agreement.

Other importers also made proposals. Switzerland – a country which had never had recourse to the MFA – identified a basic possible choice, which it suggested might be left to individual importers, between gradual phase-out of the MFA and the replacement of the bilateral restrictions applied under the MFA by more GATT-consistent restrictions. The latter idea, taken up by the United States, would have converted restrictions into equivalent tariffs, tariff quotas (under which tariff levels increase when prescribed import levels are exceeded) or global quotas (i.e. quotas for which all suppliers can compete). The United States also insisted that the negotiators look at non-MFA trade distortions, among which it identified measures taken outside GATT by Round participants, measures by non-members of GATT, safeguard measures taken to promote infant industries or protect the balance-of-payments, the existence of tariffs not bound under GATT, and preferential arrangements not approved by GATT.

Up to this point, although proposals put forward had been much more specific than in the early stages of the Round, they still lacked detail. They served, however, to develop some key ideas. Already, the predominant view in the group clearly favoured a phase-out based on gradual and supervised easing of the existing MFA regime. Exporters were not happy with the proposal for transitional safeguard rules for textiles, nor with the introduction of non-MFA issues and measures into the negotiation.

In October 1989, India made the first detailed proposal for a programme to integrate the textiles and clothing sector into GATT. It was followed in quick succession by proposals from Bangladesh (for the least-developed countries), the Nordic countries, the ITCB, the ASEAN countries and the United States. In the early months of 1990 several of these proposals were developed further, along with new ones offered by Japan and Canada. These various proposals provided the substance of negotiations on textiles and clothing right up to the Brussels meeting in December 1990.

India's proposal called for terminating the MFA on expiry of its latest extension, in July 1991, and its replacement by a five-year transitional arrangement. Under this arrangement some restrictions would be removed immediately, including those on imports from least-developed countries, handloom products, outward processing traffic, and aggregate and group limits. Importing countries would remove one fifth of the remaining number of quotas in each of the following years, and at the same time would progressively increase imports allowed under the quotas that were still in force. India also proposed a surveillance body to supervise the process but did not favour a special safeguard arrangement. Of these ideas, the distinction made by India between the removal of all MFA restrictions from certain products and the gradual easing of quota restrictions on products still under restraint, both to be undertaken progressively, foreshadowed the key provisions for "integration" and "liberalization" in the final Uruguay Round agreement on textiles.

Bangladesh, for the least-developed countries, put their case for special treatment. It proposed more rapid removal of restraints affecting them, and exemption from any new restraints during transition, as well as from any special safeguard provisions.

Other influential proposals from the exporters' side were put forward by the ITCB and by the ASEAN countries. The ITCB, developing its earlier ideas, again proposed the removal of some restrictions and practices from the beginning of the phase-out of the MFA, and repeated the proposal that elimination of restrictions might go forward by stages of processing, starting with the raw material and finishing with made-up garments. The group also proposed progressive increases in permitted growth rates and an easing of the provisions that already, under the MFA, permitted some flexibility in the way that individual quota restrictions were applied. The ITCB was prepared to envisage some sort of special safeguard arrangement, different from that available under Article XIX of the GATT, for products covered by the agreement. Finally, it saw a need for a standing body which would monitor progress in phasing-out the MFA, and help to settle any disputes that might arise. For their part, the ASEAN countries also wanted a monitoring body, and gradual phase-out of the MFA over 8½ years, with immediate removal of some restrictions and practices, and a progressive enlargement of quotas.

Some of these ideas had support also on the exporters' side. The need for a monitoring body was widely accepted, and although envisaged in different forms, everyone was aware of the highly professional precedent set by the Textiles Surveillance Body (TSB) which handled this task under the MFA. A proposal by the Nordic countries included a number of other elements in common with the exporters. Like the ASEANS, the Nordics foresaw an 8½-year phase-out of restrictions, gradually increasing growth rates for restricted products, and faster removal of some restrictions, such as those affecting the least-developed countries and small suppliers. They too felt it best to move to a liberal system directly through dismantling of the familiar rules of the MFA. Unlike the exporters, however, they shared the European Community's concern that MFA liberalization should go hand in hand with strengthening of GATT rules and disciplines, to ensure that markets would be opened, and that fair conditions of competition would prevail. They also thought that special safeguard provisions might be needed to handle surges in imports of textiles during the transitional period. Japan was another supporter of an 8½-year phase-out and of moving to liberal trade through gradual easing of MFA restrictions, with new and strict rules to govern any bilateral agreements negotiated for the transitional period.

The United States developed its earlier ideas in proposals put forward at the end of 1989 and early in 1990. It argued for a 10-year phase-out, and suggested that, rather than gradually easing bilateral restrictions under the MFA, a better approach would be to move in the transitional period towards increasing reliance on global quotas or tariff-rate quotas that would affect all suppliers equally and thus conform to the basic GATT rule of non-discrimination. It spelled these ideas out in detail. The United States continued to insist that liberalization must not be limited to restrictions under the MFA, but should cover all restrictions that were not explicitly authorized by the GATT. Liberalization should also go hand in hand with strengthening of GATT rules and disciplines. A Canadian proposal carried further the idea of moving towards a system of global quotas, suggesting that the MFA should be terminated when it reached its current expiry date of July 1991, to be replaced by the possibility of introducing global quotas, similar to those envisaged under Article XIX of the GATT. Such quotas would be permitted when textile or clothing imports threatened market disruption (rather than the "serious injury" prescribed in Article XIX), and would not require compensation; however, their scope would be gradually reduced over the transitional period by progressive reduction in the range of products that could be restricted, and by provision for growth in the size of each quota.

Taken together, these proposals made in late 1989 and early 1990 set out almost all the elements that found their way into the final agreement on the future rules for world trade in textiles and clothing.

From April 1990 onwards, when the governing Trade Negotiations Committee resolved that the profile of the final Uruguay Round package should be developed by July, the pace of the textiles negotiations accelerated. The negotiating group, basing itself on a growing understanding of the elements which would need to be included in an agreement, decided to focus on six topics: how the MFA restrictions should be phased out; how to get rid of other restrictions inconsistent with the General Agreement; a transitional safeguard mechanism; a surveillance system; strengthened GATT rules and disciplines; and the time-span for the transition.

For the phase-out, it was fairly clear that the way forward would be through gradual dismantling of the MFA. The US-Canadian suggestion that the MFA should be replaced by a new transitional system of global quotas or tariff quotas found little support. Although its authors developed their ideas in the early summer of 1990, exporting countries felt that this approach would actually widen the already broad scope of quotas limiting trade in textiles and clothing, applying restrictions to countries at present unaffected, while shielding industries in the importing countries from necessary pressures to adapt to greater competition. Many importers, too, saw no merit in a liberalization process that would broaden the scope of present restrictions. Finally, a very widespread view was that no purpose would be served by introducing a new set of temporary complications into international trade in textiles. Whatever one thought of the MFA, traders and governments were used to it. The least trade-disruptive means of moving towards a more liberal trade regime, in this view, would be to dismantle the MFA by stages. Japan argued for a somewhat different approach to phase-out, under which MFA restrictions as such would be abolished immediately, to be replaced if necessary by transitional restraints.

Phase-out of restrictions covered neither by the GATT nor by the MFA was obviously going to be awkward. The existence of these restrictions was often not publicly known, and some were probably GATT-illegal. A Nordic proposal suggested they could best be handled by bringing them into the open through notification requirements, and then phasing them out in the same way as restrictions imposed under the MFA.

Ideas about the kind of safeguard mechanism that would be required during the phase-out were becoming clearer. As far as its scope was concerned, most countries agreed that it should apply only to products still covered by the agreement: once a product had been "integrated", any safeguard action against it would have to be governed by the standard GATT rules. Safeguard action against restricted products should be on lines similar to that permitted under the MFA, but should be harder to justify and should allow faster trade growth.

For surveillance, the European Community proposed a modified version of the Textiles Surveillance Body of the MFA. This approach was widely supported. However, the EC also proposed a "verification mechanism". This would establish a process by which the progress of individual countries through the various stages of transition from the MFA to full integration would be subject to review of how they were fulfilling the commitments they had undertaken both in the textiles negotiations and in those to strengthen GATT rules and disciplines. In effect, the proposal served to put teeth into the EC's already controversial view, which it now repeated, that MFA liberalization must go hand in hand with other measures for a "fairer, more predictable and more liberal trading environment", including market opening by all and an effective GATT safeguard mechanism.

Although a fairly wide range of possible periods for phase-out of the MFA was still being mentioned, ranging from five to ten years, most countries were ready to start the process either when the present MFA expired (July 1991) or when the main Uruguay Round agreements entered into force (probably January 1992).

Ahead of the July 1990 meeting of the Trade Negotiations Committee, several of the main players put forward revisions of their earlier proposals. The ITCB, with support from developing countries in general, called for phase-out over 6½ years. It proposed that all MFA restrictions be carried over into the transition. However, this step would be followed by an immediate start on elimination of some restrictions, beginning with least-processed products and then moving on, through four stages, until the most fully finished products were removed from restriction. Trade in products still under restriction would be allowed to grow increasingly rapidly, with the permitted annual increase moving up each year from an initial 6% to 25% in the sixth year, with higher growth rates for cotton. It allowed for a general easing of flexibility and other provisions widely applied under the MFA, such as sub-division of quotas and restrictions on outward processing traffic. A transitional safeguard would be available to importers, but only in the case of serious injury, and normally only for one year. No other measures were to be used against restrained products. The ASEAN countries made a separate proposal that contained similar elements, although it envisaged an 8½ year transition. Importers criticized the proposals as unrealistically ambitious, and because they did not deal with GATT-inconsistent restrictions, or with strengthening GATT rules and disciplines. The European Community countered with its own outline proposal, which echoed some of the ITCB's ideas: a mixture of staged integration of some products with gradual liberalization of the remainder, combined with some easing of the MFA's flexibility provisions, and special treatment for products of the least-developed countries. But the outline fell well short of the ITCB proposal in its specific provisions. The EC also incorporated its earlier ideas on verification and on linking phase-out of the MFA with strengthened GATT rules and disciplines; it did not specify how long the phase-out should take.

Taken together, all these proposals covered more or less the full range of elements that were needed to build a complete agreement that would fulfil the negotiating group's mandate. On some issues, such as gradual phase-out of the MFA, the views of governments were clearly converging. However, informal meetings by the chairman (Lindsay Duthie of Australia) with key delegations showed that convergence had not progressed far enough to develop the requested "profile" of the outcome of the negotiations. The best he could do was to send the TNC, in July 1990, a text which, although for the first time it set out the shape of a formal agreement, included all the alternative proposals made to the group. Like most other Uruguay Round groups, the textiles negotiators were still a daunting distance away from the agreement they were supposed to reach before the end of the year. Indeed, real negotiation had scarcely begun.

Over the next three months, the chairman worked with a dozen key delegations, reporting back at intervals to the whole group, to narrow the differences between positions, and to pin down the precise implications of the outstanding proposals. In September, the group agreed, at last, that the transition should be based on gradual phase-out of the MFA, with the existing individual restrictions as the starting point for increasing growth and flexibility. It also agreed that non-MFA restrictions would have to be covered somehow, that a safeguard mechanism would be needed, and that some of the products covered by the MFA, such as handloom and handicraft products and children's clothing, might be able to be integrated immediately. However, it was unable to decide exactly how these principles should be applied. A further advance took place in October, when Canada suggested a new basic concept on safeguard action which, although not accepted at first, was to find its way into the final agreement. Under the Canadian approach, the justification for introducing safeguards would be established at two levels: a global test to show that the domestic industry was being damaged by imports, taken as a whole, of a particular product; and a test to justify action against imports of the product from particular suppliers.

On other matters, however, deep differences persisted. The exporters pushed for integration and liberalization rules that would remove all barriers smoothly over the transition period, so that the MFA would, in effect, self-destruct. Importers were not prepared to force rapid adjustment on their domestic industries, preferring as long a transition as possible, even at the cost of major adjustments (a final "cliff") when the MFA disappeared. On safeguards, exporters and importers disagreed on whether their use would be justified only by "serious injury or threat thereof", or by the lesser standard of "market disruption or real risk thereof". They also disagreed on the products that could be subjected to safeguard action, the duration of such action, and on whether safeguards could be imposed without prior approval, or by countries which, like Japan, had not so far imposed restraints under the MFA. Exporters remained opposed to the importers' desire to link MFA phase-out with a strengthening of other GATT rules and disciplines and for a "verification" process that, as the exporters saw it, would subject them to constant threat that the liberalization process would be halted. They continued to argue that the staged elimination of restrictions should proceed by degrees of processing; the importers preferred to advance by removing restrictions from a given percentage of trade under restraint.

With the Brussels deadline looming, the chairman made successive revisions of the draft agreement he had put forward in July. His first revision made the key choice of adopting the approach of phased and progressive removal of existing restrictions on trade in textiles and clothing, but still included large numbers of the square-bracketed words and passages that indicated continuing disagreement. A second version, following another round of negotiations, went further: it outlined a liberalization process that would combine complete removal of some products from MFA coverage with the gradual liberalization of others, and also set out key elements of the safeguard mechanism and detailed lists of the products to be covered by the agreement. Finally, a third and last revision tentatively filled in some critical numbers in the "economic package", suggesting that 10% of the total volume of imports of the listed products should be integrated when the transitional period began, with a further 15% and 20% at the beginning of the second and third stages, and that existing growth rates for products remaining restricted should be raised at the same time by 16%, 21% and 26% respectively. This third revision, which went forward to Brussels, also included provisions on avoidance of fraud and circumvention of the new rules, and on special and differential treatment for developing countries. There were still, however, blank spaces and square brackets scattered throughout the text. More important, no government yet backed the draft as meeting its objectives. They were prepared to use it as a basis for further negotiations, but each had serious difficulties with many of the provisions it proposed.

As the textiles negotiators prepared to travel to Brussels, a long list of unresolved questions remained, each of which would need to be settled if an agreement were to be reached there. Most of the technical work had been done, but many hard choices had still to be made, each of which would have an impact on the future of the textiles and clothing industry worldwide. They included decisions on the time-span for the phase-out of the MFA, the list of products to be covered by the transition rules, the principles to guide selection of products for integration, what special treatment might be given to certain suppliers such as least-developed countries, the criteria for use of safeguards, and the verification issue ("review procedures") by which importers still sought to link MFA liberalization with market opening by the exporters as well.

Agriculture

The agreement on agriculture, reached in April 1989, served to re-launch the Uruguay Round as a whole, provided a broad framework for the coming negotiations, and set a timetable. It settled little else. Interpretations offered by each of the main participants showed that none had abandoned their objectives.

The first few months after Montreal were largely devoted to work on some key technical issues. The European Community and others set out ideas on use of an aggregate measure of support (AMS) as the basis for negotiations on the main sectors of agricultural products. With the same aim of making subsequent negotiations on market access more straightforward, the United States offered proposals on "tariffication", the technique by which non-tariff barriers to imports might be converted to a tariff of equivalent effect. A further proposal from the EC on GATT rules and disciplines affecting agriculture focused on the subsidy rules of Article XVI of the General Agreement. Japan, Switzerland and the Nordic countries put their case for special treatment as countries whose agricultural policies were governed largely by non-commercial concerns, and argued that they should be allowed to contribute to the Round's objectives by means other than a general reduction of support to agriculture. There was some discussion of the needs of developing countries, and particularly of the net food-importers, although in both cases it was understood that decisions on special treatment for these countries could be reached ouly when it was known what commitments the major participants in the negotiations would assume. However, the agricultural negotiations were to a great extent marking time until participants produced the detailed proposals which they had undertaken to provide by December 1989.

The proposals, when they came, showed that the gulf between the positions of the major participants was as wide as ever.

First detailed proposals

The United States, first to come forward, repeated its call to phase out export subsidies completely over ten years. On market access, it proposed that all non-tariff barriers, including the variable levies that were the main EC measure affecting imports, be tariffied, bound against increase, and negotiated down to lower levels, with a minimum access for imports of 5% of the domestic market. Internal subsidies should be disciplined under what became known as a "traffic light" system: the most distortive ("red") should be phased out altogether over ten years, while less distortive ("yellow") subsidies should be disciplined, and only those "green" subsidies which had minimal trade effects, such as domestic food aid or disaster relief programmes, would escape action. Developing countries would be given longer than developed countries to adapt to the new disciplines.

The Cairns Group was not far from the US position, arguing for a freeze and subsequent phase-out of export subsidies, and for "substantial progressive reduction" in the most trade-distorting internal policies, although with flexibility on how the reduction would be achieved. On market access, it wanted a phased reduction in aggregate support that would reduce tariff and non-tariff barriers and include all those products which countries had, in one way or another, managed to exclude from previous liberalization efforts in

GATT. (On this last point, Canada differed in wanting to keep protection for "fresh products at a primary level".)

The European Community's proposal was less specific, and far less ambitious. The AMS was proposed as a flexible means to reduce both domestic and export subsidies, with an overall target reduction to be agreed, but with each participant free to decide how this objective was reached. For market access negotiations, the Community accepted that tariffication could be a useful tool, but also wanted to harmonize its tariff structure by re-balancing (that is, raising certain tariffs that it felt were so exceptionally low as to distort markets), and to allow tariffs to be adjusted in response to large changes in currency exchange rates.

Proposals from the other main participants in the negotiations showed that positions had not really changed as a result of the mid-term agreement. Japan, Korea and others were ready to support the removal of export subsidies, which were not an important feature of their own policies. However these countries, along with many of the non-EC Europeans, saw no reason to remove domestic subsidies if these did not distort trade, and insisted on the need to provide support for land preservation, the environment, rural communities and food security. Similar arguments were put for continuing to restrict imports of some agricultural products to their markets, and Canada and others called for clarification of the GATT rules (in paragraph 2(c)(i) of Article XI) that permit such restrictions when domestic production or sale of similar agricultural or fisheries products is limited by governments. The non-Cairns developing countries repeated their earlier views.

This process of putting forward detailed proposals continued into the early months of 1990, by which time the scheduled final meeting of the Round in Brussels was only about nine months away. From April onwards, following agreement in the Trade Negotiations Committee that a complete profile of the Uruguay Round package should be developed by the week of 23 July, an informal group of eight of the main participants met to clarify the proposals and try to agree on how each element of the reform programme might be negotiated. At the same time, a separate working group on sanitary and phytosanitary measures tackled the issue of regulations on food safety and animal and plant health.

Sanitary and phytosanitary measures

In contrast to the main agricultural negotiations on market access, domestic support and export subsidies, the group on sanitary and phytosanitary (generally abbreviated to SPS) measures made excellent progress, reflecting a great deal of fundamental agreement on the objectives sought.

No one questions that governments have a duty to protect their citizens against unsafe food, and to prevent the spread of diseases and pests that affect animals and plants. The GATT rules expressly recognize (in Article XX:(b)) that measures "necessary to protect human, animal or plant life and health" are justified. Such protection is part of the wider responsibility of governments to require that goods of all kinds meet certain standards, particularly of safety. In the case of agricultural products, with their direct effect on health and on ensuring food supplies for the future, the need for action is particularly obvious. Imported agricultural products, like domestic produce, must be safe and free from diseases and pests. Moreover, it is accepted that countries should play safe: if there is any real doubt whether imports might bring – for instance – a cattle disease or a plant pest into a country or region free from that disease or pest, then those imports may be banned. However, just because sanitary and phytosanitary measures are applied everywhere, and public fears about food safety, in particular, are easily aroused, they are open to misuse as a barrier against competition from imports. With the Uruguay Round expected to reduce tariffs and subsidies affecting agricultural trade, there was a danger that countries would be tempted to make increased use of SPS measures as an alternative form of protection. There was also concern, reinforced by some specific disputes brought to GATT that, in response to consumer or other pressures, governments might introduce SPS measures to ban imports produced with the use of particular techniques or ingredients about which fears had, without scientific justification, been aroused.

By the time of the mid-term review, discussion of the subject had advanced sufficiently for ministers to agree on the long-term goal of "harmonization" of national SPS regulations. By this, they meant that national SPS requirements should as far as possible be consistent with internationally established standards, guidelines and recommendations developed by scientists and government experts working together in the specialized international bodies concerned with these matters. They also agreed that GATT Article XX had to be strengthened to make sure that measures permitted by it were based on sound principles and scientific evidence. In particular (adopting well-tested principles familiar from many other GATT agreements), they wanted notification and consultation arrangements to ensure that national SPS measures were generally known, could be discussed with other countries, and could be properly reviewed in case of dispute.

Proposals on how to meet these objectives were included in the broader agricultural proposals for the Round put forward in late 1989 and early 1990. Actual negotiations on this largely technical matter, however, took place in a separate working group, chaired by Gretchen Stanton of the GATT Secretariat, in which trade experts were joined by government officials responsible for drawing up and administering national SPS measures, and by representatives of the organizations involved in establishing international standards.

In strong contrast to the broader agricultural negotiations, there was always much common ground among the various proposals on SPS measures, with differences mainly in emphasis on one or other aspect of the mid-term goals. The US proposal stressed that SPS measures should be scientifically justified, and should recognize other countries' standards if these ensured substantially equivalent levels of safety. The EC proposal, on similar lines, suggested consultation and notification arrangements for SPS measures similar to those under the Tokyo Round code on technical standards. The EC also argued that, because countries which had achieved high health standards would find it difficult to accept moving to lower standards, they should, where appropriate, be allowed to apply SPS standards more stringent than those agreed to internationally. This was to be an important issue later in the negotiations when outside critics expressed fears that harmonization on inadequate standards could prevent countries from giving proper health or safety protection to consumers. The Cairns Group countries differed from this approach mainly in stressing that importing countries were responsible for justifying their SPS measures. Most developing countries favoured the widest possible use of international standards, to avoid creating unnecessary trade barriers. Japan, in contrast, suggested that geographical and dietary differences between countries would justify differences in national requirements, and that internationally agreed standards should serve mainly as guidelines.

In spite of these differences of emphasis, the SPS working group advanced rapidly. By May 1990, it had outlined the elements which seemed likely to be needed in an agreement on preventing SPS measures from being an unnecessary hindrance to trade, had reviewed what the various national proposals had to say on each element and, on some, had already reached tentative agreement. By July the group was working on a complete draft text. By October, the number of unsettled issues was already quite small. The group had agreed on most of the basic disciplines needed: international standards should be used when appropriate; more stringent measures should have scientific justification; measures should be based on assessment of actual risks; when alternative measures were available, the least trade-restrictive should be chosen; measures should be fully publicized and not discriminate between suppliers, and there should be a standing international body to consult regularly on their application.

By November, the draft agreement included only a few unsettled issues. How wide should the agreement be: should it (as the EC suggested) go beyond consumer concerns to regulate measures to protect animal welfare and the environment? Should national governments be made responsible for ensuring the consistency of SPS measures applied by regional or local governments with the new rules? (This was a problem particularly with rules about food additives and contaminants.) Should national rules more stringent than international standards be acceptable, and to what extent should product approval procedures take trade considerations into account? These and a few other questions remained, but the draft SPS agreement that was sent to ministers at the Brussels meeting was essentially in good shape, and ready for final decisions.

The same could not be said of the negotiations on the other three elements in the proposed agricultural reform programme: border measures, domestic support and export subsidies.

Impasse in the main agricultural negotiations

No meeting of minds was achieved in the informal discussions in which, from April 1990 onwards, a small group of key participants tried to reach agreement on the kind of commitments to be undertaken to increase market access and reduce domestic and export subsidies. With positions still far apart, and time running out, De Zeeuw decided to put forward his own proposals for a framework within which countries could make concrete offers. His six-page paper, circulated late in June, concentrated on setting out principles that could provide a basis for negotiations in each area of the agricultural negotiations. In practice, this required that he focus on border measures and on subsidies since the SPS negotiations were going well and action on such other issues as the concerns of net food-importers would depend on the content of the reform programme as a whole.

For border measures, De Zeeuw opted for the basic principle of tariffication as giving the best possibility of meeting the objective of more market-oriented trade policies. He allowed, however, for negotiations to meet non-trade concerns through "specific solutions" for some products, as well as for safeguard provisions to handle import surges or exceptional movements in world prices. For internal support measures, he identified the basic problem as being "where to draw the line between those such as market price support and deficiency payments which should be subject to the full reform commitments and those which are intended to offer a permissible way for governments to pursue policies of assistance to the agricultural sector, the rural community and the environment". The concept of decoupling support from production would be important, but was not "water-tight". De Zeeuw's proposed solution was to permit maintenance of some support policies, provided they did not exceed an overall ceiling and met specific criteria, such as being based on taxes rather than transfers from consumers, and not being linked to production. Examples of such permitted policies would be "services of a generally beneficial public nature to agriculture and the rural community", environmental and conservation programmes, and regional development and income safety-net programmes. All other internal support – market price supports, direct payments to producers, including deficiency payments, and other measures – would be subject to "substantial and progressive" reduction in terms of the aggregate measure of support (AMS) given to each commodity in 1988. Crucially, however, the paper did not specify whether separate commitments would be called for within the AMS total. For export subsidies, De Zeeuw accepted that although most countries wanted to see them eliminated as being the most trade-distorting form of support, others believed that they were necessary as long as world and internal prices continued to diverge. His proposal therefore would allow them to continue to exist, but with bigger reductions than to other forms of protection; he did not, however, offer a figure for the percentage reduction that should be made.

On 11 July, at the end of the Houston Summit meeting, the leaders of the world's leading industrialized countries paid a rare tribute to the work of an identified civil servant by agreeing in their final communiqué to "commend to our negotiators" the De Zeeuw text as "a means to intensify the negotiations". They also promised their personal involvement and political leadership "to ensure the successful outcome of these negotiations".

Unfortunately this endorsement was not enough. The United States and the Cairns Group were broadly in favour of De Zeeuw's framework proposals, although they were unhappy with his AMS proposal, because it would permit protection for some products to be retained or even increased. The European Community, however, insisted that no breakthrough had been achieved in Houston, and Ray McSharry, the EC Commissioner responsible for agriculture, warned in a speech that the Community's common agricultural policy was "under unprecedented and coordinated attack" in the Round. Meeting a few days later, the negotiating group on agriculture could not reach agreement on the proposals, although they adopted the Houston formula of using the paper "to intensify the negotiations". They undertook to submit "country lists" by the beginning of October that would set out information on their border measures and domestic and export subsidies. But it was clear that these would not be actual offers to liberalize, and that there was still no significant narrowing of positions. In effect, the negotiators had agreed to push on with their technical work, but at the cost of postponing to the last minute any bargaining on the critical and painful political choices without which no Uruguay Round agreement on agriculture would be possible.

In spite of pressure by Dunkel at the TNC meeting in July, and further subsequent meetings of the negotiators both in the framework of the Round and elsewhere, no progress was made on the fundamental problems. In its internal discussions on how to proceed, the European Community encountered disagreements among its twelve member governments, and inside the Commission itself, that prevented it from producing any proposal in Geneva until the first week of November, exactly one month before the Round was due to end. When the proposal came, it differed little from what had been found unacceptable by its trading partners a year before: on market access it offered replacement of variable levies by a fixed tariff plus a variable corrective tariff; on internal support it proposed a 30% reduction on 1986 levels (of which some two-thirds was already in effect because of changes since 1986), and it made no offer at all on export subsidies. Meanwhile the United States and the Cairns Group had also put forward proposals that showed very little change from the years before. The United States softened its stand only to the extent of calling for a 90% reduction in export subsidies, rather than their total abolition, and minimum market access of 3% rather than 5%; it coupled these proposals with a 75% reduction in "red" internal supports and a 30% cut in "yellow" supports. The Cairns Group matched the US proposal on export subsidies, and called for full tariffication of border measures and reduction of the resulting tariffs by 75% by developed countries and 45% by developing countries. Both the US and Cairns proposals would be put into effect over ten years by developed countries, and 15 years by developing countries. Other participants in the negotiations submitted widely differing offers, still reflecting their earlier positions. They had no incentive to move as long as the EC and US, in particular, were unready to compromise.

The agriculture negotiations were clearly in crisis, and with them, the Uruguay Round as a whole. On 8 November, Dunkel began intensive consultations on the main outstanding issues in the Round, starting with agriculture. The United States and Cairns negotiators told him bluntly that they had difficulty in continuing negotiations on what they described as inadequate offers, particularly that from the European Community. As Dunkel told the TNC four days later, they questioned whether the EC offer was consistent with the commitments undertaken in Punta del Este and at the mid-term review. They expressed concern that, in some ways, it would mean a deterioration in their present trading position and their GATT rights; they also called for more precise commitments on market access and export subsidies. No movement took place as a result of the consultations. At the TNC meeting, Dunkel summed up the position as "deadlock".

With the Brussels meeting now imminent, and the political stakes obviously very high, the US and EC multiplied their contacts. When President Bush and the EC Council and Commission Presidents pledged in Washington on 13 November to make every effort to ensure successful conclusion of the Round, there was no doubt that agriculture was the central issue they had in mind. Further negotiations continued between the two sides. But there was no sign of a breakthrough.

On 26 November, Dunkel sent a series of questions to governments, in an attempt to elicit a clear stand by them on the main issues that clearly had to be resolved before a substantial agreement on agriculture could be reached. Most of the questions concerned the form and content of the reform commitments in market access, domestic support and export assistance, as well as the treatment to be given developing countries. Governments were asked to reply in writing, and to indicate their priorities.

The basic document for Brussels sent by Dunkel to governments on 3 December, the "first approximation to the Final Act embodying the results of the Uruguay Round", made all too clear the immense distance that would have to be travelled if ministers were to reach agreement on agriculture. The agriculture section consisted essentially of Dunkel's list of questions, De Zeeuw's unaccepted framework paper from the summer, a 14-page descriptive summary of the disparate national offers made in October and November and – the sole encouraging element in the package – the draft SPS agreement.

The new subjects

For two of the three "new subjects" of the Uruguay Round, the mid-term review had comparatively little impact on the negotiations. The ministerial text on TRIMS had actually been settled in advance of the Montreal meeting, since the negotiating group needed no guidance at that time on how to continue its work. The services text had been agreed without too much difficulty. This did not mean that either the services or TRIMS groups faced an easy task: in fact it was an indication of slow progress that they had yet to reach a stage where governments needed to make difficult choices. For TRIPS, on the other hand, the hard-won mid-term agreement marked the end of sterile confrontation over the scope of the negotiations on intellectual property. Differences in national concerns and objectives of course remained but, from the spring of 1989 onwards, governments had a broadly shared view of where they were headed and progress was rapid.

Services

The main value of the Montreal agreement on services lay in the timetable it laid down for subsequent negotiations, and its identification of the key principles and concepts that would need to be considered in drawing up agreements. In fact, the timetable was to slip badly over the next year and a half, and the principles and concepts had already emerged fairly clearly during the long period of fact-finding and discussion in 1987-88. But the agreement helped to kick the negotiations into life. A second factor that gave the negotiations greater purpose and dynamism was the shift in attitude by many developing countries, in services as in many other areas of the Uruguay Round, away from defensiveness and sometimes obstruction and towards an active search for solutions that would allow them to participate fully in whatever gains the negotiations might bring. After Montreal, the battle lines of the services negotiations ceased to be drawn on exclusively North-South lines. Instead, there was a sharpening of differences on many issues among the developed countries.

The Montreal timetable set the end of 1989 as a key date: the GNS was "to endeavour" by then "to assemble the necessary elements for a draft that would permit negotiations to take place for completion of all parts of the multilateral framework and its entry into force by the end of the Uruguay Round". The timetable also proposed compilation of a Secretariat reference list of sectors by April 1989, and submission of indicative lists of the sectors of interest to governments by May 1989. These steps were to be followed by examination of how identified concepts, principles and rules might be applied to particular sectors.

The agreement also helped to cut down the number of alternative approaches to a services agreement from the almost infinitely wide range that had been discussed earlier. Ministers accepted that the multilateral framework could cover not only cross-border movement of services, but also cross-border movement of consumers and factors of production. This ended the debate over whether the negotiations could legitimately extend to services delivered by firms and individuals within the host country. It was also agreed that, in considering the coverage of the framework agreement, no sectors would be excluded in advance. Overriding considerations might, however require some sectors to be excluded in whole or in part.

The largest part of the Montreal agreement was devoted to setting out a list of familiar "concepts, principles and rules", and providing guidance on how these should be applied in drawing up the future multilateral framework.

The principles listed were transparency, progressive liberalization, national treatment, non-discrimination, market access, increasing participation of developing countries, safeguards and exceptions, and the regulatory situation. They were accompanied by a commentary which in several cases was more informative in what it left out than in what it included. For instance, ministers called for inclusion in the framework agreement of a provision on non-discrimination (most-favoured-nation treatment), but said nothing about the extent that exemptions or waivers from this provision might be permitted. Similarly the Montreal text recognized that provisions might be needed for safeguards, for instance for balance-of-payments reasons, and for exceptions to respond to security and cultural policy objectives, but did no more than accept that negotiations on these matters would be needed.

The first meetings of the GATS after the resumption of work in April 1989 were largely devoted to efforts to pin down more clearly the implications of each of these concepts. For the first time, the negotiators looked together at the special problems and issues affecting trade in a number of sectors, in order to understand how the general principles being worked out for the framework agreement might apply in practice. This sectoral testing exercise, covering telecommunications, construction, transportation, tourism, professional services and financial services (including insurance), involved study – with the help of experts – of the pattern and structure of trade in each sector (for instance, whether it required cross-border movement of consumers or suppliers of services) and of the kind and degree of government regulation in force. It also included such questions as how the aim of progressive liberalization might be achieved, how foreign and domestic suppliers could be put on an effectively equal footing (national treatment), and whether the sector covered activities of particular interest to developing countries.

The testing exercise showed that several of the key concepts, such as non-discrimination would, if applied, result in profound changes in the basis of international trade in that sector, usually because at present it was largely regulated through bilateral agreements. One lesson learned, among many, was that liberalization would in many cases be meaningless unless it gave foreign service suppliers the right to establish branch offices or station key personnel in the host countries. The meetings also helped in understanding which barriers to trade in services offered more promise than others as subjects for negotiation. In transport services, for example, it was made clear that port services and computer reservation systems might well be opened up, whereas cabotage (shipping services between domestic ports) and bilateral air transport agreements would almost certainly not be put on the negotiating table. In the case of telecommunications, the exercise demonstrated the sharp distinction between basic telecommunications – the communications network itself, in many countries, operated by a government-owned monopoly – and "value-added" telecommunications services which need to make use of the network. In construction services, developing countries underlined the strong links between construction contracts and the cross-border movement of labour. Their suggestion that these links meant that labour should be included as a service sector for the negotiations was received without enthusiasm by developed countries which had no intention of negotiating on their immigration laws. The discussion on financial services made it clear that this would be a particularly difficult sector for negotiations for several reasons: the generally recognized need for strong government regulation, for prudential reasons; the importance of the sector for national economic policy; and the very wide range of attitudes towards the entry of foreign financial suppliers (especially banks). Many countries were strongly attached to highly restrictive policies while others, such as the United States and the Europeans, were keenly interested in gaining entry to their markets.

While this aspect of the sectoral examination went well, and taught a great deal, little was achieved in the discussion of national indicative lists of sectors in which the countries concerned were interested.

In the autumn, the GNS turned attention to the task set by ministers of assembling the elements for the framework agreement. This involved a good many issues, not least of which was how to combine in an acceptable manner the ideas and structural approaches submitted in some 15 separate papers put forward between September and the end of 1989 by as many delegations. These included proposals from both New Zealand and Switzerland on the general structure for the framework agreement, and a text in legal form from the United States, all of which, together with a later proposal from Korea, were notable for introducing into the negotiation for the first time a name for the proposed framework – the "General Agreement on Trade in Services" – that underlined the ambitions of its sponsors. The US text, welcomed as the first near-complete legal draft, was criticized for provisions that would allow governments to exclude specific sectors from their national schedules, and to place reservations on particular provisions of the agreement, as well as for its failure to include special provisions either for developing countries or regional agreements.

One issue quickly raised was whether the framework, whatever its title, was to cover all services, and if not, whether its coverage should be established by building up a list of sectors for inclusion (a "positive list") or by assuming that all except a specified ("negative") list of sectors would be included, and therefore subject to commitments. The United States and the European Communities backed the negative list approach, because it would require a broad effort by all countries and would widen the scope of the agreement as a whole; developing and smaller countries preferred the positive list precisely because it would not require them to open up a large number of sectors. Other questions were raised by developing countries, with India in particular insisting that the services framework must provide a balance of interests by helping to strengthen the services capacity of developing countries, not least by providing support for infant industries. Similarly, Singapore said that developing countries should be given extra time to put services concessions into effect, and should have some discretion in giving preference to domestic service suppliers. Brazil argued that the service framework should provide for some transfer of technology and for preferential financial arrangements to help developing countries to build up their service sectors. Discussions continued on the broad principles identified by ministers in Montreal – market access, national treatment and so on – without any meeting of minds: an internal Secretariat report on a lengthy discussion in the October meeting of the GNS noted that "there existed almost as many perceptions as there were interventions and in important respects many of the views are far apart".

With some difficulty, the negotiating group managed in the final weeks of 1989 to "assemble the necessary elements", as requested by ministers, for the multilateral framework of rules and principles for trade in services. Inevitably, square brackets abounded, reflecting the wide range of views on most questions, and not all of the 15-page draft document that emerged from the discussions was fully developed; but at least the main issues were defined by the numerous alternatives set out. Three reasonably detailed sections covered the scope and definition of the framework, the concepts, principles and rules that might be embodied in it, and its coverage and application. A fourth section on institutions consisted only of a set of headings for later discussion.

The new document helped to clarify and organize discussion in the New Year, but did nothing to resolve differences, either about the structure and coverage of the framework agreement itself or about what other matters would need to be dealt with in the services negotiations before the end of the Uruguay Round. One fundamental disagreement concerned whether negotiation of the framework agreement was the sole task of the GNS or not. Most developed countries felt that a worthwhile outcome to the Round would require that participants take on a substantial first package of specific commitments to ease trade in services, although they envisaged that the process of progressive liberalization would be carried forward in subsequent further rounds of negotiations, to be conducted in accordance with rules that would be set out in the framework agreement. Brazil, Egypt, India and some other developing countries argued that the mandate of the GNS did not go beyond negotiating the general framework of rules and principles, leaving any negotiation of specific commitments to the years after the Round was concluded. Linked with this split in views was a disagreement as to whether countries should at least undertake to freeze their existing service regulations, and if so, whether developing countries should be exempted from such a standstill requirement on the ground that their present regulations required further development. Discussion continued on these issues, and there was a gradual acceptance that at least some general obligations such as transparency should apply as soon as the framework agreement took effect. However, the difference of approach was such that it is easy to understand why the services negotiations never reached the stage of bargaining on the easing of specific trade obstacles within the original time-frame of the Uruguay Round.

Most of the time remaining up to the meeting in Brussels was thus spent on negotiating the framework agreement, and on discussions on how to accommodate the special characteristics of particular service sectors. In practice, the issues became closely intertwined, and this was reflected in the development of several sectoral annexes to be attached to the basic framework document.

The main landmarks of the 1990 negotiations were submission in February of a Latin American draft for the framework agreement, providing a counterbalance to the earlier US text, meetings of sectoral working parties from May onwards, preparation by the chairman of a draft framework text that was sent to the TNC in July, and – in common with the other Uruguay Round negotiating groups – nearly non-stop meetings in the autumn to develop a text for ministers to consider in Brussels.

The Latin American text, a full draft running to 34 articles and 19 pages, clearly illustrated the opposite extreme from the US position, giving great prominence to special provisions for developing countries, and stressing MFN treatment. Among provisions for developing countries, it included flexibility to open fewer sectors or liberalize fewer types of transactions, the right to provide incentives and export subsidies to domestic suppliers of services, priority in negotiations to measures of particular interest to them, the right to establish preferential arrangements among themselves, and commitments by developed countries to provide financial and technical assistance. "Parties to the Framework, and in particular developing countries," it stressed, "shall have the right to regulate the provision of services within their territories in order to implement national policy objectives." The paper's basic definition of services included cross-border movement of both services and consumers, but provided for cross-border movement of factors of production only for specified purposes, distinct transactions and limited duration. This important paper was to be supplemented in May by a proposal from seven Asian and African countries, including India, China and Egypt, which foresaw that liberalization would initially be undertaken mainly by developed countries, with developing countries joining in as their own services exports felt the benefits of the earlier opening of markets in developed countries.

The renewal of sectoral discussions reflected recognition that some sectors presented problems that might prevent them from being opened up for trade unless special provisions were negotiated for them. Closely related to this concern was a growing belief that, as long as these problems were not fully understood, general rules drawn up in the broader framework agreement might later prove hard to apply to those sectors. There was also – and this was sometimes disconcerting for the traditional trade negotiators engaged in work on services – a strong interest on the part of specialists in finance, telecommunications and other sectoral matters in ensuring that non-specialists did not commit them to changes that would ignore considerations that they thought important. From time to time, there was a tendency for some sectoral discussions to become dominated by the experts, and somewhat detached from the mainstream of the services negotiations. As in the 1989 discussions, much attention was given to financial services, including both banking and insurance, with the focus on prudential issues and the need for service suppliers to establish offices in the host country, as well as on the view of some developed countries that liberalization could not be on a fully MFN basis unless most countries offered substantial commitments. For transport services, many countries wanted to see a move from bilateral agreements on sea transport towards a more multilateral opening up of markets; in contrast, most countries accepted that air transport would for the foreseeable future remain dominated by bilateral agreements. Some countries felt, having discussed questions of labour mobility, that a special annex to the framework agreement would be needed, particularly to deal with movements of essential personnel. Later troubles with trade in audiovisual services (which for the most part consist of films and television programmes) were foreshadowed by disagreements over the need or otherwise to protect "cultural identity", either by covering the sector in a special annex, or by a general cultural exception to be included in the framework. Other meetings of experts looked at the special aspects of trade in professional services and tourism – the latter, by some estimates, the world's largest industry.

By June, work in the services group was directed mainly towards producing its contribution to the July objective of a "profile" of the package to be put to ministers in Brussels. In the case of services, this was agreed to mean a complete draft for the framework agreement, and an indication of what sectoral annexes or annotations might be needed. During the month, Switzerland, and then the European Community, produced their own full draft texts for a General Agreement on Trade in Services. They had much in common, with broad coverage, minimum exceptions, an initial freeze on existing measures affecting trade in services, and provision for a first set of national liberalization commitments to be attached to the GATS, as well as for periodic further negotiations to open up national markets for service suppliers. The EC proposal also called for recognition of the objective of achieving a higher degree of liberalization through customs unions or free trade areas. Japan, too, produced its version of a GATS agreement in July.

With this wide variety of proposals to draw upon, Felipe Jaramillo, chairman of the GNS, developed his own proposed text for a framework agreement. Following a final week of intensive discussions with delegations, he sent it to the Trade Negotiations Committee on 23 July, as the services element of the promised profile of the Brussels package. It ran to 35 articles, divided over six sections. Four sections (scope and coverage, general obligations and disciplines, specific commitments, and progressive liberalization) were complete; the other two, on institutions and final provisions, consisted only of headings. Jaramillo pointed out that the whole text was subject to further consideration. He identified as issues on which agreement was now urgently needed, the questions of scope or definition, coverage (on which he noted that "some delegations" felt that countries should be able to exclude sectors), MFN treatment, stronger provisions for developing countries, progressive liberalization, and the negotiation and application of commitments. As can be seen, this formidable list was virtually identical with the headings of the four complete sections of his draft.

This chairman's proposal cut usefully through a large number of secondary questions, but – as an internal Secretariat note pointed out – most of the major issues remained open. Among sectors whose coverage remained in doubt, because of hesitations by one country or another, were land, sea and air transport, financial and audiovisual services. Developing countries continued to insist on the need for balance between commitments on establishment and those on labour mobility. The United States and the European Community emphasized that the framework agreement should be accompanied by initial commitments to remove obstacles to trade in services. The United States had actually put specific requests to 15 of its negotiating partners. It also did not want to adopt a straightforward MFN provision for services, mainly because it envisaged that it and other interested countries might negotiate higher-level commitments in certain sectors. All these matters were important, and to a great extent they were also linked to one another. Few countries, for instance, were ready to start negotiating specific market-opening commitments as long as the agreement's sectoral coverage and rules on non-discrimination remained unsettled.

Discussions in the July TNC served only to reveal the extent of disagreement. A long string of contradictory declarations on services are recorded in the Secretariat's official note on the meeting in the classic form of "some thought..." and "others thought..." (and sometimes, "yet others"), covering all the points mentioned by Jaramillo, and more as well. In his summing up, Dunkel recalled these points, and put his finger on the most divisive question of all: "The vast majority of participants do not favour ... excluding sectors, in total or in part, from the coverage of the agreement." For substantive negotiations to proceed, he said, the question of coverage had to be settled, as well as the role that MFN treatment would have in the process of liberalization.

These two questions – sectoral coverage and MFN – were to dominate the services negotiations up to, and well beyond, the Brussels meeting.

As far as individual sectors were concerned, a further series of meetings took place in the early autumn, with each working group asked to decide whether its sector had special characteristics that would need to be covered by a separate annex to the framework agreement, or by special notes. The discussions proved difficult, with views divided in practically every case. There were particularly sharp differences over how to treat financial services and whether there was a need for special annexes for this sector as well as for telecommunications, transport and audiovisual services. In each of these areas, one or more of the participating countries showed themselves unwilling to apply some of the basic rules of the framework agreement. Usually, the objection was to application of the MFN rule. The immediate implication was that some countries would be unable to enjoy the benefits of market openings negotiated in that sector. The broader and even more disturbing implication was that the eventual services agreement might not offer a broad balance of advantage to a significant number of countries.

One negative conclusion was reached: there would be no time to negotiate specific liberalization commitments for trade in services before Brussels. It was agreed that this should be a first priority for the early months of 1991.

Negotiations on the framework also achieved no breakthroughs. True, Jaramillo completed his text by adding provisions on dispute settlement and on institutions to run the services agreement. Considerable work was also done on putting the draft into more final, legal language. But these were peripheral issues. A number of important, but not central, questions were discussed without reaching clear conclusions: they included safeguard provisions to be applied in emergencies or balance-of-payments difficulties, government procurement, and rules on the use of subsidies. A complete new draft text was circulated for the final pre-Brussels meeting of the GNS at the end of October. However, disaccord on the central questions of coverage and MFN treatment remained: indeed, it grew deeper.

In the last weeks before the Brussels meeting, it became known that the United States, in particular, had hardened its position: it was now firm in its wish to exclude some sectors altogether from the services agreement, and to tie MFN treatment to the exchange of specific commitments, rather than make it a general obligation linked to acceptance of the agreement as a whole. This stand was greeted with dismay by most other countries, and had the effect both of halting the sectoral negotiations and of generating pessimism about the prospects for the services negotiations as a whole.

Green-room discussions proved unproductive: no country was ready for compromise, presumably because the issues were important in themselves, and because any concessions were being reserved for a final bargain involving other key subjects such as agriculture and textiles.

At least the section on services in the consolidated draft agreement that went to ministers now bore the title "General Agreement on Trade in Services", and was of a length and complexity indicating clearly that the services negotiations, if successful, would give birth to a new set of international rights and obligations comparable to those of the GATT itself. But the text came forward only on the responsibility of the GNS Chairman, and a multiplicity of square brackets made all too clear that, as Jaramillo said in his commentary, there remained "many divergences of views among participants". Chief among the decisions left to ministers was the question of MFN treatment. Was MFN to be "a general obligation to extend the benefits of any measure on trade in services from any country to all parties" or would it (as provided by alternative language reflecting US views) just apply to specific benefits negotiated with another country? Depending on the answer to that question, what provisions would be needed in sectoral annexes to permit countries, in some circumstances, to discriminate against some others? Draft annexes were provided on maritime, inland waterway, road and air transport, on basic telecommunications and telecommunications services, on labour mobility and on audiovisual services. An annex on financial services was conspicuously missing, even though it was agreed to be needed.

All in all, the draft services agreement was not, most officials in Geneva agreed, in a state of which they could be very proud. Ministers in Brussels, they correctly forecast, were going to be highly critical of a text in which (as the EC delegate put it at the final TNC at official level on 26 November) "the ocean of brackets" made it "well-nigh impossible to distinguish substantive political options from mere technicalities". And although the delegates found a number of specific points to criticize or emphasize, they were largely agreed in their opposition to the US stand on MFN treatment: its maintenance, the EC said, would lead to the failure of the services negotiations.

TRIPS

The mid-term review decided that the goal of the TRIPS negotiations, while still always carefully expressed in terms of "trade-related aspects" of intellectual property rights, was to reach agreements on matters central to any system of intellectual property protection. "Adequate" standards and principles (what kinds of intellectual property should be covered, what rights should be available, and how could they be exercised), "effective and appropriate" means to enforce intellectual property rights, and "effective and expeditious" procedures to resolve disputes between governments multilaterally were now accepted subjects for negotiation. Added to these matters was the negotiation of rules to prevent trade in counterfeit goods. There were of course provisos as well. Until the end of the Round, there would be no decision on whether GATT or another institution would administer the resulting agreement. Due consideration had to be given to "the underlying public policy objectives" of national systems for the protection of intellectual property: in other words, to the arguments which had led many developing countries, in particular, to limit the protection they gave to owners of patents, trademarks and other forms of intellectual property so as to encourage such aims as the growth of technologically based domestic industries and the supply of low-cost medicines to their populations.

With these new ground-rules the TRIPS negotiations could at last get down to hard discussion and bargaining, aimed at a deal whose basic elements had now been identified. The North-South confrontation that had marked the TRIPS discussions up to 1988 eased, even if it never died away, and in any case was diluted as new issues arose that created different lineups of interest.

Work re-started with a deluge of national proposals which left no doubt that negotiations were now fully engaged. By the end of 1989, 15 detailed proposals had been made on standards for intellectual property rights, eleven on enforcement, and several more on other issues. Some of the proposals were already in the detailed and precise language of a draft treaty. With these proposals as basis for discussion, the negotiating group was able to work its way systematically through the issues, to understand what each participant wanted, and to identify the differences that would have to be resolved.

One question was how far the basic principles of GATT might be applied to intellectual property rights. GATT and the Berne (copyright) and Paris (patent) Conventions all provided broadly for national treatment: foreign goods or nationals were to be treated the same as those of national origin. But only the GATT provided for MFN treatment, meaning that no distinction could be made between foreign countries. There had been cases, resented by those who were not among the beneficiaries, in which better protection was given to the intellectual property of one country's citizens than to that of others. Some participants therefore sought to include an MFN rule in any TRIPS agreement. Many developing countries also wanted explicit recognition of their special need, as they saw it, to have flexibility in providing protection to intellectual property so as to be able to pursue important national policy objectives. Some argued that a TRIPS agreement should give weight to the obligations, as well as the rights, of owners of intellectual property, and suggested that rules were needed to require patent holders to work their patents, to discourage restrictive business practices, and in particular to prohibit licensing agreements that placed limitations on trade and development. In reply, developed countries argued that developing countries would actually gain by giving better protection to intellectual property, because this would attract foreign investment, research, and transfer of technology that would support their economic development. This discussion formed part of a long-running exchange over whether a TRIPS agreement could respond adequately to the needs of developing countries just by giving them more time than developed countries to adapt to its rules, or whether it should provide permanently different rules for them.

On the issue of standards or norms of protection, proposals were made for minimum standards in areas which effectively covered all the main categories of intellectual property: copyright and related ("neighbouring") rights, trade-marks, geographical indications, industrial designs, patents, layout designs for integrated circuits, and trade secrets. In general, these proposals aimed to strengthen protection, for instance by requiring a minimum and, if possible, standard patent life, tighter rules to limit compulsory licensing, and a ban on the use of geographical names for products actually originating elsewhere. While each proposal tended to reflect particular national interests and existing legislation – thus aimed at changing the laws and practices of other countries which gave less protection to those interests or at defending that existing legislation – some were much more controversial than others. The strongest disagreements were expressed over patent protection for pharmaceuticals. Several developing countries did not grant patents for pharmaceuticals at all; others required that licences to manufacture a patented pharmaceutical be granted. Two strongly held views clashed head on: developing countries argued the primacy of public health needs; the manufacturers (to a large extent American and European) pointed to the huge research costs and long delays in approval as justifying lengthy patent protection.

Proposals for enforcement of intellectual property protection revealed much smaller differences of view. Participants recognized that no country was going to make fundamental changes in its legal system because of an agreement on intellectual property. The focus was on setting obligations that would be compatible with the basic features of different national legal systems but be sufficiently precise to ensure some essential requirements. These included fair, straightforward and reasonably rapid procedures; adequate civil remedies, such as damages and injunctions; provisional remedies to prevent irreparable damage; and, in cases of flagrant disregard of property owners' rights, criminal penalties or suspension of imports of goods that infringed rights. The concern to protect intellectual property rights had to be balanced against the risk that any measures introduced might be misused as a means of harassing and blocking legitimate trade.

As long as no decision could be reached about the institutional framework for whatever TRIPS agreement would emerge, it was hard to agree what approach to adopt to a multilateral dispute settlement procedure. One possibility was to follow the GATT model, with or without the possibility of permitting the withdrawal of GATT rights to compensate for a failure to live up to TRIPS obligations (i.e. cross-retaliation). Another was to rely on some other institution, outside the TRIPS framework, to handle disputes. A related issue – and a spur to reach agreement on a multilateral procedure – was the concern to block the possibility of unilateral action.

By the beginning of 1990, the TRIPS group was in the happy situation of being clearly ahead of many other Uruguay Round groups. The main issues and proposals had all been explored, the points of difference (numerous: by the count of a Secretariat checklist, more than 500 in all) were known, and there was every prospect that a very substantial agreement could emerge from the negotiations. The time had apparently arrived to start putting together all the elements that would have to go into a final agreement on TRIPS, and to begin serious negotiations to bridge differences. On the other hand, some delegations, particularly from developing countries, were reluctant to continue so fast as long as other areas of the negotiations in which they felt greater interest were lagging behind. There was an awkward period of some weeks during which the negotiations marked time, only informal talks were possible, and precious weeks appeared to be slipping away.

This standstill phase ended quite quickly when first the European Community in March, and then the United States, Switzerland, Japan and a group of 14 developing countries each put forward draft legal texts for a full TRIPS agreement. The four developed-country proposals were similar in approach, differing mainly in specific provisions on standards. They provided for a TRIPS agreement integrated with the GATT itself, and therefore sharing its dispute settlement arrangements. Parties to the agreement would be required to accept the provisions of the Paris and Berne Conventions, as well as strengthened standards and enforcement obligations. Their specific differences, however, showed that they still had many problems to resolve among them. These included the question of whether the United States could be persuaded to change its basic rule on the grant of patents from "first to invent" to the "first to file" standard of other countries, the efforts of the EC and Switzerland to obtain better protection for geographical names applied to wine and other products, and several important copyright issues. One question already attracting outside attention from environmentalists was whether the TRIPS agreement should give protection to biotechnological inventions. This inspired an outbreak of graffiti on Swiss highway bridges urging "GATT: no patents on life!" and a Greenpeace stunt in which the GATT headquarters building was draped for much of a day in a huge banner.

The 14 developing countries (seven from Latin America – Argentina, Brazil, Chile, Colombia, Cuba, Peru and Uruguay – together with China, Egypt, India, Nigeria, Pakistan, Tanzania and Zimbabwe) were those who all along had been most reluctant to negotiate stronger protection for intellectual property in GATT, and their proposal reflected this. They offered quite strong rules, to be incorporated into the GATT system, on counterfeit and pirated goods, and general provisions on enforcement. On standards, they stressed the obligations of holders of intellectual property rights, and offered no minimum level of protection for patents or copyright. Their proposal left open whether the rules on standards and enforcement would be taken into GATT or put into effect through another organization.

By midsummer, most work on TRIPS was concentrated in open but informal negotiations on a "composite draft text" assembled by the chairman and Secretariat. This 100-page paper put the provisions of all five draft legal texts into a single text, using square brackets or alternatives to indicate differences. About 25 delegations were involved in the first round of discussions, which resulted in some useful minor cleaning-up of some proposals, and a considerable advance in allowing the negotiators themselves to gain a clearer view of the issues that would have to be resolved to reach agreement. However, very little was achieved in actually settling differences of substance, partly because negotiators were not prepared to play their cards as long as other Uruguay Round negotiations were not moving, and more particularly because there was no sign that the two largest players, the United States and the European Community, were yet ready to settle the considerable differences that divided them. Moreover, the basic difference of approach between the four developed-country texts on the one hand, and the draft by the 14 developing countries on the other, remained unresolved.

Over the remaining months before the Brussels meeting in December 1990 positions narrowed, the single draft text was revised several times, and gradually shrank in length, but remained in status a chairman's text, with no country committed to it. Indeed, not one point was clearly agreed to by all participants. The TRIPS text that finally went forward to Brussels was in better shape than those on many other Uruguay Round subjects, but it still represented a negotiation that was far from finished. While the majority of differences had been settled, the key ones remained outstanding. Anell's covering "commentary", besides underlining the continuing difference between the 14-country approach and the other proposals, identified a long list of further "major outstanding issues on points of substance". They included the several decisions needed on copyright questions (e.g. on the protection of computer programs, rental rights, the rights of performers and the length of protection of sound recordings), "considerable" differences on geographical indications, a large number of "basic" and other questions on patents (e.g. on coverage, term and compulsory licensing) and, in addition to a number of miscellaneous issues, essential decisions about transition and other arrangements to be provided for developing and least-developed countries.

TRIMS

The mid-term review made little difference to the trade-related investment measures (TRIMS) negotiations, which had still not found a focus or aim. Early meetings of the group in 1989 led some observers to believe that the strongest opponents of new disciplines to regulate TRIMS might be coming round to acceptance of substantive negotiations. At the same time, a number of developed countries were meeting informally in Geneva as "Friends of TRIMS", trying to define the coverage of an eventual agreement that would be generally acceptable. By the autumn, however, there could be few illusions of converging views.

In July, the United States and Switzerland both came forward with proposals that would prohibit certain measures that inherently had trade effects, and make others subject to lesser disciplines. A paper from Singapore argued in favour of consultation and dispute settlement to handle the trade distorting or restrictive effects of TRIMS, but rejected any outright prohibitions. A meeting of the group in September reviewed three further proposals that had little in common. Mexico, which had traditionally made considerable use of TRIMS, suggested a practical exercise: pilot studies of two measures (it suggested export requirements and local equity requirements) to assess their trade effects and how these might be avoided, taking into account development aspects. Japan, working on similar lines to the United States, proposed a framework of disciplines for seven TRIMS that would at a minimum require that they be applied without discrimination and transparently, and would prohibit those which restricted or distorted trade unless they were clearly consistent with GATT provisions. India's statement, a long and closely argued account of its whole approach to the TRIMS issue, did envisage substantive negotiations, but insisted that prohibition was inappropriate. Only four TRIMS – essentially export performance requirements, local content requirements and variants on these – could, in its view, have direct and significant adverse trade effects; but these would not always occur, and any disciplines negotiated would have to take full account of development considerations and be matched by disciplines over the restrictive business practices of multinational corporations.

There was little change in this situation in the following months. Those developed countries which sought strong disciplines to regulate TRIMS continued to bring forward new proposals or refine old ones, while the developing countries that were determined to preserve their ability to regulate investment held essentially to their existing positions. Only in the middle was there evidence that common ground might emerge. Among the developed countries, the Europeans had more limited ambitions than the Americans and Japanese, partly because they themselves had used local content requirements, especially to regulate Japanese investment. Several developing countries in Latin America and East Asia showed themselves ready to discuss the possibility of limited but effective disciplines on the use of TRIMS. Both the European Community and the Nordic countries put proposals forward in November. The Community's proposal covered eight measures, most of which it believed were already governed by GATT rules. The major exception was export performance requirements, which it conceded were not clearly covered by the GATT, but felt ought to be prohibited.

The Nordics believed that local content rules were already prohibited by the GATT rules, and that requirements on export performance (and trade-balancing, whose effects they viewed as almost the same) should also be banned as having clearly adverse effects on trade. For the remaining TRIMS, they proposed "second-level" disciplines that would be less constraining but would be combined with the possibility of dispute settlement action if the measures were shown to be causing damage to the trade interests of other countries.

On the face of it, the TRIMS group was now beginning to establish a real basis for negotiating an agreement, an impression reinforced when, in January 1990, the United States tabled a draft agreement, based on GATT Articles and principles but going beyond them. The main features of the draft, foreshadowed by earlier US proposals, were prohibition of most of the identified principal TRIMS, on the ground that they inherently restricted or distorted trade. Those not prohibited would be governed by obligations to apply them in a non-discriminatory way, and not to use them at all if they adversely affect the trade of another country. Developing countries would be given longer than developed countries to adapt to the new disciplines, but would not be exempted from them. Other developed countries welcomed the US proposals as a basis to get serious negotiations started, even if they doubted whether such strong disciplines would ultimately be negotiable. However, developing countries generally objected to the US draft's reliance on prohibition of many TRIMS and its failure to recognize their arguments that these measures had a legitimate place in development and industrialization policies.

The strength of developing-country opposition to restrictions on TRIMS emerged clearly in March, when eleven countries, soon joined by several others, co-sponsored a statement which declared that the negotiating group had not finished its first task of identifying the trade effects of TRIMS and examining them in the light of the GATT rules. The statement's sponsors, including Argentina, Brazil, China, Egypt, India and Nigeria, accused the developed countries who were now proposing new disciplines for TRIMS of ignoring the negotiating mandate. They argued that development considerations out-weighed whatever adverse trade effects TRIMS might have, and that no new GATT provisions to regulate them were needed. Developed countries did their best to interpret the statement as a comprehensive exposition of developing-country views and a constructive approach to further dialogue, but many in fact saw it as arguing (as one delegate said) "that basically the group did not have to do anything".

The Round was supposed to end in Brussels in December; in April the GNG agreed to seek "the profile of a final package" by July. As chairman, Kobayashi had to seek a compromise between the views of participants. Some countries were ready for this, but there was little sign of common ground between the United States on one side and Brazil, India and their allies on the other. Only the United States had put forward a clear negotiating proposal, and this had already been rejected as a basis for negotiation by most developing countries. The negotiating group remained split over such fundamental questions as whether some forms of TRIM should be prohibited or not, and whether developing countries should come under whatever disciplines might be negotiated. Kobayashi concluded that he would have to put forward a draft proposal of his own, even though it was bound to be criticized heavily by at least one side, and probably both.

Kobayashi circulated his first proposal informally in May. It provided for the phase-out and eventual elimination of local content requirements contrary to GATT Article III and of trade-balancing requirements and export restraints contrary to Article XI, although both were open to justification under the infant-industry rules of Article XVIII:C. It also provided for phase-out of export performance requirements. Immediately, it ran into the expected objections. For the developing countries most opposed to disciplines on TRIMS, the prohibitions would be an unacceptable and unjustified extension of the GATT rules, the development provisions were inadequate, and the lack of reference to restrictive business practices made it unbalanced. For the United States and Japan, it was simply far too narrow and unambitious.

Consultations in June brought out clearly that although many developed and developing countries were prepared to negotiate on the basis of the chairman's paper, the group led by Brazil and India was not. Moreover, as long as this situation persisted, the United States, too, would insist on standing by its own proposals. Discussions allowed the chairman's paper to be developed and refined considerably. However, at the June meeting, twelve developing countries, broadly the same as those which had produced the March paper, presented a "Draft Declaration on Trade-Related Investment Measures" that represented their idea of a suitable outcome to the negotiations. The draft Declaration underlined the negotiating mandate and stressed that the final result of the TRIMS negotiations would apply only to "the direct and significant adverse trade effects" of investment measures directed at affecting trade flows. It affirmed the sovereign right of any country to decide what investment it would permit, and set out 13 wide-ranging development objectives which would justify developing countries in continuing to employ investment measures which served those ends. The only discipline proposed for TRIMS, apart from limited transparency requirements, was a provision of the classic "best endeavours" variety, lacking any real binding effect: countries should "seek to avoid" applying TRIMS in a manner which directly and significantly distorted trade and caused significant injury to the trade interest of another GATT member, or which might hinder attainment of GATT objectives. India, presenting the draft, underlined that it reflected the case-by-case approach that his own and other countries had supported all along as the proper way to handle the TRIMS issue. The United States described the draft as a proposal for no result at the end of the negotiations.

Matters got no better in the following weeks and months, in spite of concentrated negotiating sessions that gave rise to fleeting moments of comparative optimism. In July, the chairman was only able to send forward to the GNG a report on the TRIMS negotiations which put side-by-side his own text and the two rival statements of extreme opposing views: the developing-country draft declaration, and the US proposal. Numerous further meetings took place in September, October and (after a TNC meeting to which the latest three-alternative text was submitted) in November. Drafting efforts were concentrated on the chairman's text, but the sponsors of the draft declaration maintained their central demands that no TRIMS be prohibited outright, that problems be dealt with only on a case-by-case basis, and that development considerations be given a central place in any new rules, not treated simply as a possible exception to prohibition. (Australia and South Africa joined in support of the first two arguments.) These developing countries also continued to argue that TRIMS could not fairly be regulated unless matching action were taken against the restrictive business practices which they were designed to counter.

On top of all these differences, another came to the fore. Should rules on TRIMS apply only to measures that were required by law, or should they also cover requirements that an investor might accept for other reasons – for instance, as a condition for receiving a subsidy? Once again, this was an issue which split the participants. It also introduced a complication into the Round as a whole, since it was an issue that concerned both TRIMS and the subsidy negotiations.

On 9 November, following a final meeting of the TRIMS group and further informal discussions, and with just a month to go to the Brussels meeting, Kobayashi forwarded his last version of a proposed agreement. It was now in fairly straightforward form, and no longer contained the US version, but – four years on from the start of the negotiations – still offered starkly contrasting alternatives on the main issues.

Along with other disputed texts, the TRIMS proposals were discussed during November in the green-room meetings of heads of delegations. Following a first round of discussions, he asked the representative of Hong Kong, Keith Broadbridge, to consult further and try his hand at a re-draft. However, Broadbridge's draft proved unacceptable as an alternative basis for negotiations, even though he left for ministerial decision the key questions of whether any TRIMS should be prohibited, whether export performance requirements should be covered, and whether restrictive business practices should be mentioned.

No negotiating text of the Uruguay Round went to Brussels in worse shape than that on TRIMS, although some others were equally unready for decision. Indeed, formally no TRIMS text went to Brussels at all, although the various alternatives were of course well known to governments. The "first approximation to the Final Act" included just one page of "commentary" on TRIMS, which noted that "basic divergences of view continue to exist" on points which it summed up in seven questions, and that no text had emerged that had been accepted as an agreed basis for negotiations.

Institutions

In the near-shipwreck of the Montreal meeting, only three really encouraging events had occurred. One, the agreement on a package of early trade concessions for tropical products exported by developing countries, was the sole result of substance to emerge from the whole range of Uruguay Round negotiations on market access and on improved rules for world trade. Both of the other unalloyed successes came from the negotiations on institutions. The dispute settlement negotiators had produced an interim package of mainly procedural improvements that was to be put into effect immediately, and which it was hoped would produce quick results, not least in smoothing and speeding up the progress of the record number of dispute cases currently going through (or blocked in) the GATT machinery. The FOGS group had developed the basis for a completely new and major GATT activity: the regular, systematic and detailed review of every member country's trade policies, not in connection with any particular dispute or other development, but as part of a continuous surveillance of trends in international trade policy. Both of these agreements were adopted in April 1989, following the agricultural agreement that allowed completion of the mid-term review. In the case of the new Trade Policy Review Mechanism, several weeks of further intensive and sometimes difficult negotiations were needed, in a technical group chaired by the Secretariat, to reach agreement on the format which defined the information that countries under examination would have to provide in their reports to the Council. In July 1989 the GATT Council adopted the agreement, and the way was clear for country reviews to begin. They soon became a regular and important feature of GATT's work, and although introduced provisionally, their continuation at the end of the Round was never to be questioned.

Real though these institutional achievements were, however, they had been achieved so early because they reflected wide and genuine agreement on the objectives sought. Both the dispute settlement group and the FOGS group had been working, in the packages approved at the mid-term review, on matters which everyone agreed were both important and – crucially – of interest to all participants. This made it possible to reach agreement on them in isolation, without regard to progress on other matters under negotiation in the Round. Although the remaining issues already raised in the two institutional groups were still, on the whole, less controversial than those being discussed elsewhere in the Round, there could be no certainty that they would be handled as smoothly as the two packages agreed to in Montreal. As it turned out, certain countries had much more ambitious ideas in mind than they had yet revealed. Moreover, some of these ideas could only be made effective through action that would cut across the somewhat artificial demarcation lines that separated the mandates of the dispute settlement and FOGS groups.

Dispute settlement

The Montreal package of improvements to the dispute settlement procedures was made up of proposals on which agreement could fairly easily be reached. But there were also others on the table, for which varying degrees of support had been expressed, and which required further study before serious negotiations on them would be possible. Moreover, the world was not standing still. In the United States, the new trade legislation voted by Congress in 1988 had provided the US Administration with the authority it needed to negotiate agreements in the Uruguay Round, but had also actually strengthened the Section 301 powers widely resented by other countries as a standing incitement to unilateral action in disregard of America's commitments under the GATT rules. At a GATT Council meeting in September 1988, not long before the Montreal meeting of ministers, the European Community, Japan, Brazil, India and many others expressed strong misgivings about the new "Super 301" provisions. The United States defended the provisions as being aimed at coping with issues not adequately covered by present GATT rules, but which it sought to discipline through the Uruguay Round. The Community had from the first pushed strongly in the dispute settlement negotiations for a clear prohibition on unilateral action on matters covered by the multilateral rules. From this point onwards, that objective became a priority both for it and for other countries, not only in the dispute settlement negotiations but also in those on safeguards, subsidies and anti-dumping. In all these areas, there was a general concern to make sure that the rules were drawn tightly enough to prevent any country from making its own judgements and punitive decisions without reference to the GATT rules and appropriate approval from the GATT membership as a whole.

A second development was that several Uruguay Round groups were negotiating the modification or introduction of dispute settlement arrangements distinct from the standard GATT procedures. Even before the Round began, some participants had been worried about the fragmentation of dispute settlement between the basic procedures under GATT Articles XXII and XXIII and the separate arrangements established under many Tokyo Round codes. A particular problem, shown up in a running US-EC dispute over subsidies for civil aircraft production, was that aggrieved countries might pick and choose ("forum-shop") among alternative sets of procedures according to their judgement of which would be most likely to produce a favourable result. Now, further refinements of the Tokyo Round arrangements under discussion in the Round, as well as the introduction of the major new subjects of intellectual property and services, threatened to fragment the dispute settlement rules of the international trading system even further.

During 1989, work in the negotiating group on dispute settlement tended at first to regress to a general discussion of principles rather than genuine bargaining. This was perhaps inevitable. The mid-term ministerial decisions had identified a long list of dispute settlement issues for further negotiation. Explicitly, they called for a closer look at how panel decisions could be made effective, and at the rules for compensation of injured parties. A further discreet reference, probably unintelligible to the casual reader, told the negotiating group to continue work on the unresolved issues of domestic legislation incompatible with the GATT dispute settlement rules and on the requirements for adoption of panel reports. Julio Lacarte, chairman of the group, lengthened the list still further at the first post-Montreal meeting, when he reminded negotiators of their concern that all GATT dispute settlement procedures should if possible be integrated into one text, as well as of other problems such as the status of non-violation complaints and the possibility of making greater use of arbitration. Even his list proved far from exhaustive. Taken together, these questions were much more difficult than those dealt with in the Montreal agreement.

From the resumption of negotiations until early 1990, the group gave most attention to how panel reports should be adopted and how their recommendations should be put into effect. Although the fundamental issue was still whether decisions should be taken only on the basis of consensus (in other words, with no country explicitly objecting), there were others. Should a panel judgement apply only to the case under review, or should it set a precedent for similar future cases? What if the panel's conclusions were poorly argued, or frankly wrong? One answer, already explored on past occasions, might be to improve the quality of panellists by establishing a fixed pool of qualified potential panel members, going beyond the roster which had already been built up, and perhaps including many more non-governmental panellists. More daringly – and here a completely new theme was introduced into the negotiations – would the legal quality and precedential value of dispute settlement cases be improved if there existed the possibility of appealing a panel decision to some kind of higher body? The European Community was an early supporter of appeals to eminent legal experts when panel decisions were "erroneous or incomplete", and it found an ally in the United States. Although some countries were hesitant to endorse the idea of an appellate body, mainly because they feared it might slow down still further the dispute settlement process, it was discussed in detail from late 1989 onwards, with the proposal gradually crystallizing as a standing tribunal that would be called on to review and pass prompt and binding judgement on disputed conclusions reached by panels on purely legal issues.

Another subject debated at length was how, and how rapidly, a losing party in a dispute ought to comply with panel recommendations. Countries differed over whether losers should be encouraged to give compensatory trade concessions to offset injury done by a trade measure. Some insisted (following a traditional GATT line of argument) that the primary aim should be to get rid of the injurious measure. Others agreed, but thought compensation well suited to redressing injury done to developing countries which in practice had no real prospect of effective retaliation. Another justification seen for compensation was as a means of restoring the balance of advantage in "non-violation" complaints, in which a country might claim that GATT benefits to which it was entitled were being nullified or impaired by another country's trade measure, even if that measure was not actually contrary to GATT, and therefore could legally be maintained. Finally, how long was "a reasonable time" before corrective action need be taken?

Still further specific proposals came from Bangladesh and from Switzerland. Bangladesh proposed permanent special procedures to benefit least-developed countries involved in disputes. It met sympathy, but most participants preferred to envisage applying the standard procedures flexibly to the least-developed countries, rather than introducing new arrangements that could further complicate a situation which they were trying to simplify. Switzerland suggested that private persons and companies should be given rights through domestic law to have their interests taken into account in hearings, decisions and the implementation of GATT disputes. This proposal did not get far, mainly because other countries did not want to extend GATT's essential character beyond that of an agreement between states.

At last, in April 1990, major and far-reaching negotiating proposals were put to the group. Within a few days of one another, the European Community and United States each put forward their visions of an overhauled GATT dispute settlement system. These were notable both for their differences and their common features.

The EC proposal adopted as its broad theme the establishment of a balance of rights and obligations over the whole field of action of the Uruguay Round. In this perspective, new dispute settlement rules were to go hand in hand with the end of the "grandfather clause" and all special derogations from the GATT rules, and with "an unequivocal and irreversible undertaking" by all parties to fully respect their GATT and code obligations "and to bring their legislation into line with the obligations concerned" and "refrain from unilateral measures which are incompatible with a multilateral approach to the settlement of disputes". Unsurprisingly, this stand, widely supported by other countries, was not reflected in the United States proposal.

Other points, however, in the two proposals showed quite strong similarities. Both backed strengthened arrangements for the composition of panels. Both favoured an appeals body to rule on disputed legal points. Both made suggestions for various deadlines to help move the dispute process along, and both envisaged compensation, and if necessary the right to retaliate, if the losing country in a dispute did not remove its offending measures within a reasonable time. On the problem of blockage of panel reports, the European Community proposed retention of the rule of consensus. The United States, accepting that this was the single most difficult issue facing the negotiating group, set out bolder alternatives. One, it suggested, could be automatic adoption provided the losing party did not object strongly or appeal to the appellate body. A second would be consensus adoption but with the losing party excluded from the decision. Broader decisions on legal interpretation might be left to later formal sessions of the GATT contracting parties.

Many of these ideas were picked up and further crystallized in proposals by Canada and Mexico, which again, as before Montreal, played a significant role in pushing the negotiations along. From this point onwards, moreover, discussion increasingly took place in informal sessions – a nearly invariable characteristic of GATT negotiations as they reach the stage of real bargaining, and participants seek to explore alternative possibilities without being forced to adopt rigid positions. By July, when Lacarte (like other group chairmen) reported to Dunkel on the "profile" of the agreement that seemed likely to be possible by the end of the year, he was able to indicate much common ground on the issues, and a fair degree of convergence on possible solutions, even if full agreement was still lacking even on widely supported proposals such as the suggested appellate body. Positions were perhaps furthest apart on whether adoption of reports should be automatic, on whether non-violation complaints (in which, by definition, no GATT rule was being broken) should have the benefit of the proposed new procedures, and on the demand by most countries that all should undertake to refrain from unilateral measures and bring their domestic legislation into line with the GATT dispute settlement procedures. On the last point, Lacarte recorded the US view: "one delegation considers that unilateral measures include procedural unilateralism employed with respect to dispute settlement, such as blocking at any stage of the process" and could be addressed "only where there are clear rules ... that eliminate opportunities for delay and blockage". Other open issues, still to be discussed properly, included the question of whether the new common procedures being developed could be applied to dispute settlement under the Tokyo Round agreements.

The draft agreement for Brussels took shape in informal negotiations during September and October, on the basis of a Secretariat text that covered all the points discussed since Montreal. (It was agreed that the Montreal agreement itself would be woven into the final text in due course.) The outcome was a text that went forward to the TNC, in Lacarte's name, on 19 October. To a great extent, it reflected agreement on many of the questions that the group had been discussing since 1987: for instance, the appellate review body was included, and compensation issues were largely resolved. But it still had gaps, such as the lack of any indication of whether the new procedures would apply to dispute settlement under the codes, and square-bracketed language indicated that some major decisions were still needed.

Further work before Brussels, including green-room discussions, succeeded in getting rid of a few of the less important brackets. But the text that went to Brussels was essentially that which had emerged from the group on 19 October, and it left unresolved the same three basic issues identified by Lacarte in July. First, and most directly important for the functioning of the dispute procedures themselves, was the question of how decisions should be taken on the adoption of panel and appellate body reports and on the authorization of retaliation. The alternatives, which in fact contained the seeds of the solution eventually to be reached, were stated (in the case of panel reports against which no appeal was lodged) as adoption "unless ... the Council decides [otherwise] [by consensus] [not to adopt the report]". The second major issue was the perennial question of a pledge against unilateral action, where the US position was covered by a footnote that made its acceptance subject to an agreement being reached on decision-making. The third, far less politically sensitive, was the problem of how non-violation complaints should be handled.

Functioning of the GATT system

In most sectors of the Uruguay Round, the intensity and pace of negotiations increased after the mid-term review. This did not happen in the FOGS group, which had already achieved what proved to be its biggest success, the agreement to set up the Trade Policy Review Mechanism. Several further proposals for institutional change were still on the table as negotiations resumed in 1989, and others of potential importance were to be made in 1990. However, priorities clearly shifted elsewhere. The United States, which had no great desire to pursue most of the FOGS proposals made by its trading partners, made it known that it would be quite happy to see the group wound up before the end of the Round, to allow negotiators to concentrate on other subjects. Other countries, some of which had much greater ambitions for institutional change, felt it inappropriate to bring proposals forward until the shape of the overall Uruguay Round package became clearer. Significantly, no new negotiating proposals were submitted to the group until the very end of 1989.

Negotiations on the review "format", which would define the coverage of reports that governments would submit for the trade policy reviews, kept the FOGS negotiators busy up to June 1989. Little else was discussed. At the suggestion of Julio Lacarte, who was now chairing both the institutional negotiating groups, discussion of proposals for a small ministerial-level group was set aside since there was clearly no immediate possibility of progress. This decision left as the main outstanding issue the third objective in the group's mandate: "To increase the contribution of the GATT to achieving greater coherence in global economic policy-making through strengthening its relationship with other international organizations responsible for monetary and financial matters."

The mid-term FOGS agreement fleshed out this objective, by calling for a dialogue between GATT and the monetary and financial organizations "to facilitate policies and actions which enhance the complementarities that exist between them". It asked the Director-General to explore with the heads of the IMF and World Bank ways in which GATT's relationships with them might be strengthened, and to report back by September 1989, taking into account "the views, issues and proposals" raised in the FOGS group. A meeting of the group in June, at which widely varying, if not contradictory, advice was proffered on the matters which Dunkel should cover in his report, gave notice that whatever he said was likely to displease more than one government.

Dunkel's report, sent to the FOGS group in September, was the result of discussions over several months between senior staff of the GATT, Fund and

Bank, including meetings between Dunkel and the Managing Director of the Fund, Michel Camdessus, and the President of the Bank, Barber Conable. Dunkel was careful to describe the report as "exploratory", and to note that in taking up with the Bretton Woods agencies the "coherence" issues raised in the FOGS group he was not himself necessarily endorsing the views that delegates had expressed. The report set out eight major concerns which had been stated in the group. These included the contradiction between protectionism and efforts to relieve the debt problem, the belief that exchange-rate fluctuations inhibited trade liberalization, and the desire of developing countries reducing protection to obtain negotiating credit in GATT for what they did under Fund and Bank programmes, with some assurance of financial support if they ran into adjustment difficulties as a result of joining in multilateral liberalization.

Dunkel emphasized that although the role and character of GATT differed greatly from those of the Fund and Bank, they had large shared interests, among which were the concerns he had set out earlier (apart from the argument about exchange-rate fluctuations, with which, he noted, the heads of the Bank and Fund "cannot associate themselves"). While these policy inconsistencies called primarily for better cooperation among governments, the three agency heads agreed that they themselves could help to make the trade and financial communities aware of the interlinkages between policies. Contacts between the heads and staffs of the Fund and Bank, on one side, and the GATT on the other, could "help to alert each side to national trade, financial and monetary developments that may have an impact on the economic and trade interests of other countries". Dunkel recalled proposals in the FOGS group for meetings of trade and finance ministers, but also pointed out that "policy coordination begins at home", with national finance and trade policies that are mutually consistent. He went on to look at how GATT views might be brought to bear when the Fund and Bank were drawing up trade reform objectives under their loan programmes. The report discussed possibilities of obtaining for developing countries GATT negotiating credit if they liberalized their trade unilaterally and Fund or Bank financial support if they did so as part of the Uruguay Round. Finally, Dunkel reviewed various practical ways in which, pragmatically and gradually, working-level cooperation between the GATT Secretariat and the Fund and Bank staffs might be built up.

The report was received without enthusiasm. Predictably, it exposed the basic divergence in the group over the "global coherence" issue: was the group's mandate to define, debate and seek solutions for the great policy issues of protectionism, debt and so on, or was it to look for helpful practical improvements in GATT's relations with the international financial institutions? The report clearly leaned towards the second interpretation, disappointing delegations who had hoped for endorsement of their own policy views on "global coherence". But even those who, like the Canadians, had given priority to institutional links and had called for enlarged and more formal cooperation arrangements, were disappointed by what they saw as the timidity of the report's proposals. Some developing countries attacked the report. India offered root-and-branch denunciation: the report had "left unaddressed ... the mandate of bringing about greater coherence in global economic policy-making" yet also proposed a role for GATT for which it was not conceived or equipped, and which would "only result in worsening the situation of the developing countries". India objected most strongly to allowing the Secretariat to comment on the trade policy elements in Fund and Bank loan programmes, a proposal which it believed would add to the existing "harassment" of governments by "conditionalities and cross-conditionalities". Dunkel made a statement to the negotiating group which corrected some of the more extreme misconceptions about the Secretariat's tentative and limited suggestions, but which must have further disappointed those countries which wanted an early strengthening of formal links with the Fund and Bank. In all, this discussion of the report served to focus attention on some issues which were later taken up elsewhere in the Round, such as whether negotiating credit could be given to developing countries for unilateral liberalization and whether the Fund and Bank could help countries that were net importers of food to adjust to an anticipated rise in world prices. Otherwise, its only real outcome was agreement that the ideas it sketched would need to be explored much further before conclusions could be reached.

In subsequent meetings in early 1990, the group returned to the "coherence" issue and to the report. Lacarte urged the negotiators to define more precisely the matters that they would want Dunkel to take up in further talks with the heads of the Fund and Bank, but could not get far in the face of the fundamental disagreement over the group's mandate on the subject. For his part, Dunkel was content to leave matters as they were. The reception given to his report had shown that any follow-up report would probably be equally divisive and misunderstood, and might even put at risk his vitally important standing as mediator in the Uruguay Round. Moreover, he was convinced that a more equal and satisfactory relationship with the Fund and Bank would be easier to achieve after a successful conclusion of the Round, when GATT's rules, scope and standing should all have been greatly reinforced. Many countries thought the same. The final and uncontroversial outcome was that the Ministerial Declaration drafted at the end of 1990 simply invited Dunkel to review with the heads of the Fund and Bank "the implications of GATT's future responsibilities for its cooperation with the Bretton Woods institutions, as well as the forms such cooperation might take, with a view to achieving greater coherence in global economic policy-making", and report back. This language was to survive essentially intact through the remainder of the Round, and was included in the final outcome.

Before this conclusion was reached, however, the European Community tried another approach to the "global coherence" issue. In February 1990, it proposed that a joint declaration be negotiated and adopted at ministerial level by GATT, the Fund and the Bank. The declaration would define principles for the conduct of trade, monetary and financial policies, as well as establish the basis for institutional cooperation. The Community set out its ideas on both subjects, once again including in its policy prescriptions the highly controversial emphasis on exchange rate stability that had caused difficulties in Montreal. Other countries showed little enthusiasm, not only because they disagreed with the suggested content of the declaration, but because they, along with the Fund and Bank staffs, foresaw great practical difficulties, and little real advantage, in negotiating such a joint statement. The Community persisted with the proposal until late in the year, and then converted it (without explicitly abandoning the objective of a joint statement) to a lengthy draft declaration on "global coherence" to be made by GATT ministers alone. Much effort was then devoted to negotiating a statement which all countries could accept, but the text that went to Brussels was well garnished with the square brackets indicating disagreement. The strongest objections to the EC draft were raised by the United States.

The FOGS group was able to clean up all outstanding issues under the first ("surveillance") heading of its mandate. Picking up earlier discussion, Australia, Canada, Hong Kong and New Zealand formally proposed that ministers in Brussels should endorse the value of domestic monitoring of trade policies. Many countries were ready to agree, provided it was made quite clear that implementation would be entirely voluntary. A few delegations grumbled that GATT was a contractual arrangement, and should not concern itself with non-binding commitments, but their reluctance was overcome without much difficulty, and an appropriate paragraph drafted for ministers' approval. This survived the later vicissitudes of the Round without significant change, and was incorporated into the Marrakesh text on the trade policy review mechanism. Another largely uncontroversial agreement was negotiated on the improvement of notification procedures, following up on the ideas which the United States and others had put forward before the mid-term review. On this issue, the Secretariat, at the group's request, put forward a draft agreement which in the event was approved with little change. It reaffirmed the responsibility of governments to keep one another informed of changes in a defined range of trade policies and regulations, introduced a central registry to track and request such notifications, and provided for a general post-Round review and streamlining of notification requirements.

Much the most far-reaching proposals made in the FOGS group in 1990, however, were those from two separate sources for a new international trade organization that would embrace all the results of the Uruguay Round and at last put the GATT on a solid institutional footing. Although in time they were to lead to what Dunkel's successor described as "the crowning achievement" of the Uruguay Round, they initially attracted scepticism and minimal attention.

The idea of establishing an umbrella organization that would at the same time end the anomalous position of GATT, tidy up the messy situation left by the Tokyo Round, embrace the full results of the Uruguay Round, and apply uniform dispute settlement rules to the whole range of new and old trade agreements concerned had attracted some attention among scholars and governments.

Among the scholars, the best-developed and most recent ideas were those of John Jackson, an American jurist and acknowledged authority on GATT legal issues. Jackson published his proposals on *Restructuring the GATT System* in 1990, but had been discussing them with others for some time beforehand. His proposed "World Trade Organization" reconciled the elements which then seemed likely to emerge from the Uruguay Round by placing a central assembly, limited-membership executive council and unified dispute settlement arrangements over a number of sub-agreements which, like the Tokyo Round codes, need not necessarily be accepted by all members. His ideas were received with respect, but not widely seen as likely to come to fruition in the near future. Moreover, as was soon to become clear, his own country's government was not at all anxious to create a powerful new international agency.

From late 1989 onwards, however, it became clear that some governments, too, were beginning to think seriously about providing GATT and the expected results of the Uruguay Round negotiations with more appropriate institutions than its existing makeshift arrangements.

One set of ideas was developed inside the European Commission, where proposals were developed for an organizational treaty that would give GATT a proper institutional basis, overcome the fragmentation (and two-tier system of obligations) introduced by the Tokyo Round codes, cover all the expected results of the Uruguay Round and – not least – provide more effective curbs than the GATT on unilateral trade action. In February 1990, the first public support for such an organization w as voiced by the Italian trade minister, Renato Ruggiero. Soon afterwards, in April, the Canadian trade minister, John Crosbie, put forward proposals for a world trade organization at an informal meeting of trade ministers, held in Puerto Vallarta, Mexico. The Canadian paper suggested that ministers take a decision in principle to set up the new body at the final Uruguay Round meeting in Brussels in December, leaving the details to be negotiated afterwards. The trade ministers' communiqué acknowledged the proposals, but stated no agreed view on them. Although the paper was also circulated in Geneva, the proposals were not put to the FOGS group.

By early summer, however, the European Commission's ideas had borne fruit with the EC member states. At the June meeting of the FOGS group, the Community put forward an official proposal for "establishment of a multilateral trade organization (MTO)". The Community's short paper was mainly devoted to setting out six main arguments for a new organization. These were:

· the need for a proper legal basis for the GATT;

· the value of putting the Tokyo Round codes into a common institutional framework;

- the advantages which a single dispute settlement system could provide;
- the fact that GATT was being extended beyond its contractual nature by its new role as the international body for review of trade policies;
- the desirability of finding an integrated framework for all the Uruguay Round results, including services; and
- the appropriateness, if ideas of closer cooperation with the World Bank and IMF were to be pursued, of giving GATT a strong institutional basis to match theirs.

The Community proposed that all these purposes could be met by a purely organizational convention without substantive provisions. Its main elements would be provisions on membership and organizational structure, a legal basis for putting into force the results of negotiations and for adopting common dispute settlement procedures, establishment of a Director-General and Secretariat, and provisions on the organization's budget and legal capacities.

Introducing the proposal, the Community representative was careful not to ask for immediate reactions. Many were given nevertheless. Canada was supportive, recalling its own informally circulated proposals. Most other countries were concerned that the proposal might divert attention from more pressing matters. The United States was frankly hostile, arguing that GATT was in practice already an established institution, that the fragmented nature of the GATT system reflected a political problem – the refusal of some countries to accept new or clarified obligations – rather than a legal one, that unified dispute settlement rules did not require a new organization, and that only political will was required to bring a services agreement under the GATT.

The debate on the proposed "MTO" was to go no further in the FOGS group, although the subject was raised briefly again in the autumn. The fact that the European Community's paper itself stressed that the new organization was only meant to provide a framework for existing trade agreements, and would not alter the substantive rights and obligations of their signatories, meant that the proposal was not regarded with great interest. It received little attention from the press. The strong US opposition voiced at the June meeting made many people doubtful that anything could be achieved. Most important, there was a genuine fear in many delegations, shared strongly by Dunkel, that the chances of completing negotiations on the many difficult substantive issues still open in the Round would be reduced if attention were diverted to this new subject. The existence of the proposal was conscientiously noted in reports, and the FOGS group provided a point in its draft agreement for Brussels at which ministers could, if they so decided, attach an agreement on future work on institutional matters. Effectively, however, the group set the issue aside. It was to re-surface later.

As the final ministerial meeting approached, the position reached in the negotiations on the functioning of the GATT system looked reasonably good. The FOGS group had successfully completed substantive work on the first item in its three-part mandate, with the agreements on domestic surveillance and on notifications, and the much bigger mid-term agreement on trade policy reviews. On the improvement of GATT as an institution, there was agreement only to hold regular ministerial sessions. However, the question of a possible new trade organization had by general consent been postponed until after the Round, although some hoped that ministers might endorse the idea in principle in Brussels. A formal proposal by the United States to establish a limited-membership GATT Management Board, equipped with decision-making powers on some issues, was put forward very late, only days before the final meeting of the FOGS group in October. It was received with hostility by developing countries, as an attempt to revive a concept (described by one delegate as "hegemonic") which they had firmly rejected before the mid-term review. Other developed countries, unanimous in this respect, said that the idea should be looked at only later, in conjunction with the proposals for a multilateral trade organization. On the third issue in the mandate, "coherence in global economic policy-making", there was agreement that the Director-General should resume discussions with the IMF and World Bank, and there was the draft Ministerial Declaration based on EC proposals. Although the latter was by no means agreed, there seemed no reason to fear that any FOGS questions would seriously trouble the final bargaining over the Uruguay Round package.

Chapter VI

Brussels and after

As the last weeks of 1990 slipped away and the Brussels ministerial meeting grew inexorably closer, the 15 negotiating groups held their final meetings. Their chairmen forwarded to Dunkel, as chairman of the TNC, whatever texts, agreed or partially agreed, were available. The negotiations, however, did not stop. Informal meetings continued in the hope that a few more days, and the pressure of the Brussels deadline, might push delegates into working out agreements that had previously eluded them. In green-room meetings with the heads of key delegations interested in each subject, Dunkel confronted them with the central issues and choices. He recruited individual senior representatives to explore with their colleagues options and possibilities of movement on particular subjects, and to put forward their own proposals. Many of these green-room meetings lasted into the early hours of the morning. Some progress was achieved, but not much. Governments were all too clearly not yet ready to take the key decisions on the most sensitive subjects, and until these decisions were made they would not risk weakening their bargaining position by making concessions even on less controversial matters.

As the agreed texts, partially agreed texts and explanations of why no agreements had been reached emerged from this final pre-Brussels bargaining, they were brought together in a single working document of the Trade Negotiations Committee. This "first approximation to the Final Act embodying the results of the Uruguay Round of Multilateral Trade Negotiations", as it was described by its cover note, soon grew to massive proportions. Even in the absence of any texts on anti-dumping or TRIMS, and with no agreement on agriculture, it ran to nearly 400 pages. Moreover, very many of those pages were liberally scattered with the square brackets denoting disputed language: some brackets embraced a succession of brief alternative formulations, while others marked off long passages which had been endorsed by some governments but rejected by others. Most texts were preceded by a commentary describing the main issues still open. Far from constituting the "final and complete package" which TNC members had agreed in July should be ready by 23 November, this Draft Final Act, issued on 3 December – the opening day of the Brussels meeting – impressed most readers more by the huge range of matters still unsettled than by the few complete agreements it recorded. A new introductory text – the proposed Final Act itself – carried no more conviction, and received little attention. The product of informal meetings in the last weeks, this text dealt with issues of great importance: the relation of the Uruguay Round texts to one another; whether acceptance of any would require acceptance of all; the desirability of a new multilateral trade organization or (the less ambitious alternative) a new organizational structure, and whether its coverage would extend beyond trade in goods; and the obligations of least-developed countries. But none of these matters had been settled.

A final pre-Brussels meeting of the TNC in Geneva, on 26 November, did nothing to raise expectations. Delegates of one country after another recorded their disappointment with the results that had emerged from the negotiating groups. Many of them took the opportunity to re-state in strong terms the positions they had defended so long on the key questions on agriculture, services, investment, anti-dumping, safeguards and the other most difficult issues.

Brussels

The ministerial meeting in Punta del Este had been big; Montreal was bigger still; and Brussels was even bigger than that. The joint hosts, the Belgian government and the European Community, took over a large part of the sprawling exhibition centre at Heysel in the Brussels suburbs. One vast building became the main concourse and reception centre (complete with an artificial canal running down its centre). Another two large exhibition halls, filled with temporary offices, housed the majority of delegations; two more accommodated tented meeting rooms, the Secretariat and the press; another held the plenary meeting hall. Elsewhere on the site, non-governmental organizations established their first official presence at a GATT or Uruguay Round meeting. Many of these organizations, Third-World-oriented and still partisans of policies which developing countries themselves had largely abandoned, announced their opposition to a threatened Brussels "GATTastrophe". Official delegates to the meeting numbered some 1,600, including about 90 ministers. Some 1,300 journalists from all over the world, including television teams from virtually every major broadcasting organization, swarmed over the proceedings.

Initial attention focused on the formal proceedings of the meeting, launched by a plenary session that was attended by the King of Belgium and addressed by the hosts and by ministers of the major participating countries. Plenary sessions continued over the next days, with heads of each country's delegation taking their turn to highlight their concerns, stress the importance of the Round and its possible consequences, and call for political courage and resolve to overcome the outstanding problems. The spotlight, however, shifted away from the plenary hall to the smaller meetings where delegates grappled once again with the familiar Uruguay Round draft texts.

Introducing the massive consolidated document, Dunkel had taken an optimistic stand. "We have in our grasp", he said, "all the ingredients necessary for a substantial package of results". He acknowledged, however, the shortcomings of the text: the absence of even draft agreements on agriculture, TRIMS and anti-dumping, and the need still for key political decisions to complete work on many other subjects. There was no option, he concluded, "but to negotiate, negotiate and negotiate, and waste no time in political shadow boxing or mutual recrimination".

Hector Gros Espiell, Foreign Minister of Uruguay and ministerial chairman of the TNC, quickly parcelled out responsibility for pushing forward negotiations on an informal basis to seven of his fellow ministers. Each took either a single major subject or a group of subjects, which in turn were generally handed over to smaller groups which brought together ministers and officials both from capitals and Geneva. At intervals, over the next three days, Gros Espiell called meetings of heads of delegations to report progress.

Although all the Geneva texts received some attention, and there was intense bargaining on a number of subjects, the heart of the negotiations in Brussels was the critically important issue of agriculture.

Agriculture aroused fiercer passions and more difficult political and economic issues than any other sector of the Uruguay Round. It set the largest participants in the Round against one another and divided among themselves not only the members of the European Community but also the domestic interests of many individual participating countries. (This latter point was underlined by a massive demonstration by thousands of farmers in the streets of Brussels during the meeting.) For the first time in any GATT negotiation, there were countries so determined to reach a substantial and constructive outcome in negotiations on agricultural trade that they would veto any other result that might be obtained in this round of negotiations unless a satisfactory conclusion for agriculture formed part of the package. They had proved their determination in Montreal in 1988. Yet the Geneva negotiators had not managed even to assemble a single text on agriculture on which ministers could negotiate; indeed they were still so far from that goal that a long list of "principal issues for discussion" put together by Dunkel listed over 20 open questions under ten headings and, even then, ended inconclusively with a series of dots. Nevertheless, hopes still persisted that an agreement on agriculture could, somehow, be reached. Was it possible that governments which had expended so much time, energy, political capital and credibility on the Round, and had assembled in Brussels in this immense final meeting hosted by the European Community itself, would fail to reach a meeting of minds, and put at risk the whole enterprise?

The Brussels meeting was dominated by the crunch on agriculture. On certain other issues, substantial negotiations went forward and progress was made, although delegates were careful to insist that any agreement could be no more than tentative. These issues were for the most part those which still clearly required so much work that they could not be left aside until an agricultural agreement might clear the way for decisions on them. In the Brussels negotiations on other subjects for which agreement required only a political signal and quick choices among known alternatives, there were always participants who made it clear that they would not move until breakthroughs had been achieved on more difficult issues.

Agriculture

The agriculture negotiations got off to a reasonably good start, with informal consultations chaired by the Swedish agriculture minister, Mats Hellstrom. Although the agriculture texts sent to ministers provided no agreed basis for negotiations, Hellstrom's exploratory discussions with the US Secretary of Agriculture, Clayton Yeutter and the EC's Ray McSharry suggested that both might be prepared to contemplate an agreement that would provide for an initial five-year reform programme that might include a 30% cut in internal support levels, a similar reduction in border protection, and some sort of cutback in the quantities of agricultural products receiving export subsidies. Hellstrom put together a tentative paper reflecting these elements. The paper's existence became known, encouraging optimism among delegates and in the press; but in fact its potential as a basis for agreement was not tested since negotiations on it were never really engaged.

What proved decisive for the agriculture negotiations, and for the Brussels meeting as a whole, was the set of answers provided by the European Community to the chairman of the meeting in response to the questions that Dunkel had asked all participants in Geneva. These questions went to the heart of the differences that had divided the negotiators throughout 1990. The EC responses were encouraging at first sight, but closer analysis showed that the Community was still essentially offering agricultural reform commitments in terms only of reductions in overall support (the AMS), rather than on specific products and measures. Thus its readiness to reduce border protection would depend, it said, on whether the products concerned were covered by the AMS or not; it was not prepared to make a separate commitment on limiting total export subsidies; and it would give specific commitments on tariffication and on export subsidies for particular products only if its demands to rebalance tariffs on some non-grain feed ingredients were met. By Thursday afternoon, 6 December, it had become clear that negotiations on agriculture could not advance further on a basis which many exporting countries would accept. As in Montreal, it was the Latin American countries of the Cairns Group which took the decision that it was no use going on. On Thursday evening, they ordered their delegates in every area of the Brussels negotiations to withdraw from meetings. The instructions did not reach all delegates for some time, and one or two groups continued for several hours, but by late evening negotiations came to a halt.

Breakdown

In the early afternoon of 7 December, Gros Espiell told a silent plenary meeting that the Uruguay Round would have to be prolonged. The Brussels meeting, he said, had made a substantial contribution to advancing the negotiating process, but participants needed "more time to reconsider and reconcile their positions in some key areas of the negotiations". He proposed that Dunkel be asked to "pursue intensive consultations in the period from now until the beginning of next year with the specific objective of achieving agreements in all the areas of the negotiating programme in which differences remain outstanding". Dunkel should reconvene the TNC "at the appropriate level to conclude the negotiations at the date he considers appropriate in the light of his consultations". Gros Espiell's proposals were accepted, and the Brussels meeting broke up.

Although the difficulties in the agriculture negotiations, and their eventual breakdown, hampered all other negotiations in the Brussels meeting, useful progress was made on some issues. Suspension of the meeting meant that even clear agreements reached there could not be confirmed, and more tentative movements towards compromise were in danger of being lost. One of the main objectives of the Secretariat in the months that followed was to ensure that when negotiations resumed they would do so with the benefit of whatever agreements or fresh initiatives had emerged in Brussels. The hope was that these would provide a new point of departure for the negotiating groups in Geneva, and help to overcome the blockages which had prevented agreements from being reached before the meeting. The following paragraphs look briefly at what happened during the meeting in areas of the negotiations other than agriculture.

Market access

The essential unity of the negotiations on tariffs, non-tariff measures, natural resource-based products and tropical products was recognized by giving responsibility for work on all four subjects in the Brussels meeting to a single green-room group. Bilateral and multilateral discussions took place, with the ambitious – some would say unrealistic, in view of the complexity of the task – aim of completing the negotiations by the end of the week. Given the close link between these negotiations and progress on other matters, particularly on agriculture, it is not surprising that little was achieved.

The one unqualified success on market access was the full agreement reached on the two multilateral non-tariff measure texts – preshipment inspection and rules of origin. On the first, a compromise package was found to settle the outstanding questions. The most difficult, concerning price verification, was solved by spelling out in some detail the conditions under which inspection companies could compare contract prices with those of similar exports from the same country. On rules of origin, another compromise agreement included settlement of the key issue of whether the principles set out would apply to rules of origin governing preferential as well as non-preferential trade. The outcome was that they were made applicable only to non-preferential trade but that, at the European Community's suggestion, a "common declaration" was agreed in which governments undertook to follow many of the same basic principles in applying origin rules for preferential trade. This completed work on the two agreements, and although they were not formally adopted until the end of the Round, no substantive changes were made to the Brussels texts.

Rules

Negotiations on safeguards in Brussels brought substantial advance, and a new draft was before ministers in a green-room session at the moment when the meeting collapsed. Several questions appeared to have been cleared away: the debate about whether tariffs, quotas or adjustment measures should be the preferred instrument for action was dropped; a number of missing figures were filled in; and total exemption of developing countries from safeguard action was no longer sought. There was even conditional agreement on the phase-out of grey-area measures, with a new twist: the possibility that some such measures would be allowed to stay for eight more years, rather than three or four. Little movement, however, had taken place on the central question of selectivity. The issue was now posed in less objectionable terms: indeed, new language stated flatly that "safeguard measures shall be applied to a product being imported irrespective of its source". But the idea of quota modulation was maintained, with the usual square brackets, elsewhere in the text. One can only speculate on whether, in different circumstances, a safeguards agreement could have been reached in Brussels. At least the central issue of selectivity was a matter of fairly straightforward political choice: this was not a case where much technical work needed to be done. The fact that the choice had not yet been made when the meeting broke down was only to be expected, since it was sufficiently important to have been reserved for the final bargaining along with agriculture and other major issues of the Round.

For the negotiations on subsidies and countervailing duties, the link with agriculture was even closer. There was no possibility that agreement could be reached, particularly on the central remaining question of how to define and treat the most-and least-acceptable ("red" and "green") categories, as long as deadlock persisted on the treatment of agricultural subsidies. No changes were made to the draft subsidies text during the Brussels meeting.

Modest progress was made on secondary anti-dumping issues, but none on the critical questions. The negotiators decided to tackle the easiest questions first, and the most difficult last. A first batch of questions concerning evidence, provisional measures, price undertakings, notice of determinations and judicial review was tentatively settled, and the negotiators moved on to rather harder matters. However, they had not even begun on those matters pinpointed in the commentary to the Brussels document when the meeting as a whole broke down. Had an anti-dumping agreement been reached in Brussels, it seems improbable, given the limited time available, that it could have gone much beyond secondary issues.

Some minor points on the standards agreement were cleared up, but the necessary compromise on the obligations of second-level governments had not been found by the time the meeting ended. On the other, essentially secondary, rules issues that had remained unsettled in the document that went to ministers, no significant progress was made.

Textiles and clothing

Intensive negotiations on textiles and clothing took place during the Brussels meeting and considerable progress was made, although the blanks in the economic package, concerning such key matters as the length of the transition period for phasing out the MFA and the rates at which products would be integrated into GATT or have their MFA quotas eased, had not yet been filled in when work was halted by the impasse on agriculture. Nevertheless, given the clear understanding that existed of the issues for decision, and the way in which negotiations in fact proceeded in 1991, it appears more likely than not that the textiles negotiators would have finished the job in Brussels in December 1990 if the huge political impetus of an agreement on agriculture had been provided.

Services

The negotiations on services also made good progress. The Mexican Minister for Trade and Development, Jaime Serra Puche, chaired a series of consultations which suggested that a way could be found around the apparent roadblock created by the earlier US reluctance to accept a general obligation to give MFN (non-discriminatory) treatment to all signatories of the new General Agreement on Trade in Services. The United States said that it would accept unconditional MFN, provided other participants came forward with satisfactory offers on market access commitments. For their part, all the ministers consulted by Serra Puche said that they would make such offers, in some cases very soon, provided the principle of unconditional MFN were adopted as a guiding principle for the GATS. On the annexes to the GATS, there was constructive discussion about the negotiating approach to be adopted for basic telecommunications and financial services, and about the possibility of adding an annex on labour mobility. Two new draft proposals on financial services were put forward in Brussels: one by Canada, Japan, Sweden and Switzerland, and the other by Southeast Asian countries. The first was notable for introducing the idea of what became known as "the two-track approach", in which those participants that were able to agree among themselves to take on additional commitments – by recognizing measures of other countries, aligning their national measures with those of others, or entering into cooperative arrangements – would be able to do so. The ministers also consulted on how to keep to a minimum the exceptions from MFN treatment that were being sought by some countries in the sectors of transport and audiovisual services, and a consensus seemed to be beginning to emerge that the GATS should provide for later efforts to review whatever exemptions might initially be unavoidable, and if possible to negotiate their removal.

By Thursday evening, 6 December, agreement had been reached in a green-room meeting to clean up the GATS text on the lines suggested by the consultations, and a drafting group set to work on the task. Its efforts were halted after barely an hour by the collapse of the agriculture negotiations.

Again, one can speculate about what would have happened if the halt had not occurred. Obviously, many difficult problems remained to be solved before an agreed GATS text could have been achieved, but equally obviously the negotiations on services were moving ahead in a way that had never been seen in Geneva. Given the fact that the aim on services for the Brussels meeting was in any case only to reach an agreement on the framework text, with the market access negotiations left to the early months of 1991, it seems likely that services would not have stood in the way of the meeting's success. On the other hand, so much more was achieved in the services negotiations between Brussels and the end of the Uruguay Round, including improvement of the framework agreement well beyond what was envisaged in December 1990, that the Brussels breakdown may perhaps be regarded, as far as services are concerned, as a blessing in disguise.

TRIPS

Negotiations on TRIPS went well in Brussels, but never reached the point of trying to resolve the most critical issues, which required tough decisions at the highest level that were never going to be forthcoming except in a context of general breakthrough. As long as there was no deal in sight on agriculture or textiles, developing countries in particular were not going to discuss the patenting of pharmaceuticals, or the inclusion of the full TRIPS agreement into GATT (with its implied possibility of cross-retaliation in dispute cases). Nor would they settle the issue of transition periods. Consultations suggested, however, that the key ministers were equipped with enough flexibility to have reached the major compromises necessary for overall agreement if an agricultural breakthrough could have been achieved. On lesser matters, a drafting group in Brussels made progress in defining possible compromises on many points, including a number of issues on standards, and virtually all outstanding problems on enforcement. It was still hard at work when the negotiations as a whole were halted.

TRIMS

The deep and persistent disagreements on trade-related investment measures, demonstrated vividly by the lack of any proposal to ministers, inevitably suggested to some people that this was one negotiating subject, at least, on which the Uruguay Round might produce no result. However, consultations among ministers in Brussels quickly showed that most developed countries were not prepared to accept such an outcome. They also showed that some, but not all, of the key developing countries would probably be able to ease their opposition to prohibition of any TRIMS, provided satisfactory results were emerging on Uruguay Round subjects of interest to them. A green-room proposal would have been put forward on Friday morning of the Brussels meeting, but was never put to the test, since by Thursday evening the impasse on agriculture had brought all negotiations to an end.

Institutions

Very little happened in Brussels on institutions. On dispute settlement, the major questions of decision-making and the proposed pledge not to resort to unilateral action were not discussed. Meetings of legal officials concentrated mainly on the question of non-violation complaints, and in the absence of any political signal to reach conclusions resulted in only minimal progress. The largely political issues still outstanding on the functioning of the GATT system fared even worse: a single brief meeting showed that major participants were not ready even to enter into discussion of them. The new "Draft Final Act" text, with its bracketed alternatives on new institutions and on links between acceptance of the various Uruguay Round agreements was cleaned up a little, but left unchanged in its essentials.

Getting back on track

The Brussels decision to give governments more time "to reconsider and reconcile their positions in some key areas of the negotiations" gave Dunkel the sole responsibility for deciding when it would be worthwhile to re-start the negotiating process in Geneva. Gros Espiell's statement had envisaged that Dunkel's consultations "until the beginning of next year" – in other words, over a period of barely three weeks – might yield agreements on the outstanding issues of the Round. This was a forlorn hope. It served to bring the Brussels meeting to a decent conclusion: after all, ministers could scarcely acknowledge that three weeks was an insufficient period for their governments to reach agreements that they had been ready, earlier in the same week, to conclude within five days. However, there was never any chance that the fundamental differences over agriculture, in particular, could have been resolved without a prolonged review by governments of the positions they had taken in Brussels, followed by the reopening of substantial negotiations. Moreover, the momentum (to use a favourite term of international negotiators) of the Uruguay Round had been lost. The brief interval in which the Round had attracted top-level political attention, and thus the possibility of quick decisions, had passed, and instead the participants had become all too well aware of the great amount of work that remained to be done, not only on the most immediately controversial issues, but also on those for which less-than-satisfactory draft agreements had been patched together in October and November.

The immediate need was to find a basis on which negotiations could resume at all. Since the suspension in Brussels had been brought about by the breakdown on agriculture, this had to be the main focus of Dunkel's efforts to bring governments back to the negotiating table. But he had also to seek an understanding on which to re-launch negotiations on the other unresolved issues of the Round. Each of these was of particular importance to some governments who would insist that any renewal of negotiations on them should come properly to grips with outstanding problems. In substance, this meant that Dunkel had to establish, and obtain consent to, a fresh work programme for this new concluding phase of the Round.

For nearly three months, no official Uruguay Round meetings took place. The annual GATT session, later in December, and a regular GATT Council meeting that was dominated by disputes over agricultural questions, provided ample opportunity to delegations to deplore the impasse in the Round, and to point out the need for agreed and modernized rules for world trade. It was left to Dunkel, however, to travel and talk endlessly with governments, individually and in broader consultations, in order to gauge their intentions and minimum needs, as the basis for his own proposals. By early February he was able to report, in a speech in Davos, his conviction that "the consensus in favour of a successful conclusion of the Round remains intact". The Brussels meeting had at least led to "a much clearer perception of the major stumbling blocks", and "changes or adjustments" had occurred in national positions.

The key breakthrough came some two weeks later, when a formula was found to overcome the critical difficulty encountered in Brussels. The EC at last accepted that the agricultural negotiations and, with them, the Uruguay Round as a whole, would fail unless it accepted the need to undertake separate commitments to reduce not only its domestic supports but also export subsidies and border measures. It was allowed, however, to make this shift of position without explicit acknowledgement that it was doing so. On 20 February, a meeting at GATT of some 30 delegations accepted a proposal from Dunkel on the negotiating approach to be adopted for the remainder of the agricultural negotiations. With this agreed, Dunkel held a series of green-room sessions over the following days to reach similar agreements on the ground-rules for negotiations on other outstanding issues: textiles and clothing, services, GATT rules, TRIMS, TRIPS, market access, dispute settlement and the institutional issues to be covered by the Final Act of the Round. On 25 February he was able at last to convene a meeting of the Trade Negotiations Committee, to tell delegates that "all the elements necessary to enable us to put the Round back on track" were now at hand, and to distribute to them a paper that summed up the agreements reached in his informal consultations. Deliberately, Dunkel did not read out his proposals, saying only that the text provided a basis for re-starting the negotiations in all areas in which differences remained outstanding, as well as a proposed agenda for work in each area. He asked the TNC to agree to continue the negotiations "with the aim of concluding them as soon as possible", but at this time suggested no target date for conclusion, since "experience has taught us that fixing target dates is not always helpful". Without discussion, and therefore without having to give explicit support to the proposals in Dunkel's document, the TNC formally "*agreed* with the statement made".

The Uruguay Round had been re-launched.

Chapter VII

Extra time: 1991

The Uruguay Round changed in character after Brussels, and it was to change again at the end of 1991. The months in between – effectively, from February to December 1991 – were a period of transition, both for the negotiations in Geneva and in the context of world economic and political events in which the Round took place.

Changes in Geneva

In Geneva, the agreement reached by the Trade Negotiations Committee in February 1991 put the Uruguay Round back on track, in the sense that governments had found a common basis on which to resume negotiations. It was agreed, moreover, that the decisions taken in 1986 at Punta del Este and in 1989 in the mid-term review still stood. The Trade Negotiations Committee, the GNG, GNS and the surveillance mechanism would continue to be needed. However, it was clear to all that the negotiations on specific issues would have to be organized differently.

For services, there was still much work to be done, and the GNS would continue to be needed; indeed, its workload was such that it was soon given a co-chairman. For the negotiations on goods, however, there was little sense in maintaining 14 separate negotiating groups. On several subjects, little or no further work was required: they had been settled, subject to completion of the Round as a whole, or they required only final decisions that would not be taken except as part of the final package. Others had reached a point at which it no longer made sense to deal with them in isolation. Tariffs and non-tariff measures, natural resource-based products and tropical products, for example, were all part of the same task, the reduction of trade barriers at national frontiers. Most important, unless the number of negotiating groups competing for attention and meeting space were cut back drastically, each would be able to meet only at intervals of three or four weeks. This would imply a pace of negotiation, as Dunkel told the GNG in April, "visibly, and alarmingly, out of tune with the political commitment that all participants have shown towards bringing the Uruguay Round to a successful conclusion as soon as possible".

The solution reached was to reduce the number of groups to six. Three – for textiles, agriculture and TRIPS – continued to deal with a single subject; and three were set up for the remaining negotiations on goods – one for market access (tariffs, non-tariff measures, natural resource-based products and tropical products), one for "rule-making" (the issues covered by the earlier groups on safeguards, subsidies, GATT Articles, the Tokyo Round codes and TRIMS), and one for institutions (the Final Act, dispute settlement and FOGS). To underline the expectation that delegations would henceforth be single-mindedly negotiating among themselves, the task of each group's chairman was defined simply as being "to moderate negotiations in this area".

New authority for the negotiators

Agreement in Geneva on these changes took time. Also time-consuming were other steps, taken elsewhere, that were essential to a successful restart of the negotiations.

One was renewal by the United States Congress of the negotiating authority given to the President by the Trade Act of 1988. That authority was to expire in June 1991, but its procedural provisions meant that the US delegation had, by the beginning of the year, already lost the power to negotiate in Geneva. A two-year extension was voted in May.

Meanwhile, governments everywhere reviewed their objectives in the Round in the light of what had happened over the previous four years, not only in the negotiations but also in their trade, their economic development, and their national policies. One aspect of this review was to be critically important for the Round. Within the European Community, faced by the continuing rise in the budgetary cost and distortions of the common agricultural policy, the twelve member countries began to discuss CAP reform. These discussions were to continue into 1992, but they bore early fruit in May 1991 when cuts in price support for some products were agreed. Although some EC member countries were always insistent that there was no connection between the CAP reforms and negotiations in the Uruguay Round, the two processes were mutually helpful. In Brussels, reform was encouraged by the knowledge that it would ease trade difficulties with the rest of the world, and provide bargaining leverage for the Round. In Geneva, the CAP reforms gave greater authority and credibility to the Community's negotiators, and encouraged confidence that they would be able to make the commitments agricultural exporters believed essential to the success of the Round.

The players in the negotiations changed. In terms of participation, the number of countries active in the Round increased, partly because of new accessions to the GATT, but more importantly because of dramatic shifts in the economic policies of many developing and Eastern European countries that made them far more interested in the predominantly market-oriented reforms that the Round was trying to achieve, and in some cases caused them to reverse long-held positions on important issues. In addition, there were big changes in the Geneva cast of individual negotiators. With responsibility for most of the Uruguay Round issues reshuffled, and distributed among fewer negotiating groups, most of their original chairmen returned thankfully to their normal duties as national officials. Among national representatives, there was also a large turnover, since most delegates had been in Geneva since 1986 or earlier, representing a full normal diplomatic posting. For the last stages of the Round, there were to be few negotiators who had been participants from the first. The newcomers brought fresh enthusiasm and ideas, but there was also a less helpful loss of continuity. A similar turnover occurred among the staff of the GATT Secretariat, in particular with the simultaneous retirement of Dunkel's long-serving deputy, Madan Mathur, and of several senior officials directly responsible for negotiating groups.

The Round in a new perspective

World events altered the perspective in which governments viewed the Round. Economic growth slackened in the developed countries, with the United States first to go into recession. As already noted, large numbers of developing countries were shifting from inward-looking economic policies, characterized by high protection, government direction of the economy and great suspicion of foreign investment, to liberal and market-oriented policies. These moves to open up their markets (a widely noted GATT report in April 1991 recorded trade liberalization by 30 developing countries since the beginning of the Round), and the example of dynamic growth set by East Asian developing countries made some developing countries that had been sceptical about, or even clearly hostile to, GATT involvement in some subjects such as services and TRIPS far readier to contribute constructively to negotiations, and eager to use the bargaining power for market access negotiations with which their own liberalization efforts had equipped them.

Two other factors affected government attitudes to the negotiations, working in opposite directions.

One factor, which encouraged completion of the negotiations as quickly as possible, was the perception that the Round's agenda was in danger of being overtaken by events. Most strikingly, its multilateral approach to trade relations seemed threatened by an extraordinary wave of moves to establish new regional trading arrangements. In Europe, where regional free trade already extended effectively over the whole Western half of the continent, new agreements were multiplying with and among the Eastern European countries and soon afterwards were in prospect with the new countries that were to emerge after the collapse of the Soviet Union. Canada and the United States had agreed to form a free trade area, and were negotiating its expansion to include Mexico. Latin American countries were engaged in their most serious efforts yet to remove trade barriers among them, and similar moves were being discussed in

Southeast Asia and by other developing countries. Regional trade agreements, as Dunkel frequently pointed out, were not contrary to the GATT. They could happily coexist with the multilateral trading system. But coexistence required that the multilateral system itself be in good shape, with strong rules and low worldwide trade barriers to ensure that trade relations did not become, as some apocalyptic commentators suggested, a nightmare of warring blocs.

A further spur to action was the threat that in the absence of agreed and up-to-date rules, especially in the new areas of the Round, the largest countries would take coercive unilateral measures to achieve their national objectives. This threat took concrete shape in US legislative provisions, the so-called "Super 301", which authorized the President to restrict imports from countries whose trade policies he found unfair. Yet another element was the evident hostility to the Round of certain non-governmental pressure groups. Some suggested that the Round's objectives were contrary to the interests of developing countries, a view they usually put forward on grounds that the governments of those countries had conspicuously abandoned. Others, often with support from unions in the industries concerned, argued that low-cost imports would not only result in loss of jobs but would perpetuate denial of adequate wages and working conditions to workers in the exporting countries. Another theme, which aroused more general sympathy, was that neither the Round nor the GATT as a whole gave proper attention to environmental concerns. While some of the environmentalists' objections were felt to be unfounded (and were suspected by developing countries, in particular, of being a smokescreen for protectionist interests), they were a reminder that, as long as the Uruguay Round continued, it would be difficult to get to grips with trade issues that had been left out of the Round's agenda and now needed attention.

A second factor, however, was not helpful to bringing the Round to an early conclusion. The Round had missed too many deadlines. The failure in Brussels was in this respect particularly damaging. More and more, people recalled past GATT experience, and especially the Kennedy and Tokyo Rounds of the 1960s and 1970s. In those negotiations, only the imminent expiry of the United States legislative authority to negotiate had finally driven the participants to face up to the critical political choices and thereby reach agreement. Renewal by Congress in 1991 of the US authority to negotiate – effectively until the beginning of 1993 – postponed pressure on the participating countries to wind up the Round before then – and by unhappy coincidence ensured that the Round would become an electoral issue not only in the United States but also in France, the country which was finding it hardest to accept the direction that the agricultural negotiations were taking.

Fortunately, these negative influences, however real in their effects, could hardly be acknowledged publicly. The annual economic summit of the seven most powerful industrialized countries, held in 1991 in London in July, produced the strongest pledge yet to complete the Uruguay Round successfully.

The seven leaders called for completion by the end of the year, and this time promised to be personally involved in the process.

Putting the package together: the Draft Final Act

It was against this much-altered background that in June and July 1991, a full half-year after the breakdown in Brussels, that Uruguay Round negotiating groups began to meet again. The work of each group during the remainder of the year is described in later sections of this chapter. The problems and progress on each negotiating subject are best understood, however, against the background of developments in the Round as a whole over the same period. These were the months in which the Uruguay Round package took shape, in a process governed essentially by decisions of the Trade Negotiations Committee.

The first stage of the process was launched in June, when each negotiating group was told to concentrate on the questions where breakthroughs were needed. The aim, as Dunkel put it, was to help participants "to judge their capacity to conclude the Round successfully by the end of 1991 – a target which more and more governments are beginning to see as feasible and desirable for different reasons".

At the end of July, the TNC met again to review progress. Dunkel reported that in areas such as agriculture, textiles and clothing, market access and services, although a "tremendous amount" of substantive work remained to be done, negotiators were in a position "to move with determination in the phase of negotiations proper". (His choice of words suggests a view that these groups had yet to get down to real bargaining.) For other subjects – notably rule-making and TRIPS – on which texts were available, the preparatory work had largely been done, and matters were "ripe for the final political trade-offs". Even in areas where there was still no common negotiating text, such as TRIMS and anti-dumping, agreements should fall into place fairly quickly, once the essential political decisions had been taken. Dunkel also suggested that the time had come to focus on dispute settlement and institutional arrangements. In summary, it appeared that participants had at hand "all the elements necessary to finally carry the Round to a successful conclusion". On this basis, Dunkel put forward an autumn programme of meetings for all the negotiating groups, and called for "intensive informal, bilateral, and plurilateral negotiating sessions, ending in concrete results leading up to formal meetings of the groups to take note of these results and move the negotiations further along". Backing this approach on behalf of developing countries, Brazil called for political decisions as soon as possible on the main elements of the agricultural negotiations, priority for the textiles negotiations and quick progress also on other issues of particular concern to developing countries who "had already walked the extra mile in the negotiations, first by negotiating in a flexible and constructive spirit on issues like services ... and secondly by opening their markets, without waiting for the conclusion of the Round".

This July TNC meeting successfully set the pattern for work in the final months of 1991, to the extent that everyone agreed that non-stop meetings at all levels were going to be needed, and that the months of October and November, in particular, were going to be the time for "deal-making". What the meeting could not ensure was that governments would in the event be ready to make all the decisions essential to securing final agreements.

Dunkel's hope was that sufficient progress would be made to allow a complete revision of the Brussels draft agreements to be issued early in November. Much was in fact accomplished by then, but the breakthroughs needed were not achieved. In some of the most difficult areas, such as agriculture, governments had still not accepted that major shifts in their positions were unavoidable. This situation in turn prevented agreement on other subjects, because no participant was prepared to give up even a small part of the potential negotiating leverage on major issues provided by their continued withholding of assent on minor ones. Work on some other issues, and particularly on dispute settlement and institutions, was behindhand simply because there had not been enough time to reach conclusions on matters that had not been looked at in detail before. At a further meeting of the TNC in early November, Dunkel reported that there was still not "a sufficient basis for compromise solutions on the essential substantive issues". In a lengthy statement, which had been put together with the help of the chairmen of each of the negotiating groups, he listed the main issues that remained to be settled in each area of the negotiations, and announced that from 11 November onwards, negotiations in all these areas would become "continuous and simultaneous", with the aim of reaching results across the board by the end of the month.

The task in fact took a little longer, in spite of what became effectively non-stop negotiations. The climax was reached in mid-December, with several of the negotiating groups working through successive nights in which they hammered out agreements on many of the issues that had defied solution for so long. On most of the unresolved issues, they carried the negotiations to a point at which only a very few further choices were required. On 18 and 19 December, each of the chairmen, armed with a deep knowledge of national positions acquired through months of negotiation and consultation, and relying on their judgement of what would constitute, for all participants, a reasonably balanced and acceptable outcome, made their own decisions on all the questions still unsettled. The GATT Secretariat gave advice, but these final decisions were those of the individual chairmen. Only the texts dealing with institutional questions were left in an unfinished state, and even these had advanced to the point at which fundamental choices had been made, bringing all the results of the Round together in a single package.

On 20 December, the Trade Negotiations Committee met to receive a complete and consolidated text, the "Draft Final Act Embodying the Results of the Uruguay Round of Multilateral Trade Negotiations". As Dunkel pointed out, the document was the outcome both of intensive negotiation and of arbitration and conciliation: "negotiation among you, the participants, and arbitration and conciliation by the chairmen when it became clear that, on some outstanding points, this was the only way to put before you the global package of results of this Round. Even more importantly, it offers us, for the first time, a concrete idea of the scope and scale of the benefits of broadbased liberalization and strengthened multilateral rules which are within our grasp." As a comprehensive text, which sought to strike the best possible balance across the board of the whole Uruguay Round agenda and which incorporated the substantial progress made during 1991, it was, he said, a much more important document than that sent to ministers in Brussels. It required completion, since it still lacked the national schedules of specific commitments that had yet to be agreed on in the market access negotiations, for agriculture, and for services. These negotiations still lay ahead. But he asked governments to give the package represented by the Draft Final Act "the most serious and urgent consideration, at the highest political levels".

The Committee adjourned for three weeks, to give time for governments to decide whether they would accept the package of results. But in spite of Dunkel's expression of confidence that "if we continue to share the vision which brought us together in Punta del Este five years ago, your governments will judge the package favourably", first reactions from some quarters, and especially from Brussels, gave warning that at least some of the draft agreements were not going to be judged generally acceptable.

As usual, the principal problem was agriculture.

Agriculture

Resumption of the Uruguay Round negotiations after Brussels had been made possible by the breakthrough agreement on the aims of the agriculture negotiations announced by Dunkel in February 1991. This agreement provided, crucially, that participants "conduct negotiations to achieve specific binding commitments" on domestic support, market access, and export competition and to reach an SPS agreement. It also set the agenda for the restart of work in the negotiating group on agriculture. This immediate work was essentially technical – a matter of achieving a common understanding of what options were available under each heading of the negotiations – but it was essential to any decisions on exactly what commitments were finally to be undertaken, and it was to occupy the group until the autumn. The result was a set of "options papers". They covered a long list of issues. For domestic support policies, they dealt with such questions as which policies should be judged non-distortive, and therefore to be excluded from reduction commitments, and how the aggregate measurement of support (AMS) should be defined and used. As the basis for possible decisions on market access, the agriculture group discussed how commitments on tariffication, as well as on minimum access to markets, could be applied in practice. For export competition, the issues were which policies should be treated as subsidies, and how subsidy commitments could be enforced without cutting into genuine aid shipments. In all three areas, the group looked at how the relevant GATT rules might be reinforced. The group also began drafting a declaration, to form part of any final package of decisions, in response to the concerns of the net food-importing countries.

By the time the Trade Negotiations Committee met in November, most technical issues had been resolved. What remained were the hard decisions, which could only be made at a political level, and which clearly demanded shifts in the national positions that had been taken in Brussels. Dunkel set them out. In the area of market access, early agreement was needed above all on the extent to which tariffication would apply. In other words, would all obstacles to imports have to be reduced? The challenge here was above all to Japan, Korea and the other countries, particularly Canada and the non-EC Europeans, who claimed that special factors required that they retain absolute barriers against some imports. On domestic support, what policies would be accepted as "green" in terms of the traffic light concept, and thereby escape the need for change? At stake were some major elements in support given to farmers by the European Community, the United States and many other countries. What export subsidies should be disciplined? Finally, when all these points had been decided, there remained the crucial numbers to be filled in: by what percentages should domestic supports, import barriers and export subsidies be cut; what figures should be taken as the basis from which the cuts were calculated and over what period should the reductions be made?

Answers to these questions were sought in discussions between the United States and the European Community, notably in an early November meeting in Washington between President Bush and the EC Commission President, Jacques Delors. It was reported that the United States was now ready to accept a 35% cut in the volume of subsidized exports, and a 30% reduction in domestic subsidies; but the export reduction, at least, was unacceptable to some Community members. Moreover, the Community still wanted to rebalance some tariffs, and to see its compensatory payments to farmers under the CAP reforms classified as "green", and therefore not subject to reduction. No agreement could be reached in Washington, and the deadlock continued in Geneva over the following month.

It was in this situation that Dunkel, who was himself chairing the agriculture group, had to "arbitrate and conciliate" by proposing, for the draft agreement on agriculture that went into the Draft Final Act, answers to all the unsettled issues. There was no chance that he would please everyone: the differences in views were obviously still very wide, and the subject was the most politically explosive single component of the Uruguay Round. The hope, however, was that governments might on reflection accept a package of choices that represented an honest effort to suggest a fair and balanced outcome.

The key choices made by Dunkel to complete the draft agricultural agreement were:

- for domestic support: "green" status (exemption from reduction) for payments involving no transfer from consumers, and no price support to producers. All other subsidies, except for product-specific subsidies worth less than 5% of total output, to be reduced by 20% from their 1986 levels over the period 1993-99.
- for market access: full tariffication, with resulting tariffs reduced on average by 36%, and individually by at least 15%, over the period 1993-99, with access to at least 3% of the national market from the beginning, and to 5% by 1999.
- for export subsidies: by comparison with the period 1986-90, total spending to be reduced by 36%, and volume of subsidized exports to be reduced by 24%, over the period 1993-99.

Dunkel's choices on these central agricultural issues, incorporated into the Draft Final Act, were to be heavily attacked in the following months. The criticism came mainly from importing countries, but also from observers who felt that different decisions might have assured much earlier success in the Uruguay Round. There will always be room for argument. Certainly, he failed to find a compromise package that all participants could accept, and the final Uruguay Round result on agriculture differed from his proposals in a number of important respects. Against this, at least two considerations should be placed. First, his proposed package was much closer to the final outcome than anything previously on the negotiating table, and included some crucial elements (for instance, full tariffication and no rebalancing) which were to survive unchanged. Second, the extreme political difficulty encountered over the remainder of the Round in reaching an agreement on agriculture strongly suggests that the many people who in early 1992 were inclined to blame the continuing stalemate in the negotiations on Dunkel's arbitration of the draft agriculture text were simply indulging in wishful thinking. Key participants in the negotiations were not yet ready to settle.

Although the agricultural negotiations held the centre of the stage throughout 1991, they were in fact only one element among many in the intense negotiations that took place from mid-spring onwards.

Market access

For market access, the only clear achievement of the Brussels meeting had been to reach agreement on the two multilateral non-tariff measure texts on pre-shipment inspection and rules of origin. Developed countries were reported to be aiming at removal of all tariffs affecting pharmaceuticals and some construction products. A large number of national offers of reductions in tariffs and non-tariff barriers had been on the negotiating table since the autumn, but they were conditional on the responses of those to whom they were addressed. In some cases, they clearly fell short of the overall objectives set in Montreal, and left unsolved the questions, particularly important to developing countries, of how credit would be given for binding tariffs and for liberalization already carried out. What this meant was that the real bargaining on tariffs and non-tariff measures had not yet really started.

It did not start in 1991. As Dunkel told the TNC in February, "some major political decisions" would be needed before the market access negotiations could be successfully concluded. In fact, the situation remained as it had been the year before. Most countries had no incentive to put their cards on the table as long as key elements in the final bargain remained completely unknown and, in particular, while the big countries were making no offers on agricultural products, textiles and clothing.

In these circumstances, the chairman of the new market access group, Germain Denis of Canada, had a depressing story to tell the TNC in June: although over 50 participants had by then submitted proposals and offers which constituted an initial basis for negotiations, there had been "no substantial progress" since the Brussels meeting. His frank and lengthy survey of problems showed that none of the difficulties and differences that had dogged the work of the four market access groups from 1987 to 1990 had gone away, except perhaps for some procedural differences that ceased to be relevant now that the four groups had become just one. He called for intensive bilateral and plurilateral meetings, good-faith bargaining, and regular reviews to keep track of progress and ensure transparency.

Numerous meetings in fact took place during the final months of 1991 and, at times, participants reported an encouraging impression that governments were closer to being ready to show their hands, negotiate seriously, and reach deals. Offers were refined; possibilities of further action were explored. Observers also noticed greater overall interest in the potential outcome of the negotiations. For more than four years, the market access negotiators had laboured in comparative obscurity, their efforts overshadowed by more novel subjects such as services and by the battle over agriculture. Now governments were recalling the economic and political advantages of substantial cuts in tariffs and non-tariff barriers. But this reassessment was not enough to start effective negotiations. Other steps had to be taken first, as Dunkel acknowledged in the TNC in November, just as the final sprint to complete the Draft Final Act began: "The immediate problem is to set the scene for an effective negotiating process involving broad-based exchanges of concessions on the basis of the MFN principle, taking into account the immediate needs of developing countries." One trigger to start the process, he argued, would be agreement on methods, including tariffication, of negotiating market access as part of the agricultural reform programme. Another would be agreement on how to go about liberalizing trade in textiles and clothing, and bringing the sector into GATT.

Both triggers should have been pulled by the Draft Final Act. Denis made his own contribution, too, by taking decisions that ended a long debate on three ground-rules for the negotiations. For the draft Uruguay Round Protocol, he specified that trade barriers should be removed over just five years, and that future problems of compensation for changes in bound nontariff measures should be handled through the same GATT procedures (in Article XXVIII) used when tariff bindings were modified. Separately, in a paper setting out "chairman's guidelines" for the negotiators, he settled a major issue for developing countries by providing a formula to measure against the Montreal targets the negotiating credit they should be given for binding tariffs and for liberalization already introduced. In an optimistic statement in the market access group on 18 December, he judged that negotiations in the previous weeks had "significantly improved" the prospects of achieving "a substantial and broad-based market access package". He set a tight timetable for final negotiations in the New Year, with final schedules to be ready for attachment to the Uruguay Round package by 31 March.

Rule-making

The new negotiating group on "rule-making" inherited the remaining work of no less than five of the original 15 negotiating groups: GATT Articles, the Tokyo Round codes, safeguards, subsidies and TRIMS. Full agreement had been reached on some of the Articles and codes, and little remained to be done on others. But five subjects remained on which views were still far apart: safeguards, subsidies, the redrafting of the anti-dumping code, the GATT balance-of-payments rules and TRIMS. Anti-dumping and TRIMS shared the sad distinction of being so controversial that no working text had been sent from Geneva to Brussels, while for the balance-of-payments rules there was no decision on whether negotiations should even begin. George Maciel, the immensely experienced Brazilian former diplomat who had been chairing the Safeguards group, was appointed chairman of the new rule-making group.

The group got down to work in June. On the largely technical issues still outstanding on matters such as standards and rules of origin that had been virtually settled in Brussels, it made good progress. Once again, these matters were dealt with largely in informal groups (chaired by Peter Williams, the recently retired Secretariat official previously responsible for the subjects) and, by the time Dunkel's Draft Final Act was put together in late December, nothing further remained to be done to the agreements concerned. For standards, the missing compromise on second-level governments was found in keeping the broad "best endeavours" obligations of central governments, but increasing their responsibility to see that standards activities at the lower level were properly notified. On the five difficult subjects, however, progress was very limited in spite of several formal meetings of the group and intensive consultations by the chairman. Summing up at the end of the group's fourth meeting in late October, Maciel commented that while the difficulties in each area might be different, "a common element was that there either had not been significant progress in the informal consultations, or the progress made was not of such a substantial nature that it could be reflected in text".

Almost a month later, little had changed. On 26 November, 30 countries, representing virtually all the most active participants in the Uruguay Round apart from the Quad, sent the group a "Communication on GATT rules and procedures" that expressed their "deep preoccupation about the state of the Uruguay Round negotiations on rules". An additional negotiating effort was needed, they insisted, toward clearer and more precise rules.

These were required to provide the trading system with predictability and stability, to give a sound legal basis and a guarantee against setbacks to the reform efforts of developing countries and the economies in transition in Central and Eastern Europe, to underpin increased market access opportunities, and to revitalize the system, notably by bringing unilateralism to an end. For each of the five main rules issues still under negotiation, the 30 countries set out succinctly and even-handedly what they saw as the elements most important for success. They asserted finally that "a substantial package on rules remains the cornerstone of the multilateral trading system". The statement was an extraordinary effort by a large number of countries, many of which had regularly been on opposite sides of deeply divisive negotiations over the previous five years, to find common ground and express their alarm about the way that the rules negotiations were going.

Nevertheless, and in spite of near-continuous negotiations, none of the five issues had been settled by mid-December. As in other areas of the Round, it fell to Maciel as chairman of the rules group to make crucial decisions on the outstanding questions in each agreement, exercising his judgement, in the light of what he had heard in formal meetings and innumerable consultations with delegates, as to what would produce a fair, balanced and acceptable package.

Safeguards

Very little true multilateral negotiation on safeguards took place after the Brussels meeting. The draft text worked out in negotiations in Brussels, which had achieved tentative agreement on a good many of the issues outstanding at that time, was introduced officially into the rules group in June. By common consent, work on safeguards was set aside at first, in favour of the other four difficult subjects, on which it was felt more could be done at that stage. In October, Maciel held some consultations on safeguards but broke them off when he concluded that further negotiations were needed among delegations, "particularly in the light of the global linkages or trade-offs with other areas", and that no significant progress was possible at the time.

The joint declaration by 30 countries at the end of November held firmly to the majority view on what was needed for success: "An unambiguous non-discriminatory safeguard mechanism and a clear, staged and binding programme for dismantling grey-area measures." However, these two linked issues of selectivity and grey area, together with the rules to govern how safeguards should apply to developing countries, remained unsettled in the negotiating group to the end.

Maciel's decisions were few but important. He accepted the principle of quota modulation, but hedged it about with conditions considerably stiffer than the European Community had envisaged. Only under the supervision of the Safeguards Committee, in the case of actual injury, when imports from some countries had increased disproportionately more than imports as a whole of the product concerned, and only for a maximum of four years could restrictions be shared out on a basis that did not correspond with each supplier's share in trade. Emergency measures against imports other than those permitted under Article XIX were banned, and existing grey-area measures should be phased out or brought into conformity with the new rules within four years. Each country could maintain, with the agreement of the supplier concerned, one specific grey-area measure until the end of 1999. (This provision was designed to help the European Community swallow the pill of the new rules for, in its case, the exception was the maintenance of limitations on automobiles from Japan.) Imports from a developing country were to be exempt from safeguard measures as long as that country's share in total imports into the affected market was less than 3% (the Brussels figure had been much lower, at 1%), provided such countries did not collectively account for more than 9% of total imports. Developing countries were also allowed to maintain a safeguard measure for two years beyond the normal maximum of eight, and were allowed to re-introduce safeguards after a shorter interval than developed countries.

The Maciel decisions on safeguards were not challenged. The safeguards text included in the Draft Final Act was to some extent changed in form at the end of the Round during the legal drafting process to which all the agreements were subjected, but its substance was not touched. Essentially, the agreement is a compromise between the strict rules of a little-used but legal GATT procedure and the convenient but dangerous alternative of trade management through grey-area measures. If the new rules live up to the hopes placed on them, the multilateral trading system should in future be fairer, more predictable and more open.

Subsidies

The issues remaining open in the negotiations on subsidies and countervailing duties were more numerous and complex than those on safeguards, and there had been no progress in Brussels. A good deal of consultation and discussion took place in and around the rules group during the summer of 1992, centring on more than a dozen such issues which Maciel listed in July. They were almost all technical in form, but in substance were, with few exceptions, linked to the two basic questions of how to define and treat particular subsidies in terms of the "traffic-light" categories of prohibited, actionable and non-actionable practices, and how to treat developing countries. For example, Maciel's first item, "disciplines in the use of subsidies based on rebuttable presumption of the existence of serious prejudice", was the attempt to pin down a category of "amber" subsidies which, because they represented a large proportion of a product's value, might be assumed to distort competition seriously unless it could be proved otherwise. On these questions, however, as on the other critical issues before the rules group, no real progress was made. In late October, Maciel reported that although consultations on key issues had brought some potentially helpful suggestions, there was still not a sufficient basis for a compromise solution. A few days later, Dunkel suggested to the TNC that a solution for two issues – the acceptability of a non-actionable "green" category, and treatment of developing countries – would permit other outstanding matters to be resolved. During the final days before the Draft Final Act was put together, the United States and the European Community were reported to have tried but failed to reach agreement on defining the "green" category and the basis for action against "amber" subsidies. In the event, Maciel had to make the choices.

The Draft Final Act text on subsidies and countervailing duties provided answers to all the outstanding questions. Essentially, it followed the Brussels text. It defined a subsidy as requiring a government financial contribution (thus rejecting the wider US and Australian proposals), and left out of the agreement's disciplines all subsidies that were not "specific". In the prohibited ("red") category, it banned subsidies contingent on export performance or the use of domestic over imported goods, and reproduced an amended, but still only "illustrative", version of the Tokyo Round's list of such subsidies. Developing countries and countries transforming to a market economy were given special treatment. Least-developed countries, along with others with *per capita* incomes of less than $1,000 a year, were left free to use export subsidies. Most other developing countries were given eight years, and perhaps more, to remove them, except that those richer developing countries which had reached "export competitiveness" in any product were to get rid of subsidies to that product within two years. Countries in transition to a market economy were given seven years. The question of what action might be taken against prohibited subsidies was resolved in favour of allowing countervailing action or whatever countermeasure a dispute settlement panel might recommend – but not both. In the actionable ("amber") category, action was to be taken only in the event of injury to a domestic industry, nullification or impairment of benefits, or serious prejudice. For serious prejudice, previously undefined in either GATT Articles or the subsidy code, Maciel kept close to the Brussels draft: prejudice should be "deemed to exist" if a product were subsidized by more than 5%, or if the subsidy covered operating losses or provided direct forgiveness of debt. These last two alternatives were in fact the "particularly egregious practices" raised by the United States just before Brussels. As exceptions to the rules, debt forgiveness by economies in transition was not to be actionable for seven years, positive evidence would be required to show that a developing country's subsidy caused serious prejudice, and developing countries were also given some leeway for subsidies to support privatization of an enterprise. A carefully defined non-actionable "green" list, specifying maximum admissible percentages, included subsidies for research and development, and for disadvantaged regions, but (unlike the Brussels draft) not for structural adjustment or adaptation to environmental requirements. Even-handedly, Maciel made the new rules on serious prejudice, the list of non-actionable subsidies, and a provision for consultations if such subsidies have adverse effects on another country's industry – all applicable only for five years – with a review at the end of the period to decide if they should be made permanent.

On countervailing duties, most of the provisions in the Draft Final Act had been tentatively agreed on, subject to the United States getting what it regarded as essential on subsidies. Maciel's main contribution here was to provide some missing figures. These included *de minimis* limits, below which a subsidy would not be actionable. Thus subsidies of developed countries would be considered negligible only if they amounted to less than 1%, whereas imports from developing countries would not normally be actionable if they received subsidies of less than 2% (3% for the poorest countries), or accounted for less than 4% of total imports of the product concerned. Maciel accepted the argument that several small subsidized suppliers could have a cumulative effect, and allowed countervailing action if the imports concerned together amounted to more than 9% of total imports.

As a whole, the Draft Final Act text on subsidies and countervailing duties represented a most delicate balance of interests. Many countries were being asked to reconcile themselves to decisions by the chairman that at best gave only partial recognition to arguments which they had expressed strongly over five years of difficult negotiations. Moreover, last-minute developments elsewhere in the Round, in the negotiations on institutions, meant that the new subsidy rules would apply to all countries, unlike the earlier Tokyo Round code which only a few developing countries had accepted. Would some participants be so dissatisfied that they would insist on reopening discussions on the text?

Anti-dumping

The anti-dumping negotiations proved exceptionally difficult. No text had gone to Brussels, and none had emerged, except for a tentative agreement on a few of the least controversial issues. This meant that there was no immediate basis on which negotiations could resume in the rules group. Worse, the negotiations re-started at a moment when tensions were running high because of several strongly disputed anti-dumping cases.

As the Nordic countries were to point out a few months later, anti-dumping action, and the somewhat similar countervailing actions, had become the leading form of measure taken with reference to the GATT rules, with nearly 1500 cases initiated during the 1980s. During the twelve months from July 1990 to June 1991, the number of anti-dumping investigations initiated by signatories to the existing code nearly doubled. In the period July-December 1991, when the Uruguay Round negotiators were struggling to complete the task left unfinished in Brussels, six new dispute panels were established under the anti-dumping and subsidy codes. Earlier unsettled disputes continued to fester, the worst in relation to the negotiations being the EC-Japan case in which a panel had in 1990 found unjustified the Community's anti-dumping action against products of Japanese-owned assembly plants in Britain and France. The Community refused to comply with the panel's recommendations until the GATT rules were amended to include anti-circumvention provisions. Japan for its part was said to have stated that it would accept no such provisions as long as the Community continued to ignore the panel's findings. Dunkel undoubtedly had this case, among others, in mind when, reporting to the GATT Council in November 1991, he insisted that panel reports were interpreting existing rights and obligations, that they had to be acted on whatever might be under negotiation in the Round, and that the Quad countries, involved in 95% of all panel cases, had a special responsibility to conform with their recommendations. In this climate of mutual distrust, each side in the anti-dumping negotiations believed that the other was condoning unfair trade practices, and that concessions to their demands could even throw into doubt the value or desirability of market access commitments under negotiation elsewhere in the Round.

On the face of it, the anti-dumping negotiations went forward in line with work on other issues. There were discussions in the rules group, and consultations in an informal group chaired by Rudolf Ramsauer, a Swiss diplomat. In late October, Ramsauer held intensive consultations with a high-level group of officials, trying to find common ground through discussion of the final pre-Brussels text that the delegations of New Zealand, Australia, Mexico and Switzerland had put together in an attempt at mediation. However, these consultations were unsuccessful; they produced little beyond re-statements of well-known positions and, in some cases, even a hardening in those positions. Maciel had to report to the rules group that positions were still far apart on the essential substantive issues, and concluded that "the present situation with regard to anti-dumping has not evolved substantially since the ministerial conference in Brussels". Dunkel's summary of the situation in the TNC on 7 November, when he re-stated the essence of the problem in anti-dumping in terms which he could well have used a year earlier, showed that these negotiations were going nowhere. This was confirmed at the end of the month, when a draft drawn up by Ramsauer, based on the mediators' text of the previous year and the few points agreed in Brussels, proved unacceptable, mainly because the United States and the European Community were dissatisfied by its anti-circumvention provisions. At this point, multilateral negotiations on anti-dumping effectively came to an end.

The tentative agreement on anti-dumping in the Draft Final Act that went to the TNC in mid-December was thus very much an arbitrated text, not a negotiated one. In the circumstances of deadlock and suspicion in which it was drawn up, the arbitrators could not be bold: their task was essentially to give each side enough to make the changes from the existing code on balance worth having at all. Carefully treading a middle path, the draft offered some tightening of disciplines on findings of dumping and injury, as well as on the initiation and ending of anti-dumping action, balanced by compensating innovations that allowed action against circumvention and explicitly accepted some current practices not provided for in the existing code.

Among changes that tightened the disciplines on users of anti-dumping action, the draft laid down that the existence of dumping could not be assumed just because below-cost sales of the same product sometimes took place in the ordinary course of trade in the home market or third-country markets, or because selling prices in the importer's market were not always promptly adjusted to reflect changes in exchange rates. Curbs were imposed on comparing isolated export selling prices with average prices in the home market, unless evidence could be produced that the sellers were targeting particular regions, purchasers or periods for dumping. For injury determinations, the new text put more weight than the old code on the need to be certain that imports, rather than other factors, were causing the difficulties of the domestic industry. Investigations were not to be launched without evidence that this was desired by the whole industry, normally defined as the producers of all the products comparable with those said to be dumped, or as those producers whose collective output accounted for a major share of domestic production. Among other points welcome to exporters as being likely to reduce harassment: cases were not to be pursued if the dumping margin was *de minimis* (defined as less than 2%) or negligible in volume; a sunset clause provided that no anti-dumping duty should remain in force for more than five years (some US actions had been maintained for 20 years) unless a review showed that it was still needed to prevent injury.

The principal response to the demands of the importers was the introduction of provisions against circumvention. Subject to fairly strict conditions, anti-dumping action could be taken against "country-hopping" circumvention, where companies found to be dumping shifted their sources of supply to an affiliate in a third country. Action could also be taken against the technique of exporting dumped-price parts to a third country for assembly there before sending on the finished product. Anti-dumping duties could be levied, if a product had been found dumped, on parts or components shipped to the importing country for assembly by a related party which met the definition of a screwdriver plant: sudden expansion of output and imports for the purpose of assembly, most parts (at least 70%) sourced in the home country, and small value added. Another aim of the importers was met by permitting sampling for establishing dumping margins in a fragmented industry, although limits were put on the duties that could be imposed on exporters left out of the sample.

There were no illusions that the draft anti-dumping agreement would be popular. The hope was simply that all participants would like it enough, and be sufficiently relieved that someone else had taken the decisions for them, that they would accept what they did not like.

Balance-of-payments rules

The position reached before Brussels in discussion of the GATT balance-of-payments articles had been even worse than on anti-dumping. Not only was there no text; there was no agreement even to negotiate. In the immediate aftermath of the Brussels failure, no such agreement could be envisaged until participants in the negotiations were reasonably confident that the Round as a whole was moving forward. The subject was left aside until the autumn when, it was reasoned, deals on agriculture and textiles might be emerging, and the previously reluctant developing countries might be more amenable to accepting a modest agreement.

This judgement proved sound. During September, Maciel consulted informally with the main countries interested to identify the elements of a possible agreement. In October, this effort led at last to actual negotiations. Even then, they did not take place within the rules group, but alongside it, mainly among just four participants of strongly opposed views. The principal negotiation took place between the European Community and India; the United States and Brazil were also involved. The fragile compromise that emerged was presented to the main group at the end of October, and was subsequently carried without substantial change (other than addition of a short preamble which reassuringly "recognized" the existing GATT provisions) into the Draft Final Act and thereafter into the final results of the Round. For the most part, it deals with the procedures for balance-of-payments consultations, but also requires countries introducing restrictive measures to announce a timetable for their removal (or to justify not doing so), to give preference to measures which least disrupt trade, and to seek to avoid introducing further restrictions. The agreement also makes clear that countries resorting to the balance-of-payments provisions may still be subject to complaints under the GATT dispute settlement procedures if they do not follow the rules. As a whole, the agreement is a far cry from the ambitious, controversial and ultimately non-negotiable proposals originally put forward by some countries. But it stands as (in Maciel's words) "a serious effort to clarify the existing provisions and procedures without undermining the right to use balance-of-payments measures".

The "grandfather clause"

One tentative Brussels agreement in the GATT Articles group did not survive into the Draft Final Act. This was the draft agreement on the Protocol of

Provisional Application. In substance, however, its aim of ending the special cover given by the Protocol to some measures inconsistent with the GATT was encompassed by the tentative agreement on a new multilateral trade organization that, as described later in this chapter, emerged from the negotiations on institutions.

TRIMS

Work on TRIMS re-started after Brussels on an unpromising note. The green-room agreements of February 1991 sought to put the Uruguay Round back on track by concentrating first on technical issues. For TRIMS, this required the negotiators to discuss how a "trade effects test" might be developed and applied in order to identify trade-related investment measures that were having adverse effects on the interests of other countries. A test of this kind would be essential to the case-by-case approach, favoured by developing countries, under which countries which felt their trade interests damaged by existence of an investment measure would have to prove this through the dispute settlement procedures of GATT. However, the main precedent for this approach, the Tokyo Round subsidy code, was discouraging. Experience of the ambiguities of the code's definitions, the difficulties of showing that subsidies rather than other factors were responsible for trade problems, and the long delays in carrying through dispute cases, had persuaded many governments that it was much better, if possible, to clearly prohibit or permit trade practices rather than leave them to testing through the disputes procedures. Similar arguments could be applied compellingly for TRIMS, whose influence on trade flows was always likely to be difficult to separate out from other factors. A second argument against the case-by-case approach, in the view of most developed countries, was that some TRIMS such as local content requirements were clearly illegal under GATT, and ought to be banned outright.

Fortunately, the TRIMS negotiations did not continue down this road. From the middle of 1991, in the context of the new rules group and with the general push to complete the Round, there was a sharp change in the climate of the negotiations. Belatedly, and under pressure from Maciel to stop discussing technical matters and instead seek to bridge their remaining differences, the negotiators adjusted their ambitions to the need for an agreement.

To a great extent, these changes in national negotiating positions and objectives on TRIMS reflected the same kind of economic and other shifts that had affected attitudes to the Round as a whole. Countries' interests had altered since the mid-1980s. Crucially, the United States was no longer a huge net exporter of capital, concerned to remove barriers faced by its investors. On the contrary, US public opinion was now deeply worried about the growing role of Japanese and other investment in the United States. For their part, many developing countries that were opening up their economies and embracing free markets were now keen to attract foreign investment. On both sides, the hardest-line countries no longer held such passionate views, and were far readier to accept a modest compromise in the TRIMS negotiations.

From September 1991 onwards, Maciel put forward successive draft TRIMS agreements in a search for common ground among the participants. Starting from a point near to the Kobayashi draft of November 1990, he pared down the proposals to an essential core, throwing out elements such as the lengthy definitions of TRIMS on which agreement appeared impossible. During this process, none of the participants publicly abandoned their earlier stated priorities. However, informal consultations made it possible for Maciel to decide what was essential (and what was not) to an acceptable conclusion.

The TRIMS agreement sent forward by Maciel to the Trade Negotiations Committee and incorporated into the Draft Final Act of December 1991 was not a negotiated text. The key decisions it incorporated, answering the questions put to ministers a year earlier, were Maciel's. His central decision, without which many countries would have regarded the TRIMS agreement as not only worthless but actively dangerous, was that investment measures contrary to Articles III or XI of the GATT should be banned, the ban extending not only to measures that were legal requirements, but also to those applied as a condition for receiving an advantage. Five such measures, mainly involving local content or trade balancing requirements, were explicitly listed; countries maintaining them were to notify them and phase them out, developing countries being given longer to do so than developed countries. For these measures, the principle of prohibition had been accepted, and the case-by-case approach discarded. On the other hand, export performance requirements were not covered at all. Whatever might be said about their effects on trade, they were not contrary to existing GATT rules, and there was no basis for agreement to extend the rules to them. Finally, the draft agreement offered something to views at both extremes: it provided that five years after its entry into force, talks should begin on whether to complement it with provisions on investment policy and competition policy.

This compromise text brought the Uruguay Round negotiations on trade-related investment measures to their end. It was not subsequently challenged, and was incorporated without substantial change into the package approved in Marrakesh. In itself, the TRIMS agreement is a useful if somewhat meagre result from five years of tough negotiation. It does little more than clarify a GATT prohibition that, even if frequently ignored, had always existed. But it allows continuing discussion of investment issues that affect trade, and in the longer run it opens the door to fully fledged negotiations both on investment questions and, in the guise of competition policy, restrictive business practices. Already, it seems likely that such negotiations will take place.

Textiles and clothing

For the textiles negotiators, the first order of business in early 1991 was not the Uruguay Round but the urgent need to decide the immediate future of the

Multifibre Arrangement. The MFA had been extended in 1986 to run to July 1991, when it was expected that the Round would be over. Exporters wanted a very short extension, to end-1991; the United States preferred end-1993. Agreement on a 17-month extension, with no change in the MFA's rules, was finally reached only at the last possible moment, on 31 July. Even then, however, serious negotiations were slow to start. Many participants felt that prolonged discussion would risk unravelling what had already been agreed to before and during the Brussels meeting.

Substantive negotiation therefore began only in mid-September, with the focus initially on the safeguard provisions. The new negotiating group, chaired by Dunkel, that had been set up by the TNC in April played only a small part in the process: delegations preferred to meet informally, although they often did so in quite large groups. By the beginning of October, the whole draft agreement had been reviewed. The choices that each government would have to make were clear. The key remaining issues were the duration of the phase-out, the rates at which products would be integrated into GATT and at which imports of products still restricted would be allowed to grow, the rules for safeguard action during the transition, and the link to be established between liberalization of textiles trade and the strengthening of the GATT rules.

As in other areas of the Round, the final bargaining took place during the first half of December, with compromise agreements struck as negotiators balanced concessions in one area against gains in another, and with an eye on what was happening on issues other than textiles. The economic package was left until last, and the final figures were not formally agreed, but filled in by the chairman in the light of discussion and a general understanding of how they were likely to emerge. The results of the whole negotiation were put forward – following a final all-night negotiating session on 17-18 December – as a chairman's proposal to be incorporated in the Draft Final Act. Unlike some other texts, the textiles agreement was, apart from the figures inserted by the chairman, a fully negotiated text, and it was to be carried with very little change into the Final Act of December 1993.

Because the later changes were so small, it seems appropriate to describe at this point the outcome of the December 1991 negotiations on the last, key, issues. As far as the rather complex economic provisions are concerned, the result represented a balance of interests. Coverage of the agreement was set by an annexed list of products (Annex II), which essentially consisted of those products for which restrictions under the MFA were in operation. The phase-out period was set at ten years, starting with the expected entry into force of the Round as a whole, and divided into three phases of three, four and three years respectively. During this period, each restricting importer was to integrate (i.e. remove from coverage by the agreement) just over half of its total imports of the products listed in Annex II, each time drawing on products at each stage of processing. An initial 4% exclusion of products from

Annex II coverage was to be followed at the beginning of each of the three transition phases by integration of a further 12%, 17% and 18%, making 51% in all. (Later, in the Final Act, the 4% exclusion was combined with the initial 12% integration.) Growth rates for MFA quotas – which in practice varied greatly from country to country and product to product – were to be increased by 16% in the first stage, 25% in the second stage, and 27% in the final stage. Taken together, these integration and liberalization rules meant that final removal of all MFA restrictions at the end of the ten years would still involve a sizeable and sudden, although fully foreseeable, change in competitive conditions for the domestic industries of importers, and for those less-competitive exporters who were protected by reserved MFA quotas. But this "cliff" was a recognized part of the bargain, even if it left lingering doubts about what would happen at the end of the transition.

The transitional safeguard provisions that would govern trade in products not yet integrated into GATT were shaped by several considerations. One was that the Uruguay Round was a single undertaking, covering far more countries than the signatories of the MFA. The safeguard rules, like the rest of the textiles agreement, would bind all participants in the Round. They had to be drawn up in a way that allowed non-MFA countries to use them but, at the same time, avoided encouraging the appearance of new restrictions. In general, the objective was to encourage liberalization to go forward by providing assurance that relief could be provided in exceptional cases. The basic justification for safeguard action under the textiles agreement would be that increased imports of a product, from all sources, were causing or threatening serious damage to a domestic industry producing like or directly competitive products. However, safeguard action against particular supplying countries had to be justified by separate criteria that included the trend and size of imports from that country, as well as other factors such as whether the country was a small supplier, or whether products were being re-imported after processing. The safeguard provisions were complex, but this was because they too represented the results of an equally complex balancing of interests.

The concern of the importing countries to link phase-out of the MFA with strengthening of the GATT rules and disciplines was reflected in Article 7 of the agreement. The Article provided assurances (slightly amended between the 1991 and 1993 versions) that all countries would abide by GATT rules and disciplines to improve market access, ensure fair and equitable trading conditions, and not discriminate against the textiles sector in their import policy; and that compliance with these assurances would be monitored by notification requirements and discussion. However, no explicit link was established between compliance and the MFA phase-out and, in general, the strengthening of market access, rules and disciplines was sought in the other Uruguay Round negotiating groups, rather than through the textiles negotiations.

Services

The failure to agree in Brussels was not an unalloyed tragedy. For the services negotiations, which had lagged badly, it provided an opportunity to catch up with other areas of the Round. The year 1991 was that in which the future General Agreement on Trade in Services largely took shape, even though many of the most important issues were not to be settled until the very end of the Round.

Negotiations focused on all three basic elements of the emerging agreement: the framework text (the GATS itself), the annexes felt necessary to meet the special characteristics of a number of service sectors, and the schedules of specific national commitments to provide trade opportunities to foreign service suppliers. The three elements were interlinked, and work on them moved forward broadly in parallel during 1991.

Negotiations on the framework agreement had reached a fairly advanced stage before the Brussels meeting, and further progress had been made there in consultations among ministers. The services negotiators adopted the aim of settling the GATS text by midsummer, so as to provide a firm basis for negotiation of detailed commitments. This objective eluded them: all elements of the services package were too closely linked to permit one to be fully defined before the rest.

Some of the work on the text in any case proved irrelevant to the final outcome of the Round. Much discussion took place on how closely the provisions for settling disputes should resemble those of the GATT, and whether and how retaliation should be allowed for trade injury caused by breaches of the agreement. Even in early 1991, however, there were hints in the services negotiations of the broader deal that was to be reached in the Uruguay Round on dispute settlement. The United States suggested that there would need to be a possibility of cross-retaliation between services and goods. New Zealand envisaged a hierarchy of possibilities for retaliation, preferring a withdrawal of concessions affecting trade in the same services sector, but with the alternative, if necessary, of retaliation in any services sector or, failing that, in the area of goods.

Much more to the point was the year-long discussion on how to handle the fundamental issue of MFN treatment. As a Secretariat internal note of late July recorded, this was "by far the most troublesome" of the outstanding services problems, and it was to remain so up to, and even beyond, the end of the Round. The United States, which all along had taken the hardest line on the issue, had shifted its position somewhat in Brussels. With others, however, it remained worried by the implications of a general obligation to give MFN treatment to all signatories of the services agreement. An unconditional MFN obligation was seen as requiring that signatories of earlier bilateral agreements extend their privileges to others, without any counterpart, and as diminishing the incentive to negotiate seriously because it could permit countries with comparatively closed services markets to enjoy a "free ride" on the concessions of others. The United States felt this particularly strongly because in some services sectors – notably financial services and telecommunications – it believed that it was already offering much freer access to foreign suppliers than most countries.

As the chairman of the GNS put it, the question was how to meet the particular concerns of some countries without resorting to widespread derogations from the MFN rule. Could this best be achieved by provisions in the GATS itself, or by specific exemptions? For a long time, those arguing the need for MFN exemptions pressed for this to be achieved through separate sectoral agreements, to take the form of annexes to the GATS. But other countries were strongly opposed to this approach, which they foresaw would lead to sweeping exceptions to the MFN rule widely regarded, in the case of GATT, as the cornerstone of its success in spreading worldwide the liberalization of trade in goods, and which they now hoped would have a similar effect on trade in services. Instead, the idea took hold that the best means of giving whatever MFN exemptions might prove unavoidable would be to identify individual national measures, rather than whole sectors of activity, that might need temporary derogation. By July, the discussion had crystallized to the point of inviting each country to indicate the sectors or activities for which it would seek exemption, and for how long. But there was still no agreement on how far such exemptions would be permitted.

With this exception, work on the framework agreement progressed reasonably well. In early November, Jaramillo circulated a complete proposed text, including drafts of important articles to govern the preparation and content of national schedules of concessions. More than a month later, however, on the eve of the supposed completion of the negotiations, there was still no agreed GATS text. In part, this was because the broader Uruguay Round discussions on institutional questions had reached a point at which previous assumptions about the need for separate governing bodies and dispute settlement rules for services had been thrown into doubt. More importantly, it had become clear that several countries did not believe that the framework rules could be regarded as definitive as long as the other elements of the services package – the sectoral annexes and the schedules of initial national commitments – remained unsettled.

Four service sectors attracted most attention and controversy: labour, finance, telecommunications, and maritime.

For many developing countries, the questions of labour services was of intense concern. The negotiators had agreed that the GATS should cover four "modes of supply" of services, of which the fourth was supply through "movement of natural persons". Liberalization under this fourth mode would logically consist largely of easing rules which prevented foreign nationals from working in the country concerned. Yet most initial offers in this category by the major developed countries provided openings only for managers, executives and specialists. Countries such as India and Pakistan insisted that balance or symmetry in the services package required that developing countries be able to benefit from their principal competitive advantage, their low-cost labour force. They were careful to underline that they did not seek changes in national immigration laws, but only to allow less-skilled labour to be brought in temporarily to help in fulfilling contracts for services such as construction work.

Financial services was another key sector. Two new proposals had been put forward in Brussels. One, by Canada, Japan, Sweden and Switzerland, reflected discussions among a dozen countries, including some of the largest developed and developing participants in the negotiations. It included a proposal for what became known as the two-track approach to liberalization of financial markets. A lower-level track, following the general rules laid down in the GATS framework agreement, would govern commitments by countries with low *per capita* income. Richer countries would be expected to undertake tougher "fast track" commitments, to be set out in a special annex. Although the sponsors of the proposal saw it as a means of achieving greater liberalization than under the normal GATT rules, some other participants, including a number of the rising economic powers among the Asian developing countries, regarded it as a threat. They feared that it would be used to bring pressure on them to liberalize prematurely a sector which they regarded as fundamental to their economic independence and development. The views of these countries were reflected in the second paper, which also stressed that in the financial sector, prudential considerations must be given priority over liberalization.

Telecommunications and maritime services both presented problems, but of very different kinds. The United States was again the country with the strongest views: it initially proposed that both sectors be left out of the services agreement, the first because it did not want to undertake commitments which it believed others with less open markets would fail to match, and the second because domestic legislation greatly limited what it could offer. On telecommunications, the immediate concern was to reach an agreement allowing reasonable and non-discriminatory access to, and use of, public networks and services. Negotiations made quite good progress, and by the autumn led to drafting of a special annex that set conditions under which participants would allow service suppliers of other countries to link up with, or use circuits and equipment of, national public telecommunications systems. The annex also provided for support and assistance to developing countries seeking to establish efficient, advanced telecommunications systems. Maritime services were more difficult to handle. In September, the Nordic countries suggested a "common approach" for the sector, "to confirm the liberalization already achieved and to facilitate further liberalization of trade". Their approach called for a general binding commitment not to impose new restrictions, combined with commitments to remove cargo reservation requirements and other restrictions affecting international shipping services within three years, and to negotiate specific commitments on coastal shipping services (cabotage) and on auxiliary services such as tug and lighterage services, and cargo handling. This proposal had a mixed reception, especially from developing countries. Some favoured liberalization, although the three-year time period suggested was widely regarded as unrealistically short, while others were opposed to the ending of cargo-sharing arrangements which they valued as a support for their own shipping lines (and which in fact often followed guidelines negotiated under the auspices of the United Nations). The differences were too great to be bridged at this stage, and no special provisions were drafted.

The third element of the services package was the schedules of initial commitments. Here the negotiators were in largely unknown territory, in a situation comparable to that of the GATT negotiators of the Tokyo Round who mounted the first comprehensive assault on non-tariff barriers to trade in goods. The obstacles to trade in services themselves varied greatly, and differed according to the type of service and the way in which it was delivered. Some regulations, such as those governing the grant of work permits or access to foreign exchange, might operate across sectors, but others were specific to a particular sector. Much would depend on which of the four recognized "modes of supply" was relevant. If the service was to be delivered across national borders, with no movement of capital or labour, the way to liberalization might lie in the removal of communications barriers, regulations on materials and on payments. Movement of consumers might require easing of foreign exchange rules for tourists. Commercial presence could for instance involve rules on non-portfolio investment and foreign exchange. Movement of natural persons raised the kind of issues discussed above in connection with the proposed annex on labour services, as well as rules on professional qualification. On the whole, it could be left to individual countries to identify the specific barriers that they wished their negotiating partners to remove, but there remained the problem of how commitments were to be identified and recorded. This had to be decided before countries could begin to come forward with offers, and in the long run would be crucial to the enforcement of the concessions agreed. A long and technical discussion in the GNS, as well as in informal meetings chaired by David Hawes, the Australian co-chairman of the GNS, led to the emergence of understandings on these matters. The guiding principle was established that participants would list the services they were prepared to liberalize, and that the degree of liberalization would be defined by the general rules embodied in the GATS, except to the extent that limitations were spelled out in the national schedules. On this basis, and with the completion of the GATS Articles on scheduling of commitments, countries were able to begin preparing their initial offers. By autumn a steady stream of such national offers was under discussion in bilateral negotiations.

As the year-end approached, and all the Uruguay Round negotiating groups were meeting almost continuously in the effort to assemble the full package of agreements, it became obvious that the services negotiations could not be completed in the same sense as most of the others. As an internal

Secretariat briefing note commented, the value of the services agreement as a whole would depend on what exemptions from MFN treatment were claimed, and what initial commitments the participants were prepared to take on. This could not be known until the market-opening negotiations had been completed (at earliest February 1992). Another such note pointed out that many countries would not be interested in the services package if there were no disciplines on open-ended exemptions and sectoral non-application. Yet the United States, for one, apparently wanted the framework agreement which would govern these matters left open until the initial commitments had been negotiated. Moreover, it had further ideas to put forward: at the very last moment it proposed new provisions on subsidies for the GATS. They were not well received.

In the end, for services as for the other areas of the Round, it was left to the chairman in mid-December 1991 to make final choices on the text to be included in the Draft Final Act. For Jaramillo, the crucial decisions concerned MFN exceptions and sectoral non-application. He decided that participants would have to be allowed to take open-ended exemptions from MFN in some sectors, without being subject to disciplines to restrict such action. However, such exemptions (which would have to be clearly stated in the national schedules of commitments that had still to be negotiated) would have a ten-year limit, after which any extension would be subject to negotiation and compensation. Offsetting this less-than-ideal decision, his draft did not allow any sectors to be left out of the GATS altogether. This pair of fundamental choices was in its essentials to stand, and is reflected in the GATS agreement that emerged at the end of the Round. Jaramillo dealt with financial services by providing for separate decisions on institutional arrangements and possible fast-track liberalization; with air transport by an annex that preserved the sanctity of bilateral agreements; and with maritime services by omitting an annex but stressing the importance of reaching an agreement in this sector.

The services agreement that appeared in the Draft Final Act was far from definitive. But it represented a great advance on the text that had confronted ministers in Brussels, both in completeness and scope. For the first time, it was obvious that the negotiators were bringing to birth a completely new inter-national agreement of far-reaching significance: an agreement that promised to launch an opening-up of global trade in services that might one day compare with the achievements of GATT in liberalizing world trade in goods.

TRIPS

In spite of Dunkel's assessment in July 1991 that the intellectual property negotiations appeared "ripe for the final political trade-offs", serious negotiations did not re-start until the autumn. To general relief, the TRIPS negotiators then picked up largely where they had left off in Brussels, working in theory on the text that had gone to ministers, but in practice taking account of the compromises that had begun to emerge there on many issues.

Most of the discussion from September onwards took place informally, both in the TRIPS group and among the Quad countries. The Quad discussions were seeking mainly solutions for essentially "North-North" problems, including the protection of geographical indications (an issue that centred on the use by US and other wine producers of names originally applied only to French wines), rental rights (which pitted US recording companies against the Japanese practice of allowing taping of rented compact disks), and the copyright protection of performers and broadcasting. The broader negotiations among TRIPS participants as a whole continued to focus on what had always been the big issues: On what basis would countries accept an obligation to give patent protection to pharmaceutical products? What special arrangements would developing countries be given? What minimum standards would be set for the length of patent protection? How would the rules be related to the GATT system, and how would the dispute settlement provisions operate? No decisions emerged on key issues of this kind: indeed, the view in October of the group's chairman, Lars Anell, was that delegations were "not yet ready to negotiate in earnest". A month later the situation was still much the same but, at the same time, the informal discussions were steadily narrowing down the range of serious options on these and less controversial questions.

During the second week of December, the TRIPS negotiators, like those working on other subjects, began a non-stop series of informal consultations and meetings that produced a rapid movement towards agreement on virtually all secondary issues, and a sharp narrowing of differences on even the most difficult problems. In this, they were helped in particular by progress in the separate institutional negotiations, which resolved the relationship between TRIPS and GATT by placing both on an equal footing, in the wider framework of a new multilateral trade organization, and providing for a single integrated dispute settlement system which in the last resort would permit cross-retaliation. On 18 December, the TRIPS group held its last meeting, with a draft text before it that was 95% negotiated. Anell announced that he would, like the other group chairmen, make the final choices for the text that would go forward in the Draft Final Act the following day, and told the group what most of those choices would be. Only on three points, decided the following day, were his decisions unknown to the negotiators until the text was published and, although these choices were not wholly welcome, they proved to be so well balanced that they were never overturned.

As it turned out, the TRIPS negotiations were effectively over. The text included in the Draft Final Act of December 1991 proved to be the definitive result of the Uruguay Round negotiations on intellectual property, except for two small modifications of substance in the final stages.

By mid-autumn 1991, the general shape of the TRIPS text had become clear and many points had been effectively settled. Perhaps the most important decisions made in the final days of negotiation in December concerned the minimum levels of protection, the question of patent coverage (and thus of pharmaceuticals), geographical indications, and transitional periods. Patent protection, probably the most controversial single issue in the whole TRIPS negotiation, was to be available for 20 years for products and processes in all fields, except that it did not need to be extended to certain animal and plant inventions. Developing countries which had not allowed patents on pharmaceutical products were allowed ten years to introduce such protection but, in recognition of the long testing period before new pharmaceutical products get marketing approval (averaging over ten years), would have to grant protection at that time for inventions made from the time of entry into force of the Agreement. In general, developed countries were to have one year, developing countries five years, and least-developed countries eleven years, to meet the requirements of the agreement. On geographical indications, a compromise was struck that generally gave protection against misleading use and unfair competition, and gave still stronger protection to wines and spirits.

Two earlier issues fell away at the end. The introduction of a broad-ranging agreement on intellectual property made unnecessary a separate agreement on counterfeit goods, and the questions of dispute settlement and the relationship with GATT were effectively resolved by the Uruguay Round decisions on institutions.

Institutions

The new institutions group inherited three sets of tasks. The most nearly complete consisted of the work passed on by the group on the functioning of the GATT system, which had produced agreements on all matters of immediate substance, leaving unfinished only a political declaration on the relationship between trade, monetary and financial policies. Among dispute settlement issues identified before Brussels, the most difficult by far were the two linked questions of whether governments should accept a commitment not to use unilateral measures and whether automatic, unblockable procedures should be introduced for the establishment of panels, the adoption of panel reports, and the authorization of retaliation. The third group, on which least work had been done, was covered by the Final Act text that had been put together in the last weeks before Brussels. This very short text had posed, without answering, some crucial questions about how the agreements negotiated in the Round would be applied. Should the post-Round organizational structure include (as already proposed in the FOGS group) a new multilateral trade organization to administer all or some of the agreements? What was to be the relationship between the GATT agreements and the agreements reached on the "new subjects"? Could governments pick and choose among agreements, or must the whole outcome of the Round be accepted as a single undertaking?

When the Uruguay Round negotiations as a whole resumed in the Spring of 1991, the TNC accepted Dunkel's judgement that the main questions still open on institutional matters could be answered only towards the end of the Round, and that most required essentially political decisions. As this left for discussion only a few secondary and essentially technical issues on dispute settlement, the institutions group did not meet until late September. Meanwhile, however, the urgent need to reform the GATT dispute settlement rules, and to complete the negotiations, was underlined by a surge in the number of individual disputes brought to GATT, and by the failure of losing parties to act on five adopted panel reports. Whereas only one panel was active in late 1990, eleven were at work in November 1991, of which six (related to the Tokyo Round codes) had been set up during the preceding four months. Significantly, the blocked panel reports, all of which dealt with disputes among the Quad countries, concerned the application of policies on agriculture, dumping and intellectual property – all likely to be affected by the outcome of the Uruguay Round. As the Council chairman pointed out, however, the disputes concerned measures taken under existing treaty obligations. One delegate put it bluntly: a situation where member countries did not adopt or implement panel reports was "tantamount to a paralysis of the GATT system".

The September meeting of the institutions group produced agreement to review the Brussels dispute settlement text, along with some tentative and minor amendments that had been discussed at the ministerial meeting and afterwards. It also allowed participants to stake out positions not only on the recognized questions of automaticity and unilateralism, but also on another issue which carried broad implications for the institutional structure of the post-Round trading system.

Delegations had already agreed in principle, two years earlier, that all GATT dispute settlement procedures should be integrated into a single text, to prevent a proliferation of different sets of rules and discourage "forum-shopping". To help discussion on this point, the Secretariat had put together a paper that showed provisions on dispute settlement developed in other negotiating groups on such matters as anti-dumping action and technical barriers. Some countries quickly widened the issue by declaring their support for an integrated dispute settlement procedure that would cover not only all agreements on trade in goods, but also the "new subjects", particularly services. Strictly, as one delegate quickly pointed out in response, the negotiating group had been set up under Part I of the Punta del Este agreement, and thus had no mandate to stray outside the area of trade in goods. But the cat was effectively out of the bag: the distinction between negotiations on goods and services was breaking down as the elements of the Uruguay Round package began to be assembled; it was probably inevitable that this occurred first in discussion of the institutions to be put in place after the Round.

From this point onwards, as the United States and other countries pushed for an integrated dispute settlement system, the main issues still open on the institutions of the future multilateral trading system almost inevitably became interdependent, and could be resolved only as a package. If a single dispute settlement system would be applied to trade in goods, services and intellectual property, it was logical that a single institutional framework should also be developed to cover all three. Moreover, if the Uruguay Round results were to be tied together in a single legal and institutional package, governments and legislatures would insist on knowing the shape of that package before they accepted the results. It was no longer realistic to postpone discussion of a possible new multilateral trade organization until after the Round.

This situation in turn made it timely to put two questions which, once posed, demanded clear answers. First, should a country participating in the institutional framework be allowed to pick and choose among the agreements covered by that framework? And second, should the dispute settlement rules allow a country injured by the failure of another to live up to its obligations under one agreement to retaliate, if all else failed, by withdrawing concessions under another? Neither question was new, but now they had to be squarely faced.

The first question, it could be argued, had been largely answered by developments over nearly five years of negotiations. All the more active participants in the Round, including the developing countries, had helped to shape each of the agreements. Their acceptance of the emerging texts implied that most would in the end sign on to them. But there was no certainty that they would do so. Unless the agreements were presented as a single package, the Uruguay Round risked actually worsening the fragmentation of the trading rules brought about in 1979 by its predecessor, and perpetuating a situation in which countries had widely different levels of obligations, with some countries "free-riding" on the benefits of liberalization accepted by others. Fortunately this matter was far less controversial than it had been when developing countries generally believed that economic liberalization was not in their interests, and still hoped they could negotiate effectively with the developed countries without offering commitments in exchange for those which they demanded. They could now see both economic and bargaining advantages in accepting the new rules, particularly since they had played a full part in drawing them up.

On the second question – whether "cross-retaliation" should be allowed – there was less identity of interest. The right to seek redress in one sector when a country did not live up to its obligations in another was, however, important to some participants. If, for example, one country failed to prevent counterfeiting of another's products, and the offending country had few trademarked or patented products of its own, the country that was injured would have no effective means of hitting back unless allowed to withdraw concessions affecting goods or services, rather than intellectual property. For those participants in the Round who might have preferred not to concede a right of cross-retaliation, there were at least two reasons why they should do so. Over 40 years of dispute settlement in GATT had not produced a case in which retaliation had actually happened. And, if other countries were so keen on cross-retaliation, the implication was that acceptance of it would provide a bargaining chip to be cashed in for concessions elsewhere in the Round.

All active participants in the negotiations on institutions were aware that these issues were posed, and they were discussed informally during October 1991. It was late in the year, however, before any real movement occurred. At the TNC's stock-taking meeting on 7 November, Dunkel reported that three major questions still had to be resolved on dispute settlement: the degree to which the process should be automatic and binding, the question of doing away with unilateral measures, and "the application of the dispute settlement process across the board to the package of the Uruguay Round results, particularly if all the results must be accepted as a single undertaking". He was much less explicit on what he called "the institutional support necessary for implementing the results", noting only that "a very well coordinated approach is essential ... to fulfil the requirements of notification, monitoring, surveillance and dispute settlement arising from a large number of Uruguay Round agreements".

Resolution, at least in principle, of all these institutional issues came in a series of bargaining sessions during the final days and nights before the Draft Final Act was put together in late December 1991. Effectively, the institutions group split into two, with informal negotiations going forward in two small and crowded rooms, one hammering out new dispute settlement rules and the other working mainly on organizational proposals. Lacarte shuttled between them, or took delegations aside to mediate the resolution of particular difficulties. Nevertheless, each group worked in the knowledge of what was happening in the other room, and also in the decisive negotiations on other Uruguay Round issues that were taking place at the same time.

Early in the morning of 19 December the institutions group produced a package of five tentative agreements, all of which had been accepted by consensus and which therefore, unlike many other Uruguay Round texts, were able to be incorporated without change into the consolidated text that went to the TNC on the following day. Two of the texts required comparatively little effort. The "Final Act" itself, intended to tie the Uruguay Round package together and commit governments to submit it to their legislatures for approval, was shorter and much less controversial than its Brussels equivalent, since the big questions raised by the earlier text were now answered by a separate agreement. The group also completed the work of the earlier group on functioning of the GATT system, as the result of compromises between the United States and European Community which cleared the way for agreement on the declaration on "greater coherence in global economic policy-making". Because the negotiators had run out of time, work on the other three texts was not finished. Nevertheless, the essential decisions had been taken. Together, these amounted to a major re-shaping of the institutions of GATT. It was to be some time, however, before their full significance was appreciated.

The main text on dispute settlement was essentially a completed and refined version of that which had gone to ministers in Brussels. It dealt with the settlement of disputes in GATT itself, laying down detailed rules on consultations and timetables for panels, and the introduction of appellate review. It resolved the issue of how non-violation complaints should be handled. Negotiators resolved the crucial question of what kind of agreement should be required to set up a panel, to adopt a panel report, and to accept a report from the appellate body, by combining two of the alternative possibilities proposed in Brussels. In effect, they retained the consensus rule, but turned it on its head. Whereas consensus had been required in order to move the dispute settlement process forward at each stage, they provided that, in future, consensus agreement would be required *not* to move. The effect would be to end the possibility of a country unilaterally blocking the dispute mechanism, and to build automaticity into the progress of a dispute through the system, unless all countries agreed that the process should be halted. The counterpart of this decision was acceptance of a previously disputed provision, significantly titled "Strengthening of the GATT system", which prohibited unilateral action to redress violations of the trading rules or the nullification or impairment of agreed benefits. Countries were not to make their own determinations that GATT rules had been violated, nor to decide for themselves that action on panel reports had been unreasonably delayed, nor, if such action were not taken, to suspend concessions without Council authorization. The new provision was more explicit than the Brussels version, but left out the earlier requirement that domestic legislation be brought into line with the proposed new rules. This change eased acceptance by the United States, which could retain its Section 301 powers, while acknowledging that they should not be applied in practice to trade matters governed by the new rules.

Had the Brussels text gone only as far as this, it would still have been regarded as a great success. But now the negotiators went much further. In a second draft agreement, left as a separate document because there was not enough time to build its provisions into the main dispute settlement text, they set out the "Elements of an integrated dispute settlement system". These were to include a single Dispute Settlement Body (DSB) to handle all disputes under the GATT and its subsidiary agreements, as well as those arising under the General Agreement on Trade in Services and the agreement on trade in intellectual property. The DSB was to have comprehensive authority "to establish panels, adopt panel and appellate body reports, maintain surveillance of implementation of rulings and recommendations, and authorize suspension of concessions and other obligations". The text also recognized an injured country's right, in some circumstances, to suspend concessions in a sector of trade other than that in which its rights had been violated. This right to "cross-retaliate", effectively balancing off a loss of rights under one agreement by reducing obligations under another, was to be permissible only if the injured party found it "not practicable or effective" to suspend concessions in the same trade sector. Further rules defined the sequence and conditions to be followed in choosing what concessions to suspend.

The group's fifth text was a draft "Agreement establishing the Multilateral Trade Organization". During November, Canada, the European Community and Mexico had revived their 1990 proposals for a new trade organization to put GATT for the first time on a firm institutional basis and to bring all the Uruguay Round results under a single umbrella. Not all countries were sympathetic with this approach. The United States, while less adamantly opposed than it had been during the FOGS discussions, was not convinced that a new organization was needed, and was concerned – rightly, as events were to show – that the proposal would arouse opposition in the US Congress. Japan was also unenthusiastic. Nevertheless, they agreed to take part in negotiations on the form such an organization might take. A text gradually took shape.

By the final night of negotiations in December, a draft "MTO" agreement had been developed. It ran to just 16 articles, many very short, preceded by a preamble based on that of the GATT and followed by a list of the agreements that it would cover, and which were to become "an integral part of this agreement". The GATT, GATS and TRIPS agreements, the agreements on dispute settlement and on trade policy reviews, and all the other texts negotiated in the Uruguay Round were defined as "multilateral agreements", to which all members of the new organization would have to subscribe. Only four of the original Tokyo Round agreements – those on government procurement, civil aircraft, beef and dairy products – were put into a different category, still under the same organizational umbrella but defined as "plurilateral agreements" whose acceptance would not be compulsory. (This was because these four texts had not been taken up in the Uruguay Round. Important negotiations took place to broaden the scope of the government procurement code, but since these were essentially only among members of the code, the results would not reflect the concerns and interests of other countries.) The MTO's functions were defined simply: it was to "facilitate the administration and the operation" and "further the objectives" of the agreements it covered, provide the forum for further trade negotiations among its members, administer the dispute settlement rules and the trade policy reviews and, reflecting a continuing EC concern, cooperate with the IMF and World Bank "with a view to achieving greater coherence in global economic policy-making".

The text gave the MTO a simple structure. At its head would be a Ministerial Conference, open to all: picking up the decision taken in Montreal, this was to meet at least every two years. Inevitably, for those who had followed the FOGS discussions, there was no provision for a limited-membership management body, either at ministerial or official level. Instead, a General Council would be open to all members. This would establish and supervise the Dispute Settlement Body foreseen in the agreement on the integrated dispute system, as well as another body to conduct the trade policy reviews, and would also guide three subsidiary Councils responsible respectively for the GATT, GATS and TRIPS. New MTO-wide bodies would replace GATT's committees for budgetary matters, trade and development, and balance-of-payments restrictions. There would be a permanent Director-General and Secretariat. Among other provisions, the text affirmed that the MTO was to respect the "rules, decisions and customary practices of GATT", including its voting practices – language meant to recall that decisions would normally be by consensus. Voting, if required, would remain on the GATT basis of one vote for each country, and generally similar, but not identical, voting requirements were envisaged. All GATT members could become members of the new organization if they accepted the MTO text and the full results of the Uruguay Round, including definitive acceptance of GATT itself. (The latter point accomplished the aim of getting rid of the Protocol of Provisional Application.) Other countries would have to negotiate their accession with the General Council.

Until almost the last moment in the December 1991 negotiations, the United States and Japan took part without accepting the principle that a new trade organization should be established. Finally, however, they raised no objection to the unfinished text being forwarded to the TNC in the name of the whole institutions group. The draft was tucked away as an annex at the very back of the massive Draft Final Act presented to the TNC.

Chapter VIII

Frustrated hopes: 1992–93

On 20 December 1991, when the Trade Negotiations Committee received the Draft Final Act, it had been possible to hope that the participants in the Uruguay Round might accept the whole package without significant change.

The 440-page document was of course incomplete in several respects. Most obviously, because the final market access bargaining had not yet taken place, it lacked detailed commitments by each country to reduce tariffs and reduce trade-distorting non-tariff measures affecting goods, and to open up specific possibilities for trade in services. Even in the nearly 30 negotiated texts of the Draft Final Act, further work was needed on the agreements on the proposed multilateral trade organization and on dispute settlement, as well as on a number of technical or lesser matters. Nevertheless, the document otherwise offered answers to all the questions that remained in dispute when the final push to complete the negotiations began in November and December. A great many of those answers were, as Dunkel was to say three weeks later, "the result of protracted negotiation in the well established tradition of give and take", and could therefore be regarded as final. As for the remaining answers, those provided by "arbitration and conciliation", they were, again in Dunkel's words, "based on informed and conscientious decisions" that he and the chairmen of the negotiating groups "had no alternative but to take". Even if some of those decisions were unpalatable, the hope was that the overall package would offer each participating country a balance of advantage attractive enough that, rather than reopen the bargaining, it would give its assent, and thus allow the Round to be brought to a swift conclusion as soon as the market access negotiations could he completed.

That hope was promptly disappointed. Some countries were indeed ready to accept the Draft Final Act as it stood, and quickly said so. Prominent among them were several members of the Cairns Group. Other countries never stated their position clearly, because they were spared the need to do so: before they had time to give a considered response, the agricultural proposals, in particular, were rejected as "unbalanced" by a meeting of trade and agricultural ministers of the European Community on 23 December.

In this situation, what was the best strategy? The first objective, clearly, was to gain for the Draft Final Act the strongest possible standing, even if some amendments were eventually going to be needed, so as to avoid a general re-opening of the negotiations. This was essential, in order to secure the real and substantial gains that had been achieved in the last weeks of 1991, not only in fully negotiated agreements but also in the large number of decisions by negotiating group chairmen which no one seemed inclined to dispute. The second objective was to launch the remaining work that everyone agreed must be done: the market access negotiations, both for goods and for services, and the tidying-up of the existing texts. Finally, and very cautiously, an opening should be created for the unavoidable minimum of changes in substance in the draft agreements.

Dunkel secured agreement to this approach in January, when the TNC held a long meeting at which the main participants in the Round gave their tentative assessment of the Draft Final Act. Crucially, all of them agreed to use the new document as the basis for completing the Round. All also said that they could not fully judge the adequacy or otherwise of the Uruguay Round package until the market access negotiations were over, so that they could see what specific new trade opportunities their negotiating partners were offering. The most anxiously awaited statements were those of the countries which insisted on changes in the Draft Final Act. Objections were largely, but not exclusively, to the agriculture text. The European Community said unspeci-fically that this text must be improved to meet "very serious difficulties". Canada, Japan, Korea, Mexico and Switzerland, along with others by implication, made it clear that they were deeply unhappy with the concept of full tariffication. The United States said the Draft Final Act did not go far enough in "reducing barriers, setting rigorous standards, or providing strong disciplines against unfair behaviour", but that it sought only changes that would strengthen disciplines or lead to greater market liberalization. Most other countries argued strongly that the agreements in the Draft Final Act were best left as they were, whatever their deficiencies. They feared that attempts to amend the package would, as Brazil put it, "start a process of unravelling that could end up in the collapse of the Round".

The meeting ended with acceptance of a "four-track" approach to completion of the Round, replacing the earlier negotiating groups. Tracks One and Two were to be the immediate launching of market access negotiations on, respectively, goods and services. Track Three was to be the textual clean-up of the Draft Final Act, with the understanding that this should not involve any changes on matters of controversy. Track Four, "by far the most demanding in terms of political commitment and political courage", was to be the task of the TNC itself, which would "examine whether it was possible to adjust the package in certain specific places".

Whatever its disappointments, this TNC meeting confirmed the successful completion of the most characteristic phase of the Uruguay Round: the arduous negotiation, among representatives of many countries, of a great number of separate multilateral agreements that together amounted to the reshaping of the rules of world trade. Most of the agreements in the Draft Final Act were left substantially unchanged by the remaining months of negotiations. In retrospect, the Draft Final Act was a very substantial achievement: a far more important landmark in the Uruguay Round than the Brussels meeting that was supposed to bring the Round to an end, and second in importance only to the final agreement that was still two years away. It was also the high point of Dunkel's leadership of the GATT and the Uruguay Round negotiations.

From another point of view, however, the January meeting of the Trade Negotiations Committee was the start of an intensely frustrating and worrying period for almost all participants in the negotiations. They found themselves unable to move the Round forward at more than a snail's pace as long as disagreement continued on fundamental questions – especially on agriculture – and, for the most part, felt themselves powerless to influence debate on how those questions might be resolved. For months, that debate amounted to little more than a succession of tense and unproductive meetings, most held far from Geneva, between representatives of the European Community and the United States. All other countries were reduced to the role of bystanders, even though the subject-matter was vital to their national interests. The market access negotiations – Tracks One and Two – were crippled because they lacked ground rules as long as the status of the Draft Final Act remained in doubt. Track Three, the clean-up of the negotiated texts, and particularly the completion of work on institutional questions, could be pursued somewhat further, but only up to the point where further progress demanded decisions that no country was prepared to face until it had to – which again meant waiting for agreement on agriculture and the other unsettled issues. And Track Four, the multilateral discussion of possible "adjustments" to the Draft Final Act, could not proceed without some meeting of minds among the countries which wanted changes, or would be most affected by them. Only at the very end of the year was discussion of any such changes attempted, and then only briefly. Meanwhile, although work continued in Geneva, it was held hostage by the inability of the two largest trading powers to agree on political solutions to the key problems still outstanding.

As early as April 1992, in private discussions with the main negotiators, Dunkel found them unanimous in the view that the Round was effectively blocked, and in danger of ceasing to be taken seriously by their governments. All agreed that, without political breakthrough, it would be worse than useless to fix further deadlines for the Round. A few days later, summing up these views in diplomatic terms in an informal meeting of the TNC, Dunkel spoke of "the widespread perception that work under Tracks One, Two and Three was losing momentum after a promising start". Mute testimony to the lack of newsworthy progress during most of the year is provided by the GATT

Secretariat's series of press notes, *News of the Uruguay Round*, of which 50 issues were published between 1987 and 1991. The 50th note, headlined optimistically "Agreements expected by end-year as negotiators start the 'final sprint'", appeared on 11 November 1991. The 51st was not issued until a year later, on 10 November 1992, when the TNC itself met formally for the first time since January.

Track One: market access

Dunkel called in the December 1991 TNC for "intensive, non-stop bilateral, plurilateral and multilateral negotiations on market access", with "an enormous effort here by all participants to ensure substantial and overall meaningful results". Germain Denis, the market access group's chairman, had already fixed a timetable that called for completion of the negotiations by 31 March. A serious effort was made to achieve this, with meetings at all levels, technical support by the Secretariat, and some 37 draft schedules of commitments submitted by the due date. The substance of many offers, however, was not impressive and, not for the first or last time, the largest countries did not comply with the agreed timetable. This failure undermined the market access negotiations as a whole. The countries concerned were, for many products, each other's principal suppliers. This meant that the level of tariff reductions offered by them would largely depend on their mutual bargaining. Until that bargaining took place, smaller participants had no incentive to put their own cards on the negotiating table, since they could not form a view of what enlarged access they were likely to gain in these major markets under the MFN role. Countries reluctant to accept that the December decision to require full tariffication of agricultural trade barriers could not be reversed also made inadequate offers (or no offers at all) on farm products.

By the end of March, the negotiations had effectively run into the ground, as the group was forced to recognize that so little hard data was available in the schedules so far submitted that they could not be meaningfully evaluated. Summing up in the group, Denis recognized bleakly that progress was being impeded by the absence of complete schedules (the main shortcomings being lack of commitments on agriculture and inconsistencies with the requirements of the Draft Final Act), by lack of line-by-line concessions in the schedules of industrial concessions by some participants, by "the unsuccessful attempts to produce political breakthroughs" in some bilateral negotiations, by "doubts about the appropriate balance between the bilateral and the multilateral aspects of the negotiating process", and by lack of adequate data for evaluation. A few days later, Denis reported to the April informal meeting of the TNC that although he still saw "good prospects" for a substantial market access package, a political breakthrough in the bilateral negotiations between major participants on industrial and agricultural products was needed to ensure progress at the multilateral level.

Over the remainder of the year, progress was minimal, even though informal consultations took place intermittently, bilateral discussions continued, and the number of comprehensive offers received crept up to 38, representing 49 countries. Nevertheless, many observers agreed with Denis in seeing good prospects for the outcome on market access, if and when a political breakthrough happened. For the time being, uncertainties about the content of the final Uruguay Round package remained too great, they agreed, for governments to make firm commitments on dismantling border protection. In the long run, however, the outlook for meeting or even beating the Montreal target of a one-third reduction in barriers seemed quite good. Moreover, they were confident that, when the time came, the market access negotiations could be carried through quite quickly, in spite of the awkward necessity of intensive bilateral bargaining, and the lack of a multilaterally agreed formula to help in shaping and evaluating offers. Asked in October 1992 how long the final negotiations would take, a senior Secretariat official closely involved offered a reasonably confident estimate: "a couple of months".

Track Two: services

A similar drift and uncertainty blighted the services negotiations, compounded by concern over the continuing insistence by the United States that it was not ready to give MFN treatment in its service offers to countries whose own offers it judged inadequate. During the early part of the year, there were three rounds of bilateral negotiations, helped along by the same pressure and 31 March deadline that were being applied for market access. In the April TNC meeting, Felipe Jaramillo, chairman of the services group, reported that 47 initial offers of commitments were on the table, of which 24 had been recently revised, as well as 32 lists showing intentions on MFN exemptions. The level of commitments, he said, had improved considerably. But many participants felt that "the scope and nature of the intended MFN exemptions proposed by one major participant" called into question the structure of the GATS and risked undermining the overall level of commitments. This situation, he said, had "contributed to the lack of impetus and the standstill currently experienced".

The standstill continued virtually throughout the year. As in the case of the negotiations on goods, there was a gradual increase in the number of initial offers of commitments, the total reaching 54, covering 67 countries, by the end of 1992. Some further work, essentially technical, was also done on the GATS text and its annexes on air transport and telecommunications. But in contrast with the underlying confidence felt about the market access negotiations, many observers had doubts about the eventual outcome on services. With the new multilateral rules for trade in services still not fully worked out, with complex and pioneering sectoral negotiations ahead, and with the largest single participant in the negotiations taking a line that dismayed most other participants, there could be no certainty that in the end the services negotiations would produce a worthwhile result.

Track Three: the Legal Drafting Group

The Legal Drafting Group, chaired by Madan Mathur, Dunkel's recently retired deputy, was more fortunate. Its stated role, as defined by the January TNC, was to review all the agreements in the Draft Final Act for legal conformity and internal consistency. This required much painstaking effort, generally uncontroversial although it occasionally brought to light disagreements of substance and quite often aroused fears, especially in the Secretariat, that close scrutiny of negotiated language might reopen sensitive issues. However, the group also found that it had a further, unacknowledged task: to continue the uncompleted negotiations on institutions.

As far as the texts on dispute settlement were concerned, there was not much more to do. The key decisions had been taken, and the main task remaining was to mesh the agreement on the improvement of dispute settlement under the GATT with that on the elements of an integrated dispute settlement system. The draft rules and procedures for the suspension of trade concessions ("cross-retaliation") also had to be woven into the new combined text, and defined more precisely. A third task was to accommodate the special dispute settlement provisions developed for some agreements, such as that on subsidies, within the overall framework of rules. Differences also remained on some secondary matters.

The draft Multilateral Trade Organization needed much more work. During the early months of 1992, up until the beginning of the summer, informal meetings of the Legal Drafting Group discussed each article of the agreement in turn, in exchanges that not only led to extensive redrafting, but also clarified everyone's understanding of the provisions hurriedly put together in the final weeks of 1991. This was an essentially cooperative enterprise, in which all the most active participants in the Round shared, with the Secretariat producing fresh redrafts and a large number of papers on particular issues between meetings. Much of the task consisted in defining precisely the relationships of the proposed organs of the new organization to one another, and in deciding how the different rules and institutions envisaged under all the agreements in the Draft Final Act would fit into the single structure established by the MTO agreement. Because the great majority of the agreements had been drafted to stand alone, they would need to be changed in form to become subsidiary parts of the all-encompassing single agreement that would set up the MTO. This meant, for instance, that the individual provisions on acceptance and withdrawal in many agreements would need to be removed, since acceptance would be automatic for all MTO members. Because the GATT itself would become an annex to the MTO, fairly large-scale redrafting of its original 1947 text seemed desirable, even though its substance would be hardly changed. This redrafting would involve deletion of superfluous articles and provisions on matters such as voting, as well as of some quaintly outdated references (the Ottoman Empire featured in Article I), and disappearance of the time-honoured phrase "contracting parties". Of the Uruguay Round agreements themselves, those on GATT Articles, as well as the future schedules of commitments on market access for goods, and the texts on agriculture, textiles and clothing, and rules would all be attached in turn to this revised GATT, together making up a single annex on multilateral trade in goods. (One of the GATT Articles agreements, that on waivers, was embodied in the MTO agreement itself.) Further annexes would attach to the MTO the GATS, the TRIPS agreement, the dispute settlement rules, the trade policy review mechanism, and the four limited-membership "plurilateral" agreements. Some other texts negotiated in the Round, such as those on the global coherence of economic policies and on help to least-developed countries, would more appropriately become separate decisions and declarations to be adopted by ministers.

As this process went forward, it defined the elements and relationships of the much wider, more complex, and more solidly established multilateral trading system that was to replace the GATT. Few participants in the meetings can have been unaware that the results of the separate and sometimes confusing negotiations that had so far constituted the Uruguay Round were coalescing before their eyes into a single, logical and impressive structure. Even if the MTO itself had been given no great powers beyond those already embodied in individual agreements, the outcome of the Uruguay Round would have a significance, taken as a whole, very much greater than the sum of its parts. For those not involved in Track Three, however, this essential unity of the Round's results was less obvious. The texts resulting from negotiations up to the end of 1991 remained bundled in the Draft Final Act in an order based mainly on the sequence of the Articles of GATT. Brief, bureaucratically titled (for reasons of inertia and lack of time, rather than deliberate choice), and obscurely positioned behind more than 400 pages of other texts, the agreement establishing the Multilateral Trade Organization was largely overlooked. Far from calling the new organization "the crowning achievement" of the Round, as his successor Peter Sutherland was later to identify it, Dunkel gave it no more than a brief mention in his introduction to the Secretariat's review of GATT activities in 1991, and the review itself gave the MTO only a short paragraph, compared with more than two pages for the dispute settlement agreement.

There were reasons for this reticence, apart from Dunkel's known reluctance to offer any encouragement to negotiators tempted to focus on institutions rather than commitments of substance. The Legal Drafting Group made good progress in defining the relationships between the MTO and the other agreements emerging from the Uruguay Round, and in settling some other problems. However, important issues remained open when in mid-1992 the group succumbed to the same paralysis that had already brought work on market access to a halt. The most difficult questions still unsettled concerned voting. The text in the Draft Final Act called for the MTO to respect the customary practice of GATT, including voting practices, which clearly meant that decisions should normally be made by consensus. Nevertheless, it prescribed that in the absence of consensus, interpretations of the MTO and its subsidiary agreements could be based on a two-thirds majority, made up of more than half the members. Waivers could be granted on the same basis. The MTO text could be amended if two-thirds of the members voted in favour, and the amendments would apply even to countries which did not accept them, although the text of any amendment should be agreed beforehand by consensus. Several possible variants on these rules were floated in the group's discussions, but no agreement could be reached. For some countries, and particularly the United States and Japan, the proposed voting rules gave inadequate reassurance against the possibility that a united group of smaller countries might force through decisions permitting themselves to escape obligations, or imposing new obligations on unwilling governments.

Further key questions about the MTO were also left open. Should all countries becoming original members of the new organization be required to submit schedules – that is, to accept binding commitments on goods and services? Should an exception be made for the least-developed countries? Given that the MTO draft called for the GATT to be accepted on a definitive basis, should certain practices hitherto protected by the "grandfather clause" of the Protocol of Provisional Application be given new legal cover? Answers to these questions, and to others, could not be found as long as the necessary political will was lacking. The drafting group managed some desultory discussion on possible overhaul of the GATT text during the autumn, but the task proved more complex than expected, and in December was effectively abandoned for the time being.

Track Four: substantive changes in the Draft Final Act

Dunkel had stressed in January that any work under Track Four – the "adjustment of the package in certain specific places" – would have to be "concentrated entirely on what we all can collectively agree to without unravelling the package". He himself had no intention of opening what could be a Pandora's box, and most countries agreed: there were things in the Draft Final Act that they did not much like, but they were prepared to accept the package as long as it was left as it stood. The European Community had made it clear at the TNC meeting that it would insist on changes to the agricultural text; several other agricultural importers were reluctant to accept full tariffication; and the United States had called for unspecified changes. In addition, a number of countries made direct proposals to Dunkel for changes in the Draft Final Act. On behalf of the least-developed countries, Bangladesh asked for their exemption from some major obligations under the textiles, TRIMS, services and safeguards agreements, as well as a broader exception in principle from any obligations inconsistent with their needs or beyond their administrative and institutional capabilities. Twenty-one African, Caribbean and Pacific countries wanted amendment of the agricultural text to ensure that the entrenched preferential advantages they enjoyed in European Community markets would be not be undermined by the tariffication requirements. Other participants, while not asking directly for changes, made it quite clear that if texts which contained features they disliked were opened up under Track Four, they would press for removal of those features.

In the following months, several governments began to come under heavy pressure from domestic interests not to accept particular elements in some texts. Violent riots by farmers against the admission of foreign rice took place in Korea and Japan, and large-scale demonstrations by farmers in Western Europe also degenerated on several occasions into disorder. The TRIPS agreement's requirement to provide patent protection for pharmaceuticals and seeds aroused fierce controversy in India, and Dunkel (held personally responsible for the Draft Final Act, known there as "the Dunkel draft") was burned in effigy. On the other hand, American pharmaceutical manufacturers found unfair the delayed introduction of patent protection for products already in the "pipeline" leading to market launch. Other US interests protested about what they saw as lax new rules on anti-dumping and subsidies, and a one-sided phase-out of restrictions of imports of textiles and clothing. In France, objections extended beyond the agricultural text to the services agreement, accused of putting the country's cultural independence at risk by easing restrictions on imports of foreign films and television programmes. Environmental campaigners in the United States, Britain and elsewhere claimed that sovereign rights to protect health, safety and the environment would be undermined by provisions in the draft agreements on the MTO, technical barriers and sanitary and phytosanitary measures.

Although no Track Four negotiations took place during most of 1992, these developments made everyone aware that, sooner or later, some adjustments of the texts would be politically unavoidable.

The Round at the mercy of external events

External events in 1992 were largely unhelpful to the negotiations.

Global economic activity slowed. The previous year had been the third in succession in which the growth rate of world trade declined, and although 1992 was to see some pick-up, this was not obvious at the time. North America was being followed into recession by Western Europe and Japan. Trade among the Central and Eastern European countries collapsed, following their political upheavals. Only demand from developing countries in Asia, Latin America and the Middle East provided a strong prop for international trade.

Trade policy-makers in North America were heavily occupied by negotiations on the free trade agreement between Canada, Mexico and the United States, finally signed in December. The American presidential election campaign ran throughout almost the whole year, with the Democratic candidate, Bill Clinton, showing sympathy for domestic interests dissatisfied with existing US trade policies. The European Community succeeded in May in reaching an agreement on reform of its common agricultural policy, but a tense political campaign in France, leading up to a referendum in late September on whether to accept the Maastricht agreement, made it hard for the Community to contemplate any compromise deal on agriculture in the Uruguay Round. Hopes that the annual summit of the Group of Seven industrial powers in July might provide new impetus for the Round were unfulfilled, in spite of a pre-meeting appeal by the International Chamber of Commerce on behalf of world business. Meeting in Munich, the leaders declared that "an early conclusion of the negotiations will reinforce our economies, promote the process of reform in Eastern Europe and give new opportunities for the well-being of other nations, including in particular the developing countries". They stated their expectation that agreement could be reached before the end of the year. Unfortunately, as the press was quick to point out, they had expressed the same expectation at their two previous annual meetings.

In fact, the year's main breakthrough in the Round was prompted in part by events in GATT itself. In April, a GATT dispute panel concluded that a new EC support system for oilseeds producers, introduced to replace earlier arrangements that had been found to deny foreign oilseed suppliers the full benefit of a long-standing zero tariff binding, was still impairing the binding's value. Very large trade interests were involved, with the United States alone claiming injury of some $1 billion a year to its producers. The Community agreed in June to negotiate compensation, and its subsequent negotiations with the United States were broadened to cover disagreements over the agricultural provisions in the Draft Final Act. Talks in Chicago early in November were reported to have come close to agreement, but broke down with noisy recrimination, not least within the EC Commission itself. At a GATT Council meeting on 5 November, the day after the elections in which President Bush was defeated by Bill Clinton, the United States asked for authorization to compensate its traders' losses by suspending trade concessions to the Community worth $1 billion, and a day later published a list of concessions it proposed to withdraw if no settlement was reached within 30 days. The situation worsened with a declaration by EC ministers in Brussels on 9 November that a US withdrawal of concessions "could only lead to a retaliatory spiral, which would damage both sides through a slump in business confidence and lost jobs".

On the following day, Dunkel called an emergency meeting of the TNC, at which he put aside his usual optimism. The Round, he acknowledged, remained blocked, and "unresolved and escalating trade disputes" made the present situation even more critical: they "put under threat even the existing multilateral trading system which is the very foundation for our ongoing efforts in the Uruguay Round". In his consultations with government representatives, he said, "an overwhelming majority of participants express deep concern and helplessness" at the inability of the Community and the United States to resolve their bilateral differences and provide "the trigger to the multilateral process". "In short, there is a deep sense of crisis, since it appears that the Uruguay Round itself is in danger of being lost." In response to his proposals, the TNC endorsed conclusions which stated that the Uruguay Round was stalled, largely because of the continuing disagreement between the Community and the United States, and that further delay to the Round – "a multilateral undertaking with a large number of major national interests involved" – might mean failure "which neither the world economy nor the participating governments can afford". The TNC appealed to the Community and the Americans "to discharge their responsibilities" as the two major trading entities in the multilateral trading system, and called on Dunkel to state its concerns in Brussels and Washington.

Dunkel did not in fact have much leverage to exert. In Brussels, in particular, the choices he had made in the agriculture text for the Draft Final Act were regarded as more sympathetic to US views than to those of the Community, and some officials both in the Commission and the member governments were reported reluctant to view him as a neutral mediator. Nevertheless, the Community and the United States both gave him a polite reception, and his insistence on the frustration and dismay felt by all other participants in the Round may have added usefully to the pressures on the two sides to agree. Both, however, were in any case anxious to achieve a settlement. They knew that unless they could do so, and then complete the Round in the few weeks remaining before President Bush left office in January, there could be little hope of achieving success before US negotiating authority expired in early March. Neither wanted to start a damaging cycle of retaliation and counter-retaliation over oilseeds. They resumed negotiations, this time at Blair House in Washington, the President's guest quarters for foreign dignitaries.

On 20 November, the negotiators of the United States and the European Commission reached an overall agreement. The oilseeds dispute was resolved by setting acreage limits for EC production. For the Draft Final Act, the United States agreed to support three important changes. Perhaps its most important concession was to accept a cutback of only 21% in the volume of subsidized exports, rather than the 24% that Dunkel had prescribed. (For developing countries, the agreement provided that the reduction percentage become 14% rather than 16%.) Although no change was proposed in Dunkel's 36% cut in spending on export subsidies, the easier volume requirement was expected to ease the Community's future problems with exports of cereals. Second, the Blair House agreement accepted that some domestic subsidies paid directly to producers, and not previously accepted as falling in the "green box", should be exempt from reduction commitments and from challenge by countervailing action or complaint. This concession would legitimize instruments that the Community had decided to use in reforming its agricultural policy, and would also (a less-noticed consequence) provide cover for some American domestic subsidies. Finally, the agreement extended the "peace clause" provisions which gave immunity against complaint to subsidies in course of reduction. The Community failed to gain acceptance of "rebalancing", which would have allowed it to reintroduce some protection of oilseeds as a partial offset to liberalization of other agricultural products. However, the United States agreed to consult with the Community if EC imports of non-grain feed substitutes, such as corn gluten, reached a level which threatened to undermine reform of the common agricultural policy.

A joint EC-US statement claimed that "we have achieved the progress necessary to assure agreement on the major elements blocking progress in Geneva". Both sides promised to complete negotiations on their country schedules quickly. They also announced that in the market access negotiations they would maximize tariff reductions by reducing high tariffs, harmonizing low tariffs and eliminating tariffs in some key sectors, and in the services negotiations would take a common approach on financial services, improve their offers, and expect others to do the same.

The initial reaction of most countries to Blair House was enthusiastic. Agricultural exporters were disappointed by the proposed weakening of the Draft Final Act's requirements, but accepted that the settlement had been essential to progress in the Round. The TNC reconvened on 26 November, and agreed to Dunkel's proposal "that substantive negotiations in Geneva be re-activated as of the present day with a view to achieving a successful political conclusion of the Uruguay Round before the end of 1992".

Euphoria was short-lived. Although market access negotiations on goods and services got under way quickly, events over the next three weeks showed that the breakthrough had been less decisive than hoped. Almost immediately, France denounced the Blair House agreement (in its eyes only a "pre-agreement", since it required endorsement by EC ministers), claiming that the Commission had exceeded its mandate and agreed to measures incompatible with the common agricultural policy. Although a threatened French veto in Brussels was averted, the ability of the Commission to negotiate effectively in Geneva was weakened. Canada, Indonesia, Japan, Korea and other countries continued to oppose tariffication. The US and Community schedules of agricultural commitments, reflecting the Blair House agreement, were not submitted until late December. Major differences persisted between them, and with other countries, over many aspects of the market access negotiations.

There was more. With the agricultural blockage at least partially cleared away, and the two largest participants pressing to complete the Round, other participants grew anxious that their own outstanding concerns would be overlooked. Already at the second November TNC meeting, India and Tanzania had warned that they were not ready to accept the MTO text as it stood: Tanzania, in particular, wanted the least-developed countries exempted from the requirement that all MTO members accept binding commitments on goods and services. Dunkel, fully aware that there was no certainty that the United States and the EC Commission could deliver on their promises, decided that the Secretariat must push the negotiators as hard as possible, and that the time had come to face the politically charged Track Four issues. Armed with assessments by the negotiating group chairmen and by his Secretariat colleagues of the issues which individual governments seemed likely to press, he took the risky step of inviting the chief negotiators of some 20 of the most active participants in the Round to state what they wanted.

Although the discussion took place at a private dinner, on 14 December, much of what was said quickly leaked out. The list of demands was long, but most of them were expected. A Secretariat meeting three days earlier had identified more than two dozen issues, some wide-ranging, some specific, that would require political decisions. However, there was shock at the extent of the changes for which the United States was asking, including what was seen as weakening of the anti-dumping agreement, tougher provisions on intellectual property, and abandonment of the Multilateral Trade Organization. On the MTO in particular, it had been known that the Americans, and others, had problems with the proposed voting arrangements, and that they feared it might fall outside the scope of Congressional fast-track approval, thus requiring the difficult process of Senate ratification. Now, however, they proposed to get rid of the new organization altogether, replacing it by a simple ministerial decision and a protocol that would require the agreements to be accepted as a package, with their unity subsequently maintained by the combined effects of the integrated dispute settlement system and of ministerial meetings every two years, with a council to handle matters during the interval between those meetings.

Although Dunkel was criticized for having provided "an invitation to all-comers to rekindle old disputes that had died down", anger was reserved mainly for the United States. At a meeting of the TNC on 18 December, its proposals were widely attacked. Opposition to its attempt to suppress the MTO, in particular, was unanimous. Most countries knew that its substitute proposals were practicable: after all, these amounted very much to a "GATT writ large". But all objected strongly to what they saw as a US attempt to retain two major reforms it wanted – a single Uruguay Round deal with no "free riders" permitted, and a unified dispute settlement system with cross-retaliation – while refusing to permit a solid institutional base for the reformed trading rules or to renounce use of unilateral weapons of trade policy. Many countries also warned that the proposals being put forward to modify the Draft Final Act were tilting the package against their interests, and that they too would have to request changes. Some spelled out their demands.

In spite of the obviously desperate lack of time to settle outstanding issues, the TNC agreed to continue negotiations and meet again in January. Hopes of early progress were briefly encouraged by a declaration issued in Washington on the same day, following a regular US-EC summit meeting. President Bush and the Community's ministerial chairman and Commission President, British Prime Minister John Major and Jacques Delors, called for a speed-up in the Geneva negotiations, with the aim of reaching "a balanced and comprehensive agreement by the middle of January". But there was no follow-through. Dunkel's own hopes dwindled when, shortly afterwards, the chief US and EC negotiators in Geneva made it clear to him that they had been given no new instructions that would help in meeting the deadline just proclaimed by their political masters. Recalling the incident privately, three months later, Dunkel judged that it had probably marked the end of the road for hopes of concluding the Round before the expiry of the US negotiating authority.

Press and public interest remained high. For the first time, the huge satellite dishes of the world's television broadcasting services were parked for days on end outside GATT headquarters. Reuters news service promoted items about the Uruguay Round to the priority category announced by a double bell-ring. Reports and rumours of developments in the Round were cited as a prime cause of movements on the London stock market.

It was not to last. As 1993 opened, there were still faint hopes that a deal could be struck. Carla Hills, the US trade representative, and Sir Leon Brittan, for the European Commission, tried to put together an agreement on tariffs which would have combined EC acceptance of zero tariffs in some sectors of interest to US exporters with American reductions in tariff peaks affecting sectors such as textiles. They did not succeed. On 19 January, on the eve of President Clinton's inauguration, the TNC met to review the position reached. Dunkel reported continuing intensive work on market access. He explained his own efforts to carry out what he called "soundings with a view to completing comprehensive political reading and review of the Draft Final Act" – a process which he insisted had not been one of negotiations or trade-offs. The Round could still, he said, be concluded quickly, provided that the immediately needed political decisions were taken, and that these did not upset the overall existing balance of rights and obligations. No one disagreed. Instead, and perhaps for the first time, several delegations suggested that if countries now wished (as Chile, speaking for the Latin Americans, put it) "to introduce new items, or even put new emphasis on existing ones, this could only be carried out in a new round of negotiations in the future". This line of thinking was developed a few days later in a proposal by Fred Bergsten, head of the independent Institute of International Economics in Washington, that "the most pragmatic course" might be to agree immediately on a Uruguay Round "mini-package", and to take up the remaining issues in a new Clinton Round.

Whether or not Bergsten's proposal might have been acceptable a few weeks earlier (and this seems doubtful, given the central importance of some of the most disputed issues to the package as a whole), it was too late. Just ten days after the TNC meeting, in a widely reported speech to a business audience in Davos, Dunkel acknowledged the inevitable: the Round could not be finished before the effective expiry of the US negotiating authority on 2 March. "We need," he said, "a bit more time." In fact, he himself had no more time: he had accepted a final six-month extension of his term of office to help finish off the Round, but that would expire at mid-year. He had already presided over his last TNC meeting.

Once again, the Uruguay Round drifted at the mercy of events. The United States had no negotiating authority. Although the new Administration promised to seek fresh powers quickly, the process would clearly take several months, and there were fears that unacceptable conditions would be attached to its renewed authority. Remembering the fatal tendency of all GATT negotiations to continue in any case until the last possible moment, some observers concluded that the Uruguay Round could well continue to 1994 or beyond. Others, listening to the emphatic rejection of the crucial Blair House agreement by all major contestants in the French general election, doubted even whether the Round could be re-started in 1993, and thought it all too possible that the negotiations would in the end ran into the sand.

At this low point in the Uruguay Round, the De la Paix Group of countries again found common ground in their desire to keep the negotiations alive and moving. A letter drawn up by them in Geneva, and signed on behalf of their governments by President Carlos Menem of Argentina, was sent on 11 March to President Clinton, to the presidents of the EC Council and Commission, and to Prime Minister Kiichi Miyazawa of Japan, as leaders of the three largest participants in the Round. The 37 developed and developing countries, still essentially the same group whose efforts had paved the way for launching the negotiations in 1986, appealed to the major countries "to display leadership at this critical time and to give the Round the priority it so clearly deserves". The letter emphasized that the basis for the final result stood largely prepared. Only the detailed package of market access commitments for goods and services needed to be settled, and the few remaining differences on the Draft Final Act resolved. The future of the Round, and of the entire trading system, was in the hands of the major economies. The signatory governments called for the US negotiating authority to be renewed on a basis reflecting the urgent need to conclude the Round, asked the three powers to negotiate constructively in Geneva, and pledged their own commitment to the Round's success.

Whatever the immediate impact of this letter, it coincided with the beginning of a slow improvement in the climate for the Round, even though the negotiations were still effectively suspended. In April, the United States and the Community settled a bilateral dispute on government procurement with an agreement to open up to each other their markets for heavy electrical equipment. The agreement improved prospects for the negotiations on government procurement which were taking place among signatories of the Tokyo Round agreement, in parallel with the Uruguay Round, and helped the atmosphere for the Round itself. In the United States, President Clinton, after consultation with other countries, asked Congress to extend his fast-track negotiating authority without alteration, to expire on 15 April 1994. The date was chosen to give long enough to complete the negotiations, but not enough time for them to be dragged out. Allowing for the necessary notice to Congress, it would require the completion of substantive negotiations by 15 December 1993. Congress approved the new authority, with effect from 30 June. After the delay inseparable from a change of Administration, the United States had a new negotiating team in place, headed by Mickey Kantor as US Trade Representative. In France, with the elections out of the way, the new government seemed ready at least to show greater flexibility in its opposition to the Blair House agreement: in June, it agreed to ratify the oilseeds part of the agreement, even though continuing to demand further changes in agricultural and other provisions of the Draft Final Act. Looking ahead to July, the annual summit meeting of the Group of Seven was to take place in Tokyo, once again raising hopes, however regularly disappointed in previous years, that the leaders of the major industrialized powers might give a decisive push to the negotiations.

A change of cast

These more promising developments, however, came too late to affect Dunkel and his deputy Charles Carlisle, both of whom left office on 30 June. Tributes were rightly paid to Dunkel for his 13-year stewardship of GATT, for his persistence and dogged optimism in leading the Uruguay Round negotiations, and for his personal role in developing the Draft Final Act. Dunkel had in fact presided over the entire period of gestation and birth of the Round, as well as nearly seven years of actual negotiations. He had served the world trading community well, and was unlucky not to see the Round through to its end. His successor was Peter Sutherland, an Irishman nominated as GATT Director-General by the European Community and appointed by consensus decision to that post, and to the chairmanship of the TNC, after it became clear that he enjoyed wider support than the other candidate, the GATT veteran Julio Lacarte.

Sutherland brought qualifications to the post different from those of Dunkel. Dunkel's entire career had been as a negotiator on international economic issues (and for more than 20 years, exclusively on trade matters); he was an economist; he seemed to work most comfortably with other trade policy professionals. The hallmark of his approach to problems was to seek consensus agreements by quiet negotiation, most typically in the informal green-room meetings. He would speak out in public when he felt this necessary, but did not usually push for decisions until certain that the time was ripe for them to be taken successfully. Sutherland, by contrast, was a political figure who, although he came to GATT from a top-level business post, had made his name first as Ireland's Attorney-General and then as its EC Commissioner in Brussels, responsible for developing and enforcing the Community's competition policy. He had acquired a reputation for being dynamic and outspoken, for pushing people hard to force decisions, for having a lawyer's quickness to master a brief, and for excellent political contacts at the highest level. He also had one undeniable advantage over his predecessor. Long years of frustrating negotiation, recurrent crises and missed deadlines had inevitably eroded Dunkel's credibility. Sutherland brought new enthusiasm, a different face, and a fresh voice to the Round. And if he lacked Dunkel's deep knowledge of trade policy issues, he moved to compensate that gap and complete the renewal at the top level of the Secretariat by appointing three new deputies, Anwarul Hoda, Warren Lavorel and Jesús Seade, who had each played substantial parts in developing the Uruguay Round policies of their respective countries, India, the United States and Mexico.

Chapter IX

Final push

Sutherland nailed his colours to the mast immediately. In a press statement within hours of his election, he declared that the Tokyo summit meeting of the Group of Seven powers would be "crucial" to a quick conclusion to the Round, and would require "deeds, not words". He followed this up with direct pressure on the main Tokyo participants. With the summit due to take place barely a week after he took office, his stand seemed to many observers brave but rash. Previous summits had done nothing for the negotiations. If, as seemed likely, Tokyo proved as vaporous in outcome as its predecessors, Sutherland risked an early and serious loss of credibility.

His gamble – if gamble it was – paid off. The Group of Seven leaders were under strong pressure from the rest of the world, and they themselves needed a breakthrough in the Round for both political and economic reasons. Sutherland's stand must have helped. At the beginning of July, trade ministers of the Quad group (who as representatives of Canada, the European Community, Japan and United States covered all the Group of Seven countries) met in Tokyo, ahead of the summit. On 7 July, they produced a broad package agreement on how they would pursue the market-access negotiations. Two days later, the summit participants endorsed the package, declaring it to be "a major step to the immediate resumption of multilateral negotiations in Geneva". They announced their determination "to achieve with all our partners a global and balanced agreement before the end of the year".

The last re-launch?

Sutherland wasted no time in picking up the challenge, calling meetings of the TNC, the market access group and the services group on 14 and 15 July to re-launch the negotiations. In the TNC, he hailed the Tokyo package as clearly signalling "an intent to put the Uruguay Round to the forefront of the political agenda during the coming months", adding that "conclusion of the Round is now an acid test of world leadership".

Not everyone shared Sutherland's confidence that the Tokyo package was a real breakthrough. Recent experience, following the Blair House agreement, did not encourage optimism. Some noted that agricultural ministers had not been present in Tokyo, and that the package had nothing to say on the crucial disputed issues of agricultural policy. Even on market access, for which the Quad ministers defined four alternative approaches to liberalization of trade in goods, there were no firm commitments. Developing countries pointed out that eight product groups identified in the Tokyo agreement as candidates for complete removal of trade barriers did not include their main export interests. The undertakings on services were noticeably less precise than those on goods. On the other hand, the Quad countries were now making proposals for goods liberalization that were more specific than they had ever put forward before, and that seemed to point towards larger tariff cuts, overall, than had been promised even by the Montreal agreement. Quad participants could also underline that the Tokyo package was based only on discussions among themselves, and that they were now eager to re-engage negotiations with other countries.

Two weeks of intensive meetings in Geneva over the remainder of July proved broadly encouraging. The market access and services groups met; more importantly, there were also many smaller meetings, including useful bilateral sessions between the four Quad members and some 30 other countries. Sutherland told the TNC on 28 July that the atmosphere had been generally positive and constructive, and that governments seemed ready to engage quickly and substantively in negotiations. He was insistent, however, that greater urgency in the negotiations was needed. "Leaving problems for the eleventh hour," he said, "is a recipe for failure. If we are to succeed in December, the eleventh hour is now." Delegations should give more information about possible concessions, even if their offers would be conditional because of linkages with the outcome on such matters as the new trade rules for agriculture and textiles. "Vast amounts" of technical work and substantive negotiations lay ahead also on other issues. He warned however that governments seeking substantial changes in texts in the Draft Final Act of December 1991 would have to exercise "maximum self-restraint and discipline", since consensus would be hard to reach.

Sutherland reported agreement with Germain Denis and David Hawes, chairmen of the market access and services groups, that these must aim for "concrete and convergent" results by mid-October. For goods, he defined a critical path for the negotiations: review by each government of its national position during August; negotiations in September both bilaterally and in larger groups; and stock-taking and consultations by the chairman in October. This should be followed by final adjustments in offers by mid-November, leaving the way clear in early December for the required review of the results of the negotiations for developing countries. For services, offers still outstanding should be made by the beginning of September, the GATS text should be finished off by the middle of the month, and two negotiating sessions in September and October, each lasting two weeks, should complete the bargaining on concessions.

Although participants in the TNC meeting accepted Sutherland's proposals, they made it clear that the big countries could not expect the others just to sign up to the Quad package. Developing countries pointed out that the goods sectors proposed by the Quad for the most far-reaching liberalization excluded textiles, electronic goods, tropical products, beef, fish and other products in which their competitive strength was greatest. They also insisted that their cooperation depended on maintaining – undiluted – the new rules in the Draft Final Act on such matters as anti-dumping, dispute settlement and textiles.

From July onwards, Sutherland kept up a punishing series of whirlwind visits to top-level political leaders in the major countries, along with press conferences and speeches to influential audiences. Having gambled success-fully on a breakthrough in Tokyo, he took an even stronger line on the 15 December deadline for completion of the negotiations. There could be no question, he insisted, of a further extension beyond that date, which was "engraved in stone": unless success was achieved by then, the Round would be dead. Many people, including some of his Secretariat colleagues, were initially sceptical. They had seen the supposedly final deadlines of 1990, 1991 and 1992 come and go. Sutherland's refusal to contemplate any alternative, however, combined with the accumulating evidence that the negotiations were at last really moving, gradually swung most participants in the negotiations behind his view. Complaints by politicians in France that the deadline was artificial, and imposed by the Americans (one minister described it as "intellectual terrorism") received little echo elsewhere. The US Administration was recognized to have drawn up its request to Congress for fast-track extension only after consulting other countries about the time needed to complete the Round. With growing acceptance that 15 December was a gen-uine final deadline, the pressure grew on each participant in the Round to negotiate seriously and to decide privately which of its present demands it would be prepared to abandon, and which concessions it could ultimately make to others. A convincing final date for the negotiations was not a sufficient condition for their success, as the collapse of the enormous and supposedly terminal Brussels meeting had shown. But it undoubtedly helped in the autumn of 1993 in driving the Uruguay Round forward, and forcing essential political decisions.

Apart from his own notably blunt speeches, Sutherland also pushed the Secretariat to take a higher profile than in the past. The change was signalled by a much-noticed Secretariat paper on the costs paid by consumers for protectionist policies, and the benefits the Uruguay Round could bring, that was distributed to the press in August. While the examples and figures it drew from a variety of sources were striking, its style ("How governments buy votes on trade with the consumer's money") was still more so.

On 31 August, the TNC met again to open what Sutherland described as "the last stretch" of the negotiations. Setting a pattern which he would follow in successive TNC meetings, he made a strong opening statement, clearly aimed at least as much at governments and public opinion as at the delegates present. Underlining the gains to be expected for the world economy from a successful Uruguay Round package and the "appallingly high" costs of failure, he appealed to governments "to face down vested interests and to place leadership before expediency". He called for immediate resumption of the negotiations on goods and services, and announced that Julio Lacarte would once again take responsibility for chairing negotiations on institutions. On the other issues of substance, he repeated his July warning that any delegation seeking changes in the Draft Final Act would have to demonstrate that proposed changes were a matter of major substance and had good prospects of attracting multilateral consensus. Sutherland also gave the TNC its first opportunity to look beyond the bargaining: he foresaw a ministerial meeting in the following April to sign the agreements reached, adopt a joint declaration, and set a programme for future work.

Once again, Sutherland's proposals were accepted. Agricultural exporters reinforced his comments on possible changes in the Draft Final Act. No doubt responding to press reports which suggested that Germany might be ready to back insistent French demands for further easing of the new rules for agriculture, they insisted that changes could be made only by consensus, and hinted that they would walk away from the Round, as they had from the Montreal and Brussels meetings, if the proposed reforms were undermined. The United States sparked strongly hostile reactions, particularly from the European Community and India, when it expressed continuing doubts that a new multilateral trade organization was needed, and argued that it would be "unwise to burden the negotiations" with the proposal.

Sutherland promised the TNC to mediate in the coming negotiations if this seemed desirable, and to deal with blockages by intervening when necessary with ministers. His top-level access was promptly demonstrated by meetings within the next few days with Chancellor Helmut Kohl of Germany and Prime Minister Edouard Balladur of France.

Negotiations September – November 1993

The TNC was to meet frequently over the next weeks. Far too large for effective negotiation, its meetings nevertheless offered an excellent means of keeping the Round in the public eye, of maintaining pressure on governments, and of reassuring even the smallest countries that they were still part of the negotiating process. Sutherland, too, continued to seize every opportunity to urge the negotiations forward. Late in September, at the annual meetings of the International Monetary Fund and World Bank in Washington, he persuaded the heads of both institutions to join with him in an unprecedented call by all three of the world's major economic agencies to governments to put aside "political hesitations and vested interests" and make the "difficult and visionary decisions" needed "to conclude the Uruguay Round and thereby contribute to substantial and sustainable economic growth".

Until about mid-November, however, the focus of the negotiations in Geneva returned to the separate groups working on market access for goods, services and institutions. Meanwhile, "political hesitations and vested interests" were much in evidence, especially in several of the European Community countries and the United States, as well as in Japan, Korea and other countries faced with demands for removal of long-standing protective trade barriers. Initial optimism that the Tokyo agreement guaranteed an early conclusion of the Uruguay Round ebbed. Sutherland, whose own estimate of the odds on completion in December had been 60-40 in mid-September, quoted no better than 50-50 to journalists in early October.

Market access

For market access, the Quad agreement on how to pursue the negotiations had been sorely needed. The Punta del Este Declaration had set broad objectives: the reduction or, as appropriate, elimination of tariffs; reduction or elimination of high tariffs and tariff escalation; the expansion of tariff concessions among all participants; and reductions in non-tariff measures and measures affecting trade in tropical and resource-based products. The first two years of the Uruguay Round had achieved little more towards these objectives than the separate Montreal agreements to seek overall tariff reductions at least as ambitious as the average one-third cut achieved in the Tokyo Round, and to make some immediate cuts in barriers facing imports of tropical products. The next two years brought a range of widely differing suggestions on how to achieve the broad goals for the market access negotiations, but nothing had been decided by the time of the Brussels meeting. Real negotiations still did not start in 1991 or 1992. The Draft Final Act of December 1991 appeared to settle some key issues, particularly by prescribing full tariffication for agricultural products and a five-year period for carrying out the tariff reductions. However, by the time the negotiations as a whole drifted to a halt in the spring of 1992, market access offers had not been received from the largest suppliers, and even those offers on the table were largely unimpressive. Only at the very end of the year, after the Blair House agreement, did the United States and European Community submit schedules showing what they were offering for agricultural products. Apart from the continuing unwillingness of Japan and others to accept tariffication, there was still no general understanding on how the targets set in Punta del Este and Montreal might be reached.

For industrial goods at least, the Quad agreement reached in Tokyo proposed answers to most of the outstanding general questions. It put forward four "minimum elements", or alternative approaches, which the Quad countries proposed to use in drawing up their offers. The most ambitious would be the complete elimination of protection. Eight product sectors, several of which had figured in a list put forward by the United States in 1990, were identified as candidates for this treatment: pharmaceuticals, construction equipment, medical equipment, steel, beer, furniture, farm equipment, and spirits. Action on steel would be conditional on conclusion of a multilateral steel agreement directed mainly at limiting subsidies, and the last three categories would have to be subject to some exceptions. A second ("harmonization") approach, somewhat less ambitious, would aim to bring national tariffs for some product groups into line with one another, at low levels. Chemicals were identified as one possible group for this treatment. Third, the Quad countries would seek 50% cuts in as many as possible of those tariffs currently standing at over 15%. This proposal, generally assumed to be particularly relevant for textiles, was made subject to the offer of "effective market access by other exporting countries". The fourth approach, applicable to all other industrial products, would seek to cut import tariffs by an average of at least one third, and in some cases by more than one half.

The Tokyo agreement was very encouraging, in that it showed that the largest countries were setting their sights high for the market access negotiations, and had concrete ideas on how they would move forward. Whatever its shortcomings, pointed out in the TNC meetings in July and August, it gave a much-improved basis for the negotiations in Geneva.

Discussions on market access during September were intensive, and promising. As seen from the Secretariat, all participants were being constructive, and were clearly keen to move ahead. However, the stage of real bargaining had not yet been reached, and many delegates complained that their concerns had as yet received little attention from the Quad countries. Doubts over whether the European Community would be able to maintain its offer, based as it was on the Blair House agreement that France was still vigorously rejecting, meant that some other countries were unwilling to come forward with their own firm offers. Rumours flew on the content and likely effect of an agreement on tariff cuts supposedly reached between the EC and US textile industries. Talk of applying the "zero-for-zero" approach (mutual and complete removal of trade barriers in particular sectors) to consumer electronics was discouraged by the European Community, which felt that its main suppliers, Japan and the United States, would first have to offer it more in other areas of the negotiations. The Community, always adept at using the press to exert influence on the negotiations, leaked its unenthusiastic internal analysis of the American offer on textiles. The United States suggested that the second Tokyo approach (harmonization of tariffs at low levels) could be applied to wood, paper, scientific instruments and non-ferrous metals, if others would join in. Australia, Canada and others showed interest. Summing up the situation in the TNC on 30 September, Sutherland reported that some 70 countries had, or would very soon have, offers on the table. The overall picture, he said, was not bad, but "much more needs to be done, and urgently", if the negotiations were to be kept on their critical path.

By mid-October, when the timetable called for a broad picture of the market access package to be visible, concern was growing. The negotiations were clearly lagging, although there was no reason to doubt the goodwill of participants. In terms of the Montreal objectives, prospects looked good, except that developing countries found it hard to assess what they were likely to gain, particularly as long as uncertainty continued over offers on agricultural products and fish, and whether tariff elimination would take place in such sectors as non-ferrous metals and electronics. Japan and Canada claimed that their offers had already reached the Tokyo goal of a one-third average cut, and the European Community and the United States were confident of achieving similar or better figures, given an appropriate response by others. The Quad countries were still supporting tariff elimination in the eight sectors proposed in Tokyo, and were ready to look at such further sectors as lumber, paper, scientific instruments, non-ferrous metals, oilseeds and toys, but warned that they would not act unless their trading partners offered reciprocal benefits. Several countries expressed doubts, on the basis of statistics offered by participants, whether offers made so far would have much impact on high tariffs.

Two weeks later, Sutherland gave a mixed report on the market access negotiations to a TNC meeting on 1 November. New or revised offers were flowing in, 72 offers were on the table representing in aggregate the great bulk of world trade, and "some quiet progress" seemed to have been made on agricultural offers. But there had been a "lamentable failure" to define the multilateral package on the basis of the Tokyo package, particularly for sectoral proposals and high tariffs, and little had emerged on textiles or natural resource-based products. Sutherland appealed to the Quad countries, especially the Europeans and Americans, to provide leadership and negotiate with others. "Mutual recrimination," he said pointedly, "is neither useful nor helpful." Mexico, for the Latin American countries, was pessimistic, speaking of "endemic crisis" in the access negotiations, and complaining that the Latin Americans were being asked to bind their tariffs and join in tariff elimination for products of no interest to them while being denied credit for past liberalization or responses to their own requests. The EC's chief negotiator in Geneva told journalists after the meeting that although increasingly confident about the outcome of the Round, he found it "scary" that so little movement seemed to be taking place on market access. In spite of these and similar comments, which were themselves part of the negotiating process, some participants remained privately optimistic that a good market access package would emerge in the end.

The picture changed little during early November. A TNC meeting on 10 November saw Sutherland once again reporting progress, but urging greater efforts by the Quad countries. Conflicting figures were exchanged on the percentage value of tariff cuts offered, showing how high average reductions could translate into much smaller figures from the point of view of individual suppliers who found little was offered on their main export products. Uncertainties about the final outcome on such politically charged issues as tariffication of agricultural products, the Blair House agreement, and the proposed multilateral steel agreement were all factors still making it hard to judge prospects. The original 15 November deadline passed with many offers still to come. There was evidence in plenty of continuing hard bargaining, particularly over possible "zero-for-zero" elimination, as well as statements by many middle-sized developed and developing participants about the tariff cuts they proposed, and promises by the United States and others to make their offers within the next few days. Many smaller countries, however, were insisting that they could not offer the improvements they were prepared to contemplate as long as "intercontinental warfare and public relations exercises" (in the words of an ASEAN spokesman) continued among the major countries, and their offers could "still not be assessed rationally".

Services

The agreement reached by the Quad countries in Tokyo had less of substance to say on services than on goods. "Subject to appropriate contributions by other participants", the Round's four biggest players were ready to build on their existing market access offers. Their views appeared closest on financial services and basic telecommunications. On the former, they announced progress in commitments towards more open markets, and called on other countries too to offer more, "including commitments which offer a real prospect of liberalization". On the latter, they reported agreement on the agenda for future negotiations beyond the Uruguay Round. For maritime and audiovisual services they promised only "to continue to work toward satis-factory solutions". Unofficial reports suggested that Japan had made con-cessions on financial services, the European Community on the principle of future negotiations on telecommunications, and the United States on partici-pation in the maritime services negotiations. On audiovisual services, it was reported that the European Commission would offer to bind (i.e. promise not to tighten further) the Community's basic rule that half of European television programming should originate in Europe, but would insist on recognition that such services had a "specific cultural" aspect, implying that they would sometimes need to be treated as an exception to the general GATS rules.

Even before serious negotiations on services re-started in Geneva in September, the Secretariat was well aware of potential problems. The GATS text itself was generally in good shape, with few significant issues still to be resolved. However, internal Secretariat notes in July and August flagged one difficulty: an apparently obscure issue concerning the right of governments to treat foreign suppliers differently from national suppliers in applying direct taxes. To meet American concerns, an elaborate footnote to the GATS rules on exceptions had been negotiated, defining the grounds on which different treatment would be justified. However, there were fears that the US Treasury, •

still worried that countries might be able to use the GATS dispute settlement procedures to challenge American tax policies, might seek a completely free hand to tax foreign suppliers differently. On financial services, the controversial proposal for a "two-track" approach, endorsed mainly by the OECD countries, was still seen by many developing countries as an attempt to press them to open their markets prematurely. The United States was well known to be dissatisfied with offers from many of these countries, and to be threatening to discriminate against those who, in its view, did not offer enough. On maritime transport, in spite of the Quad agreement, there was no certainty that the United States and Japan would be ready to make sufficiently substantial offers for a worthwhile package to be put together.

While little was heard of these questions until later in the services negotiations, disagreements on another erupted in public much sooner. Should the opening-up of markets for audiovisual services (primarily films and television programmes) be governed by special rules? Indeed, was this an appropriate subject for trade negotiations at all? For the United States, the audiovisual sector was of major economic interest: audiovisual exports were a top source of export earnings, and the industry was incidentally a formidable lobbying force. France, and to a lesser extent Germany, regarded films and television programmes as an essential part of national identity, and saw the issue, as President Mitterand was reported to have said, as "not a question of commerce but of civilization". American films had some 80% of the European market (against a tiny European share of the US market), and American programmes filled a large proportion of air time on most European television channels. But these undoubted facts could be interpreted quite differently. Through American eyes, they reflected efficiency in responding to consumers' desires. Seen from Paris, they were evidence of the overwhelming advantages of scale and language enjoyed by Hollywood. Resistance to "cultural imperialism" soon took the form of demands for a tougher line by the European Commission in the Uruguay Round, with no softening of the EC's quota limits on non-European television programming, and with a total exemption of "cultural" services from the broad GATS rules. Over a very few weeks in September and October, the audiovisual issue grew to virtually equal promi- nence in France with the continuing French objections to the Blair House agricultural agreement. A meeting of EC ministers on 4 October showed that on this issue the French enjoyed considerable sympathy.

In spite of these potential difficulties, the services negotiations made good progress in September and October. The negotiators enjoyed the unfamiliar experience of being at the leading edge of the Round, clearly advancing faster than their colleagues involved in the goods negotiations. Essentially, two processes were going on at the same time: the submission and negotiation of national offers of concessions, and the clean-up of the framework GATS text and its annexes. Although many countries missed the 1 September deadline, initial or revised offers flowed in over the following weeks. At the end of the month, offers covering 77 countries were on the table, and vigorous bilateral bargaining was in progress. A month later, on 1 November, Sutherland was able to report to the TNC that the number of countries covered was up to 81. The Secretariat was working hard to help smaller developing countries to produce offers, conscious that those who failed to do so were at risk of being excluded by other participants from benefits negotiated elsewhere in the Round, and perhaps even of being disqualified from membership in the proposed new trade organization. Work on the GATS also went well: a revised text was issued early in October – the first text, incidentally, to emerge as an acknowledged replacement for part of Dunkel's Draft Final Act – and a further and near-final revision at the end of the month.

The difficulties foreseen earlier by the Secretariat were however already beginning to surface by the beginning of November. Although the services sector was still making the running in the negotiations as a whole, many countries were dismayed by what seemed a decision of the United States, the original champion of including services in the Round, to abandon effective participation in central areas of the emerging services agreement. The United States announced that its schedule of services concessions would state its rejection of the GATS obligations on direct taxation. This "carve-out", or across-the-board refusal, of one important aspect of national treatment of service suppliers aroused a storm of objections from all other participants. A further US announcement, foreshadowed by press reports, was spelled out to Congress by the US Treasury Secretary: in the financial services negotiations, the United States would give MFN treatment in any future liberalization only to countries which offered equivalent benefits to US financial institutions. The move was interpreted by most observers as an effort to persuade developing countries, particularly in Asia, to improve their offers. It was vigorously attacked as introducing a two-tier membership into the GATS, and under-mining both the GATS itself and the basis on which many countries had put forward their present offers. Even countries which had some sympathy with US aims felt that the tactic would not work. Yet another worry about American intentions concerned the maritime services negotiations: although these were to be taken up only in late November, the United States was not yet among the 25 declared potential participants, and was known to be reluctant to offer access to shipping services.

Nor was this all. Responding to French concerns, the European Community was insisting that cultural matters must be recognized in the GATS as requiring special treatment, and that the outcome of the services negotiations as a whole would depend on resolution of this issue. Egypt and India strongly disliked, and also believed inappropriate, a provision in the telecommunications annex that called for pricing of public telecommunications transport networks and services to be "cost-oriented". A technically difficult new issue, very unwelcome at this late stage in the negotiations, arose over whether the GATS rules on national treatment would require governments to allow foreign suppliers of services a right to social security payments or to other privileges not obviously relevant to market access. This question of "the scope of the GATS" carried the danger that, if not resolved, governments might load their schedules of services concessions with long lists of measures whose benefits would not be available to foreigners.

By mid-November, therefore, there were clear signs that the services negotiations, like the negotiations on goods, were arriving at a critical point. On the whole, they had gone well. But now problems were arising which threatened further progress. Most required political decisions, and those decisions in turn were increasingly likely to be linked with judgements, in each country, on national interests across the whole spectrum of issues raised by the Uruguay Round negotiations.

Institutions

The new group on institutions started work on 21 September with agreement to base itself on the texts on the Multilateral Trade Organization and the integrated dispute settlement system bequeathed by the 1992 Legal Drafting Group. All countries but one saw the group's task as being to resolve the issues still outstanding on these texts, and thereby to bring them to the same clean and complete status as the other elements in the Draft Final Act. Apart from technical problems, the main open issues concerned, for the MTO, voting and amendment rules, qualifications for membership, possible special rules for least-developed countries, and provisions on consistency of national laws with international trade rules and on environmental issues. On dispute settlement, little of substance remained except to complete definition of the rules on cross-retaliation. The United States, however, had put all other countries on notice at the August TNC meeting that it was still unconvinced that a new international trade organization was needed at all. In the institutions group, it insisted that because the negotiations had been broken off in December 1991 for lack of time, the status of the texts was different from that of others in the Draft Final Act, and all issues had to be regarded as still open. Other countries warned that if the MTO's existence was called into question, they would feel free to open other institutional issues, with the risk of both texts unravelling. The European Community's Council of Ministers reinforced this message with a statement in Brussels that the MTO was essential to the credibility and durability of the new trading system.

During the dead months of early 1993, when the Uruguay Round was effectively at a halt, many of the delegates involved in the negotiations on the MTO text in the previous year had met on several occasions to explore possible solutions to the outstanding problems. Although the United States was not involved in these meetings, it was thought that some of the ideas developed, particularly on voting requirements, might make it easier for the Americans to accept the MTO. In spite of this prior discussion, however, initial progress in the negotiating group was slow. Lacarte had originally warned negotiators that he intended to wind up the group's work at the end of October, leaving any unsettled issues to be resolved at a higher level. He continued to push for this, both in meetings of the group and in consultations with individual delegations on possible solutions to particular problems, but made little headway. At the opening of the TNC meeting of 1 November, Sutherland suggested formally that the group be given a further two weeks "in view of the complexity and linkages between a number of the principal issues", but later provided the altogether blunter explanation that delays in the group "arose from some delegations putting forward and debating at considerable length purely technical issues without getting to the core issues". Canada, more delicately, regretted that "the creativity of some was not being matched by the flexibility of others". On the central issue of whether a new organization was needed at all, the TNC meeting showed no signs of movement: Mexico, Brazil, Canada and others insisted on the need for the MTO, while the United States reaffirmed its "inability to conclude the Round on the basis of a proposed MTO agreement" which was, "at this stage, fundamentally flawed".

Sutherland's characteristically forceful intervention, combined with Lacarte's negotiating skills, proved effective. Following a series of late-night negotiating sessions, the group met its new deadline by producing revised versions of both the institutional texts. For dispute settlement, the Uruguay Round negotiations were effectively over. Even for the MTO, solutions to most of the outstanding problems had been found. Perhaps the biggest achievement of the negotiators was to reach full agreement on voting provisions. The revised text provided that the MTO follow the normal GATT practice of seeking consensus, and required that, for decisions interpreting agreements or waiving obligations, a three-fourths majority of the full membership would be needed. This was a very tough requirement: comparable votes in GATT needed only a majority of two-thirds of the votes actually cast, with the majority comprising more than half of the members. Given, for example, a membership of 120 countries, MTO approval would require 90 votes in favour, against a minimum 61 and an absolute (and highly improbable) maximum of 80 for GATT. For votes on amendments, the provisions offered an impregnable defence against a possible tyrannous majority, since unanimity would be needed to amend such key rules as those on voting and the MFN requirements under the GATT, GATS and TRIMS. The negotiators also agreed that all MTO members would be required to make commitments on both goods and services, but qualified this requirement by stating that least-developed countries need undertake only commitments "consistent with their individual development, financial and trade needs or their administrative and institutional capabilities". (The practical significance of this language was revealed almost immediately when Bangladesh announced that it had been agreed that least-developed countries need make only token concessions, and had been given a full year from the signing of the Uruguay Round agreements to do so.) Short of time, the negotiating group left open the question of whether the original

GATT text should be redrafted, as the Legal Drafting Group had intended, or left unchanged. The only unsettled points of importance were some new draft language in the preamble stating environmental objectives, a requirement that members ensure the conformity of their laws, regulations and procedures with the new trade rules, and a provision which would allow the United States to maintain the exclusion of foreign ships from its coastal shipping trade. The first point was intended to ease the concerns of environmentalists about the aims of the proposed organization, and had so far been resisted by developing countries essentially because they wished to retain some leverage to block a further proposal to add a permanent committee on environment to the MTO structure. The second was clearly aimed at the United States. The third would provide the politically essential cover for the US Jones Act, which would otherwise become illegal under the GATT with the ending of the Protocol of Provisional Application.

Sutherland greeted the new texts as "a major breakthrough". So they were, although the United States continued to argue that the aims and operative elements of the new organization could be realized without setting up a new organization.

Track Four: should the new trade rules be changed?

Still in the background of the Geneva negotiations during this period were the issues that everyone knew would in the end have to be faced: the demands that key provisions in the Draft Final Act of December 1991 be reconsidered. Negotiations on these politically sensitive issues – what Dunkel had called "Track Four" – had never begun, although some countries had revealed in December 1992 what they would seek, and experts had discreetly explored possible changes in at least one text, the phytosanitary agreement. Some of the problems encountered since September in the goods, services and institutional negotiations were clearly "Track Four" in character: reluctance to accept agricultural tariffication underlay many difficulties in the goods negotiations; the audiovisual issue was as politicized as any; and the voting provisions for the MTO were crucial to the acceptability of the new trade organization.

The media ensured that no negotiator could be unaware of the continuing pressures in the United States to change the texts on anti-dumping, subsidies, textiles and TRIPS, or of the unhappiness of public opinion in India with the TRIPS and textiles agreements, and of Japanese and Korean farmers with the prospective opening, through tariffication, of their domestic markets to foreign rice. Reports from Brussels, Paris and elsewhere recorded the sharp and continuing EC debate on the acceptability of the Blair House agreement on agriculture and on other issues such as audiovisual services. All over the world, senior government ministers were recorded as meeting in capitals to exchange views on the Round and to enlist support for the outcome they sought. In the nearby French and Swiss countryside, delegates could see for themselves the posters and graffiti recording the indignation of farmers at the proposed

Uruguay Round agreements. In Geneva, farmers staged mass demonstrations and protests close to the GATT building. Within the TNC itself, Sutherland kept delegates under maximum political pressure by ensuring that they were aware of an extraordinary succession of communiqués from ministerial meetings of Latin American, African and Central European countries, of the IMF and World Bank, of the ASEAN, Cairns and APEC groups, from Commonwealth Heads of Government and from international business organizations – all stressing the urgency of settling the outstanding issues and concluding the Round. He himself was a leading participant in several of these meetings, helping to enlist political support for the Round. Other Sutherland journeys, such as a brief visit to India in late October, helped to counteract misunderstandings, and even misrepresentation, of the draft Uruguay Round agreements.

It was always obvious that breakthrough agreement on the most difficult political issues could only come through some kind of settlement between the United States and the European Community. This fact was unpalatable for other participants in the Round, since they recognized that their interests were likely to be at best a secondary concern in any bilateral US-EC bargaining. Nevertheless, they hoped that the two leading powers in the negotiations would at least quickly face and resolve their mutual difficulties so as to define the basis for the final multilateral negotiations in Geneva. To general dismay, however, the autumn weeks slipped away without any movement. French calls in September for renegotiation of the Blair House agreement were met by a clear refusal from the United States. Agreement among EC ministers to seek "clarification" of Blair House was followed by discussions in Washington between the chief US and EC negotiators, Mickey Kantor and Sir Leon Brittan. Optimism rose when these talks at least produced agreement to seek the largest possible market access package, and gave some promise that the two sides were ready to talk further. But there was no follow-through. In Geneva, the market access negotiations in fact lagged. In Paris, the French line toughened still further, with a strong statement by the Prime Minister to the National Assembly, and suggestions that the Uruguay Round should either be wound up promptly with a "light" package that would omit agriculture, textiles and audiovisual services, or that it should be prolonged, with 15 December regarded simply as an occasion for stock-taking. Another round of talks between Kantor and Brittan in mid-October, this time in Brussels, proved unproductive. Kantor was reported to have refused to reopen or even interpret the Blair House agreement: the Community's difficulties with it were, he suggested, an internal problem.

To outside observers, the situation was worrying. The Community appeared to be painting itself into a corner, with France in particular making demands that could not be met, and the United States adopting a rigid attitude both in its bilateral talks with the Community and in the multilateral negotiations in Geneva. Moreover, everyone knew that agriculture was not the only political issue to be resolved. Reports from Washington suggested that the United States would demand far-reaching amendment of the anti-dumping and subsidy texts, a five-year extension of the phase-out of textile and clothing restraints, and other changes. When would these matters be brought into the open? Was the United States planning, as unfriendly voices suggested, to save its demands for the last days of the Round, and then force them through by threatening to torpedo the negotiations if it were not given satisfaction?

On 10 November, the pace of negotiations quickened perceptibly, with an important meeting of the TNC. With just 35 days to go until the 15 December deadline, Sutherland in effect put the Geneva negotiations on a war footing. On his proposal, the TNC agreed that it should henceforth be permanently on call, and that informal meetings of heads of delegations should be held frequently to deal with outstanding issues and with blockages in the negotiations. Sutherland would help the process along through consultations, assisted by four "Friends of the Chair" (Denis, Hawes and Lacarte, plus Michael Cartland, chairman of the earlier group on rules). For its part, the United States at least dispelled fears that it would keep its most difficult demands for change until late-night bargaining in December. In a statement in the TNC, it put its negotiating partners on notice that it wanted changes in some texts in the Draft Final Act. The questions it wished to pursue, it insisted, were not new, and consensus on them had not been found in earlier negotiations. For those issues which were of general concern, such as anti-dumping, it would put its proposals in writing and explain them to all. The United States was ready, in return, to look at the difficulties of others. "People are talking," it said, about ideas such as deferral of agricultural tariffication: "we should have an exercise in mutual problem-solving."

The US stand, and its open invitation to other countries to formulate their own demands, clearly foreshadowed tough negotiations, and risked reopening issues apparently settled nearly two years earlier. But it was far preferable to have these matters brought into the open in good time, and discussed with other countries, than to leave them to the last moment. Most Geneva delegates agreed, after the TNC meeting, that the outlook for the Round had brightened. In a meeting with his senior staff, early in the following week, Sutherland was optimistic. Things were on the move.

End-game

On 17 November, the United States Congress finally approved the North American Free Trade Agreement, with a comfortable margin of favourable votes to spare. The decision, greeted by Sutherland as "half the battle", was enormously encouraging. The outcome had been in great doubt, and failure would have signalled a high risk that Congress would also find the results of the Uruguay Round unacceptable. The only concern in Geneva was that the approval might prove to have been conditional on undertakings by US officials to demand unacceptable changes in some of the Draft Final Act texts, or to refuse tariff concessions important to developing and other countries. The immediate effect of the NAFTA decision, however, was to relieve President Clinton's officials of what had been their most urgent international economic concern, and to permit them to give full attention to the Uruguay Round.

The following week saw the first of a crucial series of meetings between Mickey Kantor and Sir Leon Brittan that were to continue with only short breaks over a period of more than three weeks. Their efforts to resolve bilateral differences over the Round provided a counterpoint to the multilateral negotiations in Geneva.

Even before the first of their bargaining sessions, a meeting of the TNC on 19 November confirmed that the negotiations were moving into their final phase. On the previous day, Sutherland told a press conference, "The Uruguay Round is in our grasp – what remains are political issues." He stressed both points to the TNC, welcoming progress and summarizing prospective achievements, and identifying "the political choices that must be made if we are to win the prize of a success". The key to a satisfactory market access package, he insisted, lay in settling the issues of agricultural tariffication and access opportunities. On tariffication in particular it was time "for those few who continue to oppose this central element of the Draft Final Act to review their position". Other issues on market access included improvement of offers for high-tariff products such as textiles and clothing, the continuing efforts to eliminate or harmonize tariffs in the sectors identified in Tokyo, and perhaps in others, and concerns about negotiations on electronics, leather products and footwear. On services, Sutherland delivered a forceful warning that "certain positions which have been taken recently on financial services may prove to be utterly unproductive" and that unless urgently reviewed "the important progress we have already achieved may begin to unravel". Lest anyone be in doubt of the target, he called on the United States, in particular, to find "workable solutions". After repeating his usual warning that any country wanting to change texts in the Draft Final Act carried the burden of seeking the support needed "or alternatively reviewing its position," he added: "delegations that wish to embark upon this process should do so now." Several countries responded, at this TNC meeting and the next, with statements that pinpointed many, but not all, of the remaining issues to be fought out. Canada and Korea recalled their difficulties with tariffication (although Korea acknowledged that "discussions are continuing"). Mexico and Canada expressed discontent with provisions of the subsidy agreement. Spokesmen for the banana-producing countries of Latin America and the Community's associated states put diametrically opposed views on how the Community should adapt its import policies on bananas to the new tariffication rules. Bangladesh, for the least-developed countries, recalled their general request for special treatment. The United States, at last showing its hand on the anti-dumping agreement, appealed for help with this "matter of enormous importance to us", and shortly afterward distributed far-reaching proposals for change. Other countries responded to all these requests with warnings that significant weakening of any major element of the Draft Final Act could lead to disintegration of the whole Uruguay Round package.

Talks in Washington between Brittan and Kantor on 22 and 23 November were reported to have covered a wide range of issues, including agriculture, steel, electronics, textiles and audiovisual services. In spite, it was said, of secret talks beforehand in Brussels about agriculture which were believed to have explored ideas of extending the period for cutting back subsidized exports and the duration of the "peace clause", there was no agreement. The impression given, however, was that both sides were negotiating in earnest, and were well aware that their differences were holding up the Geneva negotiations. Kantor agreed to come to Brussels in the following week. Prime Minister Balladur of France, briefed by Brittan on the talks, said that none of France's concerns had been met. Sutherland warned in the TNC on 26 November that the United States and the European Community "must next week in their meeting in Brussels reach a substantive result and place a decisive contribution on the table here in Geneva. So many offers and schedules from other participants depend on that contribution. Time is now becoming as big a factor as the remaining issues of substance." He was backed by both developed and developing countries. As New Zealand put it, "we must know the deal between the majors: it sets the parameters for the rest of us".

The TNC approved Sutherland's proposed timetable for winding up the Round over the 19 days remaining until the 15 December deadline. Final consultations on market access, and review of the results for developing countries, should take place in the following week; heads of delegations should meet to discuss the critical issues in services and start clearing each of the revised Draft Final Act texts. The negotiations should be completed by 13 December, and a meeting of the TNC on the 15th should approve the whole Uruguay Round package. To most participants, the schedule sounded just possible, provided the Americans and Europeans could settle their differences and offer a basis for the Geneva negotiations to go forward. But what would happen if there were no agreement, or if the two big powers demanded, jointly or individually, large changes that would deprive other participants of expected gains from the Round? Observers noted, for instance, that even though the two-tier approach to the financial services negotiations proposed by the United States might be technically feasible, it had already prompted India to make no offer of its own for that sector of services, and had brought threats from other Asian countries to withdraw existing offers. Would the Community, which had also wanted access to the Asians' financial markets, now withdraw offers made to them, perhaps on textiles? "One negotiator" quoted in the London *Financial Times* and known by some to be a prominent figure, saw a great danger that the US objections to the anti-dumping text could lead to collapse in turn of the subsidy agreement and of the central provisions on subsidies in the agricultural package.

Reinforcing these fears, the services negotiations were running into increasing difficulties. On 22 November, a US Treasury official briefed the services negotiators on why the United States proposed to "carve out" the GATS provisions on direct taxation. The packed meeting turned out to be a dialogue of the deaf. The American representative argued that the GATS provisions would undermine bilateral double taxation agreements that at present regulated international tax questions effectively. He was met by unanimous objections that direct taxation could obviously be an important means of discriminating against foreign suppliers, that the GATS specifically gave primacy to bilateral tax agreements, where these existed, and that the GATS provisions had been painstakingly negotiated at American insistence, and satisfied everyone else. Four days later, a stock-taking meeting of the services group noted that completion of the GATS text would have to wait for agreement on whether, as the Community demanded, it should recognize the "special nature of audiovisual services". The taxation issue and the question of "the scope of the GATS" were unresolved. A decision on future negotiations on basic telecommunications was nearly complete, and 26 participants were now ready to accept commitments on maritime services. But the target date for final offers of commitments had been missed, as Hawes said, "by a very wide margin". Although 76 offers, covering 89 countries, were on the table, most were not final. Many countries warned that they would withdraw some offers unless the United States in particular adopted a more forthcoming approach. Recognizing the inevitable, the group pushed back the deadline for final offers to 9 December.

The following week saw much activity, unconfirmed reports of good progress in the renewed Brittan-Kantor talks, and strongly growing optimism about the outcome of the Round.

At the beginning of the week, press reports on the mood in European capitals and Washington gave a confusing picture. Confidence was boosted by hints of flexibility on agriculture from American sources, and of greater French readiness to accept a deal, and by evidence from both Europeans and Americans that they were preparing for their meetings with the utmost care. Some reports speculated on the price that Europe and others might have to pay for American concessions on agriculture: dismantling of tariffs on electronics and other products, defeat on the audiovisual exception clause, less liberalization for textiles and clothing, rejection of the Multilateral Trade Organization? Others even suggested that the United States was losing interest in the Uruguay Round, and would leave any real concessions to the Europeans. In Geneva, a high official of the US Treasury once again argued the case for "two-track" liberalization of financial services, and the chief American textiles negotiator sought support for a five-year extension of the phase-out of textiles and clothing quotas. Meanwhile, two important pieces of a final settlement seemed to be falling into place, with reports that both Japan and Korea might be ready at last to accept some imports of rice, under deals that would let them postpone full tariffication. Sutherland told the press that the coming talks between the Community and the United States would be "crucial". After a meeting of heads of the Geneva delegations, B.K. Zutshi, chairman of the GATT contracting parties and India's chief negotiator, sent "a message to the two of them" on behalf of his colleagues: "Get your act together. This is the last chance, more or less."

The EC-US talks resumed in Brussels on 1 December, with each side's team now reinforced and including their agricultural negotiators. The days that followed were a period of high anxiety in Geneva, as all the other participants in the Round went through the motions of negotiation while waiting for news. First reports from Brussels announced that the two sides had reached what Kantor called "outline packages" on several issues, including agriculture; that Brittan acknowledged that he had not expected to make so much progress; that the EC Council, including France, encouraged Brittan to continue; that the talks would resume in Brussels after the weekend, on 6 December. Further information leaked out, including reports that the United States might be giving up its opposition to the new trade organization, but that there was no agreement on anti-dumping or audiovisual services.

On the following day, 3 December, Sutherland welcomed the "real progress" in Brussels, but insisted that the United States and the Community could no longer negotiate in isolation from their partners in the Round. "They must," he said, "at the earliest possible opportunity report here in Geneva on the results achieved and negotiate further with over 100 other participants whose interests must also be assured and accommodated. Time is of the essence ... Not only is 'nothing agreed until everything is agreed' but agreement must also extend to the other participants in the Round and not just to the major trading partners."

The weekend saw a flurry of activity, with the French position generally recognized as central to the outcome of the US-EC talks. On Sunday both Brittan and Sutherland met Prime Minister Balladur in Paris. Balladur, who was reported to have been in touch also with President Clinton and Chancellor Kohl, let it be known that he believed "excessive optimism" had reigned about the Round. Sutherland told the press that it was "imperative" that an agreement be reached between Europe and the United States on the 6th, "or we will be in a very, very, serious crisis that would threaten the whole trade talks".

Breakthrough came on Monday, but only after talks that stretched all day. Even then, the news was initially discouraging: an agreement on agriculture was announced, but was then said to be rejected by France. Later, after a meeting of EC foreign ministers, it became clear that France would accept the deal, subject to assurances from its Community partners that French farmers would not bear costs beyond those already imposed by the agreed reforms in the common agricultural policy. With a statement by Balladur that "agriculture is no longer an obstacle to agreement in Geneva", the issue that had caused more difficulty than any other throughout the Uruguay Round effectively vanished, except for settling the question of rice imports into Japan and Korea, from the negotiators' agenda.

On Tuesday, only hours after their agreement in Brussels, Brittan and Kantor arrived in Geneva. At GATT headquarters, where their arrival was greeted by some 25 television crews and hundreds of journalists, they reported to the chief negotiators of the other Uruguay Round participants on what they had achieved, and what remained to be done. Both the market access and services groups met to hear detailed explanations of the Brussels agreements — and to allow other countries to comment. From this point onwards, although bilateral negotiations still played a large part in the continuing bargaining, the remainder of the final Uruguay Round drama was played out, as Sutherland had insisted it must be, in Geneva, and with all countries participating.

Even during the US-EC marathon, one landmark multilateral meeting had taken place in Geneva. On 3 December, the negotiators met to assess the likely results of the Uruguay Round for developing countries. The Punta del Este Declaration required this evaluation. An important part of the bargain in 1986 had been that it should take place in the GNG, thus ensuring that results on services, on which many developing countries had not wished to negotiate, would not be taken into account. Moreover, the assessment was to be "in terms of the objectives and the general principles governing negotiations as set out in the Declaration". Those objectives had been set out in very broad terms, and the principles, as far as concerned developing countries, had been stated in the boiler-plate language of past North-South negotiations, stressing differential treatment and non-reciprocity. Seven years of negotiations and of evolution in developing-country views made the evaluation exercise very different from that envisaged in Punta del Este. Because developing countries themselves wanted the services results assessed, the GNG met jointly with the TNC. Little was heard of the rhetoric of Objectives and Principles. Almost without exception, the developing countries confined themselves to sober assessment of the gains and losses which each of them foresaw in the light of the known results of the Round.

In the circumstances, assessment was not easy. As Sutherland commented, the results were a moving target. Documentation provided by the Secretariat had to be based on tariff offers on the table two weeks earlier, and on service offers which, although barely a week old, could not really be measured. The United States and the European Community remained locked in critical negotiations in Brussels. Delegates in Geneva could not know what the coming days would bring. Would it be significant further liberalization in product sectors of interest to them? (There were real hopes of progress on textiles and clothing, electronic products, fish, oilseeds, forestry products and non-ferrous metals.) Or, on the contrary, would it be disappointment of these hopes, tougher anti-dumping rules, weaker limits on unilateral trade measures, more distant deadlines for liberalization of trade in agricultural products and textiles, and a services agreement narrowed in scope and impaired in fairness?

The Secretariat's assessment fell into two parts. The first looked at the tariff and services offers in the light of the present and likely future export strengths of developing countries. The second reviewed the new trading rules and institutions expected to emerge from the negotiations, and particularly their special provisions for developing and least-developed countries. Most of the detailed figures given are not worth quoting now, since they were based on incomplete information and have since been several times revised, generally for the better. The broad picture that emerged was of cuts approaching 40% on average in tariff protection, a massive increase in security for trade because of tariff bindings and removal of non-tariff barriers, particularly for agriculture and by developing countries, and a strong overall boost to future world trade and world economic growth. However, the cuts in barriers facing exports of developing countries would in general be lower than those affecting products exported mainly by developed countries. Assessment was particularly difficult in the very important case of textiles and clothing, much the largest industrial export category for developing countries, because even small cuts in the generally high tariffs of developed countries might have a big effect, and because the end of the Multifibre Arrangement promised large gains, eventually, to competitive producers, but losses to those whose exports depended on MFA quotas. The rules changes looked generally favourable, given developing countries' particular need for stable and clear rules and strong institutions, although most agreements gave permanent exemption from obligations only to the least-developed countries.

Sutherland acknowledged that individual countries would have a far clearer picture than the Secretariat of the extent to which their specific offers had met the concerns of their trading partners, and their partners' offers in turn had met their interests. He urged them to be as specific and realistic as possible in identifying the areas in which further efforts might be made in the final week of the Round. The discussion that followed in general bore out the points made by the Secretariat. Malaysia's chief delegate, chairman of the informal GATT group of developing countries, agreed that the results were a moving target, that everyone was hoping for improvements, and that each country would have to make its own assessment at the end of the Round. His main message was a plea not to change the rules of the game by altering the anti-dumping and financial services texts. Mexico, speaking for Latin America, agreed and expressed disappointment with tariff reductions offered so far, particularly on textiles and clothing, tropical products and natural resource-based products. Egypt, for the African countries, was the most pessimistic: most were net food-importers and were likely to face higher food costs; margins of preference their exports now enjoyed in Europe and the United States would be eroded; there was little for them in the services agreement. Bangladesh expressed similar concerns on behalf of the least-developed countries (of which most, though not all, were in fact African). Many individual countries, including Brazil, Chile, Hong Kong, India and Pakistan, cited their own initial and largely discouraging assessments, insisting that the market openings they had been offered for their main exports fell well short of their own offers to liberalize. All in all, however, the statements by developing countries were perhaps no more pessimistic than might have been expected, given the market access figures then available and their natural desire to apply the strongest possible leverage for further concessions in the final days of the Round.

With the Brussels negotiators in Geneva, details of agreements they had reached began to emerge, and to be injected into the multilateral negotiations. At the same time, intense bargaining began on virtually all the issues still outstanding. Most discussions took place bilaterally, to settle market access issues, or in small groups consisting of the countries most interested in a particular problem. Sutherland chaired meetings of a group restricted to heads of national delegations, wielding his chairman's gavel with a vigour that rapidly became legendary in order to achieve clearance, one after the other, of the less controversial revised texts. The same group took responsibility for seeking solutions to general issues still open.

The TNC did not meet during these final days, but the services and market access groups did. For many delegates, they provided the only reasonably broad view of what was going on, except to the extent that they could gain snatches of news from the large number of journalists who were now permanently on the GATT premises to follow events. These press sources did not always prove reliable, since their information in turn often came from national briefings at which they were offered views calculated to influence the negotiations.

The services group passed the GATS text forward to heads of delegation with only minor changes. India and Egypt, having failed in the group to obtain removal of the objectionable reference to "cost-oriented" pricing of telecommunications services, won their case with the heads of delegation. Problems continued, however, with the sectoral negotiations. Little, if anything, appeared to have been resolved by the Brussels talks. The United States came forward with its offer on services, and even included an offer on deep-sea shipping. But it maintained its insistence on giving MFN treatment in financial services only to those countries which gave reciprocal access to American companies. Its chief apparent targets, the Asian countries, responded by threatening to reduce their own offers. Late arrival of the US offer, continuing uncertainty about what would happen on taxation, financial services, shipping and audiovisual services, and the absence of an offer from the European Community, made it impossible for other countries to meet even the postponed deadline of 9 December. On the 10th, a complex agreement was announced that settled the taxation question by acknowledging the right to treat foreign and national service suppliers differently, provided certain conditions were met. As a result, the United States withdrew its "carve-out". The European Community put forward its long-promised proposal for a provision in the GATS that would recognize cultural reasons for maintaining restrictions, and warned that it would make no offer on audiovisual services unless the text were accepted. Canada, most of the smaller non-EC European countries and Brazil supported the Community; the United States, Japan and India were strongly opposed. On this and other service issues, Brittan and Kantor were known to be still locked in negotiations, with no indication of the likely outcome. In a new development, India introduced, with support from the United States, a proposal for a post-Round examination of how qualification and licensing requirements for professional services, and particularly for accountancy, might be prevented from blocking trade unnecessarily. Criticized only for its late introduction, and with its unusual and powerful backing, the proposal was clearly well set for the approval which it later won.

A meeting of the negotiating group on goods on 8 December provided a briefing from US and EC delegates that filled out hitherto fragmentary reports of what had been agreed to in Brussels. For agriculture, it was confirmed that the two sides now proposed a slower phase-in (from which, incidentally, both would benefit through higher grain sales) of the cuts in subsidized exports, and would extend by three years, to nine years in all, the so-called "peace clause" period during which the Community's common agricultural policy would not be challenged. A variety of other points in the agricultural agreement were revealed, with new market openings and tariff cuts in prospect for grains, meat, fruit and vegetables. For industrial products, the United States and the Community sketched out their agreement. They were now proposing tariff elimination for paper and pulp, wood, toys, and also steel, but had abandoned hope for the time being of a multilateral steel agreement. Deep tariff cuts were envisaged for electronics products (but not consumer electronics), for scientific equipment, and for non-ferrous metals, with tariff elimination for tin, nickel and copper. All these proposals were conditional on similar action by others, especially Canada and Japan. Other countries expressed relief that the Round's two largest players had struck a deal, but there was fierce criticism for much of its content. Developing countries saw nothing new in it on cotton, textiles, leather or tropical products; the agricultural agreement, they said, was a further weakening of the Draft Final Act provisions; the easing of restrictions on fruit was not helpful to Southern Hemisphere producers. The decisions on pulp and paper, and on non-ferrous metals, were welcome, but the offer on tropical timber had been made conditional on action by themselves to ease export restrictions. Other countries noted that the announcements implied that the Tokyo objectives for tariff elimination would not be entirely met, that nothing had come of the proposal to eliminate tariffs on oilseeds, and that hopes of liberalization for trade in fish had not been fulfilled. In reply, they were reminded that the Round was not yet over, that there was still scope for further offers, and that they too were expected to make greater contributions in order to finish the negotiations.

On the 9th came the expected approval of the agricultural package by the EC Council of Ministers, and further unconfirmed reports that the Japanese government would accept imports of rice. Sutherland was known to be aiming to complete all work on the Uruguay Round texts by Sunday, and all bilateral discussions by the Monday, 13 December.

As the negotiations moved into their final weekend, large pieces of the Uruguay Round puzzle were clearly falling into place. Most people were now confident of final success, but several highly politicized questions remained open, time was growing desperately short, and the outcome was essentially still, all too obviously, in the hands of the European Community and the United States. The heads-of-delegations group was trying to resolve remaining differences on the several of the Draft Final Act texts, with US demands on anti-dumping the most difficult. The unsettled problems on services seemed actually to be growing more intractable. Brittan and Kantor were negotiating with one another not only on these matters, but on possible further tariff cuts and on the non-Uruguay Round issue of subsidies for civil aircraft.

The weekend brought frenzied activity, action on a wide variety of issues and in groups large and small, and assessments of progress that varied between declarations of crisis and assurances that any difficulties were no more than had to be expected. On Saturday, an EC summit meeting in Brussels adopted a tough position on remaining Uruguay Round issues, and especially on audiovisual services. The Dutch Prime Minister was reported to have suggested that it might be necessary to "stop the clock" on the 15th, earning from Sutherland the comment that this was "a misapprehension of the highest order". The Quad ministers met. In a flying visit to Geneva, the Japanese foreign minister made a last but fruitless effort to secure acceptance of continued closure of his country's rice market. Even though the US representatives were among those outwardly most confident, it was afterwards announced that President Clinton had telephoned the British, French and German leaders on Sunday afternoon to urge their support for completing the Round. Sutherland spoke to the press of the "extreme fluidity" of events. While the main issues under negotiation remained the same, others surfaced, including an unsuccessful move by the European Community to gain support for its view that Hong Kong, Korea and Singapore must now be regarded as developed countries.

A first critically important breakthrough came on Sunday, too late for most of Monday's morning newspapers, which reported the Round still deadlocked. Agreement was reached on the anti-dumping agreement. The United States had asked for eleven changes. It won several, but not all. Most important was probably an agreement on "standards of review" which provided that dispute settlement proceedings could look at how dumping cases had been handled by national authorities, but not at the facts of the case. The right of US labour unions to bring dumping complaints was recognized, but the sunset and *de minimis* provisions were changed only marginally. The anti-circumvention clause, far from being strengthened as both the United States and the European Community would have liked, was removed altogether, leaving the issue for fresh negotiations after the Round.

The success on anti-dumping, generally regarded as the hardest remaining issue after agriculture, opened the floodgates. During the same evening, Sutherland "gavelled through" more than 20 of the Uruguay Round texts in a six-hour meeting of heads of delegations. They included the agreements on agriculture, now reflecting the revised Blair House amendments, and on textiles, for which the ten-year phase-out was retained in spite of US pressure. On textiles, India and Pakistan continued to resist making tariff and non-tariff concessions themselves, but accepted a small change in the agreement that hinted at longer-term liberalization by developing-country exporters. Minor changes were made to the subsidy text to bring it into line with the anti-dumping agreement, and subsidies given to help in achieving environmental objectives were included in the non-actionable "green" category. To general relief, the agreement on the new trade organization was accepted, almost unchanged. The deal kept the environmental language in the preamble but left any decision on a standing environmental committee for the end of a post-Round work programme. The provision on conformity of national laws with the new trade rules was also retained, but modified slightly in a way which effectively left room for non-conforming laws if these did not prevent governments from meeting their obligations. To further reassure environmental and consumer interests, language in the agreements on technical barriers (standards) and phytosanitary measures was modified to make clear that signatories could apply higher standards than those agreed to internationally. A draft declaration on measures to help the least-developed countries spelled out several newly won gains, including the extra year to submit their goods and services schedules, and advanced introduction, where possible, of concessions of interest to them. Least-developed countries also gained an easing, in their favour, of rules in the subsidy and textiles agreements. For other agreements such as safeguards, the most significant fact was their approval without change, thereby endorsing the "arbitrated" choices made two years earlier by the group chairmen.

The negotiations, however, were not over. On Monday morning, the 13th, both the market access and service negotiators were hard at work, and some were far from certain that they had time to finish before the Wednesday deadline. The services negotiations, in particular, were in very serious trouble over the financial and maritime sectors. Brittan and Kantor had still not resolved their final differences: they were reported to remain deeply divided over audiovisual services and civil aircraft subsidies. The TRIPS text was held up by American pressure for tighter restrictions on the compulsory licensing of semiconductor technology and earlier introduction of patent protection for pharmaceuticals in developing countries. The TNC meeting was cancelled, and printing of the final texts held up. Few, however, had any doubts now that the

Round would end successfully on the 15th. Sutherland called it "inconceivable" that the differences between the Community and the United States could block agreement, since they paled, in his view, into "absolute insignificance" compared with the agreements on market access and new trade rules already reached among all Uruguay Round participants.

With so much else going right, the services group's meeting on the 13th was a depressing occasion. In the absence of progress on financial, maritime and audiovisual services, eleven participants, including most of the developed countries other than the European Community and the United States, announced they would withhold from their final offers concessions they had been ready to make. They felt they had little choice: the rules for the negotiations meant that at this stage, although they could make additional offers, they could not withdraw what they had put on the table. Most insisted that they were ready to offer more, but expressed frustration that they still had no clear idea, only hours before final offers were due, of what the two largest participants would offer.

Brittan and Kantor negotiated through most of Monday night, and again on Tuesday morning, and at last reached an accord that, on the final issues, amounted to an agreement to disagree. On audiovisual services, the United States refused to concede recognition of their special cultural character, and the Community in consequence announced it would make no offers. In France, the outcome was greeted as a victory. The two sides had also reached agreement on financial services and shipping, although the details emerged only later in the day. On subsidies for civil aircraft, not part of the Round, the two sides undertook to continue negotiations over the coming year.

Completion of these bilateral negotiations at last cleared the way for movement on services. The going, however, remained extremely difficult. The services group held four separate meetings on Tuesday. The Community's decision not to make an offer on audiovisual services meant that others too withdrew the specific commitments they had been ready to offer. In consequence, the whole audiovisual annex was lost from the services agreement (although, contrary to many reports, the ground-rules of the GATS would apply to this sector of services, as to others). To head off the looming danger of a two-tier system of international obligations for financial services and of a consequent mass withdrawal of offers in this sector too, a package solution was put together that essentially encouraged prompt further negotiations after the Round and meanwhile maintained on an MFN basis most of the offers that had already been made. This was done by a formula that would allow countries not satisfied by the results of further negotiations to withdraw offers, without giving compensation, up to six months after the Uruguay Round results came into effect. The agreement was promptly approved by heads of delegation. Developing countries, and particularly India and Pakistan, were pleased by an agreement to launch further services negotiations after the Round on the movement of natural persons. The maritime services agreement, however, hit a reef. The United States announced that the necessary "critical mass" of support for a deal did not exist, and withdrew its offer, at the same time proposing that negotiations on this subject too be taken up after the Round. The European Community did the same, but other countries, with Japan in the lead, called for the precedent just established for financial services be followed, whereby present offers would be maintained, but could be adjusted if the later negotiations did not produce a balanced result. No immediate conclusions could be reached, and once again the deadline for final services offers was pushed back, this time to the morning of the 15th.

The other main development on this penultimate day of the Round was the belated distribution of the massive consolidated text of the multilateral agreements. The single volume, still not quite definitive and somewhat mis-leadingly bearing the previous day's date, was confidently titled "Final Act Embodying the Results of the Uruguay Round of Multilateral Trade Negotiations". Unlike its 1991 predecessor, which until now had offered the only comprehensive view of what might emerge from the Round, the new document's structure fully reflected the proposed future shape of the international trading system, headed by the new Multilateral Trade Organization. This edition was in fact to survive only one day: by the 15th, sufficient further developments had occurred to make a revision necessary.

Although the final TNC of the Round was set for the evening of the 15th, there was still a good deal to be done. The TRIPS text was at last settled. One significant change, in response to earlier strong objections by US manu-facturers, set strict limits to the grant by governments of compulsory licences for the use of semiconductor technology. Equally significantly, no change was made in the draft rule allowing developing countries a ten-year transition period to introduce patent protection for pharmaceuticals. These decisions were reflected in the 15 December edition of the Final Act. Another, however, was not. At a meeting of heads of delegation, the United States proposed that the clumsy and bureaucratic title "Multilateral Trade Organi-zation", which had been adopted almost by default, be changed to "World Trade Organization". News of the change filtered out only slowly, and had certainly not reached a large proportion of delegates by the time of the TNC meeting. It was not the least of American contributions to the Uruguay Round package. Participants in the government procurement negotiations, which had been going on over the past months in parallel with the Uruguay Round, mainly among developed countries, announced that they too had reached agreement on a massive overhaul and expansion in coverage of the old Tokyo Round code.

There remained the final meetings of the services and market access groups. The services discussions continued tense and difficult almost to the end. Long after an 8 a.m. deadline fixed the previous day, the European Community had still not introduced its final offer. For some hours, it insisted that the proposed maritime services negotiations after the Round would be acceptable only if it were agreed that in the event of their failure, the sector should be removed from the GATS altogether. A midday meeting of the services group heard successive statements by other participants that they could not confirm their own offers as long as the Community's was still missing. Finally, the Community dropped its conditions for the maritime services negotiations, and submitted its schedules. At last, the group's closing meeting could be held, and the services offers declared final and now capable only of being improved. The mood of participants was mixed. There was disappointment at the retreat in the final weeks from the larger package that in early November had seemed within the negotiators' grasp. But as several delegates recalled, the outcome far exceeded even the most optimistic expectations of 1986. Ten years earlier, when preparation for new trade negotiations had just begun, discussion even of the possibility of opening up trade in services had been fiercely controversial. Now agreement had been reached both on the GATS, a set of binding rules for services comparable in scope to the GATT rules for goods, and on thousands of individual liberalization commitments by the great majority of the world's countries. Ahead lay a daunting, but also promising, programme of continuing negotiations.

Much the most striking feature of the market access group's last meeting was that, just three hours before the final TNC meeting, the participants were still vigorously engaged in negotiations with one another. Many were confident of reaching several more bilateral agreements by the end of the day. Even without the least-developed countries, to which the current deadline did not apply, 95 participants had deposited schedules of offers. No withdrawals would now be possible, but many countries expected to continue negotiating improvements up to 15 February, the final date for deposit of offers. (In some cases, negotiations went on even longer. A full year later, just before the Uruguay Round results came into force, the United States and the Community reached agreements with India under which both sides eased market access for textiles and clothing.) Most participants pronounced themselves reasonably satisfied already, and still hopeful of further gains. Canada, Japan, Korea and Mexico officially announced their acceptance of full tariffication for agricultural products. For Japan and Korea, the decision had been softened by agreement that they need not immediately open up their markets for rice, provided they gave minimum access opportunities to foreign suppliers. An annex to the agricultural agreement allowed Japan a six-year period over which it was required only to provide access opportunities rising from an initial 4% of domestic consumption to a final 8%. Korea, as a developing country, won a ten-year respite, with minimum access rising from just 1% to 4%. For both countries, after these periods, there would either be full tariffication or further negotiations to extend special treatment. The concessions helped Japan and Korea in reaching what was certainly, for each, their most politically difficult decision of the Round.

Nothing remained but to bring the negotiations to their formal close.

In the late afternoon of the 15th, some hundreds of delegates, the entire Secretariat (at Sutherland's insistence) and a large contingent of the world's press crowded into the same plenary hall of the Geneva conference centre in which, in 1982, GATT ministers had met and started the formal process that had led to the launching of the Uruguay Round. Sutherland outlined the agreements reached, describing them as "a major renewal of the world trading system", and a choice of "openness and cooperation instead of uncertainty and conflict" which should lead to "more trade, more jobs and large income growth for all". Many other speakers followed, some concerned to spell out specific interests, continuing uncertainties, and sacrifices made, but all recognizing the scale of what had been accomplished. For Malaysia, speaking for the developing countries as a whole, there were "areas of deficiency", lack of commitment to the agreed special treatment for developing countries, and hopes still for more market-opening measures in their favour. Nevertheless, this was "a victory for international trade which will set a new era for our future generations, to benefit and contribute to the increased global welfare". The European Community spoke of "beginning to build a worldwide economic democracy". For the United States, the agreements reached were "moving the world in a certain direction – a direction of openness and free exchange and the kind of progress and prosperity that those qualities will produce". Brazil, looking ahead, warned that "this means a new management of world trade affairs in a totally new framework, in which the complexity of the fields covered poses an even greater challenge to our countries' ability to cope with our individual and collective responsibilities".

At 7.30 in the evening, to huge applause, Sutherland brought down his gavel to signify approval of the Uruguay Round agreements and the effective end of the negotiations. It was, he suggested, "a defining moment in modern economic and political history."

"Can it be true?"

There was of course still a long way to go before the World Trade Organization, and all the other results of the Round, could be brought into force. Any further bargaining on market access for goods and services – now confined strictly to improvements in offers, with no withdrawals allowed – had to be completed, and the resulting schedules of commitments examined and verified by the beginning of March. The form and accuracy of the negotiated texts approved on 15 December had to be checked. The TNC met several times more to develop a work programme for adoption at the conference in April, held in Marrakesh at Morocco's invitation, at which ministers signed the agreements. One decision quickly reached was to advance the date for entry into force of the World Trade Organization and the other Uruguay Round agreements: the Final Act of 15 December had set 1 July 1995 as the target date, but it was brought forward by six months, to 1 January 1995. After the

Marrakesh meeting, there were months of further work in Geneva, directed by a preparatory committee chaired by Sutherland, to settle a myriad of details on how the World Trade Organization would operate, where it would be based (Geneva won, over Bonn), and how it would take over the functions and staff of the old GATT. The postponed sectoral negotiations on services, effectively a spillover of the Round, began. From Marrakesh onwards, there was also a long and sometimes anxious wait for governments to obtain the approval of national legislatures for the Uruguay Round package. Anxiety was greatest over approval by the US Congress, where some legislators argued that national sovereignty might be infringed by the new dispute settlement procedures for which American negotiators had fought so long. Only in early December did the legislation pass. On New Year's Day 1995, the World Trade Organization was born.

Reviewing the events of 1994 in its final issue of the year, the magazine *The Economist* found an apt headline for its note recording the signature and ratification of the Uruguay Round and the imminent birth of the WTO. Putting into words what was surely the dominant feeling of the thousands of negotiators, officials, politicians, journalists and lobbyists who had carried the Round from its beginnings in the early 1980s to its conclusion in the mid-90s it asked:

"Can it be true ?"

Epilogue

The WTO three years on

This history of the Uruguay Round negotiations was largely written during 1994 – that is, immediately after their completion, and before their results entered into force. A large and obvious advantage of setting the story down quickly was that it could be recorded while the story was still fresh in the minds of the author and of participants in the negotiations. An equally obvious disadvantage was the lack of perspective inevitable in an account of events that, in great part, had only just taken place.

What was achieved in the Round? What long-term consequences will it have? Three years on from the birth of the World Trade Organization, it is still far too soon to pass judgement with any certainty. But more is known now about how governments are facing up to their Uruguay Round commitments, and how the new multilateral trading system embodied in the WTO differs from the old. An observer can also offer, with a little more confidence than was possible in 1994, a personal view on whether the world community might, in the not-too-distant future, embark on another such comprehensive trade negotiation.

Are governments living up to their Uruguay Round commitments?

Signature of the Uruguay Round texts in Marrakesh meant that the negotiations were finally over, and that each participant undertook to seek the authority necessary under its national laws to put the agreements into effect. It could not guarantee that the authority would be granted or, if granted, that governments would in fact live up to their commitments.

We now know that the Marrakesh Agreement of 1994 is at any rate a more solid achievement than the Havana Charter of 1948, the previous attempt to reshape the world trading system. The Charter, and the International Trade Organization it was meant to set up, failed to win the support of the United States Congress, and consequently died, leaving the stop-gap GATT to survive in its place for nearly half a century. No such fiasco occurred after Marrakesh.

The majority of GATT members, including the United States and the other large trading powers, formally accepted the Uruguay Round package by the end of 1994. The World Trade Organization became reality at the beginning of 1995. Twelve months later, the original GATT and its institutions, already mere shadows of their former selves, were formally laid to rest. Although a few of the smallest countries among the GATT contracting parties took longer to qualify for, and ratify, WTO membership, all had by early 1997 become full members. Life was quickly breathed into the institutions of the WTO. Its General Council, together with the Council's alter-egos for dispute settlement and trade policy review, the three subsidiary councils, and the host of other bodies set up to guide the application of individual Uruguay Round agreements, have all met regularly and frequently in Geneva. A successful first meeting of the governing Ministerial Conference of the WTO, held in Singapore in December 1996, reached agreement on several controversial matters.

Most of the individual agreements reached during the Round are now fully in operation, although many are not yet biting to the extent they will in a few years' time, when phased commitments to liberalize markets or to accept more stringent rules will take full effect. (A few examples: import duties on manufactures are being brought down progressively by annual cuts over five years, with the fourth taking effect at the beginning of 1998; agricultural restrictions are being lowered over six years; for textiles and clothing, the easing of restrictions is spread over ten years; the TRIPS agreement on protection of intellectual property did not take effect for developed countries until the beginning of 1996, and developing countries will not be bound by most of its provisions until January 2000.)

In general, WTO members seem to be living up to their commitments. A very large part of the present work of the specialized bodies of the WTO is in fact directed to ensuring that this is the case. Typically, the committees responsible for individual agreements such as those on agriculture, subsidies or technical standards are engaged in painstaking review of the legislation adopted, and other actions taken, by each country to meet the detailed requirements of the agreement concerned. The reviews serve the essential purpose of establishing a common understanding of how the paper commitments signed in Marrakesh are to be carried into practice. When inconsistencies are found, the country concerned is brought under immediate strong pressure from other members to come into line. This process is less a matter of ensuring that governments do not cheat, than of restraining them from going too far in testing – as they naturally will – the limits placed by each agreement on their freedom to set national trade policies. The examinations may also reveal ambiguities in the negotiated texts that will need to be resolved, possibly by seeking understandings on how the language concerned should be interpreted.

Governments have also been living up to commitments, included in the Uruguay Round package, to complete leftover negotiations on four aspects of trade in services. The outcome has been mixed, but on balance encouraging: two unqualified successes (on basic telecommunications and financial services) reached after prolonged and very tough negotiations; one positive but very limited agreement (on movement of natural persons); and a clear failure (maritime transport services). A so-called "built-in agenda" of future reviews and negotiations to which WTO members are already committed, made up of provisions scattered throughout the various individual agreements reached in the Round, has been identified, and was given formal endorsement by the ministerial meeting in Singapore. Some of this work is already under way.

The experience of the last three years has brought both successes and disappointments, as well as some practical problems.

The WTO itself, and the new dispute settlement system, are proving far more important and effective than appeared likely in the closing stages of the Round, when attention was largely focused on final bargaining on such issues as agricultural policies, "zero-for-zero" tariff negotiations, and the dismantling of restrictions on trade in textiles and clothing. A large number of countries that showed no interest in GATT membership now seek to join the WTO. In an important new move, led by the United States, countries that account for nine-tenths of world trade in the huge and growing sector of information technology decided in March 1997 to establish full free trade by the year 2000 in the products concerned (computers and related hardware, software, telecommunications equipment and many scientific instruments). This WTO-based agreement, together with that reached a few weeks earlier on opening up basic telecommunications services, will cover international trade with a total annual value comparable to that of trade in agricultural products, automobiles and textiles combined.

Although some of the Uruguay Round agreements have encountered criticism or difficulties, it seems too early to say whether these amount to more than teething problems. The agreement on textiles and clothing has been a particular target for criticism, mostly from people who were slow to accept that the scheduled progressive dismantling of restrictions leaves most liberalization for the final years of the transition period. This "back-loading", while unwelcome to the more competitive textile exporters, was part of the Uruguay Round bargain. The agricultural agreement has also come under fire. Studies of how the agreed principles of agricultural tariffication were carried into practice have demonstrated that the new tariffs, however welcome in their simplicity and promise for easier liberalization in future negotiations, generally provide continuing very high levels of protection. The independent entity set up to resolve disputes over preshipment inspection is thus far unused. Follow-up negotiations required to fill gaps in some agreements have progressed more slowly than expected. A widespread problem, affecting almost all agreements and all WTO members, has been the heavy burden of meeting notification requirements designed to show how members are fulfilling their Uruguay Round commitments. Very many members have failed to make notifications on time, particularly on their use of subsidies. Although even large countries have admitted to difficulty in meeting notification deadlines, the smaller developing countries are most obviously ill-equipped to handle the essential duty of keeping other WTO members informed about their trade policies and practices.

The apparently humdrum issue of notification obligations highlights a wider issue: have developing countries taken on more than they may have realized in signing up to the Uruguay Round package and WTO membership? The question is not asked (as some unreconstructed critics of the old GATT continue to ask it) because of any hankering after discredited policies of economic self-sufficiency or lingering suspicions of the market, but because of concern that many countries lack the administrative capacity to apply the Uruguay Round agreements fully, or to participate effectively in the continuing work of the WTO in Geneva. As long as this is so, they risk not only being found in breach of their obligations, but also failing to gain the full benefits of WTO membership. The WTO Secretariat has built up its technical assistance to developing countries, and developing-country representation in Geneva is much greater than it was only a few years ago, but the situation is still far from satisfactory.

The trade performance of the 48 countries categorized by the United Nations as "least-developed" is a particular worry. The share in world trade of these countries, most of which are in Africa, was never large, and is now well below 1 per cent. Their share in world output is smaller still, having fallen by a third since 1980 to 0.4% in 1993, and they attract less than 1% of international flows of direct investment. Although the Uruguay Round seems unlikely to have done them harm, it probably will do them little good. Harm might come from the erosion of their preferential access to developed-country markets that must follow from the general reduction in MFN import duties, or from higher prices they might have to pay for food imports. Neither factor, probably, will cause great difficulty: existing tariff preferences given by developed countries have not protected them from loss of market share to more competitive exporters, and research suggests that subsidy cuts negotiated under the Round will not significantly affect world prices for agricultural products. Least-developed countries were themselves largely exempted from liberalization commitments, and from the disciplines of the new WTO rules. But against this, they appear, by common consent, ill-equipped to gain much from the trade liberalization now taking place under the Uruguay Round agreements. For the most part, they lack the expertise, administrative capacity, infra-structure and investment needed to seize the market opportunities being opened up. The WTO, as the pre-eminent organization dealing with the world's trade problems, cannot ignore the marginalization of the least-developed countries. The Singapore meeting adopted a so-called "Comprehensive and Integrated WTO Plan of Action" that encourages member countries to help the least-developeds, through measures to improve not only their market access opportunities but also, more fundamentally, their capacity to compete effectively on world markets. Regrettably, the Plan of Action, unlike the new trade rules negotiated in the Round, imposes no binding commitments. (In the diplomatic jargon, it is a "best endeavours" agreement.) The WTO's reputation and credibility will suffer if those member countries which confidently expect to benefit from the results of the Round ignore the difficulties of least-developed countries for which the Round was, perhaps, largely an irrelevance.

Is the WTO all that different from the GATT?

Much about the new World Trade Organization is recognizably derived straight from the GATT. Its manner of work is much the same; so are the relative roles of national delegates and secretariat. As national delegates are fond of saying, the WTO, like the GATT, is a "member-driven" organization, differing in this from the Bretton Woods twins, the IMF and World Bank, with which the same delegates sometimes compare it. Physically, it remains housed in the same 70-year-old grey office block by Lake Geneva, and very many of the people involved in the Uruguay Round are still at work within the new organization. The provisions of the "GATT 1994", as the General Agreement on Tariffs and Trade is known in its post-Round form, are not all that much changed from those of the GATT of 1948. Nevertheless, the WTO is a very different animal from its predecessor. Its scope is far wider than that of the GATT, and yet it provides a single and coherent set of institutions and rules to govern multilateral trade relations. Its provisions apply to more countries, and with greater force. Above all, the WTO has teeth. Taken together, these characteristics give the WTO an international standing and influence that the GATT never attained.

Even in the traditional GATT field of trade in goods, the Uruguay Round has resulted in commitments that go far beyond the results of earlier negotiations such as the Kennedy and Tokyo Rounds. To give just one example, the negotiations on agriculture invaded highly sensitive areas of domestic policy, and their outcome gives the WTO a continuing right and duty to concern itself with these matters. The General Agreement on Trade in Services, a completely new set of disciplines and liberalization commitments, is already comparable in scope with the GATT of the 1950s or 1960s, and is explicitly pledged to future successive rounds of negotiations aimed at achieving "a progressively higher level of liberalization". The TRIPS agreement has established yet another body of new disciplines, in this case for the protection of intellectual property. These three distinct sets of commitments – on trade in goods, trade in services, and the protection of intellectual property – are bound together by the new central instutions introduced by the Marrakesh Agreement: the General Council, the integrated dispute settlement system, the trade policy reviews, and regular political-level input through the WTO's Ministerial Conference. Whereas the GATT was not strictly an organization at all, the World Trade Organization is a full-fledged international agency, so confident of its own unique character that it has by choice stood apart from the United Nations family of institutions.

The WTO's field of concern appears likely to expand still further. When, in September 1986, governments adopted the Punta del Este Declaration that established the coverage of the Uruguay Round, they could not agree to take up investment or competition issues. In Singapore, ten years later, they agreed to start discussions on trade-related aspects of both investment and competition. They took care to underline that this work "shall not prejudge whether negotiations will be initiated in the future", but that very statement suggests quite a strong possibility that negotiations will in fact follow. In 1986, Ministers could not agree to negotiate on trade in high-technology products; in 1996, they welcomed the imminent free-trade agreement on information technology, a prime element of the high-technology sector. (Not all disagreements, however, have faded away in the space of a decade: in Singapore as in Punta del Este, developing countries remained adamantly opposed to any discussion of the issue of workers' rights, now relabelled "labour standards".) Environmental issues, ignored in 1986, are now high on the public agenda. With only limited success, the WTO's members have been trying for some time to reach understandings on how to handle possible conflicts between its rules and international and national efforts to protect the environment. Multilateral efforts to preserve the ozone layer, national laws to discourage fishing methods that endanger dolphins or sea turtles, bans on sales of foods produced with the help of genetic manipulation or hormone treatment, requirements that packaging be recyclable, and campaigns to limit patent coverage of controversial biological techniques: all these current concerns could pit vocal environmentalists and consumers, as well as their governments, against WTO rules. The old GATT provisions, too, were relevant to many of these matters, but in the last resort could be ignored because dispute settlement rules were ultimately unenforceable if blocked by a party to a dispute. That is no longer the case. In spite of the potential for acute disagreements and unpopularity, including the danger of reopening North-South differences between member countries, increasing WTO involvement in environmental concerns appears unavoidable.

The WTO differs also from the GATT in its membership. True, the GATT had 128 members in its last days, but many of these joined only at the end, in order to ease their passage into the WTO: membership remained below 100 until the early 1990s. Few countries that were not GATT signatories have yet completed the arduous process of accession under the WTO's Article XII procedures, but there are some 30 such applicants for membership, including China, Russia and Saudi Arabia, nearly all of the former constituents of the Soviet Union, and several other significant trading countries. Almost all should be WTO members by the year 2000. Once they are in, total membership will be over 160, giving the WTO strong claims to effective universality. Many of the applicants seem likely to be persuaded, as condition for entry into the

WTO, to take on commitments which many present members have refused, including liberalization of government purchasing through membership of the agreement on government procurement, and acceptance of existing sectoral agreements such as that on information technology products. All members of the WTO, whether former signatories of the GATT or new entrants into the web of multilateral trading rights and obligations, have taken on much wider, and more binding, commitments than were involved in GATT membership.

Perhaps the most striking difference between the GATT and the WTO has become obvious only in the the past year or so. The credibility of WTO rights and obligations has been greatly reinforced by the demonstrated effectiveness of the new dispute settlement system. Dispute settlement under the GATT could work very well, provided the countries involved did not care too deeply about the outcome. On occasion, a country might even privately welcome a panel conclusion which went against it, if the effect was to require withdrawal of an unwise trade measure originally introduced under domestic pressure. When major or particularly sensitive issues were at stake, however, formal GATT dispute settlement procedures often were blocked or delayed, and panel decisions effectively vetoed by refusal of the losing party to accept them. The possibility of blockage or veto no longer exists. The new dispute settlement agreement also sets deadlines for completion of each stage of examination of a dispute. Even if the process is extended by an appeal to the standing Appellate Body, the brief delay involved is more than compensated by the enhanced authority of the final conclusions.

The influence of the dispute settlement procedures on the reputation and standing of the WTO has been startling. Now that governments on the losing side have bowed to a succession of decisions by dispute settlement panels, in most cases following an unsuccessful appeal, the WTO is perceived as having teeth, and in consequence commands respect. The procedures are being tested by a far higher volume of complaints than was ever experienced under the GATT: 25 requests for formal consultations were made in 1995, and 39 in 1996, and 47 in 1997. The pattern emerging is that roughly two-thirds of complaints are settled at the consultation stage. The remainder go on to be examined by panels. A small but rapidly increasing number have now passed through the entire process of successive consultations, panel examination, findings, appeal and final adoption of the conclusions by the Dispute Settlement Body. In all cases so far in which complaints were finally upheld, the country found at fault has either taken the necessary steps to put the situation right, or has undertaken to do so within an agreed period. Along the way, the Appellate Body, in particular, has won plaudits for the quality of its reviews of the legal soundness of panel reports, and this has helped ease final acceptance. As under the GATT, the United States and the European Union have figured in most disputes, but an increasing number have involved developing countries as complainants (in about one-third of all cases so far), respondents, or both.

There can be no certainty that the record on dispute settlement will continue to be so encouraging. A severe test was averted, for the time being, when President Clinton decided to suspend operation of a provision of the Helms-Burton Act that was particularly resented by other governments. The Act's conformity with WTO rules was about to be reviewed by a panel whose right even to consider the matter was – most controversially – denied by the United States on the ground that the issue was one of national security. The European Union faces a painful and politically charged choice in seeking to reconcile its WTO obligations with its desire to support several very small developing countries economically dependent on banana exports to Europe. A number of other such potential test cases are working their way through the dispute settlement process, and more will no doubt surface in the years ahead. Some practical criticisms of the system are also being heard: the increasing complexity of cases, the shortage of suitable panellists ("suitable" in the sense not only of competence but also of perceived neutrality), the difficulty for small countries of arranging adequate representation. But all in all, experience of the WTO dispute settlement arrangements so far is overwhelmingly favourable. The lawyers who so often despaired of GATT do not despair of the WTO.

The WTO's role as the accepted point of reference in global trade relations, its near-universal membership, its binding rules and perceived effectiveness, have already made it one of the heavyweights among international agencies. It may not yet have achieved full parity with the Bretton Woods institutions, but it comes reasonably close, and it has no rivals in its own field.

Towards a new Round?

Will we ever see another trade negotiation on the scale of the Uruguay Round? Or was the Round not only the largest, but also the last, of the recurrent cooperative efforts by which the world community has ensured during the past half-century that trade barriers continue to fall, and trade rules be kept abreast of evolving needs?

Some people argue today that the huge expenditure of time, effort and political capital needed to carry an enterprise such as the Uruguay Round to success is unnecessary and unjustified. They suggest that the Round itself has put in place all the institutions and instruments necessary to govern multilateral trade relations for the foreseeable future. As they see it, the WTO offers a permanent negotiating forum, in which issues and opportunities that require negotiation can be taken up as part of its day-to-day activities. As confirmation, they point to recent successes in reaching independent and far-reaching agreements in the WTO to liberalize trade in information technology products, basic telecommunications services and financial services.

Much the same view was taken in the early 1980s, in the aftermath of the previous marathon trade negotiation. Those who took it then were quickly proved wrong.

Certainly, there seems no immediate prospect of a new comprehensive effort on quite the scale of the Uruguay Round. The institutional structures of the WTO, and its interlocking system of rights and obligations, have only just been put in place, and should not need far-reaching overhaul for some time. Moreover, with the tide still running strongly in favour of liberal trade policies and open markets, there may well be further opportunities to negotiate liberalization in some sectors of trade in goods or services. There must be suspicion, however, that the negotiations on information technology, basic telecommunications and financial services were special cases, in which an unusually wide common interest in a successful outcome allowed stand-alone agreements to be reached. The similar negotiations to liberalize trade in maritime transport services failed, because participants had no such shared desire for their success. Certain components of the Uruguay Round results, too, might have been negotiated separately. The early decisions reached on trade policy reviews and ministerial meetings, for example, reflected very broad support. But it is almost inconceivable that the agreements on agriculture or on textiles and clothing, to name just two of the main elements of the Marrakesh package, could have been achieved on their own, rather than as part of a larger package that allowed all participants to set off painful concessions made in one agreement against a perceived balance of advantage on another, and so to be able to secure an overall result acceptable to their legislatures and public opinion.

Already, the WTO is committed, in and around the year 2000, to open new negotiations on a wide range of subjects. The "built-in agenda" bequeathed by the Uruguay Round includes negotiations from 1999 onwards to continue the reform programme for agricultural trade; the first of the successive rounds of progressive liberalization of trade in services, starting not later than January 2000; and reviews, also beginning not later than January 2000, of the WTO's dispute settlement provisions, the TRIPS and TRIMS agreements, and the important MFN exemption clause that allows some services concessions not to be extended to all WTO members. By that time, the discussions on trade-related investment and competition issues may be ripe for decisions on whether to move to the negotiation of commitments. Another Singapore decision, to study what is delicately described as "transparency in government procurement practices", also calls for the development of "elements for inclusion in an appropriate agreement": more plainly, for a further negotiation. The present discussion of environmental issues may well have matured, in three years' time, to a point when negotiations will seem desirable. So could "trade facilitation", an apparently uncontroversial concept also placed on the WTO agenda in Singapore in order "to assess the scope for WTO rules in this area".

Nor need the list end there. China, Russia and other countries which today have no influence on the WTO agenda should by the year 2000 be full members, and will wish to see due attention given to their particular interests and concerns. Governments which feel that the WTO should look more closely at the present proliferation of preferential trade agreements will be able to draw on whatever conclusions emerge from the discussion of systemic issues now in progress in the WTO's committee on regional trading arrangements. The prospect of sweeping moves to liberalize trade among members of such regional groupings as APEC, ASEAN and the proposed Free Trade Area of the Americas may, like the dismantling of tariffs within Western Europe in the 1960s and 1970s, stimulate fresh initiatives to reduce MFN trade barriers worldwide. Several Uruguay Round agreements require decisions in the next few years on whether to maintain or alter particular provisions, and these decisions may well require negotiations. Moreover, if some members feel that an emerging decision would alter the balance of an agreement to their disadvantage, they might make compensatory claims for adjustments elsewhere. Finally, the prospect of a new round of negotiations would prompt legislatures, business interests and environmental groups to press the inclusion of additional issues, almost inevitably controversial.

The "package" approach to trade negotiations has clear disadvantages. Like a convoy of ships, a big negotiation covering a range of subjects takes time to assemble and, once on the move, can only progress at the pace of its slowest element. Its agenda is usually overloaded; it is easily held hostage to doubts or delays in a key participating country. Nevertheless, the Uruguay Round showed that such a negotiation can finally achieve impressive results on a large number of highly controversial issues which, tackled individually and without the political impetus of a broader enterprise, would probably not have been resolved. The WTO faces negotiations in the near future on just such an array of issues.

Nothing is certain in international economic relations. The launching of multilateral trade negotiations, in particular, requires that each major player decide for itself that participation would be worthwhile, and that it be equipped with whatever mandate and authority it may need to join in the negotiations with its trading partners. Abundant evidence, not least from the Uruguay Round, suggests that no such negotiation can have much prospect of success without the willing participation, and preferably leadership, of the United States and the European Union. Other countries, too, must be persuaded that participation will be in their interest. These conditions may not be met, in which case the WTO could face a more difficult and clouded future than its present situation suggests. The odds, however, appear on balance to favour a new WTO round. Even if an enterprise on the massive scale of the Uruguay Round seems improbable, the new millenium is likely to find the members of the WTO once again embarking on multilateral negotiations to bring their trade policies and the rules of the trading system abreast of evolving needs and opportunities.

Annex

Ministerial Declaration on the Uruguay Round

Ministers, meeting on the occasion of the Special Session of the CONTRACTING PARTIES at Punta del Este, have decided to launch Multilateral Trade Negotiations (The Uruguay Round). To this end, they have adopted the following Declaration. The Multilateral Trade Negotiations will be open to the participation of countries as indicated in Parts I and II of this Declaration. A Trade Negotiations Committee is established to carry out the negotiations. The Trade Negotiations Committee shall hold its first meeting not later than 31 October 1986. It shall meet as appropriate at Ministerial level. The Multilateral Trade Negotiations will be concluded within four years.

Part I – Negotiations on Trade in Goods

The CONTRACTING PARTIES meeting at Ministerial level

DETERMINED to halt and reverse protectionism and to remove distortions to trade

DETERMINED also to preserve the basic principles and to further the objectives of the GATT

DETERMINED also to develop a more open, viable and durable multilateral trading system

CONVINCED that such action would promote growth and development

MINDFUL of the negative effects of prolonged financial and monetary instability in the world economy, the indebtedness of a large number of less-developed contracting parties, and considering the linkage between trade, money, finance and development

DECIDE to enter into Multilateral Trade Negotiations on trade in goods within the framework and under the aegis of the General Agreement on Tariffs and Trade.

A. Objectives

Negotiations shall aim to:

(i) bring about further liberalization and expansion of world trade to the benefit of all countries, especially less-developed contracting parties, including the improvement of access to markets by the reduction and elimination of tariffs, quantitative restrictions and other non-tariff measures and obstacles;

(ii) strengthen the rôle of GATT, improve the multilateral trading system based on the principles and rules of the GATT and bring about a wider coverage of world trade under agreed, effective and enforceable multilateral disciplines;

(iii) increase the responsiveness of the GATT system to the evolving international economic environment, through facilitating necessary structural adjustment, enhancing the relationship of the GATT with the relevant international organizations and taking account of changes in trade patterns and prospects, including the growing importance of trade in high technology products, serious difficulties in commodity markets and the importance of an improved trading environment providing, *inter alia*, for the ability of indebted countries to meet their financial obligations;

(iv) foster concurrent co-operative action at the national and international levels to strengthen the inter-relationship between trade policies and other economic policies affecting growth and development, and to contribute towards continued, effective and determined efforts to improve the functioning of the international monetary system and the flow of financial and real investment resources to developing countries.

B. General Principles Governing Negotiations

(i) Negotiations shall be conducted in a transparent manner, and consistent with the objectives and commitments agreed in this Declaration and with the principles of the General Agreement in order to ensure mutual advantage and increased benefits to all participants.

(ii) The launching, the conduct and the implementation of the outcome of the negotiations shall be treated as parts of a single undertaking. However, agreements reached at an early stage may be implemented on a provisional or a definitive basis by agreement prior to the formal conclusion of the negotiations. Early agreements shall be taken into account in assessing the overall balance of the negotiations.

(iii) Balanced concessions should be sought within broad trading areas and subjects to be negotiated in order to avoid unwarranted cross-sectoral demands.

(iv)   The CONTRACTING PARTIES agree that the principle of differential and more favourable treatment embodied in Part IV and other relevant provisions of the General Agreement and in the Decision of the CONTRACTING PARTIES of 28 November 1979 on Differential and More Favourable Treatment, Reciprocity and Fuller Participation of Developing Countries applies to the negotiations. In the implementation of standstill and rollback, particular care should be given to avoiding disruptive effects on the trade of less-developed contracting parties.

(v)   The developed countries do not expect reciprocity for commitments made by them in trade negotiations to reduce or remove tariffs and other barriers to the trade of developing countries, i.e. the developed countries do not expect the developing countries, in the course of trade negotiations, to make contributions which are inconsistent with their individual development, financial and trade needs. Developed contracting parties shall therefore not seek, neither shall less-developed contracting parties be required to make, concessions that are inconsistent with the latter's development, financial and trade needs.

(vi)   Less-developed contracting parties expect that their capacity to make contributions or negotiated concessions or take other mutually agreed action under the provisions and procedures of the General Agreement would improve with the progressive development of their economies and improvement in their trade situation and they would accordingly expect to participate more fully in the framework of rights and obligations under the General Agreement.

Special attention shall be given to the particular situation and problems of the least-developed countries and to the need to encourage positive measures to facilitate expansion of their trading opportunities. Expeditious implementation of the relevant provisions of the 1982 Ministerial Declaration concerning the least-developed countries shall also be given appropriate attention.

C. Standstill and Rollback

Commencing immediately and continuing until the formal completion of the negotiations, each participant agrees to apply the following commitments:

Standstill

(i)   not to take any trade restrictive or distorting measure inconsistent with the provisions of the General Agreement or the Instruments negotiated within the framework of GATT or under its auspices;

(ii)   not to take any trade restrictive or distorting measure in the legitimate exercise of its GATT rights, that would go beyond that which is necessary to remedy specific situations, as provided for in the General Agreement and the Instruments referred to in (i) above;

(iii) not to take any trade measures in such a manner as to improve its negotiating positions;

Rollback

(i)   that all trade restrictive or distorting measures inconsistent with the provisions of the General Agreement or Instruments negotiated within the framework of GATT or under its auspices, shall be phased out or brought into conformity within an agreed timeframe not later than by the date of the formal completion of the negotiations, taking into account multilateral agreements, undertakings and understandings, including strengthened rules and disciplines, reached in pursuance of the Objectives of the Negotiations;

(ii)   there shall be progressive implementation of this commitment on an equitable basis in consultations among participants concerned, including all affected participants. This commitment shall take account of the concerns expressed by any participant about measures directly affecting its trade interests;

(iii) there shall be no GATT concessions requested for the elimination of these measures.

Surveillance of standstill and rollback

Each participant agrees that the implementation of these commitments on standstill and rollback shall be subject to multilateral surveillance so as to ensure that these commitments are being met. The Trade Negotiations Committee will decide on the appropriate mechanisms to carry out the surveillance, including periodic reviews and evaluations. Any participant may bring to the attention of the appropriate surveillance mechanism any actions or omissions it believes to be relevant to the fulfilment of these commitments. These notifications should be addressed to the GATT secretariat which may also provide further relevant information.

D. Subjects for Negotiation

Tariffs

Negotiations shall aim, by appropriate methods, to reduce or, as appropriate, eliminate tariffs including the reduction or elimination of high tariffs and tariff escalation. Emphasis shall be given to the expansion of the scope of tariff concessions among all participants.

Non-tariff measures

Negotiations shall aim to reduce or eliminate non-tariff measures, including quantitative restrictions, without prejudice to any action to be taken in fulfilment of the rollback commitments.

Tropical products

Negotiations shall aim at the fullest liberalization of trade in tropical products, including in their processed and semi-processed forms and shall cover both tariff and all non-tariff measures affecting trade in these products.

The CONTRACTING PARTIES recognize the importance of trade in tropical products to a large number of less-developed contracting parties and agree that negotiations in this area shall receive special attention, including the timing of the negotiations and the implementation of the results as provided for in B(ii).

Natural resource-based products

Negotiations shall aim to achieve the fullest liberalization of trade in natural resource-based products, including in their processed and semi-processed forms. The negotiations shall aim to reduce or eliminate tariff and non-tariff measures, including tariff escalation.

Textiles and clothing

Negotiations in the area of textiles and clothing shall aim to formulate modalities that would permit the eventual integration of this sector into GATT on the basis of strengthened GATT rules and disciplines, thereby also contributing to the objective of further liberalization of trade.

Agriculture

The CONTRACTING PARTIES agree that there is an urgent need to bring more discipline and predictability to world agricultural trade by correcting and preventing restrictions and distortions including those related to structural surpluses so as to reduce the uncertainty, imbalances and instability in world agricultural markets.

Negotiations shall aim to achieve greater liberalization of trade in agriculture and bring all measures affecting import access and export competition under strengthened and more operationally effective GATT rules and disciplines, taking into account the general principles governing the negotiations, by:

(i)   improving market access through, *inter alia*, the reduction of import barriers;

(ii) improving the competitive environment by increasing discipline on the use of all direct and indirect subsidies and other measures affecting directly or indirectly agricultural trade, including the phased reduction of their negative effects and dealing with their causes;

(iii) minimizing the adverse effects that sanitary and phytosanitary regulations and barriers can have on trade in agriculture, taking into account the relevant international agreements.

In order to achieve the above objectives, the negotiating group having primary responsibility for all aspects of agriculture will use the Recommendations adopted by the CONTRACTING PARTIES at their Fortieth Session, which were developed in accordance with the GATT 1982 Ministerial Work Programme, and take account of the approaches suggested in the work of the Committee on Trade in Agriculture without prejudice to other alternatives that might achieve the objectives of the negotiations.

GATT Articles

Participants shall review existing GATT Articles, provisions and disciplines as requested by interested contracting parties, and, as appropriate, undertake negotiations.

Safeguards

(i) A comprehensive agreement on safeguards is of particular importance to the strengthening of the GATT system and to progress in the Multilateral Trade Negotiations.

(ii) The agreement on safeguards:

- shall be based on the basic principles of the General Agreement;

- shall contain, *inter alia*, the following elements: transparency, coverage, objective criteria for action including the concept of serious injury or threat thereof, temporary nature, degressivity and structural adjustment, compensation and retaliation, notification, consultation, multilateral surveillance and dispute settlement; and

- shall clarify and reinforce the disciplines of the General Agreement and should apply to all contracting parties.

MTN Agreements and Arrangements

Negotiations shall aim to improve, clarify, or expand, as appropriate, Agreements and Arrangements negotiated in the Tokyo Round of Multilateral Negotiations.

Subsidies and countervailing measures

Negotiations on subsidies and countervailing measures shall be based on a review of Articles VI and XVI and the MTN Agreement on subsidies and countervailing measures with the objective of improving GATT disciplines relating to all subsidies and countervailing measures that affect international trade. A negotiating group will be established to deal with these issues.

Dispute settlement

In order to ensure prompt and effective resolution of disputes to the benefit of all contracting parties, negotiations shall aim to improve and strengthen the rules and the procedures of the dispute settlement process, while recognizing the contribution that would be made by more effective and enforceable GATT rules and disciplines. Negotiations shall include the development of adequate arrangements for overseeing and monitoring of the procedures that would facilitate compliance with adopted recommendations.

Trade-related aspects of intellectual property rights, including trade in counterfeit goods

In order to reduce the distortions and impediments to international trade, and taking into account the need to promote effective and adequate protection of intellectual property rights, and to ensure that measures and procedures to enforce intellectual property rights do not themselves become barriers to legitimate trade, the negotiations shall aim to clarify GATT provisions and elaborate as appropriate new rules and disciplines.

Negotiations shall aim to develop a multilateral framework of principles, rules and disciplines dealing with international trade in counterfeit goods, taking into account work already undertaken in the GATT.

These negotiations shall be without prejudice to other complementary initiatives that may be taken in the World Intellectual Property Organization and elsewhere to deal with these matters.

Trade-related investment measures

Following an examination of the operation of GATT Articles related to the trade restrictive and distorting effects of investment measures, negotiations should elaborate, as appropriate, further provisions that may be necessary to avoid such adverse effects on trade.

E. Functioning of the GATT System

Negotiations shall aim to develop understandings and arrangements:

(i) to enhance the surveillance in the GATT to enable regular monitoring of trade policies and practices of contracting parties and their impact on the functioning of the multilateral trading system;

(ii) to improve the overall effectiveness and decision-making of the GATT as an institution, including, *inter alia*, through involvement of Ministers;

(iii) to increase the contribution of the GATT to achieving greater coherence in global economic policy-making through strengthening its relationship with other international organizations responsible for monetary and financial matters.

F. Participation

(a) Negotiations will be open to:

  (i) all contracting parties,

  (ii) countries having acceded provisionally,

  (iii) countries applying the GATT on a *de facto* basis having announced, not later than 30 April 1987, their intention to accede to the GATT and to participate in the negotiations,

  (iv) countries that have already informed the CONTRACTING PARTIES, at a regular meeting of the Council of Representatives, of their intention to negotiate the terms of their membership as a contracting party, and

  (v) developing countries that have, by 30 April 1987, initiated procedures for accession to the GATT, with the intention of negotiating the terms of their accession during the course of the negotiations.

(b) Participation in negotiations relating to the amendment or application of GATT provisions or the negotiation of new provisions will, however, be open only to contracting parties.

G. Organization of the Negotiations

A Group of Negotiations on Goods (GNG) is established to carry out the programme of negotiations contained in this Part of the Declaration. The GNG shall, *inter alia*:

(i) elaborate and put into effect detailed trade negotiating plans prior to 19 December 1986:

(ii) designate the appropriate mechanism for surveillance of commitments to standstill and rollback;

(iii) establish negotiating groups as required. Because of the interrelationship of some issues and taking fully into account the general principles governing the negotiations as stated in B(iii) above it is recognized that aspects of one issue may be discussed in more than one negotiating group. Therefore each negotiating group should as required take into account relevant aspects emerging in other groups;

(iv) also decide upon inclusion of additional subject matters in the negotiations;

(v) co-ordinate the work of the negotiating group and supervise the progress of the negotiations. As a guideline not more than two negotiating groups should meet at the same time;

(vi) the GNG shall report to the Trade Negotiations Committee.

In order to ensure effective application of differential and more favourable treatment the GNG shall, before the formal completion of the negotiations, conduct an evaluation of the results attained therein in terms of the Objectives and the General Principles Governing Negotiations as set out in the Declaration, taking into account all issues of interest to less-developed contracting parties.

Part II – Negotiations on Trade in Services

Ministers also decide, as part of the Multilateral Trade Negotiations, to launch negotiations on trade in services.

Negotiations in this area shall aim to establish a multilateral framework of principles and rules for trade in services, including elaboration of possible disciplines for individual sectors, with a view to expansion of such trade under conditions of transparency and progressive liberalization and as a means of promoting economic growth of all trading partners and the development of developing countries. Such framework shall respect the policy objectives of national laws and regulations applying to services and shall take into account the work of relevant international organizations.

GATT procedures and practices shall apply to these negotiations. A Group of Negotiations on services is established to deal with these matters. Participation in the negotiations under this Part of the Declaration will be open to the same countries as under Part I. GATT secretariat support will be provided, with technical support from other organizations as decided by the Group of Negotiations on Services.

The Group of Negotiations on Services shall report to the Trade Negotiations Committee.

Implementation of Results Under Parts I and II

When the results of the Multilateral Trade Negotiations in all areas have been established, Ministers meeting also on the occasion of a Special Session of CONTRACTING PARTIES shall decide regarding the international implementation of the respective results.

Index

In the following Index, references for some entries are noticeably absent: the European Community, the United States, developing countries, developed countries, and Arthur Dunkel. Rather than cite long columns of page numbers, suffice to say that their presence in this history is ubiquitous. There are few pages that do not record their active participation in the proceedings of the Round. Also, as noted in the Foreword, key negotiating subjects (market access, agriculture, services, etc.) are best tracked through the table of contents, where sections covering them are indicated.

M

Market access 156-168
  Brussels 241-242
  developments 1989-90 156-168
  Draft Final Act 257-259
  negotiations September-
    November 1993 307-310
  Track One 288-289
Mid-term review 141-151
  completing 147-151
  Montreal 142-147
**Ministerial Declaration on the
  Uruguay Round** 343-351
  functioning of GATT system
    349
  implementation of results 351
  negotiations on trade in goods
    343-351
    general principles 344-345
    objectives 344
    rollback 346
    standstill 345-346
    surveillance of standstill and
      rollback 346
  negotiations on trade in services
    351
  organization of negotiations
    350-351
  participation 350
  subjects for negotiation 346-349
    agriculture 347-348
    dispute settlement 349
    GATT Articles 348
    intellectual property rights
      349
    MTN agreements and
      arrangements 348
    natural resource-based
      products 347
    non-tariff measures 347
    safeguards 348
    subsidies and countervailing
      measures 348-349
    tariffs 346
    textiles and clothing 347
    trade-related investment
      measures 349
    tropical products 347

Monitoring 122
Montreal 142-147
Multifibre Arrangement 89-90
  developments 1989-90
    192-199
  effect 89
  extension 23
  phase-out 192-199
  signatories 89-90

N

NAFTA
  approval 317-318
National security 81-82
National trade policies
  main feature 12
Natural resource-based products 33,
  42-45, 166-167
  Australian proposal 1987 45
  developing countries 43
  developments 1989-90 166-167
  double pricing 44
  exporting countries 43
  oil 44
  separate group 43-44
  special interests 43
**Negotiations September-November
  1993** 306-317
  institutions 313-315
  market access 307-310
  services 310-313
  Track Four 315-317
Negotiators
  new authority for 250-251
Non-application of GATT
  developments 1989-90 189-190
Non-tariff barriers 32
Non-tariff measures 31-34, 39-42,
  161-166
  appropriate recognition 161
  developments 1989-90
    161-166
  information on 39-40
  negotiation approach 40
  preliminary work on 39
  preshipment inspection 41,
    162-163
  recommendations 42